Philosophia

Claus Beisbart, Christoph Halbig, Carole Maigné,
Simone Zurbuchen (eds.)

Vol. 2

Jamil Alioui, Matthieu Amat
and Carole Maigné (eds.)

The Idea and Practice of Philosophy in Gilbert Simondon

Schwabe Verlag

Published with the support of the Swiss National Science Foundation

Open Access: Unless otherwise stated, this publication is licensed under the Creative Commons Attribution-NonCommercial-NoDerivatives 4.0 International (CC BY-NC-ND 4.0) licence.
Any commercial exploitation by others requires the prior consent of the publisher.

Bibliographic information published by the Deutsche Nationalbibliothek
The Deutsche Nationalbibliothek lists this publication in the Deutsche Nationalbibliografie; detailed bibliographic data are available on the Internet at http://dnb.dnb.de.

© 2024 by the authors; editorial matter and compilation © 2024 Jamil Alioui, Matthieu Amat, Carole Maigné, published by Schwabe Verlag Basel, Schwabe Verlagsgruppe AG, Basel, Schweiz
Copyediting: Kate Bird, Berlin
Graphic design: icona basel gmbh, Basel
Cover design: icona basel gmbH, Basel
Cover: Zunder & Stroh, Kathrin Strohschnieder, Oldenburg
Typesetting: 3w+p, Rimpar
Print: CPI books GmbH, Leck
Printed in Germany
ISBN Print 978-3-7965-4936-6
ISBN eBook (PDF) 978-3-7965-4937-3
DOI 10.24894/978-3-7965-4937-3
The ebook has identical page numbers to the print edition (first printing) and supports full-text search. Furthermore, the table of contents is linked to the headings.

rights@schwabe.ch
www.schwabe.ch

Contents

Abbreviations 7
Introduction 9

I. A New Way of Philosophising

Giovanni Carrozzini: Thinking Life, Living Thought.
Simondon's Conception of Philosophy 21

Ludovic Duhem: The Long Detour. Simondon Reader of Plato 39

Clémentine Lessard: Energetics of Philosophical Systems.
Simondon's Philosophy of Philosophy 57

Carole Maigné: Philosophising from and with the Camera.
The Wild Invention of Photography 81

Sarah Margairaz and Julien Rabachou: The Problem of
Philosophical Style. The Case of Simondon 101

II. What Is Philosophy about?

Jamil Alioui: On the Mode of Existence of Culture 121

Jean-Yves Chateau: Science and Philosophy in
Gilbert Simondon's Work 139

Michaël Crevoisier: Ontogenesis and Finitude. Remarks on
the Marginality of Philosophical Thought in Simondon 161

Sacha Loeve: "Un avènement analogue". Philosophy and "Its" Objects ... 183

Ashley Woodward: Philosophy of/as Information 207

III. Philosophy as Ethics and Politics

Matthieu Amat: Gilbert Simondon's Grammars of Value 227

Vincent Bontems: Simondon's "Right Technology". Eco-technology,
Scalability and Negative Progress 249

Xavier Guchet: Humanism, Technology and Care in Simondon 267

Taila Picchi: Individuation and History. *Transduction* of Dialectics and Historical Epistemology 285

Contributors 305

References 309

Abbreviations

MEOT Gilbert Simondon, *Du mode d'existence des objets techniques*, Paris, Aubier, 1958, 1969, 1989, 2001, 2012.

METO Gilbert Simondon, *On the Mode of Existence of Technical Objects*, translation by Cécile Malaspina and John Rogove, Minneapolis, Univocal Publishing, 2017.

ILFI Gilbert Simondon, *L'individuation à la lumière des notions de forme et d'information*, Grenoble, Millon, 2005, 2013, 2017.

ILNFI Gilbert Simondon, *Individuation in Light of Notions of Form and Information*, translation by Taylor Adkins, Minneapolis, University of Minnesota Press, 2020.

IMIN Gilbert Simondon, *Imagination et invention. 1965–1966*, Paris, Presses universitaires de France, 2014.

IT Gilbert Simondon, *L'invention dans les techniques. Cours et conférences*, Paris, Seuil, 2005.

RP Gilbert Simondon, *La résolution des problèmes*, Paris, Presses universitaires de France, 2018.

SLΦ Gilbert Simondon, *Sur la philosophie. 1950–1980*, Paris, Presses universitaires de France, 2016.

SLΨ Gilbert Simondon, *Sur la psychologie. 1956–1967*, Paris, Presses universitaires de France, 2015.

SLT Gilbert Simondon, *Sur la technique. 1953–1983*, Paris, Presses universitaires de France, 2014.

Introduction

Gilbert Simondon (1924–1989) stands in a singular place in the 20th French philosophical landscape: author of a masterly work, on a par with famous contemporaries (Althusser, Deleuze, Derrida, for example), he remains at the same time at the margin and at the centre of this landscape: at the margin, while his work is constantly being re-evaluated upwards, as if an initial misunderstanding had silenced its deep meaning; and at the centre, because the radical philosophical choice that characterises him confers on him an ever more evident actuality. The radicality of his philosophical project goes hand in hand with the singularity of his positioning: philosophy is for him, as F. Worms underlines it, a double requirement, that of an autonomous and radical activity, which transforms itself just as radically from the inside "in the light of the objects" that it thinks, notably the technical objects.[1] This radicality makes Simondon almost unclassifiable, so much is he independent of the philosophical modes of his time.

In the history of French philosophy since 1945, Simondon does not belong to any of its dominant moments although he knows them all closely, possessing an impressive curiosity and erudition. He belongs neither to the philosophy of spirit and life that precedes him (Bergson), despite a noticeable Bergsonian influence, nor to the existentialism of the post-war period (Sartre, Camus), although he considered existentialism an indispensable phase,[2] nor to phenomenology (Sartre and Merleau-Ponty), even if he follows the courses of the latter, nor to the structuralism which unfolds from the years 1960 (Barthes, Lévi-Strauss), nor to the post-structuralism of the years 1970–80 (Derrida, Lyotard, Ricœur),[3] and nor to the cognitivism of the years 1950–1960, even if he is interested in cybernetics. He thus opens a way which is neither the existence, nor the phenomenon, nor the code, nor the structure, but the form and the information, two concepts brought to seize the individuation as an operation of and in the being, common to the whole of the

---

[1] F. Worms, "Présentation", in Gilbert Simondon, *Sur la philosophie. 1950–1980*, PUF, 2016 (now abbreviated SLΦ), p. 6.
[2] G. Simondon, "Les grands courants de la philosophie française contemporaine", in SLΦ, p. 144.
[3] The issue here is not to discuss the relevance of these labels which require, like all labels, nuance and discussion.

realities in becoming, whether they are physical, vital, psychosocial, technical or even symbolic.

Gilbert Simondon followed a "typically French" path of excellence: Ecole Normale Supérieure de la Rue d'Ulm in Paris (1944), Agrégation de philosophie in 1948, Doctorat de philosophie in 1958, to which one must add studies in psychology (experimental psychology and social psychology notably). Simondon had a very solid grounding in classical literature, which did not prevent him from taking a serious and in-depth interest in all sorts of disciplines and fields that in turn nourished his own approach, which explains the abundant and apparently eclectic character of his examples. The 1958 PhD is divided into two theses (main and complementary, as was customary at the time): *Individuation in the Light of Notions of Form and Information* (abbreviated ILNFI), main thesis directed by Jean Hyppolite and *On the Mode of Existence of Technical Objects* (abbreviated METO), secondary thesis directed by Georges Canguilhem. If the second work appeared immediately, the first one knew a first truncated edition in 1964 (*L'Individu et sa genèse physico-biologique*), opening a difficult reception of the work.[4] Simondon taught at the University of Poitiers, then at the University of Paris-V (in psychology), where he created a laboratory of psychology and technology. He ended his academic career in 1983. Health problems, from the 1970s until his death in 1989, overshadowed his last years. The reception of his thought will obviously depend on the progressive but posthumous editions of his texts, notably from the 1990s, of his first thesis, his articles and his courses.

Until recently, the non-French speaking academic world had no easy access to the work of French philosopher Gilbert Simondon (1924–1989). Only a partial translation of METO was available.[5] It was not until the seventh volume of the journal *Parrhesia*, published almost thirty years later, in 2009, that a real translation process began.[6] The first full translation of METO appeared in

---

4 The more or less laborious early stages of Simondon's publishing and reception are synthetically traced in two writings available online: the "Historique de la 'simondialisation'", written by Jean-Hugues Barthélémy and once published by the former "Centre international des études simondoniennes", https://www.implications-philosophiques.org/gilbert-simondon-breve-histoire-dune-reception-difficile/, and Giovanni Carrozzini's contribution, "Gilbert Simondon: brève histoire d'une réception difficile", published in the February 2019 *Philosophical Implications*, on the occasion of the 60th anniversary of Simondon's doctoral defence, https://www.implications-philosophiques.org/gilbert-simondon-breve-histoire-dune-reception-difficile/.
5 Provided in 1980 by Ninian Mellamphy.
6 Thanks to the work of Gregory Flanders on the introduction to the main thesis and that of Arne de Boever on the text "Technical mentality". The latter text was in fact included in the book *Being and Technology*, edited by Arne De Boever, Shirley S. Y. Murray, Jon Roffe and Ashley Woodward, published in 2012 by Edinburgh University Press, one year after Drew S. Burk's translation of *Two Lessons on Animal and Man*, Minneapolis, Univocal Publishing, 2011.

2017;[7] in 2019, it was the turn of the lecture "Form, Information, Potentials";[8] the first complete translation of his main thesis, ILNFI, was completed in November 2020[9]; finally, the 1965–1966 lecture *Imagination and Invention* was translated in 2022.[10] Since then, the non-French speaking academic world has been, one might say, in a similar situation to that of the French-speaking world in 2005: it is finally benefiting from a complete version of the main thesis, but still awaits the translation of early and late texts, decisive for the understanding of the Simondonian gesture.

But the main point is that we are witnessing an unprecedented globalisation of Simondonian studies, also manifested in numerous translations of his work into other languages. The thesis on individuation was translated into Castilian in 2009, then into Korean, Italian, Portuguese and Japanese in the last five years; a translation into Turkish is underway. Six translations of METO have appeared in the last fifteen years in addition to the one into English (into Spanish, German, Korean, Portuguese and Italian) and three are in progress (into Chinese, Japanese and Russian). Other texts have been and will be translated into several languages, notably the *Two Lessons on Animal and Man* and *Imagination and Invention*. This translation undertaking accompanies the publication of monographs on Simondon in various languages.[11] In our own way, we wanted to participate in this process by sharing in this book, published in English and bringing together a panel of international specialists, a set of problems and reflections relating above all to the Simondonian determination of philosophy and to the operations, purposes and functions attributed to the latter. Such an editorial choice calls for an explanation.

If philosophy, as Simondon conceives it, is indeed the "reflexive thought" of "a real anterior to individuation",[12] and if "reflexive" does indeed mean "consti-

---

[7] Gilbert Simondon, *On the Mode of Existence of Technical Objects*, translated by Cecile Malaspina and John Rogove, Minneapolis, Univocal Publishing, 2017.
[8] Translated by Andrew Iliadis in Andrea Bardin, Giovanni Carrozzini and Pablo Rodríguez (eds.), *Philosophy Today*, vol. 63, issue 3, Summer 2019.
[9] Gilbert Simondon, *Individuation in Light of Notions of Form and Information*, translation by Taylor Adkins, Minneapolis, University of Minnesota Press, 2020.
[10] Gilbert Simondon, *Imagination and Invention*, translated by Joe Hughes and Christophe Wall-Romana, Minneapolis, University of Minnesota Press, 2022.
[11] To mention just three very recent works: Gregorio Trenti, *Estetica e morfologia in Gilbert Simondon*, Sesto San Giovanni, Mimesis, 2020; Olivier del Fabbro, *Philosophieren mit Objekten. Gilbert Simondons prozessuale Individuationsontologie*, Frankfurt M./New York, Campus Verlag, 2021; Michael Crevoisier, *Être un sujet connaissant selon Simondon. Ontogenèse et transcendental*, Paris, Classiques Garnier, 2023.
[12] The pagination for the main thesis is indicated with the page from the English translation followed by the page of the 2017 French edition, as follows: ILNFI, p. 300/ILFI, p. 263 and ILNFI, p. 319/ILFI p. 278.

tuted by a development of acts of thought that take themselves for an object",[13] then, at least in a first approximation, philosophy is operative and ontogenetic. "Operative" means that it is not a set of structures, not a set of given objects but, rather – to use the words of Étienne Souriau – a "work to be done",[14] insofar as "it is *through the individuation of knowledge* and not through knowledge alone that the individuation of non-subject beings is grasped".[15] In this way, Simondon establishes "a philosophy of nature that rejects all metaphysics of nature".[16] But this "doing" is not an "activity" or a "production" among others, at the whim of an isolated intention; like all individuation, it is an "an operation of the complete being";[17] this is the meaning of "ontogenetic". Another way of formulating things is to say that philosophy is less a practice than a technique, insofar as it requires a gesture performed according to the "φύσις"[18] and which, for this reason, cannot be arbitrary.[19] For us, then, the philosophical operation begins as the experience of a problem to be solved, not as the intention of an individual: "all real philosophy is the instinct to seek being without establishing an initial defensive choice";[20] as long as being becomes, philosophy "can"[21] crystallise into a work, one which is symbolic in the sense Hottois has shown it to be.[22] However,

---

[13] Gilbert Simondon, "Note sur l'attitude réflexive", preparatory document, ca. 1955, in *Sur la philosophie. 1950–1980*, Paris, Presses universitaires de France, 2016, p. 20, our translation.
[14] Étienne Souriau, "Du mode d'existence de l'œuvre à faire", in *Les différents modes d'existence*, Paris, Presses universitaires de France, first ed. 1943, 2009, p. 195, our translation.
[15] ILNFI, p. 17/ILFI, p. 36.
[16] Jacques Moutaux, "Sur la philosophie de la nature et la philosophie de la technique de Gilbert Simondon", in Olivier Bloch, ed., *Philosophies de la nature*, Paris, Éditions de la Sorbonne, 2000, p. 14, our translation.
[17] ILNFI, p. 3/ILFI, p. 25.
[18] As with the main thesis, the pagination of the secondary thesis follows the English translation and then the 2012 French edition, respectively: METO, p. 213/MEOT p. 278.
[19] As Jean-Yves Chateau explained very early on, it is therefore less a question of "indicating to specialists in philosophy how technology can be founded" than of showing that "technology can only be implemented as an autonomous and complete discipline by being philosophical, in the sense that the philosophical questions that can be asked about it are actually asked of it and in it", Jean-Yves Chateau, "Technologie et ontologie dans la philosophie de Gilbert Simondon", in *Cahiers philosophiques*, 43, 1990, p. 123, our translation.
[20] Gilbert Simondon, "Recherche sur la philosophie de la nature", manuscript, ca. 1955, in SLΦ, p. 30, our translation.
[21] *Ibid.*, p. 30.
[22] "The symbol is that which, while being a product of a division, connotes intensely – constitutively – the whole from which it comes and in relation to which, alone, it has meaning. Symbolically, individuation is always relative separation.", Gilbert Hottois, *Simondon et la philosophie de la "culture technique"*, Brussels, De Boeck-Wesmael, 1993, p. 43, our translation. "Culture is symbolisation. Symbolisation consists in producing partial representations of a totality that are at the same time explicitly complementary to each other." *Ibid.*, p. 90.

the philosophical concern is less the search for stability – for a mortifying[23] completion in a work – than the ambition of an effective grip on reality, of an operative modification of the totality;[24] it is in this sense that we can understand philosophy as a "symbol of being":[25] far from being a set of arbitrary signs[26] or habits derived from a "restrictive methodological tradition"[27] in which "reality is absent",[28] philosophy is a set of contemporary operations of the becoming of being; it extends the latter into a symbol and reflexively[29] and analogically[30] understands this symbol as ontogenetic information, i. e. as meaning. Philosophy, as Muriel Combes rightly points out, is therefore irreducible to "philosophy of consciousness"; it is neither "philosophy of language" nor "anthropology".[31] However, the philosophical thought of individuation brings with it the no less philosophical problem of the inventive[32] individuation of the corpus, well beyond the thorny question of the compatibility of the two PhD theses. This compatibility is now in a position to be questioned afresh, genetically, as the moment of a longer development.

---

[23] "Only death would be the resolution of all tensions; and death is not the solution to any problem. The resolving individuation is one that conserves the tensions in the equilibrium of metastability instead of nullifying them in the equilibrium of stability." ILNFI, p. 226/ILFI, p. 204.

[24] Thus, Muriel Combes, commenting on Simondon, rightly reminded us that "philosophy is not merely the mode of thought capable of understanding the individuation of human modes of being", that as "a mode of thought, philosophy participates in such individuation, taking part in such becoming", Muriel Combes, *Gilbert Simondon and the Philosophy of the Transindividual*, translation by Thomas LaMarre, Cambridge, London, MIT Press, 2013 (first French edition 1999), p. 61. Similarly, according to Bernard Aspe, this "real, effective modification of the 'sensitive' world and forms of life" is achieved through this "passage from the abstract to the concrete" of philosophy which "signifies a passage towards ethics", Bernard Aspe, *Simondon, politique du transindividuel*, Paris, Dittmar, 2013, p. 37, our translation.

[25] Simondon, "Recherche sur la philosophie de la nature", SLΦ, p. 30.

[26] Gilbert Simondon, "Note complémentaire", ILNFI, p. 402/ILFI, p. 332.

[27] Gilbert Simondon, "History of the Notion of the Individual", preparatory work written between 1952 and 1958, in ILNFI, p. 433/ILFI, p. 357.

[28] METO, p. 20/MEOT, p. 16.

[29] About reflexivity, Hottois has shown how "the philosophy thematised by Simondon tends to coincide with Simondon's philosophical practice in METO", Hottois, *op. cit.*, p. 76. Similarly, Bernard Aspe, in his politicising reading, shows that philosophy, which is eminently reflexive, must "envisage the existing in such a way that the act that supports it (thought in its dimension of self-inclusion of the thinking part of the subject) is identified as belonging to the same type of approach as that required by any being", Aspe, *op. cit.*, p. 183.

[30] Juan Manuel Heredia, "Simondon y el problema de la analogía", in *Ideas y Valores*, 68, n° 171, 2019, pp. 209–230.

[31] Combes, *op. cit.*, p. 54.

[32] It is as an inventor that Simondon practises writing and resorts to language. At least, he developed an original and remarkable style, which has been the subject of many comments.

It would be wrong, therefore, to see philosophy and its systematicity as a "constituted edifice".³³ Rather, as the young Simondon explains, it is an "act of progressive assimilation", an "activity of interpretation" polarised around a "focus", a "hot spot".³⁴ One thinks here of the Cartesian reference to the "cosmological hypothesis of primordial vortices" found in ILNFI: although it leads to errors in the Dioptric – insofar as the structures produced turn out to be inadequate in retrospect for the understanding of observations – the hypothesis finds value because it allows Descartes' "unifying two asymmetrical notions in a very fruitful association".³⁵ In other words, philosophy institutes continuity where it was thought there was none. As Bernard Aspe rightly says, it tries to "put an end to any type of ontological hiatus, including the minimal hiatus that all transcendental problematics convey".³⁶ It is adequate not when it corresponds to experience but when it brings compatibility. For this reason, Isabelle Stengers, in particular, reproached Simondon for having preferred a method that "does not in any way compel one to seek out difficulty, obstacles, or challenges".³⁷

Philosophy as an operation of "compatibilisation"³⁸ is not, however, identifiable with encyclopaedism, cybernetics, or technology, of which it is possibly only the "method",³⁹ insofar as it provides the schema of an operation of passage, of a "metabasis" going from the "spontaneous" to the "reflexive".⁴⁰ "A real philosophy cannot first of all be defined as a philosophy *of*".⁴¹ It is because it is operative and ontogenetic that philosophy is "constructive and regulative of culture".⁴² From this point of view, philosophy can be seen as a regulating idea, in the Kantian sense. As such, philosophy is interested in everything that is able to

---

33   Simondon, "Recherche sur la philosophie de la nature", SLΦ, p. 32.
34   *Ibid.*
35   These are the notions of frequency and corpuscle, ILNFI, p. 113/ILFI, p. 113.
36   Aspe, *op. cit.*, p. 100.
37   Simondon would have been wrong to allow himself "to follow the paths of compatibility", Isabelle Stengers, "Pour une mise à l'aventure de la transduction", in Pascal Chabot, (ed.), *Simondon*, Paris, Vrin, 2002, p. 143, our translation.
38   Isabelle Stengers, "Résister à Simondon?" in *Multitudes*, 18, 2004, p. 56, our translation.
39   METO, p. 163/MEOT, p. 209.
40   Gilbert Simondon, "Cybernétique et philosophie", text from 1953 in SLΦ, pp. 61–62, our translation, and METO, p. 170/MEOT, p. 218.
41   Simondon, "Recherche sur la philosophie de la nature", SLΦ, p. 30. As Chabot wrote: "There are all manner of specific philosophies: a philosophy of contemporary art, a philosophy of genetics, a philosophy of history, or even of cooking. But there is no longer a philosophy of everything." Pascal Chabot, *The Philosophy of Simondon*, translation by Graeme Kirkpatrick and Aliza Krefetz, London, Bloomsbury, 2013, p. 129.
42   METO, p. 222/MEOT, p. 290.

institute continuity and compatibility where there is rupture or conflict:[43] from the transdisciplinary epistemology of cyberneticians[44] to pedagogical thinking about the education of high school students,[45] from Haeckel's law to crystallography: "epistemological fruitfulness" takes precedence over "positive objectivity".[46] From this, it is possible to read Simondon as a philosopher of culture.[47]

But this operative interest in everything that works also leads to many problems. For example, does this mean that the "trace"[48] of philosophical operation and invention is contingent? This would explain why Simondon does not really recognise himself in the expression "history of philosophy", to which he prefers that of "filiation of doctrines".[49] The number of texts in which he takes it up and traces it back to its Ionian origins is remarkable and reveals the extent of his classical erudition and reading. This abundance of knowledge, however, does not spare him from a certain scepticism towards what he calls "literary culture",[50] which he criticises at length. Philosophy is thus enjoined to make its own this remark made about the Encyclopaedia: it "is not necessarily a book, and even less a literary genre".[51] What we call the history of philosophy appears to Simondon as a field of possible inventions: problems, concepts, symbols are drawn from it, but there is no teleology of concepts or of history, no great open

---

43 This explains why Gilles Châtelet and then Jean-Hugues Barthélémy thought of Simondonian philosophy as a "subversion of classical alternatives", Jean-Hugues Barthélémy, *Penser l'individuation. Simondon et la philosophie de la nature*, Paris, L'Harmattan, 2005, p. 19.

44 Xavier Guchet proposes a reading of Simondon polarised by the "problem of the unity of the human sciences" whose solution is to be found in a "general science of operations". This science, "also called reflexive technology [...] is already a philosophy", Xavier Guchet, *Pour un humanisme technologique. Culture, technique et société dans la philosophie de Gilbert Simondon*, Paris, Presses universitaires de France, 2010, pp. 15–16, our translation. See also Andrea Bardin, *Epistemology and Political Philosophy in Gilbert Simondon. Individuation, Technics, Social Systems*, Dordrecht, Springer, 2015.

45 And, with it, the question of general culture, as noted by Moutaux, *op. cit.*

46 Gilbert Simondon, "Réponse aux objections", text from 1954 in *Sur la technique. 1953–1983*, Paris, Presses universitaires de France, 2014 (now abbreviated SLT), p. 226, our translation.

47 Matthieu Amat and Carole Maigné, *Philosophie de la culture. Formes de vie, valeurs, symboles*, Paris, Vrin, 2021, pp. 46–50.

48 Simondon later explains that "invention" differs from "creativity" in that it "can be studied by its traces more than by psychological observation in the usual sense of the term", Gilbert Simondon, "Invention and Creativity", 1976 lecture, in *La résolution des problèmes*, Paris, Presses universitaires de France, 2018, p. 207, our translation.

49 Gilbert Simondon, "De l'implication technologique dans les fondements d'une culture", draft not included in MEOT, ca. 1956, in SLΦ, p. 374, our translation.

50 ILNFI p. 278/ILFI, p. 246 and METO, pp. 123–124/MEOT, p. 152 and pp. 159/204.

51 Gilbert Simondon, "Les encyclopédies et l'esprit encyclopédique", text from ca. 1950, in SLΦ, p. 129.

book of philosophy; systematics is not subjugated to historicity. In this sense, Simondon and his "pre-critical"[52] philosophy seem closer to Leibniz than to Kant or Hegel; they perhaps, in the words of Xavier Guchet, "open the way to another way of being modern in philosophy".[53]

Simondon does not ignore the history of philosophy; on the contrary. However, he only resorts to it as an opportunity to invent, to solve problems, to support the "entrance of new concepts"[54] into what he calls a "system of symbols".[55] Translated into an epistemological perspective, these reflections confirm a minima that "philosophy is not a field of thought that has borders with other bordering fields, and lives with them in good understanding or in war";[56] on the contrary, the "philosophical programme includes, as its only obligation, the opening of the reflexive system";[57] it is therefore senseless to want to make a philosophy "of the object and of the subject, of Nature or of Spirit".[58] The ecumenical ambition of philosophy is virtually limitless: thus philosophy appears as the post-aesthetic[59] convergence of the technical and the religious,[60] as a kind of return path, via intuition, to primitive magic;[61] philosophy can also operate the synthetic meeting of the theoretical and the practical.[62] These reconciling aspects have earned Simondon several criticisms, notably that of angelism and apolitism.[63]

---

[52] ILNFI, p. 349/ILFI, p. 302.
[53] Guchet, *op. cit.*, p. 264.
[54] ILNFI, p. 271/ILFI, p. 241.
[55] Simondon, "Note complémentaire" in ILNFI, p. 402/ILFI, p. 332.
[56] Simondon, "Cybernétique et philosophie", SLΦ, p. 35.
[57] *Ibid.*
[58] Simondon, "Recherche sur la philosophie de la nature", SLΦ, p. 29, 31.
[59] On Simondon's "aesthetics", see, in particular, the works of Ludovic Duhem, including "La tache aveugle et le point neutre. Sur le double 'faux départ' de l'esthétique de Simondon", in Jean-Hugues Barthélémy, ed., *Cahiers Simondon Numéro 1*, Paris, L'Harmattan, 2009 as well as "'Entrer dans le moule'. Poïétique et individuation chez Simondon", in *La part de l'Œil*, 27–28, 2012–2013, pp. 227–257.
[60] METO, p. 211/MEOT, p. 276.
[61] Through intuition, philosophy "recovers a relation to being which was that of primitive magic, which then became that of aesthetic activity" in that "known being, the world, is originally neither object nor subject", *ibid.*, p. 322/243.
[62] METO, p. 220–221/MEOT, p. 289.
[63] On this subject, see in particular Hottois, *op. cit.*, p. 78, 123–124, André Micoud, "Gilbert Simondon et la posture herméneutique: quelques notations", in Chabot, ed., *Simondon*, Paris, Vrin, 2002, p. 118; Chabot, *The Philosophy of Simondon, op. cit.*, p. 33–34; Alberto Toscano, "La disparation", in *Multitudes*, 18, 2004, p. 80; and Bernard Stiegler, "Chute et élévation. L'apolitique de Simondon", in *Revue philosophique de la France et de l'Étranger*, 131, 3, July 2006, p. 339.

Undoubtedly, this multiplicity of – sometimes paradoxical – determinations and modalisations of philosophy indicates, in Simondonian terms, a metastable tension, information that solicits the setting up of reflection and questioning. In order to orientate ourselves, we propose to configure the contributions according to three sets of questions:

1. What new ways and style of philosophising did Simondon introduce? What practices of philosophy and what positioning vis-à-vis the history of philosophy does he make possible?
2. What "objects" or what problems is philosophy able to appropriate? What questions is it entitled to ask? What questions should it ask? And what exactly does it talk about?
3. Finally, what practical issues can we expect from Simondon's philosophy? What political, economic or ecological stakes does philosophy, as a set of operations, have?

The contributions in this volume are intended to provide original answers to these questions, without, of course, claiming to be exhaustive. By updating Simondon in this way from the theme of philosophy, we hope to contribute to a renewed understanding of this author, especially among English-speaking readers who, for a long time deprived of access to the texts, have had to make do with a study of techniques and their role in culture without direct access to the complete philosophical problematic in which this study is nevertheless rooted.[64] This, at least, is how we would formulate the hypothesis[65] at the origin of this book: it is because Simondon was first and foremost a philosopher – in a sense that the following pages would like to shed light on – that he was led to take an interest in technical realities and their role in culture.

Jamil Alioui, Matthieu Amat, Carole Maigné   June 2023

---

[64] It should be noted that several monographs have been translated into English, including those of Muriel Combes and Pascal Chabot (in 2013).

[65] This hypothesis is not absolutely original; it was already, in a certain sense, Moutaux's hypothesis (*op. cit.*), but here it takes advantage of a then non-existent editorial completeness.

I.
A New Way of Philosophising

Thinking Life, Living Thought
Simondon's Conception of Philosophy

Giovanni Carrozzini

In his *Praise of Philosophy*, Maurice Merleau-Ponty seeks to provide an embodied, lived image of philosophy. He finds such an image in Socrates, whose life is entirely marked by an enthusiastic and problematic kind of knowledge:

> Socrates [...] works out for himself another idea of philosophy. It does not exist as a sort of idol of which he would be the guardian and which he must defend. It exists rather in its living relevance to the Athenians, in its absent presence, in its obedience without respect.[1]

Thus, in Merleau-Ponty's opinion, Socrates would be the "living body" of philosophy. Indeed, when one tries to demonstrate the link between philosophy and life in antiquity, Socrates is the example that most often comes to mind. The aim of this chapter is to show that the twentieth century had a Socrates of its own, whose name was Gilbert Simondon, insofar as his thought is inextricably intertwined with his experience, as was the case with the philosopher of Athens.

Recalling the philosophical relationship between Simondon and Gilles Deleuze, François Dosse underlines the solitary character of the philosopher from Saint-Etienne, especially in relation to the intellectual scene of his time.[2] And in his account of the "intersecting lives" of Deleuze and Guattari, Dosse points out the role that practical activity played in Simondon's existence. In fact, as a laboratory man, Simondon was more than willing to search for concrete applications of his personal philosophical perspective, "getting his hands dirty" in contact, above all, with those technical objects of which he offered an admirable examination in his "Thèse complémentaire pour le Doctorat d'Etat", *On the Mode of Existence of Technical Objects*. It is indeed the operative dimension that drives his philosophy, that determines it, that assigns it a particular character, in each of its manifestations. In this article, I will clarify this point with particular reference to the notion of "allagmatics", theorised by Simondon in his *thèse principale, Individuation in Light of the Notions of Form and Information*. Furthermore, even the fact that, as far as we know, Simondon never directly engaged

---

1   Maurice Merleau-Ponty, *In Praise of Philosophy and Other Essays*, transl. by John O'Neill, Evanston, 1970, p. 36.
2   See François Dosse, *Gilles Deleuze & Félix Guattari: Intersecting Lives*, transl. by Deborah Glassman, New York, 2010, p. 162.

with the politics of his time makes him unique in comparison to his contemporaries, who, more or less explicitly, did not disdain to "take sides". Significant, in this sense, is his approach to the French '68, at least on the basis of what emerges from a short but dense letter sent to Jean Le Moyne, just after the events of May: Simondon confessed being worried about the exponential increase in bureaucratic obligations, as well as the need to safeguard the equipment of his laboratory in the Rue Serpente from possible "attacks" by the young revolutionaries. Not a word, therefore, about the political stakes of the affair.[3] This is not to be understood as a lack of interest, but rather as a *sui generis* approach, more typical of certain Renaissance thinkers – a model explicitly mentioned by his friend and colleague Maurice Mouillaud – focused rather on their work of radical reformation of thought,[4] right from its foundations and its ontology. We will deal more deeply with the specific characters philosophy has according to Simondon: for the moment, suffice it to note that, seeking to inaugurate a "new humanism", Simondon strove to demonstrate, with his life, the possible applications of this approach. For him, "new humanism" means first and foremost expanding the domain of humanism to domains in which the human appears hidden, masked: first of all, the sphere of techniques, in which the "human part", although foundational and generative, especially in objects, is concealed. For this reason, Simondon dedicated his philosophy and his life to rediscovering this dimension. He did so by interweaving a new philosophical perspective with a rigorous knowledge of the sciences of his time and of techniques, translating his skills into concrete "operations". Wherever he could, he set up workshops in which technical experimentation was combined with a gradual theoretical and pedagogical growth. Simondon tried thus to show not only that philosophical thought has a reflective side, but also that this side cannot be dissociated from the actual context in which operates.

Simondon uses the notion of "humanism", for the first time, in a short essay of 1953, published the following year in the volume of Proceedings of the conference at which he spoke. In this context, he argues for the need to develop a cultural humanism based on the recognition of the essential cultural significance of techniques, as expressions of the human world proper. This same position then finds systematic expression in METO, discussed, and immediately edited, in 1958. In his main doctoral thesis, in which Simondon elaborates his philosophy of Nature, this notion is not equally central. Nonetheless, it is also possible to frame it in this theoretical context, starting from some necessary clarifications. First, it should be noted that Simondon's cultural humanism should

---

3   See "Lettre de Gilbert Simondon à Jean Le Moyne, datée du 29 mars 1970", in *Revue de Synthèse* 130, 1, 2009, p. 130.
4   See Maurice Mouillaud, "Frammenti per Gilbert Simondon", in *Il Protagora* 36, 12, 2008, pp. 401–404.

in no case be associated with any expression of philosophical anthropology. The living human being, in fact, is not conceived as having some "specific difference" nor, as its corollary, a presumed superiority over other manifestations of the living. Rather, it is necessary to conceive it as a phenomenon that presents a greater degree of complexity than the other manifestations of Nature. This complexity deserves a specific study of the phenomenon to which it is related and this study acquires in Simondon the definition of cultural humanism, where by cultural we mean, as specified above, the re-understanding of the sphere of the techniques, conceived as an expression of the human work in relation to its external and material context.

In what follows, I will analyse the possible applications of his multifaceted notion of philosophy to his own thought, offering for each of these applications anecdotes meant to show the connection between Simondon's way of thinking life and living thought.

1. Simondon's Conception of Philosophy Applied to his Individuation and the Role of the Notion of Milieu

In a version of the "Introduction" to his major thesis for the Doctorat d'État, written around 1955, Simondon claims that in philosophy

> reflexive does not mean abstract, as rather constituted by a development of acts of thought that take themselves as object in the same way as the primitive objects given by direct experience and integrated into the course of reflexive thought.[5]

In the same text, he argues that the philosophical act must be "phenomenological", without being "*phenomenist*". Simondon employs the adjective "phenomenological" in an original manner, not in its traditional Husserlian sense. What he intends to say is that the philosophical act must be contemporary to its object, "neither *a priori* nor *a posteriori*, but *a præsente*".[6] As Simondon himself makes clear in the Introduction to his main thesis, this philosophy consists thus in a *sui generis* mode of knowledge, insofar as it strives to grasp the phenomena examined in the very instant in which they occur, while still in the making. At the same time, however, Simondon preserves the reflective nature of philosophical thought, which – while retaining its reflexive nature which – gives the object under consideration the status of a "*sur-objet*", to use Bachelard's words, i.e. an object that transforms or "transduces" itself through the operatory process of philosophical reflection, "whose reflexive act grasps itself in its development as

---

5   Gilbert Simondon, "Introduction. (Note sur l'attitude réflexive, autour de 1955)", in SLΦ, p. 20.
6   *Ibidem.*

analogous to the object subjected to reflection".[7] This is why in Simondon process is equally important as the given object: it has a "value of being [*valeur d'être*]"[8], as he says with regard to relation during the operation of individuation in the making.

An application of this idea of philosophy is precisely the study of ontogenesis, that is, according to Simondon, the study of the "becoming of the being qua being",[9] which finds its actualisation in the study of individuation – a thought that applies to the phenomenon as studied from the inside, "in the mould", as Simondon says of his analysis of the moulding of a brick: "we have to penetrate into the mold itself in order to follow the operation of form-taking on the different scales of magnitude of physical reality".[10]

Only a philosophy that is *contemporaneous* to the studied phenomenon can legitimately theorise *its dynamics in the making*, by discovering the dark layers, the "dark zones" of the analyses of the processes once accomplished, as is the case with substantialism and hylomorphism. The dark zone theorised by Simondon corresponds precisely to that zone in which the *relationship (which has a value of being)* between the principles theorised, in particular, by hylomorphism to explain ontogenesis, i.e. form and matter, is placed. According to Simondon, for example, Aristotle did not investigate the relational dimension between these two principles. On the contrary, Simondon points out that the principle of individuation corresponds precisely to the operation of individuation that, by its definition, is located in a *median zone*, so much so that, as he observes, there is no matter that is not preformed, nor form that is not materialised. Now, the philosophy of individuation is primarily a philosophy of Nature which, thanks to the hypothesis of the pre-individual – the system in a metastable regime preceding any generation – theorises the contemporary formation of the individual and its associated milieu. Simondon underscores the importance of such a contemporaneity in a letter to Jean Hyppolite, who was to supervise this major PhD thesis:

> Indeed, it is necessary to grasp being before it is analyzed in terms of the individual and the milieu: the totality individual-milieu is not self-sufficient; one cannot explain the individual by the milieu nor the milieu by the individual, and one cannot reduce the one to the other. The individual and the milieu both belong to a phase genetically and logically posterior to a syncretic phase that is constituted by a primary mixture. Here we rediscover an intuition of the Ionian Physiologists, and in particular, Thales.[11]

---

7   Simondon, "Introduction. (Note sur l'attitude réflexive, autour de 1955)", in SLΦ, p. 25.
8   ILNFI, p. 50/ILFI, p. 42.
9   *Ibid.*, p. 26/p. 5.
10 *Ibid.*, p. 46/p. 30.
11 Nathalie Simondon, "Biography", transl. by Joe Hughes and Drew Burk, http://gilbert.simondon.fr/content/biography [10.04.2022].

The philosophical discipline which is intended for the study of the becoming "in the making" of ontogenesis is defined by Simondon as "allagmatic" or "theory of changes". Such a discipline is "capable of grasping being before any separation of operation and structure, in this state of non-division that characterises individuality, and of showing how the syncretic state is transformed by an act into an analytical state where operation and structure are distinct".[12]

Consequently, after the *syncretic* phase of the philosophy of individuation, consisting in the application of philosophy qua reflection which is contemporary to its object, there follows an analytic phase where the individual and his associated environment are the object of specific research. In fact, we can speak of milieu and individual in a proper sense only once the process is completed. For Simondon, the associated milieu consists in a sort of filter through which external stimuli pass, as well as a "portion of space" in which the individual's behaviour takes place: if, according to Simondon, in the operation of individuation *in fieri* this filter and this space are not distinguishable from the individual himself, once the individuation is complete, the associated milieu is distinguishable from the individual as such, like a sort of *aura* that surrounds him. However, as soon as this process ends, it is the associated milieu that allows to define the operational dimension of the individual.

Here we find an explicit application of suggestions drawn from Georges Canguilhem, who, in an essay later published in *Knowledge of Life* (1952), "The Living and Its Milieu", noted the importance of the notion of milieu in rethinking individuality:

> The notion of milieu is becoming a universal and obligatory mode of apprehending the experience and existence of living beings; one could almost say it is now being constituted as a category of contemporary thought [...] through a critical comparison of several approaches, we mean, if possible, to bring to light their common point of departure and to postulate their fecundity for a philosophy of nature centred on the problem of individuality.[13]

Furthermore, Canguilhem explicitly quotes Jakob von Uexküll and his theory of *Umwelt*, the world-milieu of every animal species: "The milieu of behaviour proper to the living (*Umwelt*) is an ensemble of excitations, which have the value and signification of signals".[14] To borrow the well-known image used by von Uexküll himself, the *Umwelt* can be compared to a sort of "bubble" that surrounds the living being, acting as a filter for stimuli, which, in turn, acquire meaning precisely because of this filtering; it is within this same "bubble", and

---

12   Simondon, "Epistémologie de la cybernétique" (1953), in SLΦ, p. 199.
13   Georges Canguilhem, *Knowledge of Life*, ed. by Paola Marrati and Todd Meyers, New York 2008, p. 98.
14   *Ibid.*, p. 111.

because of its function, that the behaviour of the living being is implemented. Now, it is true that Simondon's associated milieu cannot be assimilated into the *Umwelt* without taking into account the differences between the two notions. Uexküll, for example, pays no attention to the genetic process, which is central for Simondon. However, these two concepts share the idea that every individual or species, depending on its complexity, has a milieu of its own once it has completed its genesis and that this milieu is not the mere surroundings, i.e. the external milieu, the environment. To put it in Uexküll's terms, the *Umwelt* is the "soap bubble" of a species: "everything a subject perceives belongs to its *perception world* [*Merkwelt*], and everything it produces, to its *effect world* [*Wirkwelt*]. These two worlds, of perception and production of effects, form one closed unit, the *environment*".[15] In Simondon, the associated milieu, an individual's specific milieu, is in turn an *intermediary*, a filter of stimuli and a set of possible actions, the operational "activity of relationship" of every individual.

Applied to individuation, philosophy – always understood qua reflexive thought which is contemporary to its object – allows to go back to the origins of the notion of milieu-world theorised by Uexküll and prove its significance.

The importance of the animal milieu for Simondon is testified by two anecdotes told by Jean-Marie Charpentier, who was his disciple in Poitiers, and Michel Juffé, who obtained his DES in Paris with a dissertation supervised by Simondon. Charpentier tells us: "[...] while we are walking together from the faculty to the university canteen (about a kilometre), he finds a snail on the sidewalk. He takes it and carries it with him for several hundred meters until we come across a garden in which he carefully places the animal".[16] It is clear that what Simondon wanted to do was to allow the animal to find an environment where his associated milieu could function fully and in a proper manner. As to Juffé, he recalls what follows:

> [...] in September 1966, with my *licence* in hand, I had to choose a thesis director for the so-called *diplôme d'études supérieures* (DES) in philosophy, which later became the *maîtrise* and has since disappeared after the introduction of the *licence-master-doctorat* system. Without hesitation, I paid a visit to Simondon in his office on rue Serpente and asked him to supervise my thesis, without having a specific subject in mind, except that I had really liked what he said about ethology, and I told him that. He agreed and suggested me a seemingly obscure subject: "The ontogenesis of instinctive behaviour". He did not want me to stick to a philosophical account. He proposed me, but without forcing me, to study that *in vivo*, by observing and filming in the large garden of his no less large house. It was located on the side of the Palaiseau valley, in the Lozère district, with a

---

15   Jakob von Uexküll, *A Foray Into the Worlds of Animals and Humans, with A Theory of Meaning*, transl. by Joseph D. O'Neil, Minneapolis-London, 2010, p. 42.

16   Jean-Marie Charpentier, "Un contadino del Danubio. Gilbert Simondon a Poitiers. Intervista a cura di Giovanni Carrozzini", in *Il Protagora* 45, 29–30, 2018, p. 227.

metro station on the Sceaux line (we did not yet speak of RER), itself named Lozère. I went there every week, on Thursday I believe, for three or four months. There followed always the same ritual: I would play with three or four little puppies for one or two hours.[17]

Playing is in fact for animals, including the human animal, a way of "world-making", a way of enacting the relation that genetically constitutes them and, thereby, resolving problems or submitting them to the world.

This problematic approach to the world always aroused Simondon's attention. In his laboratory in rue Serpente, as told by his collaborator Patrick de Béjarry, he was surrounded by *colonies of rats* whose behaviour he studied by having them running through labyrinths. Now, from the application of the notion of associated milieu to human beings, it follows that every man – as a complex animal whose individuality is the most remarkable – filters external reality in a unique way, producing milieus that can multiply themselves according to the context. These milieus have nothing to do with the social apparatus into which we are embedded. Therefore, we can clash with them, because human society works as a sort of "surrounding environment". It is therefore true that the associated milieu makes us unique, but it can also cause social unrest, to the extent that, as we will demonstrate in what follows, they may be mutually antagonistic.

Simondon's stance towards Rosenberg and Althusser, after his internment at Sainte-Anne, should be understood in light of this theory. As to Rosenberg, his daughter Nathalie has kindly granted me permission to read an excerpt from a letter he addressed to President Eisenhower in which he states: "death is the seed of death. I don't know what justice demands, but I know for sure that peace demands that this couple be saved".[18] Regarding Althusser, Jacqueline Lanouzière, his collaborator in Poitiers and then at the Sorbonne, remembers that

> […] in 1980, the murder committed by Althusser, who strangled his wife and was interned in Sainte-Anne for two years, affected him deeply. Louis Althusser was for him a victim who absolutely had to be helped. His fate tormented him so much that, when he was denied permission to visit him, he considered rescuing him secretly. When he informed us of his project, A. M. Mairesse and me dissuaded him, not without difficulty. He suffered from not being able to do anything for his former classmate at the rue d'Ulm, imprisoned – unfairly and arbitrarily, he believed – in that hospital/prison. In-

---

17 Michel Juffé, "Gilbert Simondon: una testimonianza", in *Il Protagora* 42, 23/24, 2015, pp. 219–220.
18 Simondon, "Voyage aux Etats-Unis (Extraits sur le Pragmatisme, 1952)", in SLΦ, p. 77.

justice disgusted him and he was naturally compassionate, seeing it as a duty to help the weak.[19]

A reflective philosophy *a præsente* might well seem a paradox, but as we have just explained it opens up original perspectives upon the objects it analyses. Thus, individuation is just one of the possible applications of this kind of philosophy, which may well be extended to other subjects to be studied *in vivo*, as Simondon did with all his objects of study. This is, for example, the case of his examination of technical objects, in which one clearly sees a further application of his reflexive philosophy *a præsente*, which not by chance Simondon raises to the level of a full-fledged theory, namely "allagmatics". Allagmatics, in Simondon's writings, has no univocal definition. However, as literally a *theory of change*, it could be generally designated as that theory which applies to the study of the transitions (changes, precisely) of a structure into an operation (and vice versa) and of an operation into another operation.[20] As mentioned, Simondon employs this strategy to examine individuation. And it is in the light of this study that, with the same approach, he investigates the domain of techniques. A reflective philosophy *a præsente*, which wants to be authentically allagmatic, examines the object of study *in its making*, rather than merely taking note of its procedural outcomes. Thus, Simondon's philosophy of techniques is properly a genetic, and therefore dynamic, study of the object of analysis: it is not by chance, then, that Simondon does not assimilate, in a Heideggerian way, the technical object to a mere tool, insofar as the theoretical presuppositions of his investigation significantly distance him from this approach. That a technical object can be evaluated *a posteriori* (or *a priori*) on the basis of its *usefulness* is a legitimate theoretical perspective, but it is obviously not the one that fits Simondon's stance, inasmuch as the *reflexivity* of philosophy cannot do without that *a præsente* that distinguishes it from any other form of traditional reflective knowledge. Hence the need for a new term, "allagmatics", to denote a new way of approaching objects of study. From an allagmatic perspective, the technical object *is not the tool*, insofar as what needs to be analysed and reflected upon directly, is its constitutive process, its ontogenesis, defined, in Simondonian terms, as the *becoming of being*. The study of the *becoming of the technical being* allows to grasp, for example, the human component at play in this process, which Simondon does not hesitate to define as "invention", as well as the ways in which this component inaugurates the processes of conversion of structures into operations and of operations into operations. Thus examined, the technical

---

19 Jacqueline Lanouzière, "Gilbert Simondon", in *Il Protagora*, Mimesis Edizioni, n° 23–24, 2015, pp. 207–208.
20 See ILNFI, pp. 663–673/ILFI, pp. 559–566.

object is not a tool, but the crystallisation of a human gesture, which in turn consists of a manifestation of a human mental scheme, that of invention.

2. Philosophy: An Emancipatory Force for Technicity

At the beginning of *On the Mode of Existence of Technical Objects*, we find another, more traditional idea of philosophy, i.e. that of an activity of thought whose goal is emancipation and liberation. Philosophy as emancipatory and liberating thought – which allows us to legitimately place Simondon in the bloodline of the thinkers of the Renaissance and the Enlightenment, applies in this specific case to the conceptualisation of the various technologies:

> The modification of the philosophical way of looking at the technical object announces the possibility of introducing the technical being into culture [...]. For this reason, [technicity] can become a foundation for culture, to which it will bring a unifying and stabilizing power, making culture adequate to the reality which it expresses and regulates.[21]

Philosophy should indeed rethink technical objects as allies of man in the process of building an actual collective, that is, a genuinely democratic society which makes coexistence rather than competition its founding value, as stated by Pascal Chabot in his *L'âge de transitions*. To do this, it is above all necessary to de-alienate technical objects, which means learning to frame them as actualisations of a process of human invention rather than as mere tools, slaves of man and devoid of a human dimension.

Philosophy has thus the task of reintegrating techniques into culture, through new methods of teaching which are able to convey the importance of the operation accomplished by the inventor, in order to reproduce and disseminate it: "Encyclopedic technological education aims at giving the adult the feeling that he is a fulfilled, entirely realised being, in full possession of his means and his forces, an image of the individual man in his state of real maturity".[22] And, regarding Pascal, he adds: "To understand Pascal is to reconstruct a machine identical to his with one's own hands without copying it, even transposing it where possible to an electronic adding device, so as to have to reinvent it by way of actualizing it, rather than reproducing Pascal's intellectual and operational schemas".[23] Indeed, as he told one of his disciples in Tours, this is what he did with his wireless receiver: "I studied it, I took it apart completely and reassem-

---

21 METO, p. 21/MEOT, p. 18.
22 *Ibid.*, p. 122/p. 150.
23 *Ibid.*, p. 123/p. 152.

bled it piece by piece overnight. In the morning, it was operational".[24] It is not *only* a question of knowing how to build a technical object, but also of modifying that presumed knowledge on the basis of a constructive action: once again, in the practical act, we find a conversion of structures into operations and a possible revision of this same process.

It is within this precise theoretical framework that one should understand Simondon's experiments in Tours, Poitiers, and at the Sorbonne. Taking advantage of the French law that established the so-called "pilot classes", Simondon, then a young philosophy teacher at the *lycée* Descartes in Tours, launched a pedagogical adventure aimed at the introduction of technical education to students, as evidenced by his complementary doctoral dissertation, more precisely by a section not surprisingly devoted to the relationship between man and the technical object in which, drawing on his "field experiences", Simondon articulates a careful inquiry into the education of the child in relation to the technical object itself.[25] The headmaster of the *lycée* Descartes, where Simondon taught, sums it up as follows:

> Simondon made an extraordinary experiment. When we got the circular urging us to do manual work, we had nothing, neither the premises nor the equipment, nor the personnel [...] Simondon, *agrégé* in philosophy, graduate in psychology, former student of the École Normale Supérieure, declared himself ready to make an experiment with some of his own tools, apparatus, etc. In April, the municipality, which had been kept informed of his efforts, agreed to set up a workshop in the cellars of the *lycée* and Simondon was able to continue his experiments in less precarious conditions.[26]

This is a good example, taken from his own experience, of the link Simondon theorised between philosophy, techniques and pedagogy. Indeed, it is true that a reflexive philosophy *a præsente*, if applied, as is the case, to the domain of techniques, cannot disregard an "educational" dimension: educating to "make" techniques, that is, to construct technical objects, means, at the same time, approaching the process in accordance with that allagmatic philosophy theorised by Simondon. But the experiment at the laboratory located in Tours continued also in Poitiers. As we can read in *L'Année psychologique*, in 1955, once he arrived at the Faculty of Letters and Human Sciences, Simondon founded a Psychology Laboratory which was also a machine workshop. As Charpentier asserts, the laboratory was housed in a former laundry room and the students had to learn how

---

24   G. L., "Gilbert Simondon. Ricordi di uno dei suoi allievi di filosofia. Tours, 1950–1952", in *Il Protagora*, n° 33–34, 2020, p. 285. The author of this testimony, a former student of Simondon, is known only by his initials.
25   See METO, pp. 103–128/MEOT, pp. 121–157.
26   Simondon, "Place d'une initiation aux techniques dans une formation humaine complète", in *Cahiers pédagogiques*, 9, 2, 15 November 1953, p. 115.

to assemble and disassemble the instruments they used for psychological research:

> [...] after the acquisition of a small mansion nearby, we were allowed to use a former laundry room which we converted, under the supervision of Simondon, into the Psychology Laboratory. This episode gave him the opportunity to demonstrate his technical versatility, because at the beginning we had no credit, neither for the installation, nor for the acquisition of equipment. Simondon bought old radars refurbished by the US military. He knew how to choose those in which the cable shears had not hit any significant part and then how to make the device work again as an oscilloscope. In this way we saw our first traces on screens about fifteen centimetres in diameter![27]

Moreover, at that time Simondon continued his research on glare-free headlights for cars. Maurice Mouillaud states in this regard that Simondon installed them on his Peugeot 404 in the corridors of the Faculty's garden in order to try them firsthand: "I remember the experiments he made in the corridors leading down from the Faculty: he had dismantled an old 404 to install a generator in the trunk, while experimenting with one of his inventions, glare-free headlights". Charpentier add further details regarding this invention:

> We have indeed acid-polished numerous plastic plates which, when assembled, were to form a single large headlight. The assumption being that the lighting of a fluorescent tube would dazzle less than a normal spotlight. As the fluorescent tubes could only be powered by alternating current, the vehicle carried a small generator in the rear [...]. Of course, the experimental set had not been presented to the mining department![28]

Precisely from this hypothesis, Simondon assigned Christiane Raymond a PhD dissertation on the effects of glare. In addition, his experiments continued with the realisation of a roof rack for his car, as related by Béjarry: "for him, the invented object had to be perfect and meet all the constraints, and this often made a useless object (for example: a roof rack for his car, a Peugeot 404, certainly robust but too heavy)".[29]

After leaving Poitiers for Paris, having obtained his post as *maître ès conférences* in General Psychology at the Sorbonne, in 1965 he founded a laboratory for general psychology and technology. Jacqueline Lanouziere, who would follow him from Poitiers, recalls in particular on his office at 28 rue Serpente:

> This dark office, devoid of any luster, had nothing that could seduce those who ventured into this den and it made psychology look at first sight like an old-fashioned, poor and vary austere science. My colleagues and I used to compare that office to that of B. Palissy after he burned his furniture and his parquet floor in order to continue his research. He

---

27　Charpentier, "Un contadino del Danubio", p. 225.
28　*Ibidem*.
29　Patrick de Béjarry, "Ricordi di Gilbert Simondon", in *Il Protagora* (forthcoming).

was a stranger to any decorum or pretense and didn't seem to suffer from being badly lodged.[30]

Richard Bilhaut, adjunct physicist at Simondon's laboratory, who worked there with François Hardouin-Duparc and Patrick de Béjarry, adds further details:

> To the right, in this reception office, another door opened onto the electronics laboratory. It was decorated with a window opening onto Boulevard Saint-Germain and, although of modest appearance, it too seemed very well equipped: seismographs and an electroencephalograph stood alongside a large number of electronic components carefully arranged in shelves and many drawers, only waiting for us to dig into them. This overview gives a fairly precise account of the "Laboratory of General Psychology" of Professor Gilbert Simondon: at first glance, no one can get a sense of the possibilities of this incredible cave of Ali Baba.[31]

Philosophy as an emancipation of techniques is therefore not only the outline of a future project, but the theoretical basis for lived experience that this theorist wanted to be disseminated starting precisely from his living example. This last point leads us to reflect on a further aspect of the relations between human beings and techniques, theorised by Simondon in a short essay of 1959, "Les limites du progres humain" – an essay written in response to, and with the same title of, a 1958 paper by Raymond Ruyer. Towards the end, Simondon stresses the need to significantly modify the aforementioned relationships. If, according to him, up to now man has related to techniques as a *subject*, like for example their inventor or builder, today the need arises to change this approach, so that the human being, as a subject, also becomes the *object* of techniques, not only in *emergency* situations, such as those where he becomes the patient of a surgical operation.[32] To make oneself the object of techniques means to ensure that they are applied to support him in the process of clarifying his own "nature": a current example of this practice is the field of neuroscience, whose importance Simondon had foreseen and which inspired him to work hard for the construction of a human energetics, i.e. a discipline straddling psychology and techniques.

---

30 Lanouzière, "Gilbert Simondon", p. 207.
31 Richard Bilhaut, "Gilbert Simondon e il suo Laboratoire de Psychologie Générale", in *Protagora*, Mimesis Edizioni, n° 23–24, 2015, p. 214.
32 See Simondon, "Les limites du progrès humain" (1959), in SLT, pp. 269–278.

3. Philosophical thought as synthesis: philosophy and psychology

Another idea for conceiving philosophy, or better yet, philosophical thought in Simondon's work can be found in the third part of *On the Mode of Existence of Technical Objects*. Philosophical thought, as a "way of being and thinking the world", aims to rediscover the old original unity of magical thought by creating synergies among the different forms of knowledge in a reflective and non-immediate manner:

> Philosophical thought [...] can know the coming-into-being of the different forms of thought and establish a relation between the successive stages of genesis, in particular between the stage that carries out [*accomplit*] the break within the magical natural universe and the stage that carries out the dissociation within the magical human universe, and which is in the process of completing itself [...] philosophical thought must really accomplish this synthesis, and it must construct culture as coextensive with the final result of all technical and religious thought.[33]

One finds an application of this synthetic thought in Simondon's way of conceiving philosophy in relation to psychology. The psychology of the philosophers is a general psychology, which overcomes the barriers between different schools and finds a fundamental unity: the need to give a scientific answer to the (Kantian) question "What is man?", as he declares towards the end of an article co-authored with François Le Terrier on "Modern Psychology": "before being an object of scientific investigation, man is first of all a problem for himself, a problem to which psychology, for the moment, does not provide an objective and definitive answer".[34]

Precisely because Simondon wanted to pursue this goal, one must not conceive of general psychology as an academic discipline, but rather as the project of bringing together all scientific research on man. Due to this ambitious project, Simondon gathered around his chair a large number of psychology researchers with different backgrounds. As Émile Jalley, his collaborator since 1966, recounts,

> Simondon's team was in charge of the teaching of General Psychology properly speaking as part of the Certificate of General and Comparative Psychology (C1), which the students had to take during the third year. One of the originalities of the team is that it also opened up to clinical psychology by providing, alongside Simondon's General Psycholo-

---

33   METO, pp. 244–245/MEOT, pp. 225–226.
34   Simondon-Le Terrier, "La Psychologie Moderne", in Maurice Daumas (ed.), *Encyclopédie La Pléiade – Histoire de la science*, Paris 1957, p. 1702.

gy course and workshops [*TD*] on general psychology, a course on Methods in Personality Study.³⁵

Although he had obtained his post at the Sorbonne thanks to the support of Paul Fraisse and the experimentalists, who had co-opted him against Didier Anzieu, the candidate of the clinicians, Simondon gathered a cohort of *maîtres assistants* who coupled their philosophical formation with, in most cases, a psychoanalytic training. By "general psychology", we must indeed understand, along the lines of Simondon, a kind of knowledge where particular research, the different theoretical orientations and the contributions of all schools of the discipline harmoniously interact:

> One could…say – Simondon declares in this regard – that psychology is waiting for a method to constitute itself as science. Until now, psychology has been divided into two partially antagonistic branches: the bundle of scientific psychologies […] and phenomenology, concerned with apprehending being in its essence and governed by a concern for totality […]. Measurement of the inessential or unscientific apprehension of the essential, such is the torment of Tantalus imposed on the psychologist.³⁶

Simondon's approach thereby proves to be cross-disciplinary: his general psychology is not only a branch centred on the study of cognitive processes (such as perception, memory, etc.), but extends to the field of developmental psychology, clinical psychology and psycho-sociology, feeding on the harmonious interaction of each area of application. The aim of general psychology consists thus in the multiform inquiry into the "complete man", i.e. a man examined in each of his dimensions and who, precisely as incomplete, is an open system made of subsets, whose study and analysis trespasses the barriers between the different psychological schools. Ultimately, in this specific case, Simondon's way of envisaging philosophy as a synthetic thought applied to psychological inquiry with an emphasis on field research, in order to recover the axiomatic unity of that science: "psychology – Simondon held – will be a science from the day when it will have found a unit of measurement applicable to its object, which, as the etymology indicates, the soul or thought".³⁷

---

35   Émile Jalley, *Un franc-comtois à Paris. Un berger du Jura devenu universitaire*, Paris 2010, pp. 355–356.
36   Simondon, "Cybernétique et philosophie" (1953), in SLΦ, p. 59.
37   *Ibid.*, pp. 59–60.

4. Optimism and Pessimism in Simondon: The Role of "Generosity" in his Philosophical Framework

Simondon's philosophical thought presents an intimate coherence: in the light of the notion of allagmatics, in fact, a connection transpires between his reflections on Nature, and in particular on the process of individuation, and his analyses on techniques. While rethinking philosophy, Simondon rethinks in particular one of its dimensions, which I would dare to define as foundational: that of ontology. His philosophy is, first of all, an effort to rethink being in its relationship with becoming, to the point that, if we want to summarise the outcome of his reflection, we could say that it consists in having redefined the being in terms of a *becoming being*, that is intimately governed by a processuality, rather than in terms of a *being in becoming* – a definition, the latter, perhaps closer to the Aristotelian conception of being. Now, this radical effort to rethink being is common to many philosophers of the twentieth century. Just think of the operation carried out by Heidegger or, in France, by Merleau-Ponty, with particular reference to his last courses and writings, even the unfinished ones. If one thinks in particular of the final lines of the famous interview given by Heidegger to *Der Spiegel*, the question legitimately arises as to the *nuances* of this rethinking of being.[38] In particular, one wonders whether every rethinking of being does not imply a precise framing of this very being in an optimistic or pessimistic key. Therefore, in this last part, I will assess whether Simondon's philosophy can be deemed an optimism or a pessimism. Simondon's philosophy is in fact a reflection which presents Nature as endowed with spontaneity, such as that of Lucretius, which actualises itself in the operations of individuation, the genetic processes which embody its generative power. A generous Nature, therefore, in the sense Descartes ascribed to generosity, and that Simondon, according to Charpentier, liked to repeat to his students:

> When I think of Gilbert Simondon, I first think of generosity. Of course in the current meaning of the term: the abundance of the fruits he offered us, the kindness with which he regarded us would easily justify this feeling. But I also remember that, on several occasions, he exposed and commented on Descartes' definition: true generosity, which makes a man esteem himself to the highest degree to which he can legitimately esteem himself, consists partly in the fact the there is nothing that truly belongs to him other than this free disposition of his will, and partly in that he feels within himself a firm and constant resolution to use it properly, that is, never to lack the will to undertake and accomplish all the things that he deems to be the best. He had, I think, high self-esteem (and rightly so!) and probably thought that a certain responsibility derived from his abilities. He

---

[38] See Martin Heidegger, "'Only a God Can Save Us': The *Spiegel* Interview (1966)", in Thomas Sheehan (ed.), *Heidegger: The Man and the Thinker*, New Brunswick-London, 2010, pp. 45–68.

spontaneously showed the same nobility to his interlocutors and suffered greatly from the errors that such a postulate made him commit in his relationships.[39]

But is Simondon's philosophy really optimistic?

In a brief text, whose format is that of a report on the students work in Poitiers (1955–1963), as explained in the note that precedes it in its recent edition, Simondon deals with optimism and pessimism from the philosophical point of view and in view of the birth of morals "which present an ethical vision of the world, and which define the table of values". After briefly analysing them from a psychological, metaphysical and moral perspective, he asserts that they are above all behaviours [*conduites*] adopted in relation to the world:

> Optimism and pessimism are behaviours [*conduites*]. These behaviours can create a natural attitude, similar to an innate character trait (retraction, dilation), or engender a vision of the world.[40]

In Simondon's opinion, the pessimist is a tense being, aware of his incompleteness:

> Apparently, pessimism is a more complex behaviour [compared to optimism], endowed the prestige of intelligence or discernment (Tacitus). It is a reflex and at times reflexive behaviour, and appears in the mechanism of the internal regulation of our behaviour by itself [...]. Man does not live in the past [...]; but it makes his futures an *already past* [déjà passé] [...]. Hence the perpetual lack of being [*manque d'être*] that characterizes pessimism [...]. The essential reason for pessimism is the metaphysical limitation of individuality.[41]

Now, it is just this internal tension that can initiate a change of state in the pessimism once he encounters another person in his path: "If the pessimist encounters a soul and a worldview similar to his own and which shares a keen and deep sense of values, they can both access a new state of being. Life re-orientates itself".[42] On the contrary, the optimist is a creative generous being who

> gives room to positive feelings and actions, and the general style of which is confidence, or hope [...]. The positive feeling is that in the deployment of which we feel ourselves to be the centre of forces turned outwards, capable of conveying a message or a positive modification in the existence of the Other. This is generosity. *Optimism is therefore the structure of a perpetuated creative experience*. Its essence is the joy of becoming a creator conscious of its activity.[43]

---

39 Charpentier, "Un contadino del Danubio", p. 223.
40 Simondon, "Optimisme et pessimisme", in SLΦ, p. 111.
41 *Ibidem*.
42 *Ibid.*, p. 115.
43 *Ibid.*, p. 111.

However, in his *Individuation*, Simondon provides a rather original definition of the subject in general. The subject is not the individual: he is the whole made of the individualised layer and of the potential charge that derives from the original individuation that generated this couple; the

> Complete subject [...] in addition to individuated reality, includes within it an unindividuated, pre-individual, or even natural aspect. This unindividuated charge of reality conceals a power of individuation, which, within the subject alone, cannot conclude, whether due to the being's poverty, isolation, or the lack of a systematic whole. Gathered with other subjects, the subject can correlatively be the theater and agent of a second individuation that gives birth to the transindividual collective and links the subject to other subjects.[44]

The subject theorised by Simondon is a tense and incomplete being, aware of this incompleteness: "we [...] feel that we are not eternal, that we are fragile and transitory, that we will no longer exist when the sun will still be shining on the rocks next spring. Facing natural life, we feel that we are as perishable as the leaves of a tree".[45] But this subject may initiate new individuations thanks to its potential charge. Furthermore, Simondon's reflection is entirely marked by the importance of potentials and potential energy. This is a topic closely related to the definition itself of optimism and pessimism in a post-cybernetic key, since, as he himself states, pessimists and optimists differ according to the disposition of their energy potential. In his psychology lessons, he refers to motivation as the potential energy that drives action. Although his philosophy of Nature seems crossed by an exhilarating optimism, the subject he paints is only an incomplete being who, thanks to his potential, can create something new by *transindividuating*, through team work – a lesson Simondon drew from cybernetics: "Critical and positivist epistemology is an epistemology of the solitary scientist. Cybernetic epistemology, on the contrary, is that of the scientific team [...]. The birth of cybernetics seems to show [...] that the knowing subject can be a society".[46]

This may be why Simondon, according to Charpentier and de Béjarry, and as we have seen, did not work alone on his projects: once he had the idea, the intuition, he acted like the subject he had theorised, by sharing his projects with his students and collaborators whom he kindly listened to. But that is not why his philosophy is pessimistic. On the contrary, it should be placed halfway between an exalted optimism and the gloomy pessimism that he deplored, as one of his students in Tours underlines in his memories of Simondon as a young professor in Tours: while correcting the homework of one of his students, he

---

[44] ILNFI, p. 348/ILFI, p. 310.
[45] *Ibid.*, p. 277/p. 251.
[46] Simondon, "Optimisme et pessimisme", in SLΦ, p. 115.

warned him "to be wary of the consequences of a destructive pessimism".[47] The essence of Simondon's philosophy is a humanism that "would be [...] a mixture of maturity and youth, if we define by maturity the sense of internal proportion and by youth the sense of enthusiasm".[48]

The *new* humanism, as Simondon defined it in a short essay written in 1953 and published the following year,[49] consisted precisely in what he himself sought to embody and worked so hard for: a humanism that neither ignored nor neglected the human being in each of its expressions and manifestations. More precisely, a humanism that also grasped the human being in those spheres in which it was latent or masked, as is the case with techniques – or better still, technical objects – to which Simondon was able to devote himself with generosity, with the aim of rediscovering the man who is concealed there and to whom we must rely on for any future salvation.

---

[47] G. L., "Gilbert Simondon. Ricordi di uno dei suoi allievi di filosofia. Tours, 1950–1952", loc. cit.

[48] Simondon, "Humanisme culturel, humanisme négatif, humanisme nouveau" (1953), in SLΦ, p. 72.

[49] See *ibid.*, pp. 71–75.

The Long Detour
Simondon Reader of Plato

Ludovic Duhem

> Therefore, if the path is long, be not astonished; for it must be trodden for great ends, not for those you have in mind. Yet your ends also, as our argument says, will be best gained in this way, if one so desires.
>
> Plato, *Phaedrus*

> This necessity to close the cycle by the Ethics starting from the concrete to the abstract and going back to the integration into the built concrete, Plato has reflected it in the image of the "long detour"; at the end of the *makran odon*, the philosophical consciousness is reincarnated in the sensible.
>
> Gilbert Simondon, *Analysis of the Criteria of Individuality*

In this chapter,[1] we would first like to define the place of Platonism in Simondon's thought and to specify the meaning of a "long detour"[2] as a philosophical method. But we would like overall to understand how this *Platonical* method is relevant, although everything seems to be opposed to such a step in the positions that the French philosopher adopts to rehabilitate the becoming, the technique and the image. And if something like a "reversal of Platonism" takes place in the philosophy of Simondon, we would then show that is by an original gesture of critique, interpretation and extension; which lights up the complex and evolving relationship of Simondon to Plato during his work, renews the reading of Plato about becoming, as much as it allows us to emancipate ourselves from the potential it conceals. From this study on Simondon and Platonism, we would finally like to qualify this

---

1   This study is an extension of a previous study about the Pre-Socratics in Simondon's work. See Ludovic Duhem, "*Apeiron* et *physis*. Simondon transducteur des présocratiques", in Jean-Hugues Barthélémy (ed.), *Cahiers Simondon*, n.4, ed. Paris, L'Harmattan, 2012, pp. 33–67.

2   Simondon uses the idea of "long detour" several times in his work ("Épistémologie de la cybernétique", in *SLΦ*, p. 194; "Analyse des critères de l'individualité", in ILNFI, p. 653/ILFI, p. 555; IMIN, p. 62). Victor Goldschmidt is certainly Simondon's main source for interpreting Plato's thought through the idea of "long detour". Goldschmidt qualifies the Platonic method, that of the dialectic, of "essential detour". See Goldschmidt, *Les dialogues de Platon. Structure et méthode dialectique*, Paris, PUF, 1947.

gesture as a *transduction of philosophy*, i.e. both as an anti-dogmatic method to read the texts of the occidental tradition, a non-linear and non-dialectical way to write the history of philosophy and an unexpected method for inventing a new way of thinking the reality.

1. Individuation and Platonism

At first sight, the place of Platonism in Simondon's thought is clear: it is incompatible with his project of thinking the whole of reality through becoming and relation by adopting a radically anti-substantialist position. Thus, Simondon affirms that "the Western philosophical tradition is [...] almost entirely substantialistic".[3] However, the "model of the being as substance" of this tradition initiated by Parmenides – who is the "father of Plato's thought"[4] – is what prevents to think the becoming as becoming, that is to say without starting from the principle that the becoming is opposed to the being, that the becoming is external to the being, that the becoming is an accident for the being and not a dimension of the being, what it is (also) as being. All the attempts, even critical, that we can derive from the Parmenidean being, that is to say an absolute being, identical to itself, eternal and unalterable, leaves the becoming in a "dark zone" which makes it almost unthinkable; because it grants a privilege to the constituted individual and explains the existence and the characteristics of it through a principle that is external, superior, and posed as a given conceptual individual.

In this sense, Simondon affirms that "it is necessary to *reverse* the search for the principle of individuation by considering the operation of individuation as primordial, on the basis of which the individual comes to exist and of which it reflects the course, the regime, and finally the modalities, in its characters".[5] The becoming of the being is thus its distribution in phases, i.e. the *operation* by which the being without phase but in state of initial supersaturation rich in potentials, dephases and structures itself then by solving the incompatibility between its phases, to form finally the couple individual-milieu[6] as an active relationship. However, such a genetical and relational conception requires on one

---

3   ILNFI, p. 87/ILNFI, p 92.
4   Simondon, "Histoire de la notion d'individu", in ILNFI, *op. cit.*, p. 437/ILFI, p. 341. Abbreviated HNI. This text is explicitly structured by a reading of Émile Bréhier's book: *Histoire de la philosophie*, PUF, Paris, 1930.
5   ILNFI, p. 3/ILFI, p. 24, emphasis added.
6   In HNI, Simondon regrets on one hand that the *chora* is reduced by Plato to a "bastard, hardly believable" concept; and, on other hand, the incapacity of the *chora* and the elementary triangles to make complete organized individuals appear. This is explained according to him by the fact that Plato granted *a privilege to the structure, to the limit, to the absolute individual*, and, finally, he did not know how to integrate the physics of the Ionians.

hand the criticism of the principle of identity and of the principle of the excluded third that Platonism implies; and, on other hand, the notions coming from contemporary sciences like the conditions of metastability, the potential energy of a system, the orders of magnitude, the negentropic information – that Platonism cannot provide.

But what is particularly interesting, while being immediately surprising, is that Simondon mobilises two notions coming from Platonism to explain his theory of the being: that of the "indefinite dyad" and that of the "paradigm".

In ILNFI, Simondon mobilises the notion of indefinite dyad[7] in an explicit way to designate several things about individuation, technology or ethics. In general, it is "an informative and interactive communication between what is greater than the individual and what is smaller than him" according to a "dynamic polarity" between initially disparate and incompatible orders of magnitude. We can say that for Simondon, the indefinite dyad plays a major and not isolated role in the theory of individuation to explain how the becoming of all the levels and all the modes of reality operates according to a dynamics between two polarised orders of magnitude and the potential that lies within. We must immediately add that the indefinite dyad is also the *apeiron*, the indeterminate, that is to say the potentials of the system and not only the tension and incompatibility between two orders of magnitude that the operation of individuation will make compatible. The indefinite dyad is more than an element and more than a condition for thought, it is constitutive of the philosophical process.[8]

In his lecture entitled "Form, Information, and Potentials" where he tries to establish the conditions of an axiomatics of human sciences, Simondon proposes to "renew the principles of the indefinite Dyad, of Archetype, of Form and Matter, and bring them in line with the recent explanatory models of Gestalt Psychology, and then those of the Cybernetics and Information Theory [...]".[9] He considers then that the Form plays a constant role of the "*structural germ* with a certain guiding and organizing power", and it supposes "a basic duality between two types of reality, the reality that receives the form and that which is the form or harbors form".[10] But the "foundation of every theory of form" for Simondon, thus for Platonism in priority here, is "the qualitative, functional and hierarchi-

---

7   Marquet was undoubtedly the first to stress the importance of the indefinite dyad. See Jean-François Marquet, "Gilbert Simondon et la pensée de l'individuation", in Gilles Châtelet, Hubert Curien (eds.), *Gilbert Simondon. Une pensée de l'individuation et de la technique*, Paris, Albin Michel, 1994, pp. 91–99. Jacques Garelli also mentions it in his preface of ILFI.

8   Simondon affirms it also about the image: "the primordial character of the motor content in any image of anticipation *a priori*, in spite of the fixity of the archetypes, was latent in Plato; philosophy is also a knowledge of the mixtures, of the indefinite dyad, of the *genesis eis ousian*, according to the philosophical metric of the ideas-numbers". *IMIN*, p. 62.

9   Simondon, "Forme, information, potentiels", in ILNFI, p. 672/ILFI, p. 531.

10   ILNFI, p. 673/ILFI, p. 531.

cal asymmetry of Form and of what takes form".[11] In the Simondonian reading of the Form, there is thus a subtle *tension* between the Form as "structural germ", as informative singularity able to trigger an operation of individuation and its superior, external and asymmetrical character compared to what takes form. The Form is capable of generating, it is the cause of sensible things, but it does not degrade nor is it capable of any progress. The fundamental problem is that the Form is given, that it is perfect from the beginning, eternal and transcendent structure. Platonism constitutes in this "a system of conservation and respect of the Idea given once and for all, or else of return to the Idea", that is to say that it seeks at all costs to safeguard the "structural system characterizing the individual".[12] The resolution of this subtle tension is realised by passing from the *first Platonism*, that of the theory of Forms, to the *second Platonism*, that of the indefinite dyad. Indeed, according to Simondon, the notion of indefinite dyad "allows to explain with more precision the *metrion*, is more appropriate for sensible objects and to their genetic becoming than the *eidos*".[13] The Platonism compatible with the theory of individuation is therefore that of the esoteric and oral teaching witnessed in Aristotle's Metaphysics,[14] for it is that in which Plato seeks to reconcile himself with becoming and even to base it. Simondon goes even further by proposing to reconsider the theory of Form in general, and more precisely of the good form in *Gestalt Psychology* (heir to Platonism) in relation to the "theory of fields", as a dyad or even a "plurality of dyads coordinated together", that is to say "a *network*, a schema, something simultaneously one and multiple – that contains a correlation between different terms."[15] The theory of individuation is, in a way, a world of undefined dyads, where Platonism is at the same time extended and horizontalised, multiplied and reticulated. But to explain the nature and functioning of such a world, it will be necessary to pass from the notion of form to that of information (neither quantity nor quality but intensity), which is the very ambition of what seems a radical overcoming of Platonism and of all these forms in philosophy as in the sciences.

---

11   *Ibid*.
12   ILNFI, 678/ILFI, pp. 535–536.
13   ILNFI, p. 679/ILFI, p. 536.
14   Aristotle, *Metaphysics*, trans. D. Ross, Oxford University Press, 1924. In a passage in ILNFI on physical individuation, Simondon explicitly evokes the Ideas-numbers, but while recognising the potential of this esoteric and oral Platonism to think the becoming and to integrate it in the whole of the reality, he specifies nevertheless that this theory "still preserves the notion of the superiority of the one and the immobile one on the multiple one, and the movement as imperfection" (ILNFI, p. 86/ILFI, p. 91).
15   ILNFI, p. 688/ILFI, p. 543.

As for the notion of "paradigm", Simondon gives two meanings: the simple paradigm and the analogical paradigm.[16] The first one, the simple paradigm, is the one that has an exemplary value and can serve as an explanatory model. For instance, it is what happens with the technical object that allows us to explain the relations between form, information and potentials.[17] But this type of paradigm is the least common in Simondon, because it is the one that establishes weak relations between elements. The one that establishes strong relations is the analogical paradigm, which is the real method of thought and even invention.

In this regard, Simondon states that the study of crystallisation has a "paradigmatic value" to explain the process of individuation. But the crystallisation is not an absolute paradigm insofar as it does not exhaust all the reality that it describes, even at the physical level. Crystallisation is in this respect "the simplest image of the transductive operation". Yet, in spite of this strong limitation, Simondon considers that crystallisation indicates the necessity of founding a "new kind of analogical paradigm" allowing not only to describe an individuation operation but to think it in all its forms, and even more, to explain the passage between individuation regimes from the physical to the biological, and from the biological to the psychosocial. Now, this jump from the particular to the general, from the descriptive to the explanatory, is not a faulty contradiction. On the contrary, the new analogical paradigm that Simondon seeks to establish is one that is both ontological and methodological, the knowledge of an individuation as an object being always and at the same time an individuation of the knowledge of the subject. Moreover, in the process of knowledge, the transfer of the paradigm is accompanied by its transformation, and notably by its complexification. To understand this, it is necessary to explain the meaning of the analogy.

In his "Theory of the Analogical Act" (supplement of ILNFI), Simondon explains that an "the analogical act is the putting into relation of two operations". He leans on Plato by saying that the latter used it as a method of inductive discovery: "*paradigmatism* consists in transporting an operation of thought, an operation which is first [learned and] tested on a particular known structure (for example, that which serves in the *Sophist* to define the angler) and imparted to another particular unknown structure and object of research (the structure of the sophist in the *Sophist*)". But the most important thing is that "this act of thinking, transfer of operations, doesn't suppose the existence of an ontological ground common to the fisherman and the sophist, to aspalieutics and sophistry. It does not in any way seek to prove that the fisherman and the sophist result from the imitation of the same shared model through the Demiurge: logical

---

16   On Plato's theory of paradigm, see Goldschmidt, *Le paradigme dans la dialectique platonicienne*, Paris, Vrin, 1947.
17   ILNFI, p. 664/ILFI, p. 532.

paradigmatism is freed from metaphysical *exemplarism*."[18] What is important is to understand that Plato finds there a "means to rationalise the becoming" according to Simondon, this means allowing to know "by defining structures by the operations which dynamize them, instead of knowing by defining the operations by the structures between which they are exercised". This means that the analogy is not an association of ideas nor a resemblance established by a relation of identity, but an identity of operative relation between the two "terms" considered – these "terms" being operations of individuation and already in relation with the operations of thought that seeks to know them. According to such a conception of analogy, transduction expresses a new type of paradigmatism inspired by Plato but which is not reducible to the theory of Ideas, and even subverts it in favour of a reinscription of the philosophical method in the becoming. The method no longer consists in seeking to compose the essence of a reality starting from concepts, but in following the object to be known in its genesis by carrying out the genesis of the thought. This form of "intuition" is in this sense either deductive or inductive, because it does not look for any external principle and keeps all the information of the problem by integrating the opposite aspects in the resolution as structure and condition of meaning. But a transduction can also be combined with several types of knowledge, including deductive and inductive modes, which will then be complementary; provided, however, that the validity of the relation between these modes of knowledge is questioned.

We will thus have understood that Simondon is not satisfied to operate a negative criticism of Plato's thought. Even if these two schemes of organisation of the history of philosophy, the one of *HNI* and the one of the *Course on Perception*, place Plato's work on the side of the "structural approach" which answers the "genetic approach" inaugurated by the Ionian physiologists, the one that makes of the history of philosophy a history dominated by substantialism, the contemplative rationalism of abstract symbols and therefore the refusal to think the becoming, Plato is not definitively the one for whom the refusal becomes an impossibility. It is indeed with Aristotle that "any genetic explanation of essences is henceforth impossible", in the sense that it imposes a "system of the pure actuality" for which "the being can be conceived [...] only as already individualized",[19] that is to say that it is not only always already in act but no part of the being remains not individualised *a contrario* of the Ionian physiologists and of

---

18   Simondon, "Theory of the Analogical Act", in ILNFI, p. 664/ILFI, p. 562. This original reading of Plato could be influenced by Paul Grenet and Pierre De Solages (dissemblance in resemblance and ratio of proportion), but Simondon proposes a different interpretation (operational not structural). To compare, see Paul Grenet, *Les Origines de l'analogie philosophique dans les dialogues de Platon*, Paris, Boivin, 1948; Pierre De Solages, *Dialogue sur l'analogie*, Paris, Aubier, 1946.
19   HNI, in ILNFI, p. 440–441/ILFI, pp. 362–363.

the late Plato's thought. In any case, there is a certain *tension* between the criticism of the first Platonism (that of the Parmenidean and Socratic heritage) and the potential for invention of the second Platonism (that of the late works of the *Sophist*, the *Parmenides* and the *Timaeus*),[20] which, in order to materialise, requires both transduction and invention, insofar as the essentials are to be found elsewhere than in the Platonic dialogues, i.e. in the esoteric teachings reported by Aristotle.

2. Technics and Platonism

In the same way as for the rehabilitation of becoming by the theory of individuation, the rehabilitation of technique seems to be also in direct opposition with Platonism. We know Plato's hostility towards technique. Certainly any production, even artisanal, is not the result of chance but of a knowledge of its nature, and more precisely of its Form. The examples of the *Gorgias*, the *Cratylus* and the *Republic* testify to the fact that the concrete object results from an intellectual view which will guide the form to be imposed on the materials. The production supposes thus knowledge of the Form and capacity to act on a material. But all these examples are there only as an analogy to explain something else more important and higher. So, even if metaphors and technical analogies are numerous in the Platonic dialogues, technique always has an inferior status in the search for truth, because it is the paradigm of human activities in the sensible world. As for the technicians, they are almost all contemptible, like the craftsmen in the order of *praxis*[21] or the sophists in the order of *logos*. In this respect, the myth of "Prometheus and Epimetheus" in *Protagoras* and the myth of "Theuth" in *Phaedrus*[22] are explicit about the place to be given to technique:[23] that of the fault, of

---

20 There is another tension between the "historical" schema of Platonism in *HNI* and in "Épistémologie de la Cybernétique". In this second text, the reason given by Simondon is: "when the metrics of philosophers replace the contemplation of archetypes ideas, the norm of (*enthendé ekeise pheugein*, 'going away from here to the higher', Thaetetus, 176a) is replaced by ἐν τῷ θνητῷ ἀθανατίζειν (*en toi thnètoi athanatizein*), 'to undead in the deadful, the sensible'; the isolation of archetypes ideas is becoming participation of number-ideas [...]." SLΦ, p. 194.
21 See the famous statement in the Gorgias about the technician to whom "you would neither give your son to his daughter nor marry his daughter yourself" (*Gorgias*, 512bc).
22 See Jacques Derrida, "La pharmacie de Platon" in *Phèdre*, Paris, GF, 2000, pp. 257–287, and Bernard Stiegler, *La technique et le temps. 1. La faute d'Épiméthée*, Paris, Galilée, Chap. 1.
23 In the text "Perception and modulation" of 1968, Simondon explains in a remark that the Platonic thought of the Ideas, such as it is formulated in the "myth" of the cave, was influenced by "technological schemes". It is about the "thaumaturgic projection of straight shadows" and about the "colored and inverted projection in darkroom (*camera*)". The common characteristic of these two models, explains Simondon, is that "projected information is degraded, the

the forgetfulness, and of the illusion of true knowledge. The *Sophist* certainly proposes a theory of technique through the method of division (by distinguishing technique as *production – poièsis –* and technique as *acquisition – ktétikè –*) and this text also shows that it is useful to understand things subject to becoming, but to finally reduce it to an opposition to true knowledge, that of science (*epistêmê*). The *Timaeus* grants a certain dignity to technique, insofar as the Demiurge, "maker and father of this universe", is a "craftsman" who uses techniques analogous to those of construction and metallurgy. But the Demiurge is not a craftsman in the sense of a mortal with a soul and a body. He is a *pure intellect* whose soul and body are products of his existence. It is prior and superior to all things that exist, at least to all the sensible things that he produces, the mathematical substructures as well as time, by imitating the intelligible Forms (and that with the help of the receptacle (*chorâ*) and the becoming to make the universe pass from chaos to order). No craftsman can compare to the Demiurge who is the best and produces the best and most beautiful; at best he is the greatest engineer by giving a mathematical structure to things subject to becoming in order to give them a stable, indestructible and understandable character by reason.[24]

In his work, Simondon does not proceed to an analysis of technique in Plato nor of the complex figure of the Demiurge. In ILNFI, it is Aristotle who is the object of a criticism addressed to the hylomorphic scheme, which is less a purely technical paradigm (relation between form and matter) than a social and political paradigm (relationship between the master and the worker or the slave). As we have seen above, in the passage of *HNI* about the *Timaeus*, Simondon regrets that Plato did not preserve the *physis* of the Ionian thinkers. The cosmos comes from a finalised action of the Demiurge, producing the overall organisation and structure of the individuality of the universe, and it is even "all [...] penetrated of finality until its smallest details [...]"[25] where the mixed beings are unable to become by themselves nor to maintain themselves in themselves. The Ionian physiologists, on the contrary, thinkers of *physis* (as a dynamism of growth and an element producing heterogeneity), are at the same time sensitive to the concrete and practical dimension of the world through the

---

imitation is always inferior to the model". However, Simondon specifies immediately that this degradation, so essential in the theory of the Ideas in the relation between model and copy, is historically determined by the technical evolution and not by an essence. The ancient techniques of Plato's time to modulate and amplify produce an "enormous" loss of information by defect of power. In contemporary times, the evolution of projection techniques would make this Platonic analogy much less relevant. See "Perception et Modulation", in Simondon, *Communication et information*, Paris, PUF, 2015, pp. 193–194.

24   On the Demiurge figure, see Léon Robin, *Platon*, Paris, PUF, 1935.
25   ILNFI, p. 433/ILFI, p. 357.

operations that take place in it, mobilise technical analogies to explain the genesis of the universe and of what composes it, and above all they are themselves technicians. They are even the technicians "par excellence" for Simondon, insofar as they are the *"eumechanos eis technas"* (Plato, *Republic*, 600a), that is to say not only the best in mechanics, but those who are at the origin of a "free individual thought and of a disinterested reflection"[26]. More precisely, they "knew how to free themselves from the community by a direct dialogue with the world"[27], that is to say that they affirmed themselves as "pure individuals"[28] able to join together the two conditions of the reflective thought (thus of the philosophy) that are the "organic life" and the "technical life". The true technician is not the one who imitates a model and arranges materials, but the one who unites organic life and technical life and establishes a mediation between community and hidden object (of research). The Platonic craftsman cannot assume such a role, whereas the Ionian thinker can, to the point of being able to institute a new community, to invent not what is useful but what without which there is no true civilisation.[29]

In his great book on technique, *On the Mode of Existence of Technical Objects*, Simondon seeks to rehabilitate technique by applying the theory of individuation developed earlier. In all coherence, the technical object is considered as an individual to be understood through its genesis and its relation to a milieu. The difference with the Platonic approach to the technique is thus double: on one hand, the technical object is thought through the becoming rather than as what results from an operation requiring a pre-existing structural principle (the

---

26   ILNFI, p. 340/ILFI, p. 411. In his *Cours sur la perception*, Simondon thus affirms that "Neither Pythagoras, nor Plato are operators, architects, craftsmen; they contemplate and isolate themselves in meditative leisure, founding esoteric groups and reserving their teaching; in their doctrines, the ethical importance shows that the World counts less than the Man". Further on he affirms in the same sense that "the Pythagorean sage [from whom Plato takes his inspiration] leaves perception as trade with objects in the operative exchange, in the vulgar manipulation, to rise radically above that by which perception is reception of information, reception of diversity, meeting of contingencies, openness to the occurrences that the present brings, and intentional movement towards the near future". The Platonic thought is certainly not without any relation with the perception but it excludes any relation to the operative which supposes a direct and manipulative contact: "The first and last intuition of the principles is, in Plato as in the Pythagoreans, defined by analogy with the perceptions given by the senses acting at a distance of the object: the use of these senses does not imply, indeed, of constructive operation, of manipulative action, of vital participation which binds the subject to the destiny of the object [...]" See Simondon, *Cours sur la perception* (1964–1965), Paris, PUF, 2013, p. 13 and p. 15.
27   ILNFI, p. 411/ILFI, p. 340.
28   See Duhem, "L'idée d'"individu pur" dans la pensée de Simondon, *Appareil*, n. 2, 2008. https://journals.openedition.org/appareil/583
29   See IMIN, Introduction, about the *pinax*.

Form); on the other hand, it is thought out of the finalist principle of utility as a system in internal resonance existing through a functioning. It is necessary to add to this that the technical object keeps in its structure a link with *physis*, both in the form of an internal dynamic and of an indeterminacy (*apeiron*) or evolutionary potential; and by the act of invention that gives birth to it, the technical object is not a pure *poiesis*, in the sense of a passage from non-being to being, nor only of an arrangement of matter by the imposition of a form imitating an archetype, but the resolution of a problem mobilising the vital force of the inventor, the laws of nature, already technical elements and functioning schemes that are rationally known at the same time as simulated in their coherent activity within the object to come. There is no production by imitation in technical invention, but problem solving by transduction and feedback.

Simondon's most explicit stand against Platonism in his technical thought is less about the invention or the mode of existence of the technical object, than about the role of philosophy itself. In the third part of METO, Simondon assigns to philosophy the role not only of knowing the meaning of technical objects through their genesis, but above all of restoring the unity of culture by integrating them to take humanity out of the alienation at the time of the industrial complexes and the informational networks. More precisely, its vocation is to ensure the convergence and to institute a mediation between "technicity" and "religiosity" which are henceforth incompatible following a second dephasing of the system of culture (after the magic unity has dephased into technicity and religiosity during the first dephasing, technicity has dephased into theory and practice and religion into ethics and dogma during the second) that prevents their integration. This requirement of convergence and mediation requires to deepen the "sense of becoming" and to constitute a "reflexive technology". But to achieve this, a new theory of knowledge is needed. To know the technical objects in their functioning and in their evolution is not enough. The awareness of the "genetic character of technicality" implies in reality that philosophical thought restarts the problem of the relations between idea, concept and intuition, and, correlatively, to "correct the meaning" of nominalism and realism.

According to the diagram of the phase theory, technical thinking and religious thinking are incompatible: technical thinking provides the paradigm of inductive thinking; while religious thinking provides the paradigm of deductive thinking. Technical thought is the one that makes intelligible the elements "taken one by one" and their combination through the mutual relations constituting the whole. For such an operative thought, "the real to be known is at the end of the effort of knowledge, it is not a mass given at once in its totality".[30] Religious thinking, on the contrary, starts from "an overall function recognized from the outset as having an unconditional value, and which can only be made explicit,

---

[30] METO, p. 240/MEOT, p. 318.

but not constructed and produced by the subject who thinks".[31] Simondon specifies that this deductive model is above all a "contemplative" model, insofar as the reality of the being can never be completely known but only represented. The knowing subject is thus held in respect, maintained in a situation of inferiority and incompleteness compared to the being. Simondon specifies then that this mode of knowledge is "the base of the idealist realism" of which Plato is the greatest representative. That is translated by the fact that the *eidos* is "a view of being, a structure of being that exists for itself before being thought; it is not essentially and, from the start, an instrument of knowledge [...]".[32] And although there is an analogical relation between the sensible things and the Ideas, and even between the Ideas and the Good, the human knowledge must carry out an ontological course reversed to the direction of the becoming.

This criticism of Platonic idealism which imposes an ontological regression, a separation of the knowing subject and the being, and especially a real given as an absolute structure in relation to which the subject will always be in a position of inferiority and incompleteness, is not absolute. We can understand this through the position adopted by Simondon in relation to the operative thought of the inductive type. If reality is given as an absolute for contemplative knowledge, it is relative to a construction for operative knowledge. Similarly, instead of being what precedes all knowledge and remains separate from the knowing subject, the real is what follows knowledge and involves the subject in its constitution. In this sense, contrary to the idea, the concept is the result of an operation, that of a "gathering" implying "abstraction" and "generalisation", which cannot be constituted without an *hic et nunc* experience. But the key point for Simondon is that this opposition between the idea defined as an absolute, given and separated structure, and the concept as a relative, constructed and integrative operation, that is to say between a deductive, idealist, realist "a priorism" and an inductive, empiricist, conceptualist and partially nominalistic "a posteriorism", is precisely what prevents to re-establish the unity of that culture, what maintains the opposition between technicality and religiosity, and what paralyses the philosophical thought to assume its role. The only way to achieve this is for philosophy to "appeal" to a "medial and superior mode of knowledge, bringing together in its unity concepts and ideas". Simondon proposes then to rethink intuition as a mode of knowledge adapted to this fundamental stake. The intuition is neither *a priori* nor *a posteriori*, but *a praesenti*, it is "contemporaneous with the existence of the being it grasps" and "which is at the same level as this being". More precisely, explains Simondon,

---

31   METO, p. 240/MEOT, p. 318.
32   *Ibid.*

it is not a knowledge by the way of the idea, for intuition is not already contained within the structure of the known being; it does not belong to that being; it is not a concept, since it has an internal unity that grants its autonomy and its singularity, preventing a genesis through accumulation; lastly, knowledge by way of intuition is really mediate in the sense that it does not grasp being in its absolute totality, like the idea, or on the basis of the elements and by combination, like the concept, but grasps being at the level of the domains constituting a structured ensemble.[33]

Intuition, as we have seen before, is an "analogy" between the becoming of the known being and the becoming of the subject, it is a method of knowledge of reality understood as a system of genetic processes. Intuition is neither intelligible nor sensible, it keeps the idea as a mode of knowledge of structural realities and their functions of totality (the background reality proper to religiosity) and the concepts as a mode of knowledge of figurative realities and their elementary functions. But it does not only preserve the idea and the concept, the intuition intervenes as *mediation* between idea and concept and ensures the genesis of the correlation between background realities and figural realities. The philosophical thought, coming after the double successive dephasing of the technicality and the religiosity, after having "exhausted the possibilities of conceptual knowledge and knowledge by idea"[34] can thus assure their convergence by the intuition of the real.

To carry out such a programme, Simondon will question the relevance of Cybernetics. It is there the last important confrontation to the Platonism regarding the question of technique. In many respects, the Cybernetics of Weiner is for Simondon a model for the building of a genetic encyclopaedism with a technological base, which is necessary to the contemporary stakes (philosophical, social and political) of knowledge and liberation. While recognising the importance of Cybernetics and its paradigmatic value in ILNFI and in METO, Simondon also insists on the limits of such a model, in particular regarding its insufficient effectiveness to establish an interscientific dialogue, regarding the erroneous postulate of the identity of the living beings and the technical objects, regarding the incompleteness of the comprehension of the relation between form and information, regarding the privilege granted to the automaton through the feedback to think the machine, regarding the problematic application of the principle of unconditional homeostasis to society. These limits express a *residual Platonism* that grants a privilege to structure, quantity, stability, finality and even to the absolute. Without Simondon affirming it explicitly, it is quite natural to deduce it from the criticisms that he addresses to Cybernetics.

But this negative residual Platonism, which limits the relevance of Cybernetics to provide a valid model in the constitution of a genetic encyclopaedism,

---

33   METO, p. 242/MEOT, p. 321.
34   METO, p. 243/MEOT, p. 323.

is paradoxically compensated by a positive Platonism, that of the Ideas-numbers. In an early text (a working manuscript) of 1953, titled "Épistémologie de la cybernétique",[35] Simondon associates Cybernetics and Platonism. Cybernetics is defined by Simondon as a "mathematics of operations", which distinguishes it from the "science of structures". Rather than imposing an *a priori* normativity to the sciences in the spirit of the negative Platonism (or first Platonism), that we find in positivism and criticism, it expresses a normativity directly resulting from the operations and which is inherent to them. Simondon considers then that "the metretics of the Ideas-numbers" already expressed an "effort of theorization of the operations of the becoming". As Plato did in his oral esoteric teaching, it is not a question of opposing "the contemplative rationality of the knowledge of the structures to the pure irrationality of the *genesis* and the *phtora*", but of accomplishing the research on an exact knowledge of the becoming by the *metrion*. According to Simondon, at the end of the *Republic* and the *Laws*, the previous isolation of the Idea-archetypes becomes a participation of the Ideas-numbers: instead of "escaping from up here" (*enthendé ekeise pheugein*), it is henceforth a question of "immortalizing oneself in the mortal, the sensible" (*en toi thnètoi athanatizein*). It follows a cascade of consequences analogous to that of the cybernetic attitude: the research on individual salvation becomes that on the balance of the city, the research on the particular essences becomes that on a paradigmatic method in the discovery of the truth, the dialectic becomes means of discovery of a relation by a group of minds. All these transformations are the expression of a "long detour", physical, epistemological and critical, which brought Plato from an initial normativity "individual like ethics, transcendent like contemplative mysticism", to a final normativity "universal like politics, immanent like becoming". Such a way was possible only with the meeting of the "Eleatic mathematics" and the "Ionian physiology" which allows Plato to form a "subtle science of the measure" which is at the same time a "knowledge of the operations of the becoming".[36] But this "long detour" is also the one made by Cybernetics, insofar as while being a science of operations, it starts from structural sciences to produce a normativity appearing at the end of the reflection. Simondon affirms it clearly: "the whole cycle of sciences is crossed when the knowledge passed from the initial normativity of mathematics to the final normativity of the cybernetic reflection by the intermediary of the sciences of the structure and the sciences of the operation: such is the 'long detour' by which the exact thought goes from the restricted normative to the universal normative."[37] There is thus an analogy in the order of knowledge, in the philosophical reflexivity itself, between the Platonic thought of the Ideas-numbers and cyber-

---

35 "Épistémologie de la cybernétique", SLΦ, pp 175–199.
36 SLΦ, pp. 193–194.
37 *Ibid.*, p. 193.

netic thought. But this analogy is neither an identity nor a resemblance that would make Cybernetics a Neo-Platonism. For Simondon, it is indeed a question of carrying out a transduction of both positive Platonism and cybernetics, which requires a transposition that is at the same time a transformation, that is to say a correction and an invention in relation to the current problematic of the crisis of reflexivity in a technological context. This is why, when Simondon affirms in *HNI* that "Plato's doctrine deserves to be taken up again and continued by means of the theory of information",[38] it is not a term by term substitution of the form for the information nor of the Platonism for a cybernetic Neo-Platonism, but a gesture of invention. If therefore the philosopher is a technician, he is not only a technologist but also the one who operates on the becoming with a new form of reflexivity of the information.

3. Image and Platonism

The rehabilitation of the image is the third and last gesture of criticism of Platonism. This gesture is far from being anecdotal, since for Simondon it is a question of *"saving the phenomena"*.[39] Such a requirement is satisfied "by reinstalling the phenomena in the becoming, by putting them back in invention, by the deepening of the image that they conceal."[40] It is a whole new thought of the image that is then proposed by Simondon. The image is neither a copy nor a simulacrum. It is neither reducible to a sign nor to a symbol. It is a reality in its own right, including as a mental image, in the sense that the image possesses a "relative independence" with respect to the subject to the point of manifesting a power of resistance to the will, acting according to its own forces, inhabiting the consciousness like an "intruder". And when it becomes objective, when it materialises in the form of object, it also possesses a power of connection, of influence and can cause the invention. This power of the image makes it rebel to the thought, insubordinate to the Idea. Image is a "quasi-organism" having power and knowledge. The only way to understand their reality is to put them back in a cycle of the imagination and to accompany them in the course of the becoming (based on a biological analogy with the ontogeny of an individual, this cycle is composed of three phases and three levels (for each phase and for the integral process): motor anticipation (biological level), perceptive experience (psycho-

---

38   HNI in ILNFI, p. 464/ILFI, p. 379.
39   This expression probably refers directly to Pierre Duhem's famous book *Sauver les apparences. SOZEIN TA PHAINOMENA. Essai sur la Notion de Théorie physique de Platon à Galilée*, Paris, Hermann, 1908.
40   IMIN, p. 14.

logical level), symbolic systemisation (formal level)).⁴¹ The image appears as living reality and inseparable from life (of the human organism in relation to the milieu) including in the form of objects, symbols, simulacra and even ghosts.⁴²

So, everything seems to be opposed to Platonism in this conception of the image. It is however possible to establish a first positive link with the status of *tertium quid* of the image. Simondon indeed considers that the image is not an isolated reality nor a given unit, it is an "intermediate reality" between object and subject, abstract and concrete, past and future. This intermediate reality means that the images participate in a certain way in the two extreme realities without belonging to them completely; they also carry out the synthesis of them without denying them or exceeding them; they can finally be mixtures reuniting the opposed terms; these different modalities are manifested according to the phases of the cycle, the conduct of the subject, the situations of life. These characteristics correspond rather well to those already met of the indefinite dyad, even if Simondon does not make explicit reference to it at this moment.⁴³ Moreover, Simondon insists that understanding the image means not reducing it to a sign, as the discussion on the nature of the denominations does in Plato's *Cratylus*, but to understand it rather as a symbol in the sense of a relation of dynamic complementarity in the manner of the primitive unity of the complete androgyne in the *Symposium* of Plato. But perhaps the most interesting thing is that Simondon applies his theory of the image to philosophical thought and to Platonism as such. In the first phase of the image cycle, that of the long-term anticipation of the experience of the object, Simondon explains that the formal level of image activity that normally corresponds to the last phase of systematisation, contains *a priori* images. These *a priori* images have the form of a motor intuition which returns to the "unique and unconditional source of the projection",⁴⁴ to the "absolute origin" of the experience. The Ideas are thus *a priori* images, but the *a priori* image is in reality more "purely unconditional" and more "perfectly unique", insofar as the true source of amplifying projection, analogous to the Sun, is the Good. Simondon explains thus that in the Platonic doctrine, "the Good is source of the intelligibility and of the participation in the world of the intelligibles". To reach the Good, it is then necessary to accomplish a violent

---

41   For a complete study, see, Duhem, "La théorie du cycle de l'image de Simondon", in Jean-Jacques Wunenburger (ed.), *L'histoire du concept d'imagination en France (de 1914 à nos jours)*, Paris, Classiques Garnier, 2019.
42   In this respect, the *daimon* of Socrates is an image with relative independence, power over the will and knowledge of its own. In HNI, Simondon concluded his study on Plato thus: "It is in his knowledge that he discovers the model of his action: the philosopher has become himself his own *daimon*".
43   The only evocation of the indefinite dyad in this text is later when Simondon analyses the *a priori* images to explain the philosophical intuition in Plato, IMIN, p. 62.
44   IMIN, p. 22.

effort of conversion which allows us to understand not only that the archetypal ideas are the model and the cause of the sensible things but that they are in truth the projection of the Good.

Simondon proposes here an audacious interpretation that could seem paradoxical both for Plato's thought, which is opposed to becoming, and for his own thought, which favours another Platonism than that of the theory of Ideas. Simondon recognises it himself for the interpretation of Plato which appears as a contemplative theory and not as the place of a "primordial image of pure movement". But it is necessary according to him to understand this theory of knowledge "starting from the progressive experience of an original model (archetype) through the various images, more or less distant, which can represent it, and which become all the more imprecise that they are more distant from the first reality, like the copies of copies, or the reflections of reflections."[45] It is therefore not a question for Simondon to change the meaning of the Platonic theory nor his position towards it, but to show that it is possible to understand it as a process, as an intuition of pure movement. Thus, philosophical knowledge is "a look that accompanies the projection in the process of being made, the demiurge in the process of being accomplished, by being no longer among the copies and in the existences in the process of becoming, but very close to the very source from which the rays leave in their unity."[46] This movement of the reflexive intuition is a pure movement in the sense that it is not a movement within the becoming, which would make the thinking philosopher a simple sensible thing impotent to rise up to the truth; nor is the demiurgic movement itself, even by participation, which would amount to being confused with the origin of everything including the Ideas or even the Good; but it is the intuition of the movement of the projection, beyond the existence and the essence. The philosophical intuition is thus for Simondon not only "the knowledge of the models (Ideas)" but "a mode of being that makes coincide the philosopher with the absolute source of the forms and the existences", that is to say the intuition in the pure state of "any projection towards the existence and the multiple".[47] This original interpretation somehow saves the image in Plato, but according to a conception quite different from his own and which conditions the philosophical operation. Simondon places this interpretation of the pure movement between an interpretation of the Platonic thought as a contemplative theory based on fixed structures and an interpretation of a second Platonic thought as a theory of mixtures, of the indefinite dyad and of the metric of the Ideas-numbers. This intermediate interpretation reveals *in fine* that the *a priori* images have the power, if they are inserted in the world as a long-term anticipation, to be fruitful for a philosophical reform after "the

---

45 Ibid., p. 58.
46 Ibid., p. 59.
47 Ibid.

long road – *tèn makran odon* – of the philosophical thought".[48] The long detour of philosophy is thus analogous to the cycle of images: the *a priori* images carry the germ of philosophical invention, which is a symbolic formalisation as well as a universalising amplification able to solve a reflexive problem in our contemporary situation.

4. After the long detour

At the end of this study, we can affirm that the place of Platonism in Simondon's thought is not marginal and superficial, it is constant and deep. The relation to Platonism is as important as the relation to Ionian pre-Socratic thought and to Aristotelian thought. From the first texts elaborating the theory of individuation and technique to the texts of the 1970s, Plato and Platonism are at the same time summoned, questioned, criticised and extended. On the one hand, everything opposes Plato and Simondon, and it would be quite easy to affirm that Simondon seeks to overthrow Platonism, not only to invert it but to destroy it by going out of substantialism, dualism, idealism, transcendentalism, universalism and the opposition to becoming, technique and image. However, it would be wrong to adopt such a position and to consider that Simondon is in frontal opposition to Platonism. In fact, Simondon differentiates himself from a kind of Platonism by differentiating several Platonisms in Plato himself.

As we have seen, there are at least two Platonisms for Simondon: the first one is the structural Platonism, the one of Socratism, which grants a privilege to Man and requires a separation from the World, which elaborates a theory of the Ideas opposed to the becoming and to the multiplicity of the sensible things, which poses as a method of knowledge the ascending dialectic and the search for essences. The second Platonism is post-Socratic, it is a Platonism which seeks to understand the becoming and to integrate it. It is always structural but also operative, giving a place and even an importance to what was excluded from the search for truth. It is the Platonism that Simondon finds in the last dialogues (*Parmenides*, *Sophist*, *Timaeus* and *Laws*) which is also materialised in Plato's attempt to concretely realise the ideal city. But, this second Platonism is not yet the one that for Simondon represents the anticipation of his own thoughts and that would be to be taken up again to extend it. It is a kind of *third Platonism*, not formalised, indirect, but quite promising, namely the one of the esoteric and oral teaching reported by Aristotle in books M and N of the *Metaphysics*. This third Platonism of the "Ideas-numbers" is the one that really integrates the becoming by immortalisation in the sensible, relativises the absolute character of the Ideas and of the individual by a mathematical mediation, provides a basis at

---

[48] Ibid., p. 62.

the same time rational and operative to found the techniques. In spite of its conjectural and reconstructed character, this third Platonism is for Simondon what is necessary to start again to elaborate a new philosophy. Without defining the whole of the elements necessary to this new philosophy (theory of individuation, genetic encyclopaedism, reflexive technology), since it requires to integrate the results of the contemporary sciences (physical and biological sciences, information sciences, and human sciences) and to inscribe itself in the current problems produced by the effects of the techno-science industrial development, this third Platonism is a reflexive potential and a source of really decisive schemes of thought.

This is why Simondon considers that Cybernetics, the model for the elaboration of his own thought, has a direct link with this third Platonism of the Ideas-numbers. But by accomplishing such a gesture, Simondon did not operate simply a historical rapprochement between two approaches to thought, nor even an enlightening analogy to understand precise philosophical stakes, in truth he operated a transduction. To really understand the place and the role of Platonism in Simondon's work, it is necessary to understand what happens through this transduction, and notably that it operates at the same time as an explanation, a transformation and an extension of Platonism. It is what explains that the third Platonism as well as Cybernetics are not to be taken back such as they are, because it is necessary to "correct" them and finally to reinvent them from their internal tensions, from their conceptual limits and from their historical determination in relation to the dominant ideas of their time and to the stage of the evolution of sciences and techniques. It is moreover this force proper to the transduction, to allow any philosophical thought to have a kind of timelessness, of potential actuality that it is a question of concretising. Thus, the Simondonian transduction of Platonism is not reducible to the prolongation of the third Platonism, since following a *long detour* it can take back the first Platonism by having passed by the second. Simondon's thought is not therefore a Platonism nor a Neo-Platonism, it is a *trans-Platonism*, a transduction of the sense of Platonism (or of Platonisms) as he did it with the pre-Socratics, Aristotle, Lucretius or Plotinus (to stick to Antiquity) ... that is to say a transduction of philosophy as invention of thought to give meaning to the becoming.

Energetics of Philosophical Systems
Simondon's Philosophy of Philosophy

Clémentine Lessard

Deleuze once wrote that "the question what is philosophy? can perhaps be posed only late in life, with the arrival of old age, and the time for speaking concretely".[1] To the contrary, Simondon's writings tell us it is rather an early question, addressed at the very beginning of his philosophical journey. Over the course of eight-odd years of preparatory work, he produced a set of texts that testify that his primary subject of thought was nothing but philosophy itself. Mostly published in *Sur la philosophie*, these texts reveal that reflexive thought, as Simondon puts it, was the first field of investigation – and even of conception – of his genetical approach. In Simondon, theory and method are so deeply interwoven that his first concern seems to have been a metaphilosophical one: how does a philosophy come into being?

As early as 1953, reflexive thought was presented as presiding over "the birth of a new individual", following the model of the ancient maieutic whose role was to "separate the new being by individualising it, by giving it autonomy of existence".[2] This subtle suggestion of a mode of existence of philosophical systems is echoed a couple of years later, when the latter became the first entities to be understood in a genetic way, in light of crystallography and embryology.[3] Under Simondon's pen, the notion of "system" is anything but innocuous, in that it is part of the collection of notions he draws from contemporary sciences, especially thermodynamics and cybernetics. From 1955 onwards, philosophical systems have thereby appeared as metastable structures defined by their transformations and their energetic relation with a milieu. This energetics of philosophical systems, as we shall call it, persisted well into the 1970s and is clearly reflected in Simondon's teaching on the history of philosophy. Thereby, this contribution aims at exploring the peculiar understanding of philosophical systems that pervades his work.

---

1   G. Deleuze and F. Guattari, *What Is Philosophy?*, H. Tomlinson and G. Burchell (trans.), New York, Columbia University Press, 1994, p. 1; *Qu'est-ce que la philosophie?*, Paris, Les Éditions de Minuit, 1991, p. 7.
2   "Cybernétique et philosophie", in *Sur la philosophie, 1950–1980*, Paris, Presses universitaires de France, 2016, now abbreviated SLΦ, p. 37. All quotations are our translation, unless otherwise stated.
3   "Recherches sur la philosophie de la nature", SLΦ, pp. 30–34.

On reflection, however, this attention to the mode of existence of philosophical systems in the preparatory works is somewhat disconcerting, especially from a thinker who puts such an emphasis on genesis and processes over structures. After all, does putting a living thought into a system not run the risk of making its dynamic operation into a dead structure? Thus, one can wonder if Simondon really envisioned his philosophical work in the form of a system. To French philosophers striving to return to the concrete in the wake of Bergson, the systematic spirit is not an attitude to embrace but rather a bogeyman and a spectre to be exorcised. Its taste for abstraction, combined with the nasty habit to squeeze reality into the narrow constructions of our mind and a certain tendency to freeze the movement of being into fixed structures, makes the systematic spirit into a hindrance to reflexive thought, conversely defined by its openness, operativity and permanent contact with experience. Therefore, the reasons behind Simondon's energetical reclaiming of the notion of system in light of contemporary sciences must be carefully examined. What new perspectives does the recourse to an energetical paradigm offer on philosophical systems, and to what extent does it reinvent the spirit of system?

To address these issues, we shall proceed in two steps. Since presenting Simondon as a thinker of philosophical systems does not go without saying, we shall first trace the emergence of this concern in his early texts. If much ink has been devoted to the unity of Simondon's work[4], few commentators have delved into his first writings on philosophy to trace his thought back to its genesis.[5] We would like to make our contribution to this point, by taking a stance on the thorny issue of the "system of Simondon". As we shall argue, understanding his energetics of philosophical systems sheds light on how Simondon envisioned and developed his own thought.

From then on, we shall attempt to grasp the originality of such an approach in relation to the philosophical panorama of the French 20th century. This investigation not only requires a comparison with the canonical, Bergsonian view of

---

[4] J.-H. Barthélémy, *Simondon ou l'encyclopédisme génétique*, Paris, Presses universitaires de France, 2008 and "Quel mode d'unité pour l'œuvre de Simondon?", in J.-H. Barthélémy (ed.), *Cahiers Simondon: Numéro 3*, Paris, L'Harmattan, 2011, pp. 131–148; J.-Y. Chateau, *Vocabulaire de Simondon*, Paris, Ellipses, 2008, pp. 7–8, 16 and 44; X. Guchet, *Pour un humanisme technologique. Culture, technique et société dans la philosophie de Gilbert Simondon*, Paris, Presses universitaires de France, 2010.

[5] Suggested by Frédéric Worms in his introduction to SLΦ, pp. 5–14, this genetical approach was recently taken up and further developed by Jamil Alioui to study Simondon's philosophy of culture. Our contribution owes much to his insight into the "radical technological reflexivity of philosophy" and the "technological reflection on philosophical writing" in Simondon. J. Alioui, *Le "numérique" à la lumière de la philosophie de la culture de Gilbert Simondon*, Doctoral Thesis submitted to the Faculty of Letters of the University of Lausanne, 2023, pp. 78–87 and 212–215 in particular.

systems as living organisms, but also calls for a closer contextualisation. From mid-century onwards, the mode of existence of philosophical systems has indeed become a real topic among French thinkers. One might mention Étienne Souriau, whose notion of the system as a *work-to-be-made*, matched with an inquiry on the different modes of existence, is not unrelated to Simondon's reflection. Nor can we forget Martial Gueroult, a renowned historian of philosophy and Simondon's professor whose "technology of philosophical systems" has been a lasting inspiration to aspiring philosophers of the mid-century. Finally, we shall appreciate the scope of Simondon's *philosophy of the history of philosophy*, to take a formula by Gueroult.

1. Towards an energetics of philosophical systems

1.1. In search of the concrete: to the root of a Simondonian issue

Understanding the ins and outs of the Simondonian energetics of philosophical systems requires to grasp the methodological concern that presided over its development. We assume it to be the following one: how to produce a concrete philosophy? Indeed, the "early research works" collected in *Sur la philosophie* show that "the time for speaking concretely", to put it like Deleuze, comes not at the end but at the beginning of Simondon's thinking. As the draft introduction written around 1955 states, "we should first investigate the condition under which a reflexive thought can be considered concrete".[6] In Simondon, the search for concreteness stems from a conception of philosophy as a reflexive activity that is deeply linked to its milieu. At a first level indeed, concrete thinking is that which reflects on experience and does not get bogged down in abstract constructions. But more profoundly, this search for concreteness may have to do with some intimate intuition of Simondon that the individual does not stand in front of the world as an insulated monad but originally forms with it a complete whole. This second sense of "concrete" lies at the core of the main thesis: the individual is not the whole of being, for the real concrete is the complete system that generated it together with its milieu.[7] This helps understand the statement that to be concrete, reflexive thought must "find in the course of its development a totality as concrete as the world it reflects".[8] Therefore, thought itself must grow in such a way that it analogically recovers the system of the individual and its milieu. We return then to the Latin roots of the term: in a third sense, concrete thinking is that which "grows together" (*concrescere*) to form a complete

---

[6] "Introduction", in SLΦ, p. 20.
[7] See ILNFI, p. 63/ILFI, p. 51.
[8] "Introduction", in SLΦ, p. 20.

whole. The exigence for concreteness thus leads to a question: how does a thought develop to reach systematic unity?

In sum, three criteria for concrete thinking can be listed: reflecting on experience, maintaining an analogical relation with the system formed by the individual and its milieu, and "growing together" into an organised whole. This last criterion draws particular attention as it recalls the traditional conception of philosophy as the production of a system akin to organic growth. Like living beings, concrete thinking seems to be endowed with a degree of internal resonance that gives it cohesion and autonomy and makes it an individual in its own right. However, defining philosophy as a construction of systems poses a challenge to anyone who seeks to fulfil the first two requirements of concrete thinking. The problem can be stated as follows: if the philosophical activity is a process by which a separate individual comes to being – becomes "concrete" in the third sense – how can it be prevented from emancipating itself from reality and sinking into abstraction? Furthermore, if the only genuine concrete is the system formed by the individual and its milieu, what degree of reality can philosophical systems claim? Finally, should we give up on the concept of systems or should we redefine it, in a way that makes it compatible with reflexive thought? This issue, that we assume to be at the root of the invention of the energetics of philosophical systems, shall serve as a guiding thread for our incursion into Simondon's early texts, using a chronological method.

1.2. Method over system, operation over structure: encyclopaedic intention vs. systematic spirit (1950)

Throughout the 1950s, Simondon seems to have grappled with two apparently incompatible philosophical concerns. On the one hand, he rejected systems and refused to see reflexive thought as a closed domain. But on the other, his writings reflect some desire to grasp reality in an encompassing way which suggests a spirit of system of some kind. This ambivalence is evident in "Les encyclopédies et l'esprit encyclopédique", his earliest published text as of today.[9] Through a reflection on encyclopaedia and dictionary considered as two ways of constituting knowledge, an opposition arises between "encyclopaedic intention" and what might be called "systematic spirit". Whereas a dictionary excels at organising a defined number of elements within a fixed structure, an encyclopaedia grows by gradually incorporating more and more operations consisting of schemas, functioning patterns and processes of all kinds. Driven by a technological interest, "Encyclopaedia is work of schematisation of operations according to an

---

[9] "Les encyclopédies et l'esprit encyclopédique", in SLΦ, pp. 117–129, written around 1950.

operation chosen as a schematisation principle", whose "intention of unifying the multiple" is based on the belief in "the existence of a real organic unity of all operative efforts".[10]

Contrasting encyclopaedia with dictionary, Simondon emphasises the former to the detriment of the latter: "To choose the operative order over the structural order, the method over the system, is to found universal humanism".[11] Although the nature of philosophy may not seem to be at stake at first glance, the many examples used – from Thales to Cybernetics via Plato, Bacon and Diderot – soon confirm it is all about finding a new way of philosophising. Beyond the rigid system of Platonism, Simondon discovers a voyaging Plato, who sets sail to Egypt and composes "this Platonic Encyclopaedia which is the *Timaeus*".[12] The widening movement of the "encyclopaedic circle", analogous to that of the navigator exploring a territory, conveys a schema of growth which captures his attention and inspires him to this quite poetical text:

> To explore and narrate one's journey is to enlarge the geographical circle of the known world; this circle of the known which represses the unknown, this circle of light which radiates into the darkness from a centre, is navigation in circles, the "journey". The encyclopaedic intention finds its operative paradigm in circular exploration. The world of the known takes the form of a circle at the centre of which is the knowing subject. [...] The navigator who explores the world does not cross boundaries, for he starts from the inside of a circle and increases the length of its radii: he is and remains, even as his knowledge progresses, within the same indefinitely expandable domain. This dilation without rupture and without μετάβασις εἰς ἄλλο ("change of plane, of order") is progress, and it is also immanence.[13]

The topological paradigm of this text deserves our full attention, as it lays the foreground for Simondon's further approach to philosophy. The themes of the circle, the journey and light, as well as the schema of dilation from a centre, are indeed to become key aspects of his thought. Afterall, is the main thesis not entitled "Individuation *in Light of* Notions of Form and Information"? Likewise, does its progression not recall that of the navigator staying "within the same indefinitely expandable domain"? In gradually transposing a crystallographic paradigm to all modes of individuation and presenting the chain of physical, vital and psychosocial individuations as a sequence of "expansions" and "dilations" of a same primitive operation,[14] ILNFI strongly resounds with this first

---

10 *Ibid.*, p. 117 and 121.
11 *Ibid.*, p. 121.
12 *Ibid.*, p. 124. See also p. 121, mentioning "this beautiful encyclopaedia which is the *Cratylus*".
13 *Ibid.*, p. 124.
14 See e.g. ILNFI, p. 178/ILFI, p. 166: "psychical individuation is a dilation, a precocious expansion of vital individuation".

study on encyclopaedia. Thus, Simondon seems to retain from the encyclopaedic spirit its postulate of the analogical unity of all operations.

But then, is it not tempting to see in such an approach a spirit of system of some kind? To shed light on this issue, let us call upon d'Alembert's distinction between "systematic spirit" and "spirit of system". Against dogmatic metaphysicians trying to fit the richness of reality into tight edifices, "the principal merit of the physicist would be [...] to have the spirit of system but never to create one": relying on "a thoughtful study of phenomena",[15] the spirit of system sticks to experience and searches for the unity of all things without ever closing in on itself. Along the same lines, one could say Simondon has a spirit of system without being systematic. His focus on encyclopaedia rather than dictionary does not prevent him from showing some interest in a method of unification of the multiple, quite the contrary. In fact, he seems to have found in the encyclopaedic intention an alternative to traditional systems that tend to freeze the operation of thought within a fixed structure, along the lines of the dictionary. Nonetheless, this parallel between Simondon and the Encyclopaedists stops here, for he does not seek to unify sciences. If there is a system of Simondon, thus, we do not think it takes the form of an encyclopaedism.[16]

---

[15] J.-B. le R. d'Alembert, "Preliminary Discourse", R. N. Schwab (trans.), in *The Encyclopedia of Diderot & d'Alembert Collaborative Translation Project*, Chicago, University of Chicago Press, 1995, p. 95 and 22.

[16] This reading differs from Jean-Hugues Barthélémy's presentation of Simondon as a "genetical encyclopaedism". To clear up any misunderstanding, Barthélémy certainly warned against the confusion between this concept and that of "encyclopaedia". Nevertheless, it designates an epistemological project of knowledge synthesis which does not define, in our view, the core of the Simondonian undertaking. In Simondon, the function of reflexive thought is not to produce a unifying synthesis of knowledge but to unravel vital problems raised by the milieu. In ILNFI, the fragmentation of knowledge and its lack of systematicity is not presented as a problem to be solved. If sciences of all kinds come together in this work, it is not in virtue of a unifying synthesis project but for the concrete perspectives they provide on the same great issue, chosen for its reflexivity, generality and high problematic content, namely the individual and its individuation (see note below). J.-H. Barthélémy, *Simondon ou l'encyclopédisme génétique, op. cit.*; *Id.*, "Encyclopédisme et théorie de l'interdisciplinarité", *Hermès*, n° 67, 2013, pp. 172–177; *Id.*, "Encyclopédisme et système de l'individuation du sens", *Klesis*, n° 42, 2018, pp. 148–181; *Id.*, "Gilbert Simondon et le malentendu de l'encyclopédisme", *iPhilo*, 2020 (https://iphilo.fr/2020/11/17/gilbert-simondon-et-le-malentendu-de-lencyclopedisme-jean-hugues-barthelemy/).

1.3. Holistic system and topology of being: cybernetics and the arising of energetics (1953)

A reading of Simondon's earliest text thus reveals some interest in topological paradigms for thinking of philosophy. So far, no energetics was at stake. The situation changed from 1952 onwards, with his choice of philosophy for his PhD thesis and the corollary choice of the individual as a main problem – we say "corollary", for it is Simondon's notion of philosophy that dictated his research topic, not the other way around.[17]

In 1953, "Cybernétique et philosophie" defined philosophy as an "unconditional reflection on any given that spontaneous experience presents as problematic".[18] On the one hand, this definition enriches the topological paradigm with a problematic dimension that allows to think of philosophy as a process of individuation: reflexive thought arises from a tense and fundamentally problematic situation which requires the invention of "a new topology of being" to be unravelled, just like the Socratic maieutic used to "separate the new being by individualising it, by giving it autonomy of existence".[19] Thus, the idea of a mode of existence of philosophical systems seems to be on the way. But on the other hand, the reflexive definition of philosophy shuffles off the idea of a stand-alone system. "Philosophy is not a domain of thinking that has frontiers with other bordering domains"[20] but an effort and a vital function of problem-solving. In light of cybernetics, the individual is described as a *"holistic system"*, that is as "a *whole* which evolves, which is able of governing itself, that is capable of governing itself or at least reacting to the impulses it receives in a particular way that testifies to an individual elaboration by the object of the messages it receives".[21] Its energetic relation with a milieu endows the individual with a degree of autonomy which allows it, by recurrence of causality, to reconfigure its way of being by changing its "structure" – Simondon then refers to Goldstein's holistic approach to biology. And as a vital activity, reflexive thought does not depart from the functioning of organisms. From this cybernetical and organological para-

---

17   See "Introduction", in SLΦ, pp. 23–24: "The notion of the individual would therefore be inherently problematic in nature. [...] There is a certain content of reflexive concern with the individual in all philosophical reflection, even if the consideration of the individual does not seem to be the direct and explicit object of this reflection". See also this 1952 letter to Bachelard: "Since this spring I have been working on the notion of individuality. This subject seems to me to be deeply reflexive, and therefore philosophical." N. Simondon, "Biographie de Gilbert Simondon", on *Gilbert Simondon. Site d'information sur l'œuvre et les publications* (http://gilbert.simondon.fr/content/biographie).
18   "Cybernétique et philosophie", in SLΦ, p. 35.
19   *Ibid.*, p. 37.
20   *Ibid.*, p. 35.
21   *Ibid.*, p. 42.

digm, it is defined as the act of invention by which an individual recomposes the territory of his thought to solve a problem posed by its milieu. Thus, the "new topology of being" is not that of a closed system but that of the individual itself.

Although no idea of a philosophical system seems to be at stake, a final reference to Hegel turns the tables: "philosophical effort in its encyclopaedic intention, following the Hegelian sense of the term, modifies the individuality of problems by tending towards the most synthetic and highest problematic".[22] This passage does not mean that Simondon intends to construct, like Hegel, a system of knowledge in the form of a philosophical encyclopaedia. Rather, it suggests seeing any genuine philosophy as Hegel envisioned his *Encyclopaedia of Philosophic Sciences:* that is, as a work which does not exist alongside the others but brings them all together in a single system. "The latest philosophy, chronologically speaking, is the result of all those that precede it and must therefore contain the principles of all of them. This is why, if it is philosophy at all, it is the most developed, richest and most concrete philosophy".[23] This Hegelian formula helps us understand that in their search for the concrete, philosophers do not *produce private systems,* they *do philosophy:*[24] this is the lesson Simondon seems to have learnt from Hegel.[25] Thus, philosophy is a networking activity that "integrates a hitherto isolated system into the immense society of systems [...] and brings an end to the solitude of problems to create the world of problems".[26] Philosophers do not produce insulated systems for they do not think alone: to solve peculiar problems, they bring with them the universality of culture that primarily consists of this great reservoir of concepts, schemas and doctrines which is the history of philosophy. One after another, they keep recomposing the topology of being in light of new milieus.[27]

---

22 *Ibid.,* p. 62.
23 G. W. F. Hegel, *Encyclopedia of the Philosophical Sciences in Basic Outline,* K. Brinkmann and D. O. Dahlstrom (eds.), Dahlstrom and Brinkmann (trans.), Cambridge University Press, 2010, §13, p. 42.
24 See *Ibid.,* §14, p. 43: "Many philosophical writings limit themselves to expressing [...] merely *attitudes* or *opinions.* – By a *system* one wrongly understands a philosophy built on a narrowly circumscribed *principle* distinct from other such principles; contrary to this, however, it is a principle of any genuine philosophy that it contains all particular principles within itself".
25 See "Introduction" and "Recherche sur la philosophie de la nature" in SLΦ, pp. 19–20 and p. 30.
26 "Cybernétique et philosophie", in SLΦ, p. 62.
27 This sheds light on the introduction to ILNFI and its peculiar treatment of the history of philosophy. In fact, the opening pages on the two dead-ends of philosophy do not target Aristotle or ancient Atomists, nor do they wrongly attribute concepts they never used, ideas they never claimed. The target of this text is the entire philosophical culture, reflected from the problem of individuation and faced with its inability to provide convenient solutions. In dis-

The whole point is thus to grasp reality in its completeness, without mutilating it nor cutting into the concrete. Can we produce a philosophy that maintains "this contact, this taking of things over the individual and of the individual over things",[28] to quote a formula by Simondon in a different context? We quote here a quite poetical note composed in 1953 after a trip to the USA, which brought to the table decisive elements on the topology of being. Putting down on paper the "impression of the sovereign reality" left by "the journey, the light, the sun", Simondon writes: "It must be said that the individual is in a field, a plurality of fields, but that there is a certain relation between its own field and the field of beings as it is in a place. There must be centres of field, units, like the centre of a city".[29] We suggest reading this passage as follows: for the individual is not a monad but a holistic system defined by its relation to a milieu, an energetical relation connects its field to that of beings. The two fields connect at privileged points of experience, crystallising at times and places where the world makes a strong impression on the individual, such as the "high, analogical house" that marked Simondon in New York.[30] We think that this view is finally applied to philosophical systems, as a criterion for concreteness. If we are right, here are the requirements for a concrete thought: to remain concrete, thought must organise its own field in a way which is analogous to that of beings; it must grow around privileged points of contact with being: there must be centres of systems, like there are centres of cities, and the topology of being must be completed with an energetics.

1.4. Symbols and metastability: systematisation as an individuation (around 1955)

This issue is addressed around 1955 in "Recherche sur la philosophie de la nature", which can be read as an attempt to save the idea of philosophical system. The subject is broached from the distinction between signs and symbols, defined as two ways of referring to being:

> [...] philosophical thought can be intended as a symbol of being but not as a systematisation of the signs of being. If it begins with the knowledge of symbols of being, then

---

missing the traditional notions of substance and form as being "part of the same system of thought", before replacing them by those of relation and information, Simondon does nothing but recompose the topology of being in light of a new milieu, so as to grasp more than an "impoverished real". ILNFI, p. 16/ILFI, p. 35.
28 "Impression de la réalité souveraine", in SLT, p. 24.
29 *Ibid.*
30 *Ibid.* We find this conception later on in Simondon's theory of the magic universe: METO, pp. 177–178/METO, pp. 227–228.

continues with a systematisation of signs, it leaves philosophical research to become a thinking exercise, when the symbol degrades into an organisation of signs. It is this degradation that generally occurs during the construction of a philosophical system: a philosophy is a philosophy of that from which it draws the primitive symbols, of that of which it is itself a symbol; it is only a system in relation to the complementary domains of the symbolic domain, in which it is an organiser of signs only.[31]

A system of signs, as we shall call it, is a closed structure based on the internal referral of its elements that makes sense on its own. But this apparent autonomy ends up in abstraction: to organise signs only, as systems constructors often do, is to take reality illusorily as a domain or a finite set which can be subjected to thought. Contrary to signs, symbols remain concrete for they maintain the relation to being. In accordance with the ancient meaning of *sumbola*, they are fragments of a same reality which only make sense from their relation. It is thus on the path of symbols, carrying an energetic dimension, that the idea of a philosophical system will be saved. To remain philosophical, a system must present itself as the incomplete symbol of its complementary domain, which is its milieu. A system maintains the relation to its milieu by drawing from it its "primitive symbols", presented as the "privileged points" of its relation to being. Serving as "paradigms" as well as "permanent terms of reference", the latter kick off an operation of systematisation such as crystalline germs direct processes of crystallisation.[32] In this light, the best paradigm is the one which spreads and radiates beyond its original territory into the richest gradient of significations, to reach "*systematic unity*":[33]

> The system must then be studied not as a constituted edifice but as an act of progressive assimilation from a focus that would be the "hot spot" of this interpretive activity. A philosophical system would then be organised according to a gradient, leaving outwardly more and more obscure zones, less and less penetrated by meaning: from which we can conjecture that the real structure of a system is that which corresponds to its genesis: a system is a polar structure.[34]

The topological schemas of irradiation, dilation and expansion previously encountered reoccur here to take on an energetic dimension. From crystals to living organisms, polarisation is indeed the condition of any individuation, allowing an individual to differ from itself and grow into a certain direction.[35] Thus,

---

[31] "Recherche sur la philosophie de la nature", in SLΦ, p. 30.
[32] Ibid., p. 34.
[33] Ibid., p. 31.
[34] Ibid., p. 32.
[35] See ILNFI, p. 109/ILFI, p. 88 and "History of the notion of the individual", in ILNFI, pp. 648–649/ILFI, p. 519, whose section on Romanticism connects the notions of polarisation, symbol and topology of being.

to describe philosophical systems as polar structures is to consider them as genuine individuals. Inviting to read "the organogenesis of a system",[36] Simondon then presents the paradigm as a germ or a seed that incrementally differentiates to engender a living organism. Therefore, "one could speak of a nature of each philosophy, as there is a nature of the seed which will be able to develop into a tree and even a forest", and a system is limited by its initial paradigms: "In the choice of paradigms is thus partially contained the expressive and reductive fate of a philosophical thought".[37]

As far as we understand, the organic paradigm allows to save philosophical systems from abstraction. Indeed, how can the degradation of a philosophy into a system of signs be prevented, if not by growing it as a living being? Here we can refer to ILNFI and its use of thermodynamics. Whereas a crystal can only degrade once the whole potentials of its mother liquor is exhausted, an organism keeps transforming throughout its existence owing to energetic exchanges with its milieu. Contrary to stable systems which cannot fight against entropy because of their lack of energy input, living beings are defined by an energetic mode of existence which allows them to delay their final degradation by remaining metastable. Just as plants are like inchoate crystals,[38] would it be possible to speak of philosophy as an inchoate system? Thus, philosophical thought would be a perpetually delayed process of systematisation. Tending infinitely towards a systematic mode of existence that it never reaches, it would be a system of signs *in the nascent state that is amplified without stabilising*.[39] Strictly speaking, a system would only exist as a "veritable individual" during its operation of individuation,[40] so long as it remains the symbol of its complementary domain. This is the approach we think Simondon chose for his main thesis: philosophy as a perpetual work in progress.

1.5. From the concrete to the concrete: the concretisation of thought (around 1958)

Yet, ILNFI does not exactly follow an organogenetic paradigm. In his main thesis, Simondon is not content with letting grow a set of germs that would determine the nature of his thought and limit its "fate", like the seed already contains

---

36 "Recherche sur la philosophie de la nature", in SLΦ, p. 34.
37 *Ibid.*, p. 31.
38 ILNFI, p. 164/ILFI, p. 152.
39 We transpose a formula by Simondon, *Ibidem.*
40 See *Ibid.*, p. 49/p. 61: "the veritable individual exists for a mere instant during the technical operation: it lasts as long as the form-taking. After this operation, what remains is a result that will begin to degrade, and not a veritable individual; this is an individuated being rather than a real individual".

the tree. If he certainly refers to thinking in terms of individuation and metastability, he is far from letting the initially chosen physical paradigm propagate spontaneously to all modes of individuation. Leafing through the second chapter, we learn that if this paradigm turns out to be "metastable", because it cannot be directly transferred to other modes of individuations, it will be modified and transposed using reflection: "A real thought is self-justifying but not justified before being structured".[41] In that, the paradigm serves less as a germ than as a foundation stone for a construction which is self-justifying. As an invention and a reflective operation of construction, philosophy is not determined by the scope of its initial domain nor limited by its initial paradigms.

As "Analysis of the Criteria of Individuality" indicates, Simondon eventually opts for a constructive approach inspired by Descartes and the scientific method. In our view, this paradigm reshuffle addresses the shortcomings of the biological paradigm, which left in the dark zone the active role of the philosopher and downplayed the inventive dimension of reflexive thought. Explaining his method by analogy with that of Descartes, he writes: "Like decision in provisional morality, the initial notional choice is invested with a self-justifying value; it is defined by the operation that constitutes it more than by the reality that it objectively seeks, like the cosmogonic hypothesis of vortices, which does not need to be true to be legitimate".[42] Thus, the value of a system does not lie in the validity of its paradigms, which are necessarily relative to the philosopher's preferences, to the value scale of one's society and to the current state of sciences and technics. Rather, it lies in the inventor's ability to construct, by means of reflection, a coherent and organised whole that analogically recovers reality, and do so not by achieving absolute knowledge but by being itself *real*, that is stemming from a process of *realisation*. Reality is not something we know, but something that is realised: to reword a formula by Simondon, we cannot know reality, we can only *realise*.[43]

To Simondon, if sciences are a model to philosophy, it is not for their "prestigious work of formalising knowledge" but for their "no less essential capacity [...] to concretise the abstract by realising it".[44] The concrete resulting of such a construction is not a "fact" but an "effect", a constructed concrete that is perpetually modified by reflection in contact with experience. On the model of sciences, one could say a philosophy is valid when it is able to put theory into practice to produce realities that function according to the laws of nature. "This necessity to close [...] the cycle that moves from the concrete to the abstract, so

---

41   Ibid., p. 77/p. 84.
42   "Analysis of the Criteria of Individuality", in ILNFI, p. 654/ILFI, p. 524.
43   See ILNFI, p. 17/ILFI, p. 36: "we cannot know individuation in the ordinary sense of the term; we can only individuate, be individuated, and individuate within ourselves".
44   "Analysis of the Criteria of Individuality", in ILNFI, p. 655/ILFI, p. 524.

as to then return to an integration into the constructed concrete",⁴⁵ found by Simondon in Plato, lies at the core of his own undertaking. A philosophy is concrete when, at the end of the "long detour" through the abstract, it is "reincarnated in the sensible":⁴⁶ calling upon Plato, Simondon insists on the necessity, for the philosopher flown to the sky of ideas, to go back down into the cave and to transform reflection into a concrete work. This concretisation of thought into a separated object, designed to be transmitted and provide new norms for action, allows the philosopher to participate in the work of culture. Thus, it is no coincidence if ILNFI closes on ethics.

Finally, we come up with the idea that to reach the concrete, philosophy itself must be a process of concretisation. With all due caution, could we appeal to the concept of "concretisation" developed in METO to describe technical objects that tend to an organic mode of existence? From this angle, the vital paradigm would not be abandoned but complexified to do justice to the inventive dimension of reflexive thought. If this analogy holds good, the existence of internal resonance, the multi-functionality of the elements, the non-self-destructive functioning and the relation to an associated milieu, which all characterise concrete machines, could be applied to well-constructed systems and provide norms for evaluation. By analogy with machines, which also result from a vital process of invention, could we see the system as "a deposited fixed human gesture"⁴⁷ whose detachable elements, in the form of schemas and notions, cross the ages to integrate other systems and pervade other cultures? To put this hypothesis to test, let us now turn to the second part of this contribution. Navigating through physical, organic and technological paradigms, Simondon stands out by a peculiar take on the mode of existence of philosophical systems that deserves to be placed in the panorama of the French 20th century to be fully grasped.

2. On the mode of existence of philosophical systems: Simondon's take on a French issue

2.1. Simondon and the French ambivalence towards the spirit of system

"Does French philosophy have a spirit of system?", wondered Jean-Luc Nancy a few years ago.⁴⁸ Although this question seems neutral at first glance, to Nancy it is quite the contrary: "if the system is the object of the desire of the spirit of

---

45 Ibid., modified translation.
46 Ibid.
47 METO, p. 151/MEOT, p. 138.
48 J.-L. Nancy, "Le système, hier et aujourd'hui", Les Temps Modernes, n° 682, Gallimard, 2015, pp. 180–197, p. 180.

system, it is not only the opposite but also the enemy of all philosophy".⁴⁹ As a closed edifice grounded on limited principles, the system would be simply incompatible with the essence of philosophy, defined by "the necessity to legitimately open a limitless examination of everything that can be invoked, constructed, discovered or recalled as a principle".⁵⁰ Hence the rejection of the spirit of system by most French philosophers advocating for a return to the concrete, in the wake of Bergson. However, remarks Nancy, French thinkers from the second half of the 20th century do not totally dismiss the spirit of system. Instead of heralding the death of systems, Deleuze and Derrida seek to "open" them, by replacing the logic of identification by that of multiplication and the model of absorption by that of opening.⁵¹ From the 1950s onwards, we observe Simondon contributing to this opening up of systems. Refusing ideologies, totalitarianisms of thought and -isms of all sorts on the grounds that they forestall reflection,⁵² he nevertheless makes room for a spirit of system that does not close on itself nor gives in to the fury of assimilation. In considering philosophical systems as metastable structures defined by their individuation process, Simondon actually addresses a double concern of his time: in him, the Bergsonian distrust towards systems as closed edifices is matched by the willingness to rehabilitate them by embracing their dynamics and tracing the movement of their genesis.

Thus, we hold that it is possible to situate Simondon in the philosophical context of his time, largely driven by questions on the nature and the fate of the discipline. After the Liberation, as human sciences were gaining autonomy and gradually appropriating objects that were previously attributed to philosophy, the latter had no choice but to withdraw into its own history. Deleuze, a year younger than Simondon, wrote: "I belong to a generation [...] that was more or less bludgeoned to death by the history of philosophy. [...] Many members of my generation never broke free of this; others did, by inventing their own particular methods and new rules, a new approach".⁵³ While Deleuze broke free of it through the development of a creative practice of the history of philosophy, Simondon did so by renewing the old conception of philosophical systems and inventing a new way of philosophising. From this perspective, the whole work on individuation can be read as a response to the question: what is philosophy? It is no coincidence, then, if the constellation of notions forged in ILNFI, including the energetic and topological schema of the propagation from a centre to a

---

49   Ibid., p. 182.
50   Ibid., p. 183.
51   Ibid., pp. 195–197.
52   See "Introduction", in SLΦ, pp. 19–20.
53   G. Deleuze, *Negotiations*, M. Joughin (trans.), New York Chichester, Columbia University Press, 1997, p. 5/*Pourparlers*, Paris, Éditions de Minuit, 2014 [1990], p. 14.

periphery, found its first echo in Deleuze's geophilosophy.[54] Thereby, when Deleuze claims in 1991: "Today it is said that systems are bankrupt, but it is only the concept of system that has changed",[55] this change partially owes to Simondon, who was clearly ahead of the curve in the 1950s when he suggested to understand systems as metastable structures based on an inchoate operation of transduction.

In giving attention to contemporary biology, cybernetics and information theory of his time, largely driven by a systematic and holistic approach, Simondon participates in revamping the old view of systems as living organisms. His role in the renewed interest in systems does not go unnoticed by Nancy, who remarks that "from the viewpoint of history, it would probably be necessary to dwell at length on the importance of the various successive cybernetic models and the development of several forms of interest in systems of interaction, correlation and transduction; we must of course think in particular of Simondon and Canguilhem, and we thus touch on a certain French specificity of the 1950s".[56] However, the use of cybernetic paradigms does not necessarily lead to considering systems as "autonomous and closed functioning[s]",[57] as Nancy seems to imply. Simondon is a case in point, and his energetics of philosophical systems provides food for thought. As we shall see in the university courses from 1960–1970, the energetics of philosophical systems does not close systems on themselves but on the contrary opens them to history.

2.2. Revamping the organic view of philosophical systems: Simondon's Bergsonian legacy

"Philosophy must not be systematic!" exclaimed Bergson in 1913. To be "capable of following concrete reality in all its sinuosities", he warns, let us hold back from identifying the philosophical mind with the systematic spirit. To whoever tries to squeeze Nature into the narrow constructions of the intelligence, Bergson reminds that intelligence is part of Nature and that we just have to follow its course. "Let us then work to dilate our thought" and make sure that our ideas,

---

54 On Deleuze's debt towards Simondon, see A. Sauvagnargues, *Deleuze. L'empirisme transcendantal*, Paris, Presses Universitaires de France, 2010, p. 13 and 240–246 and A. Bouaniche, "Milieu et création dans la "géophilosophie" de Deleuze et Guattari. Trois sources d'une théorie vitaliste de la création philosophique: Nietzsche, Canguilhem, Simondon", in M. Carbone, P. Broggi and L. Turarbek, *La géophilosophie de Gilles Deleuze: Entre esthétiques et politiques*, Paris, Éditions Mimésis, 2012, pp. 145–164.
55 G. Deleuze and F. Guattari, *What Is Philosophy?*, *op. cit.*, p. 9/14.
56 J.-L. Nancy, "Le système, hier et aujourd'hui", *op. cit.*, p. 193.
57 *Ibid.*

"as they grow larger, [...] mould themselves upon reality".[58] On the one hand, this approach splits off from the spirit of system. On the other, it reinvents it. Sweeping away the critics who seek to reduce his philosophy to a single principle from which everything would have been systematically deduced, Bergson rectifies:

> I proceeded in a completely different way, following the experience step by step. [...] I had no other principle, and therein lies my whole "system". I did count a little on a certain unity or at least on a certain continuity of reality, but I would have renounced any kind of unity rather than sacrifice anything of reality. [...] None of my books could be deduced from the previous one [...]. Each of them tries to enlarge the circle of reality that the previous one studied; they are concentric essays.[59]

This attention to the concrete, this insistence on the belonging of intelligence to Nature as well as this desire to expand thought by a process of dilation following step by step the experience, are to be found in Simondon. Like Bergson, Simondon progresses in circles, cautiously, by paying constant attention to reality, to the singularity and variety of its objects. Like Bergson, his "system" is solely based on the assumption of a certain unity or continuity of reality, considered from a genetic point of view. His "genetic monism", far from sacrificing the richness of reality, is adopted only insofar as "genesis [...] presupposes unity that encompasses plurality".[60]

There is no question that Simondon was a great reader of Bergson, who was on the curriculum for the *agrégation* when he took it in 1947–1948 and remained thereafter a recurrent interlocutor and a regular source of reflection in his theses as in his teaching.[61] Furthermore, Simondon's university teaching attests to a clear knowledge of the Bergsonian view of philosophical systems, tacitly invoked in 1962–1963 in a propaedeutic course introducing young students to philosophy. Taking over the approach defended in 1911 in "Philosophical Intuition", Simondon goes as far as applying to Bergson his own interpretive method, asserting that "one could better understand Bergson by starting from Lucretius, considering the intuitive basis of the philosophy of *phusis* that exists in these two

---

58 H. Bergson, "The Philosophy of Claude Bernard", in *The Creative Mind: An Introduction to Metaphysics*, Mineola, N.Y, Dover Publications, 2010, p. 176; "La philosophie de Claude Bernard", in *La pensée et le mouvant*, in *Œuvres*, Édition du Centenaire, Paris, PUF, 1963, p. 1439. Modified translation.

59 Letter of October 30, 1912 to E. Le Roy, in J.-L. Vieillard-Baron, "Lettres inédites de Bergson", in *Annales bergsoniennes II*, Paris, Presses Universitaires de France, 2004, pp. 459–488, p. 474.

60 ILNFI, p. 303–304/ILFI, p. 266.

61 Jean-François Marquet, who was Simondon's student in high school, relates that he primarily taught Bergson. J.-F. Marquet, *Le Vitrail et l'énigme: Dialogue avec Pierre Soual*, Paris, Les Petits Platons, 2013, p. 9.

authors".⁶² With this in mind, Simondon's refusal to study the system as a "constituted edifice" in 1955 echoes Bergson's denial to see it as a "complete edifice" in 1911 even more.⁶³ The analogy between these texts is so striking that one wonders whether the former is not a rewriting of the latter. The idea of studying a system by tracing back to the single point that, in the form of an intuitive contact with being and a mediating image haunting the philosopher his entire life, furnishes the "impulse" that sets thought in movement and leads it, "by an increasing sub-division of itself, to spread out more and more over the successive planes of the mind" just like an "original cell" differentiates and multiplies to form a "complete organism",⁶⁴ is strongly reflected in Simondon, and the Bergsonian overtones of the 1955 text are blindingly obvious. When he suggests entering the system and participating to its "organogenesis", and when he observes the way thought "regains strength each time it returns to [its] paradigms",⁶⁵ Simondon certainly inherits from Bergson.

Yet, Simondon departs from Bergson on major points that deserve to be underlined. In Bergson, the incommensurability between intuition and concept leads to seeing the construction of a system as a degradation. A system being the imperfect translation of some ineffable contact with being, the original intuition would have been expressed otherwise if the philosopher had lived at another time. The peculiar problems he addressed, the concepts he created and the paradigms he drew from the sciences of his time are only "the material he was obliged to use to give a concrete form to his thought", and "it would be a strange mistake to take for a constitutive element of doctrine what was only the means of expressing it".⁶⁶ Hence, the true object of a philosophy is upstream of the system, that is inessential in itself. For his part, Simondon does not posit the existence of such an intemporal intuition: systems take form in history, from the specific problems provided by a milieu and the paradigms chosen by the philosopher. The genesis of a system is not the mere expression of some forever lost intuition, but a problem-solving activity and a process of amplification constantly revived by the metastability of the relation to a milieu. Therefore, the degradation of a system into an organisation of signs is not a necessary law but only what "*generally* occurs during the construction of a philosophical system".⁶⁷ The object of a philosophy does not pre-exist its concretisation into a system. Simondon does not only propose a re-writing but also a correction of Bergson.

---

62   "Sciences de la nature et sciences de l'homme", in SLΦ, p. 281. See p. 271 as well.
63   H. Bergson, "Philosophical Intuition", in *The Creative Mind, op. cit.*, p. 88/p. 1346.
64   *Ibid.*, pp. 89–100/pp. 1346–1358.
65   "Recherche sur la philosophie de la nature", in SLΦ, p. 30–31.
66   H. Bergson, *The Creative Mind, op. cit.*, pp. 90–91/p. 1349.
67   "Recherche sur la philosophie de la nature", in SLΦ, p. 30, our emphasis.

2.3. Technology of philosophical systems: Simondon in discussion with Souriau and Gueroult

Around mid-century, the Bergsonian conception of philosophy became a debated topic among philosophers and historians of philosophy. Two figures in particular stand out, who are not unrelated to Simondon: Étienne Souriau and Martial Gueroult, whose take on philosophical systems did not go unnoticed by their contemporaries[68] nor by Simondon himself, as we can assume.[69] In our view, the debate that took place between these authors sheds light on the Simondonian take on philosophical systems, which happens to be at the junction between Souriau's creative conception of philosophy and Gueroult's scientific approach.

As an aesthetician and an epistemologist specialising in the instaurative path of the forms, Souriau reproached Bergson for his devaluation of systems and poor approach to philosophical activity, which he rectified using an artistic paradigm.[70] Just like a sculpture does not pre-exist its realisation, a philosophy exists only in virtue of a process of concretisation that goes from an abstract and incomplete mode of existence to a real and concrete work. This "objective" approach of philosophy is recognised by Gueroult in 1952, and summarised as follows: "Instead of the key to the enigma [of a system] being sought at the starting point, in the original intuition of the subject from which the work derives and where it must finally be reabsorbed, the direction of the current is reversed and the solution is glimpsed at the point of arrival, in the object, detached from the subject, as a completed work".[71] This view was further elaborated in 1956 in a conference with a title familiar to Simondon's readers, where philosophy ap-

---

[68] See in particular G. Deleuze and F. Guattari, *What Is Philosophy?*, op. cit., p. 41/44 and M. Merleau-Ponty, *Le Visible et l'invisible : Suivi de notes de travail*, C. Lefort (éd.), Paris, Gallimard, 1964, p. 248. Gueroult's influence on the aspiring philosophers of his generation, like Althusser, Foucault and Deleuze, is to take into consideration. See G. Bianco, "Philosophie et histoire de la philosophie pendant les années 1950: Le cas du jeune Gilles Deleuze", in F. Fruteau De Laclos and G. Bianco, *L'angle mort des années 1950: Philosophie et sciences humaines en France*, Paris, Éditions de la Sorbonne, 2016, pp. 147–167, p. 154.

[69] Not only Simondon attented Gueroult's courses at the Sorbonne, but the latter also supervised his master's degree dissertation ("diplôme d'études supérieures"). As for Souriau, the proximity between his inquiry on the different modes of existence and Simondon's main thesis has been noted by commentators. See A. Haumont, "L'individuation est-elle une instauration? Autour des pensées de Simondon et de Souriau", in P. Chabot (ed.), *Simondon*, Paris, Vrin, 2002, pp. 69–88; X. Guchet, *Pour un humanisme technologique*, op. cit., p. 35.

[70] É. Souriau, *L'Instauration Philosophique*, Paris, Alcan, 1939.

[71] M. Gueroult, "La voie de l'objectivité esthétique", in *Mélanges d'esthétique et de science de l'art offerts à Etienne Souriau*, Paris, Nizet, 1952, pp. 95–124, p. 95.

pears as a "work to-be-made".⁷² With Souriau, who was at the same time a great reader and a great opponent of Bergson, Simondon seems to have shared this operative and objective view of philosophy. Moreover, the idea that thought propagates within the limits of its initial paradigms through a process of transduction may echo the "law of point of view" set out by Souriau, that the architectonic of a system is determined and restricted by the point of view initially chosen to be repeated, modulated and varied by means of an "anaphora", an operation guiding any information process from the realisation of a statue to the construction a bridge, via the writing of a book.⁷³

Notwithstanding, the paradigm chosen by Simondon to think of philosophy is not aesthetical but scientific and technical. In fact, this choice of paradigm may be reminiscent of Gueroult's critique of Souriau's work around 1952.⁷⁴ Praising Souriau's objective approach to systems, Gueroult deplored his choice of an artistic paradigm: a system is not a product of fantasy endowed with a purely intrinsic value, but a series of deductions reaching reality through the construction of a coherent edifice. In philosophy, the work is not an end but a means to solve a problem, and it is from the sciences rather than from aesthetics that philosophy draws its method. To Gueroult, systematisation is the "technique of all philosophy", a technique whose logical and architectonical principles – namely analogy, symmetry and extrapolation – allow thought to "conquer reality and constitute itself as an object", and to develop into an "organic conspiration of concepts".⁷⁵ We find here a set of themes and notions – including those of analogy and symmetry – used by Simondon in 1955.⁷⁶ But to think of systems, Gueroult refers to Kant, and here appears a point of divergence with his former student. To Simondon, placing the system under the patronage of some *a priori* idea that would determine in advance its unity and the organic growth of each of its parts in the style of an "original germ", as suggested in the "Architectonic of Pure Reason",⁷⁷ is out of the question. Despite his interest in organic paradigms, his final choice of a technical and scientific paradigm shows to what extent he distances himself from Kant. Therefore, if Simondon retained anything

---

72   É. Souriau, "On the mode of existence of the work to-be-made", in *The Different Modes of Existence*, E. Beranek and T. Howles (trans.), Minneapolis, Univocal Publishing, 2015; "Du mode d'existence de l'œuvre à faire", in *Les différents modes d'existence*, Paris, PUF, 2009.
73   Id., *L'Instauration Philosophique, op. cit.*, p. 10 n.1 and *The Different Modes of Existence, op. cit.*, p. 128/108.
74   M. Gueroult, "La voie de l'objectivité esthétique", *op. cit.*, pp. 103–124.
75   Id., "Logique, architectonique et structures constitutives des systèmes philosophiques", in *Encyclopédie française*, t. XIX, 1957, 19.24.15–16.
76   See in particular "Recherche sur la philosophie de la nature", in SLΦ, p. 34.
77   I. Kant, *Critique of Pure Reason*, P. Guyer and A. W. Wood (trans.), Cambridge, Cambridge University Press, 1998, pp. 692–693; *Critique de la raison pure*, Paris, PUF, 2012, pp. 558–559.

from Gueroult, it is not the Kantian reference nor the understanding of system as closed structure but the analogy between the method of philosophy and that of sciences, which he takes further to "open" philosophical systems.

Like Gueroult, who held the chair of "History and Technology of Philosophical Systems" at the Collège de France from 1951 to 1962, Simondon defines philosophy as an activity of problem-solving and an operation of construction inspired from scientific method. Thus, one can think that his reference to Cartesianism and to scientific constructivism as a model for his own philosophical undertaking is not unrelated to the ideas of his former professor, whose study of the Cartesian "order of reasons", reading Descartes from a mathematical paradigm, made a great impression on French thinkers from 1953 onward.[78] In a text meant to constitute an additional chapter of METO around 1956, Simondon wrote:

> It is common and certainly legitimate to consider Cartesian logic as entirely derived from the mathematical paradigm; however, one could also show that Cartesianism very often uses the paradigm of architectural construction. It is that the palace-building century discovered that the logically constructed edifice is a kind of static automaton. [...]. When Descartes states that one must adjust all one's opinions to the level of reason, he uses the paradigm of the technical construction of an edifice that is like a machine.[79]

Implicitly referring to Gueroult's interpretation in the first lines, Simondon departs from it by moving from a mathematical paradigm to a technical one. Thus, one could say he achieves the "technology of philosophical systems" giving its name to the chair of his former professor. If technical objects serve as a "paradigm of intelligibility" for reflexive thought, as Simondon then puts it, it is not in virtue of the hypothesis that "all objects have the same mode of existence and can therefore be explained in the same way as the technical object is explained" but, more simply, on the ground that the norms of technical judgment can be transposed analogically to philosophy itself.[80] In that, a system can be evaluated by the standards of a well-functioning machine without being itself reduced to a machine. At the level of operations, the technological paradigm does not contradict the organic one, nor reduce the living thought to a dead machine.

Gueroult taught that "the Cartesian order of reasons applies only to Descartes, Malebranche's combinatorics only to Malebranche", and that "every philosophy always implicitly or explicitly includes its *Discourse on the Method*".[81] In our view, it is no coincidence if, from 1953 onwards, no fewer than

---

[78] M. Gueroult, *Descartes selon l'ordre des raisons*, Paris, Aubier, 1953.
[79] "L'objet technique comme paradigme d'intelligibilité universelle" in SLΦ, p. 406.
[80] *Ibid.*, pp. 397–398.
[81] M. Gueroult, "Logique, architectonique et structures constitutives des systèmes philosophiques", *op. cit.*, 19.26.1–2.

three of Simondon's texts have referred to Wiener's *Cybernetics* as the draft of a "new *Discourse on the Method*".[82] After Descartes, one can say Simondon sought his own method in the sciences and the technology of his time. This new *Discourse on the Method* is outlined in the form of an *allagmatics*, a general theory of operations allowing to study the transformations of any system, whether it is organic, physical or, as we shall add, philosophical, by tracing its modulation into a certain structure.[83] Combining topology and energetics, this method seems to be the one Simondon chose to carry out his study on individuation.[84]

If the "palace-building century" that saw the birth of Descartes could only provide thought with static automata, the teleological mechanisms studied by cybernetics provides us with new norms and suggests a new method of philosophising. The phenomena of information, transduction and recurrent causality, with the energetic dimension they imply, must pervade reflexive thought to revamp it from the inside. Philosophy no longer has to develop into a relatively closed structure, based on an axiomatic deduction and a determined order of reasons. It can now flourish in an open system defined by its metastability, its energetical exchange with the milieu and its ceaselessly rekindled transduction.

2.4. What philosophy of the history of philosophy? The scope of the Simondonian energetics

As a professor, Simondon never ceased to teach the history of philosophy. Far from being set aside afterwards, the notions of genesis, metastability and information, as well as the transductive approach that accompany them, reoccurred in his teaching well into the 1960s and 1970s to be applied to the whole history of thought. Quite early, the genetical method and the historical approach go hand in hand. Thus, to close this contribution, we would like to question the scope of his "philosophy of the history of philosophy", to quote the title of a book by Gueroult.[85]

First, it must be noted that in Simondon, the notion of system is not defined once and for all. Instead of imposing a single model of systematisation on

---

[82] "Cybernétique et philosophie", "Épistémologie de la cybernétique" and "L'objet technique comme paradigme d'intelligibilité universelle" in SLΦ, p. 38, 197 and 416.
[83] See in particular "Allagmatics", in ILNFI, pp. 661–671/ILFI, pp. 529–536.
[84] Due to a lack of space, we simply mention Jean-Yves Chateau's interpretation that the allagmatic point of view is certainly convenient for formalising Simondon's thought, but is not the one that he chose to set out most of his philosophy. J.-Y. Chateau, *Vocabulaire de Simondon*, *op. cit.*, p. 16.
[85] M. Guéroult, *Philosophie de l'histoire de la philosophie*, Paris, Aubier-Montaigne, 1979.

all systems, the genetical method is open to variation and admits plural forms of systematisation. From navigation to architectural construction via organic growth, philosophies of all ages tend to a systematic mode of existence by inventing their own notion of the system. In a 1971–1972 course unpublished as of today, we read: "Each philosophical thought tends to constitute a system, i.e. a whole that is compatible with itself and that stands like a well-constructed building (static type system) or an animal that runs (dynamic type system) among objects that may be mobile, or an operative vision of the world and of Man (obtained by construction or by changing the state of the matter)".[86] Illustrating this typology with examples from all centuries, Simondon places the Ionian physiologists, Descartes and Marxism in the last type of systems, which from what we can infer, is also the category in which he placed his own work.

Just like the Cartesian order of reasons applies to Descartes only, allagmatics applies to Simondon only. However, several texts by Simondon show an extension of the crystallographic and organic paradigms to the general history of thought, beyond the limits of his own philosophy. What does an energetics bring to the understanding of the history of thought? Also, can such a peculiar take on philosophical systems be established as a general method? For the purposes of a 1962–1963 course, Simondon outlined a project of "genetical encyclopaedia" departing from the dialectical logic and the Marxist approach.[87] Relying on the notion of metastability, this "genetical study of the modes of knowledge" explains how systems emerge, evolve and disappear in relation to their milieu. Religion, art, technics, politics and society then appear as "non-noetic modes of knowledge" that "intervene as modifiers of the equilibrium conditions", "creating metastability" and "preparing from the outside of the systematised thought changes of structure that emerge in the form of a new system".[88] As "phases", systems "tend to persevere in their being; they perpetuate and enrich themselves by differentiating themselves, sometimes also by becoming hypertelic, but cannot find in themselves the power to operate a mutation":[89] the notion of hypertely, forged in METO to designate the evolution of technical objects whose overspecialisation prevents them from adapting to new milieus, close to obsolescence, confirms the analogy between philosophical systems and the objects produced by the technical invention. Thus, Simondon definitely makes room for the idea of a mode of existence of philosophical systems, provided with a temporality of their own while being connected to other cultural temporalities.

---

[86] "Quelques éléments d'histoire de la pensée philosophique dans le monde occidental", 1971–1972, p. 1. We sincerely thank Nathalie Simondon for providing us with this text.
[87] "Sciences de la nature et sciences de l'homme", in SLΦ, p. 219.
[88] Ibid., p. 220
[89] Ibid., p. 241.

In that, he distances himself from Gueroult's structural approach, which consists in extracting systems from the history of philosophy to consider them as indestructible edifices and eternal essences independent from other temporalities, especially those of science and technology. Since it combines a topological view with an energetics, the transductive approach to philosophical systems goes beyond the opposition, built by Victor Goldschmidt – a successor of Gueroult – between "structural method" and "genetical method", "logical time" and "historical time".[90] The transductive approach is not limited to simply following step by step the series of operations that constitute the system in the form of a crystallisation, germination or construction. It also applies, on another level, to the historical time. In 1960, Simondon wrote: "it can be said that the hylomorphic schema or the [Platonic] notion of archetype possess a high tension of information" – this "tension of information" defining "a schema's property to structure a domain, to propagate through it, to organise it" – "because they have incited structures of significations for twenty-four centuries across widely diverse cultures".[91] Thus, the value of a system does not lie in the validity of its paradigms nor, as Gueroult thought, in its ability to resist time like an eternal essence and a monument more lasting than bronze, but in its capacity to be part of a network and to participate in the collective by spreading germs for further philosophical inventions. The history of philosophy is not a mausoleum where dead systems are embalmed, eternalised and stored in the frozen form of conceptual sarcophagi, but a relay race where runners pass on torches, in accordance with a Lucretian image dear to Simondon.[92] One after the other, philosophers pass on the same flame, continuously rekindled, to pursue and amplify an infinitely unfinished work. In 1953, Simondon wrote: "it cannot be forgotten that the legacy of the Ionian physiologists, cultivated only once by Plato and Aristotle and fallen into disuse since, has retained all its fertility".[93] ILNFI can somewhat be read as the re-cultivation of the germs left by ancient thought, transplanted into the fertile ground of a contemporary milieu.

---

[90] V. Goldschmidt, "Temps historique et temps logique dans l'interprétation des systèmes philosophiques", in *Questions platoniciennes*, Paris, Vrin, 1970, pp. 13–21, first published in 1953.
[91] "Form, information, and potentials", in ILNFI, p. 689/ILFI, p. 550.
[92] ILNFI, pp. 240–241/ILFI, p. 216.
[93] "Épistémologie de la cybernétique", in SLΦ, p. 196.

Philosophising from and with the Camera
The Wild Invention of Photography

Carole Maigné

This contribution addresses a simple expectation: how the photographic image can be understood *in* and *from* the texts of Gilbert Simondon. The idea was to examine Simondon's writings on a specific type of image, the photographic image, since Simondon deploys *both* a theory of the image and of the imagination *and* a theory of technique and invention. The photographic image seemed to be a relevant place to interrogate the Simondonian text since it combines the eye, the hand and the camera, and because it cannot be conceived of without its technical invention. Curiously, as far as we know, this author never produced any theoretical studies on photography. Yet, if our research holds true, Simondon's critical potential in this field seems underestimated, as it traverses known territories along an original path, even opening up little-surveyed horizons.

Simondon proposes a philosophy *of* photography from the genesis of the photographic image:[1] its starting point is not the image made in front of us, but the one made in the camera once we enter it. Now, to enter the camera is not only to look at what is made there: it is to grasp how it inscribes itself in a transductive and metastable world. By unfolding here what Simondon says, and by passing over this image which is evoked among many other examples, we grasp at the root of what philosophy can and must do in its work when confronted with a concrete theoretical and empirical object: his texts engage a philosophy *of* photography as a process, as a theoretical object, *because it is* technical, as a theoretical object *because* here technical invention displaces the technical regime of image production. Not only can the technique not be erased, but it makes us think; it does not come after reflection but is inseparable from it.

Does this mean that Simondon is interested in the way things are made, introducing to philosophy a kind of fascination for ignored or neglected processes? After all, isn't this what historians do already, looking at objects like devices, plates and films, and the commercial and economic relays of the image? But what proves fruitful here is not only the irruption of a material historical reality, but also a logic of invention. Invention responds to a logic of information, which

---

1   This is a decisive point: not a philosophy "of" as if philosophy were plastered on the object, but a philosophy that seeks out the ontological fault lines induced by the object's operativity. I thank Jamil Alioui for referring me to the 1955 text "Recherche sur la philosophie de la nature".

unfolds and saturates itself, thus operating by leaps which, in turn, over-saturate and create other leaps. The photographic image is caught up in this informative logic and leaves the semantic terrain altogether: if it is something caught, it is not a trace, a sign; knowing what it says about the "object" photographed does not matter at all. This is obviously the effect of not ignorance, but of a decentring: the Polaroid, which will be at the heart of the subject, is less interested in the image that comes out of the camera in its supposed 'resemblance' to the object than it is in questioning the very process of producing an image, and doing so in this way. As a result, the photographic image is much more caught up in a logic of relationship and individuation than in a questioning of what it represents.

1. Polaroid and the history of photography

Simondon's analysis of the camera, and more precisely of the Polaroid Land camera, makes us think about the history and philosophy of photography. This analysis was proposed in the 1964–1965 *Cours sur la perception* [Course on Perception] and repeated identically in the 1965–1966 course *Imagination et invention* [Imagination and Invention]. We will come back to what is not a coincidence between photography, perception and imagination. We read this invention not in relation to images in the broad sense, but from the camera's focus, restricted to the photographic image.[2] What interests us is this type of image, exposed here from the precise box that is used to produce it: the camera – more precisely, the Polaroid Land camera.

An apparatus becomes an apparatus when it is detachable and transmissible, when it is shared.[3] Simondon distinguishes three layers that make up an apparatus: an inner layer, which is the heart of "wild" invention, the place of direct adequacy between the object created and the invention, "the core of productive and resistant technicality";[4] an intermediate layer, "expression",[5] which concerns local and transitory aspects, a level of reality that is half-technical and half-lan-

---

2   Jean-Yves Château, in his introduction to *Imagination et Invention*, insists on the fact that Simondon does not want to reduce all images to a vague category, to a single essence; on the contrary, he wants "to give right to the polymorphic and constantly evolving diversity of the reality of images", p. xxiv.
3   Simondon, "Imagination et invention (1965–1966) – extraits", in Idem, *L'invention dans les techniques. Cours et conférences*, Paris, Seuil, 2005 (now abbreviated IT), pp. 273–304 p. 281. See also: METO, p. 250/MEOT, p. 245: "Through technical activity, on the contrary, man creates mediations, and these mediations are detachable from the individual who produces and thinks them."
4   IT, p. 284.
5   IT, p. 282.

guage: like an engine displays its displacement, makes language for all and creates a *koiné*; and finally, an external layer, the "manifestation",[6] namely, the multiple possible appearances of the object according to versatile aesthetic criteria, linked to a semantics and a vain obsession with novelty. The internal layer is at odds with the other two, because the latter two are semantic and not *strictly* technical. In the case of the car, the intermediate layer says something about the internal layer, but by insisting on some of its parts, without considering it as a whole: in a way, as a metonymy, the engine exhibits certain properties that are valid for the whole: "there was the time of the engines with a large number of cylinders in a row, then the V-cylinder engines, then the "flat-twin" engines".[7] The outer layer describes, for example, the use of aluminium, which does not contribute anything from the point of view of invention, but brings the airplane pilot and the car driver together in a common language, that of lightness, speed, and performance: what links the two is not technical relevance (aluminium has zero technical value for the car's dashboard), but "perceptual and operative norms".[8]

These last two layers dress up and even conceal the technical content, covering it with their accessory semantics: "a large number of technical objects are dressed up as objects of manifestation."[9] They touch on uses, which are themselves correlated to a degree of knowledge: the further one moves away from the heart of the invention, the more one strays into the accessory. The use relation goes against invention.[10] Simondon associates the most advanced knowledge with what is least visible, and the falsest knowledge with what is most visible: thus, in the case of the car, what is created most purely is found "in the parts that are not very visible or unknown to the majority of users, the gears, the transmission, the electricity generator".[11] It is also precisely these two layers that make us believe that technical progress is driven by utility: "what adapts to the human being runs the risk of becoming a means of manifestation".[12]

Expression and manifestation are cumulative, both infinite in their variations and limited in their scope: they do not touch the very essence of invention, they prolong it, deploy it, "transpose" it, as the text says, into all domains.[13] They

---

6   *Ibid.*, pp. 282–283.
7   *Ibid.*, p. 282.
8   *Ibid.*, p. 283.
9   *Ibid.*, p. 282.
10 METO, p. 18/MEOT, p. 12: the use relation is stereotypy of adapt gestures, it levels, it engulfs by fixed repetition; or METO, p. 30/MEOT, pp. 24–25: "The *made-to-measure* aspect is not only inessential, it goes against the essence of the technical being, it is like a dead weight imposed from the outside."
11 IT, p. 282.
12 *Ibidem.*
13 *Ibid.*, p. 283.

are also different in terms of temporality: these two layers, which are inessential from the point of view of invention, have an increasingly rapid temporality as they develop centrifugally; they develop a world of objects that is ever more varied and colourful, but which is basically not very creative, limited precisely by their use or by their precisely prosthetic character. Their time is that of continuity,[14] of perpetual renewal. The time of invention, on the contrary, is that of rupture: the institution of the created object is characterised by universality and timelessness. Because technical invention is a leap, something acquired once and for all, for all and for all time, it is out of time and valid for all time.[15] The dynamic described by Simondon therefore consists in opposing the organic core of technical invention to the two intermediate and external layers that are its "parasites".[16] These two layers are not without effect, they "hinder", or even impose a "distortion"[17] on development. The individuation of the invented object partially dissolves in its subsequent reincorporations. It is never lost, however, and can be reinvested, since, as mentioned above, the inventive core is resistant as well as productive. The proposed model is therefore energetic, describing processes of differentiation which are all possible translations of the original inventive act, since each layer invents meaning in a generally unstable and metastable equilibrium.[18]

With this scheme, the history of photography is first of all that of a regression. We must insist on the novel and original character of this analysis, which goes against many *topoi:*[19] photography does not move towards a perfection in capturing the image. The "wild" invention, the very core of invention, gives way to an uninterrupted externalisation that looks very much like its domestication. Basically, this history is that of the diffusion of an apparatus to a public that is increasingly ignorant of its procedures, with diffusion going hand in hand with progressive automation. Simondon describes three phases of development thought of from the three internal, intermediate and external layers outlined above, the principle being the progressive distancing from the place and time of invention: the history of photography is that of repeated cleavages within the apparatus, inseparable from the uses that are differentiated.[20]. It concerns all those who are familiar with its process, from shooting to the development of the image, the scholars and the professional amateurs. The text evokes two some-

---

14   *Ibid.*, p. 282.
15   *Ibid.*, p. 281.
16   *Ibid.*, p. 284.
17   *Ibid.*, p. 282.
18   ILNFI, p. 25/ILFI, p. 28.
19   A suitable comparison here would be Walter Benjamin's "A Short History of Photography" written in 1931.
20   IT, p. 285.

what simultaneous cleavages: the delegation of printing and the invention of rolled film. They lead to a divergence between the amateur and the professional camera: the sensitive plate remains the privilege of the professional who masters it, while the amateur delegates the development of his film.[21] The third cleavage is industrialisation, which interferes in the heart of this dissociation, deepening it more and more: "major mistakes" in exposure are avoided, but the print is standardised, the singularity of the shot evaporates. Elementary optics and automatic adjustment of the diaphragm allow everyone to take over the photographic operation. Synthesising his remarks, Simondon arrives at a final tripartition: the pure internal technical layer is that of the photographic camera with film planes, and is reserved for the scholar, the professional. The intermediate layer, where expression dominates, is the domain of journalism, which includes optical adjustments. Finally, the outer layer of the event is that of the simplified, closed and automated camera, which is suitable for leisure. On these three levels, a different gesture is at work each time, which modulates the verb "to take": in the first, one "takes a photograph" fully; in the second, one "takes photographs on the occasion of a survey or a journey"; in the third, one can only take an image under the sun and with subjects situated at a pre-adjusted[22] distance. In the last case, the setting is quite sharp: it requires that the object is not too close, and assumes that it can be far away. The major constraint is to prevent blurring.

The history that is proposed takes up the opposition between a core as the "self-correlation of a structural and functional core opposed to the divergence of adaptive evolution that specialises the product according to categories of users".[23] The massification of photography is at the heart of these repeated cleavages; for Simondon, automation is indeed a dispossession. It is a dislocation of the photographic act into separate instances (camera, film, development), absorbed by the "concentrated industrial universe" of the market.[24] But the Polaroid creates a rupture as a return effect of the internal core, like a boomerang, a feedback,[25] bringing about a convergence in this history of divergences:

> The Polaroid Land camera, instead of continuing the divergent evolution that separates the manifestation aspect from the expression aspect of the fundamental camera, brings these divergent beams together in units and covers the whole range of possible uses, from

---

21 However, Simondon does not follow the arguments of P. Bourdieu et al. in *Un art moyen. Essai sur les usages sociaux de la photographie*, Paris, Editions de Minuit, 1965: usage is not the sociology of usage, what makes sense sociologically here is more a gesture and an expectation arising from the camera and not from the image (that of the worker portrait versus the bourgeois portrait, for example).
22 IT, p. 285.
23 Ibid., p. 286.
24 Ibid., p. 287.
25 Ibid., p. 279.

professional to leisure use, to journalism or similar uses, such as setting up characters before a film shot, with feedback from the photographs on the attitude of the actors. This new wave of invention in photography so increases the compatibility between the physical and chemical processes that it makes feedback possible within the shot, with an initial photograph being used to improve the framing, subject placement, and optical adjustment of the next photograph.[26]

As Simondon's lecture dates from 1965, it is not yet the famous SX 70 released in 1972, but the Polaroid invented in 1948, which underwent multiple improvements until the colour Polaroid of 1963. What Edwin Land (1909–1991) invented, starting from a reflection on polarisation, was a camera that erased the dissociation between the different moments of the photographic act: as we know, the Polaroid promoted what became known as instant photography, ensuring the development of the film within the camera body in record time. Thanks to considerable advances in research on photosensitive emulsion, especially on colour, it combines the studio and the laboratory in the very mechanism of the handheld camera.[27] In record time, it converges and contracts the technical actions distinct from the laboratory. And it does so in daylight, with no need to protect the latent image from being erased by sunlight, as the camera body ensures its preservation. The SX 70, whose slogan was "the one step photo", would integrate techniques which were *a priori* foreign to its predecessors: sonar technology operating the focus for a fraction of a second with submarine precision, an electric motor, and a battery integrated in the charger.[28] From the point of view of its use, the Polaroid is suitable for everyone, from the scientist to the amateur: it would be used as much in medicine as in leisure or in artistic practice.[29] Simondon emphasised the rediscovered freedom of the amateur who could make immediate progress through the ease of shooting photographs and who became autonomous by developing the image themself, just like professional photographers. All of this is possible only thanks to the extreme effect of industrialisation, which delivered ready-to-use film cartridges inserted into the cam-

---

26   Ibid., p. 287.
27   M. Pieuchard, *La photographie et l'automatisme: histoire d'une utopie du Photomaton au procédé Polaroïd*, PhD thesis, Université Paris 1 Panthéon Sorbonne, 2013, https://tel.archives-ouvertes.fr/tel-03007927, p. 202: One promotional campaign thus speaks of a Polaroid film capable of "self-processing". As the cited thesis makes clear, the Polaroid is obviously comparable to the invention of the photo booth.
28   M. Pieuchard, *La photographie et l'automatisme, op. cit.*, pp. 199–201; a strong link with watchmaking is underlined on p. 203. See also Luc Debraine and Olivier Lugon (eds.), *Photographie et horlogerie*, Gollion, Infolio, 2022.
29   Land worked closely with Ansel Adams, a pillar of the *f64* group since 1932. The *Library Collection*, founded in 1957, aims to collect images by artists using Polaroid photography. The Polaroid collection sold in 2009 was deposited at the Musée de l'Elysée in Lausanne and then transferred to the Westlicht Museum in Vienna.

era's housing. The height of technicality and the height of freedom complement each other.

Technical hyper-specialisation rediscovers the original core of invention, and, in a way, the Polaroid achieves the daguerreotype of the 19th century in a mastered process: "invention brings a wave of condensations, of concretidations that simplify the object by charging each structure with a plurality of functions".[30] The Polaroid illustrates what the beginning of the course states: invention is a "structuring return of the content of anticipation on the formula of the present action, it is a return of information or rather a return of organisation whose source is the order of magnitude of the result, the regime of the operation thought of as completed and complete."[31] This invention, in return – it would not be absurd to even speak of the return of invention – consists in rediscovering the scheme of compatibility initially instituted. The Polaroid is the result of both relational problems (which are resolved through use according to a progressive perfection) and problems of self-correlation proper to the regime of compatibility (which are resolved by leaps). It is this last level that reorganises the whole.[32] This is why the whole of technical progress "can hardly be continuous, it takes place by jumps, by discontinuous stages."[33] The history of photography is a loop that does not repeat.

2. The photographic image: The end of the imprint?

Simondon proposes an original position on the very nature of the photographic image: "the basis of photography as an invention must be sought not only in the camera, but in the compatibility between this reduction of the darkroom that is a camera and a photosensitive chemical surface."[34] Although the darkroom and Judean bitumen had existed long before, "the invention consisted in making light work directly and automatically on a photosensitive material inside a small

---

30 IT, p. 288.
31 IT, p. 277.
32 IT, p. 103. Here, the very notion of "problem" should be further interrogated as to its link with invention, as Benoît Turquety does in his article "Charles Cros et le problème "cinéma": écrire l'histoire avec Bachelard et Simondon", in *1895. One Thousand Eight Hundred and Ninety-Five*, 72/2014, URL: http://journals.openedition.org/1895/4801, an article that also discusses Brunet's book, *La naissance de l'idée de photographie* cited below: the problem is not as pre-existent to its solution as it appears, and is resolved in the course of the resolution (p. 22). I have not yet read Turquety's forthcoming book: *Politiques de la technicité. Corps, monde et medias avec Gilbert Simondon*, Paris, Mimesis.
33 IT, p. 103.
34 IT, p. 286.

darkroom to form a real image of the objects."[35] One might think that Simondon was repeating a very classical definition: the inscription of light on a photosensitive surface by means of an apparatus. In our opinion, this is not the case: since it poses the problem of compatibility, here between photochemistry and optical physics, the statement has a strong impact that needs to be examined in detail.

"The compatibility lies in the suspension of the chemical activity of the sensitive material between manufacture and development, which makes it possible to insert the shot into this temporal interval."[36] It is striking to note that the scope of the invention lies in the suspension of time (chemical) more than in the *graphein* and its link to light (*photo*): suspended and deferred, the chemical action loses its imperious and immediate character. Contrary to a deep-rooted vulgate, Simondon places the emphasis here not on the revelation of the latent image,[37] but on the insertion of a gesture "in-between": it is less a question of revealing than of inserting "just in time."[38] The temporality specific to this image combines suspense and quasi-instantaneity, which allows for compatibility between the chemical dimension and the optical dimension that is inserted into the former. It is therefore neither the suspension of time in the broad sense, nor the suspension of perceptive time, but the suspension of the time of the chemical reaction that makes sense here: "for photography, it is the physical process of real image formation and the photochemical process that are made compatible by the phenomenon of the latent image; this compatibility belongs to the category of states of equilibrium, authorises the temporal succession of phases through the suspension of an activity".[39] The equilibrium of the system allows us to think of what we call the instantaneous. The latter is operative here, it contracts within itself a precise process that could not take place without the apparatus.[40] The instantaneous is not finally conjugated to the present, in a present outside of time, so much so that it would freeze time for eternity; rather, it is caught in a becoming that holds all the dimensions of time, past, present and future, because the operative moment (*metaxu*) opens up the possibilities: the suspended inter-

---

35   *Ibid.*, p. 286.
36   *Ibid.*, p. 286.
37   This is to be distinguished from the mental image, which is, in contrast, "the bearer of latent meanings". *Imagination et Invention* p. 13; we will come back to this below.
38   This is the importance of what Simondon thematises in the "Allagmatics" supplement to ILNFI: "the operation is a *metaxu* or middle-ground between two structures, and yet its nature is unlike that of any structure", ILNFI, p. 664/ILFI, p. 531. What is "between", or "middle-grounded", is characteristic of any operative act.
39   IT, p. 287.
40   It would be interesting here to question photographic images taken without a camera, such as the solarisation images of Man Ray or Moholy-Nagy: are they still photography? If one advocates a chemical definition around the imprint, this is undoubtedly the case, if one advocates the chemical-optical alliance, this is less the case.

val allows for the bifurcation, the insertion *into* and *through* time of the image of a fertile hazard.

This aspect is combined with another striking feature: what finally brings the daguerreotype closer to the polaroid image, and therefore constitutes a dimension specific to photography, is the intrinsic discontinuity of the images in relation to one another. Simondon insists on the "view by view":[41] the specificity of the photographic image, by its invention, is to be made on a plate and then on another plate, which persists on the pellicle of the film and then on the Polaroid cartridge. Simondon thus speaks of the "film-plane" and the "plates" kept by the professional camera, the only place where one really "took" a photograph. The view by view of the camera draws a red thread of analysis: against automatic levelling, against stereotyping, against the commercial standardisation inscribed at the very heart of this invention that has become a mass process, it is a question of maintaining a double process of taking and disengagement, a moment of singular taking and its overcoming in another. The emphasis is therefore not so much on the reproducibility of the same through the photographic image, according to a time of copying and resemblance, but rather on the taking within the seriality. Operationally, each image opens onto another much more than it closes itself to its alter ego. By emphasising genesis, Simondon makes the film and the Polaroid cartridge a place of inventiveness and retouching. The Polaroid combines the time and place of the image's development in a few seconds, but by singling out the image: this is why it can be retroactively modified, by a shot that changes the first. This time of feedback allows us to grasp the succession of images in permanent renewal: instead of envisaging a succession of definitive fixities, Simondon opts for a sort of dialogue of images in series, responding to each other because they are successive. It is not a question of the dramatised time of loss, but of the fertile time of resumption and its overcoming. A return to re-making, each making at once singularised and de-singularised, sounding and dissonant with the next.

This converges with Simondon's developments against the hylomorphism of the mould or the imprint as outlined in *The Individuation*. There is powerful descriptive and analytical potential for photography. Individuation certainly concerns the metaphysics of the individual, but with regard to the problem of form and ontogeny, it also touches on technical invention, which is precisely characterised by its genesis.[42] The history of a technical process implies the operation of transduction, where little by little an object is individuated, in which

---

41   IT, p. 286.
42   METO, p. 26/MEOT, p. 20: "The genesis of the technical object partakes in its being. The technical object is that which is not anterior to its coming-into-being, but is present at each stage of its coming-into-being".

Simondon indissociably links technique and life.⁴³ Simondon rejects the classical schema of a clay that takes shape because the shape of the mould is applied to it:

> [I]t cannot be said that the mold gives form; it is the clay that takes form according to the mold, because it communicates with the worker. The *positivity* of this form-taking is that of the clay and the worker; it is this internal resonance, the work of this internal resonance. The mold intervenes as a condition of enclosure, limit, halted expansion, and direction of mediation. The technical operation institutes internal resonance in the matter taking form, by means of energetic conditions and topological conditions.⁴⁴

It is a question of proposing an exchange of energy and not of giving form by imprinting: the clay does not take shape thanks to the mould that encloses it, it takes shape in a system of oriented information. There is no inert matter and form coming from outside, there is a system carried by an operation, the clay object being the complete system of this operation. The error of hylomorphism is to erase the operation of mediation, like "someone who remains outside the workshop and considers nothing but what enters and exist."⁴⁵ One must enter the workshop and penetrate the camera's case.

The photographic image, as a technical product, must be grasped from this schematism of the operation.⁴⁶ There is no mystery of the black box, there is no revelation, there is a moment of contact, envisaged as resonance "during form-taking".⁴⁷ What the Polaroid does particularly well is to contract this resonance of the *metaxu* in a short space of time, which reinforces it. Pleading to think of not the mould but the modulation,⁴⁸ the photographic image becomes itself modulation rather than imprint. The achievement here is striking: Simondon goes against a whole tradition that makes the photographic image an embalming, a mortifying fixation of time, a trace of what was and is no longer – even worse, of what was and is already dismissed.⁴⁹ The scope of his reflection even seems to constitute an apex in the tradition of discourses on silver photography. Because Simondon combines the chemical and the optical from the outset, without privileging one over the other, the photographic image crystallises through the transformation of chemical micro-grains under the action of an optical light

---

43   METO, p. 26/MEOT, p. 20.
44   ILNFI, p. 28–29/ILFI p. 45.
45   ILNFI, p. 30/ILFI p. 46.
46   It must be emphasised that the schema is first of all an operation, as Vincent Beaubois points out, an individuating knowledge-action, which the author contrasts with Kant's individual schema in time (cf. V. Beaubois, "Un schématisme pratique de l'imagination", in *Apparatus*, 16/2015, p. 1), which does not preclude the fact that it is pervasively traversed by time (*Ibid.*, p. 4).
47   ILNFI, p. 31/ILFI, p. 47.
48   ILNFI, p. 31/ILFI, p. 47.
49   See for example G. Didi-Huberman, *La Ressemblance par contact*, Paris, Minuit, 2008.

directed by the camera, so that the click of the shot is indeed a system of resonance carried by the operation of the shot.[50]

The photographic image is a recording and not an automatism. The critique of automatism, which has been mentioned several times, deserves our attention. It is crucial to refuse to conflate technique and automatism in order to launch a mechanological thought: "automatism is a rather low degree of technical perfection. In order to make a machine automatic, one must sacrifice a number of possibilities of operation as well as numerous possible usages".[51] The camera's casing brings chemistry and optics together: the suspense of the chemical reaction imposes a precise technique, which means that the photographic image is not the spontaneity of the solar reality that is inscribed without the hand of man, but rather its concretisation.[52] The Polaroid exhibits this moment when artificiality finds spontaneity, by a retroactive loop, the artifice becoming natural, as much by the widespread use of the photographic activity as by the re-conquered ease of its internal mechanism.

If there is indeed a *graphein* of sunlight on a photosensitive surface, it is in a renewed sense: the process of writing is not anterior to the system formed by the camera, as if there were light and optics and then its chemical impression, it is absolutely consubstantial to it. Simondon pays particular attention to the corpuscular and granular emulsion of the photographic film where the operation between optics and chemistry is played out. The photographic image is made up of modulated grains: "in its active part, a photographic surface, which is the support of signals, is constituted by an emulsion that contains a multitude of silver grains in the basic form of a chemical combination".[53] The ability to record details depends on the fineness of the particles: "the translation of a continuous optical line into chemical reality within an emulsion is constituted by a discontinuous trail of sensible grains; the rarer and coarser these grains are, the more difficult it is to pin down a small detail with sufficient fidelity";[54] under the microscope, the emulsion shows only a shapeless mist of discontinuous grains. What is important, for photography, as for film, the tape recorder, the video recorder, is the action of breaking down into elements a global situation, recorded by physical modification. At stake here is the crucial relationship between

---

50   ILNFI, p. 32/ILFI, p. 48: "What makes it such that a being is itself, different from all others, is neither its matter nor its form but the operation through which its matter has taken form in a certain system of internal resonance".
51   METO, p. 17/MEOT, p. 11.
52   METO, p. 49/MEOT, p. 47: "Artificiality is not a characteristic denoting the fabricated origin of the object in opposition to spontaneous production in nature: artificiality is that which is internal to man's artificializing action, whether this action intervenes on a natural object or on an entirely fabricated one".
53   ILNFI, p. 265/ILFI p. 236.
54   *Ibidem.*

form and information: the photographic image does not reproduce a form, it informs.⁵⁵ By recording, it "modulates the light point by point in the same way the photographed objects modulated the film".⁵⁶ Since the signal is not information,⁵⁷ the discontinuous nature of the medium is not yet a form: "the transmission of the image of a heap of sand or the irregular surface of granite requires the same quantity of signals as the transmission of the image of a well-aligned regiment or the columns of the Parthenon [...] there is a considerable gap between information signals and the form".⁵⁸ The relationship between form and information is even reversed: "one could even say that the quantity of signals seems to increase when the qualities of the form are lost; it is technically easier to transmit the image of a square or a circle than that of a heap of sand".⁵⁹ The image takes shape, makes sense, when it passes from signal to information. This is not a magical operation: it is an orientation of perception. Photography illustrates perception: to perceive is to polarise and intensify. "It is not enough to simply say that perception consists in grasping organised wholes; in fact, perception is the act that organised wholes; it introduces organisation by analogically linking the forms contained in the subject to the signals received: to perceive is to retain the greatest possible quantity of signals inside the forms most deeply rooted in the subject".⁶⁰ There is thus analogy and not resemblance, a crucial distinction in Simondon.⁶¹

The photographic image is conceived here not from the index,⁶² from the trace, the sign, the discursive. It is not a restitution of what is photographed in the sense of what pre-exists the image. Here Simondon shatters the idea of photography as resemblance by contact, as adherence of the image to the real. Here nothing adheres anymore, because it is a question of modulation. Nothing adheres, because something is done: if Barthes' "it has been" is dismissed,⁶³ it is not because the image says nothing, is silent, but rather because it is, on the contrary, situated in a system of information and relations. The photographic image is

---

55   METO, p. 137/MEOT, pp. 122–123 contrasts the living memory of man and the memory of the machine to note that the machine does not preserve forms, but a translation of forms by means of a coding, which is what the silver grains of photographic film are.
56   ILNFI, p. 249/ILFI, p. 223.
57   Ibidem.
58   Ibid., p. 267/p. 237.
59   Ibidem.
60   Ibid., p. 269/p. 239.
61   Jamil Alioui, "Interfaces and analogy", in *Arkhaï 2021 – Texte-Image-Interface*, Lausanne, pp. 167–193.
62   The notion of index is from Peirce: it designates a sign by physical connection; the icon, a sign by resemblance, and the symbol, a sign by convention.
63   R. Barthes, *La chambre claire, Note sur la photographie*, Paris, Cahiers du cinéma, Gallimard, 1980, p. 120.

indeed an energetic regime,⁶⁴ a system in the process of becoming while the energy is being actualised,⁶⁵ and as such, a complete but singular system, since individuation is "the singular manner in which the internal resonance of *this* matter about to take *this* form is established".⁶⁶ The photographic image is therefore not a transparency where its technicality is erased: if Barthes could say that we see the photographed and not the photograph,⁶⁷ it is clear that Simondon's perspective never erases the camera in the reflection on the image, and therefore departs from many discourses on photography that Brunet has rightly qualified as "a-technical".⁶⁸ The proposed analysis cannot promote a fascination for the acheropoietic image that photography has engendered since its beginnings, precisely because there is always technique and apparatus. The photographic image is not an open window, open to the point of erasing its own frame, of saying without showing that it does so: it is *in the very camera*.

3. Photographic gesture and wild invention

Against the automatic writing of the surrealists who used photography to bet on a surreality beyond the normalised and visible reality of everyday life, photography is not automatic writing, because it is a recording technique. We must go even further: the photographic image is not a *ready-made*, in the double sense imposed by Duchamp of that which bursts in by incongruity and questions the nonsense of a modernity that has become mute. The ready-made is totally machine-like and not technical, as Simondon⁶⁹ subtly tells us. The photographic image is not here a monstration of a rupture of meaning, it has nothing of the found object that questions the very process of signification by closing in on itself: it is articulated to a background that never ceases to make sense, it is not an emptied sign. And yet it does break through, it is not confused with any im-

---

64   ILNFI, p. 31/ILFI, p. 47.
65   ILNFI, p. 32/ILFI, p. 48.
66   ILNFI, p. 32/ILFI, p. 48.
67   R. Barthes, *La Chambre claire, op. cit.*, p. 18: "Whatever it shows and however it is taken, a photograph is always invisible: it is not what we see. In short, the referent adheres".
68   F. Brunet, *La naissance de l'idée de photographie*, Paris, PUF, 2012.
69   Simondon sees in surrealism the last attempt to defend a pure art: it is striking to read that surrealism constructs "an object that is stable, self-organised like an automaton, independent from its creator and indifferent to the one who encounters it. Surrealism, so to speak, is in the hyper-functional manner of constructing the object: this object is neither useful nor agreeable; it is consistent unto itself and turned back to itself, and it is absurd that it has not complied with the obligation of signifying in a reality other than its own. The object is endowed with internal resonance, which is palpable even in poetic forms or in painting. The surrealist object is an absolute machine". It is "extraordinary" because it makes a being appear detached from any function, breaking up a whole: ILNFI, p. 416/ILFI, pp. 343–344.

age: it imposes itself, it returns on its own invention. Simondon joins Hubert Damisch and Rosalind Krauss in the urgency to conceive of an original image that cannot be confused with the painting, he allows to make photography a "theoretical object". But it is not a sign that breaks its reference at the very moment it is exhibited; the Polaroid theorises an image taken in a constellation that is always already meaningful.[70] To define the photographic image from the surrealist object is therefore to break the technical logic of invention, to think of this image from that which can only isolate it. On the other hand, what surrealism shows is the domestication of invention by habit, by use. One way out, offered by Simondon, is to reintroduce the technical into the machinic and the machinal: to find not the mercenary who wants to subdue the apparatus, but the one capable of carrying the wildness of its invention, or even its emancipating character.[71] Against the domestication of invention, we must reactivate its active core. This shows the extent to which the wild and the vital are intertwined in this philosophy of technique: recording is a vital matrix, photography loses its thanatographic relationship to reality, and resolutely moves away from the embalming gesture that Bazin attributed to it.[72]

A thought of technical gesture contains an implicit ethics: because there is gesture, act, operation, there is free action. To take an image is not so much to possess, to capture, as to engage another image and another than oneself by engaging a meaning. The photographic act becomes an incessant and ever-renewed opening: the beautiful pages that Simondon devotes to the ethical act make sense

---

70   H. Damisch, *La Dénivelée. À l'épreuve de la photographie*, Paris, Seuil, 2001, especially the article on R. Krauss, "À partir de la photographie", p. 38. Déotte points out that Simondon's critique of the psychology of form rests precisely on the primacy of form, which forgets about the substance: the substance is not in the background, it is not a simple support, it is a binding power, cf. Jean-Louis Déotte, "Simondon: les appareils esthétiques entre la technique et la religion", in *Cosmétiques: Simondon, Panofsky, Lyotard*, La Plaine Saint Denis, Editions des maisons des sciences de l'homme associées, 2018, p. 14 (http://books.openedition.org/emsha/222); see METO p. 58; we share less the idea that Simondon is only interested in the self-regulated machine.

71   ILNFI, p. 416/ILFI, pp. 343–344: "The surrealist object tends towards a positive surreal, and one of the paths of this surreal is that of the technical being, which is extraordinary because it is new and beyond utility. The technical being reproduced and disclosed through industry loses its surreal value to the extent that the anesthesia of everyday use deprives perception of the object's singular characteristics [...] Thus the technical object is a surreal, but it can only be felt as such if it is grasped by the pure individual, by a someone who can be creative and not by a user who treats the technical object as a mercenary or a slave".

72   We will explore this point further in an article to be published in the proceedings of the Cerisy conference "Beauté vitale", organised by Clélia Zernik and Anne-Lise Worms (July 2022): C. Maigné, "Sauver les phénomènes: la beauté vitale en photographie. À partir de Simondon et de Marker". We defend the idea of a vitality of technique in Simondon that finds an astonishing expression in Chris Marker, who in turn can be described as a technologist.

here, in an original way. "There is only a centre of the act, there are no limits of the act. Each act is centred but infinite; the value of an act is its breadth, its capacity of transductive expansiveness":[73] Simondon invites us to think of a freedom through photography, *because* it is a theoretical and technical object, according to a double plan: the possibility, through the Polaroid, of returning to the image taken, of re-taking it, but also that of putting images in resonance, the indefinite series spread out by the photographic act becoming an exchange of information and not the withdrawal of each image into itself. The serial character of photography does not imply the reproducibility of the same, nor the freezing of the instant: it is possible to see in it the exercise of a freedom, in the very sense of the triggering of the shot, for "there are no islands lost in the becoming, no regions eternally closed in on themselves, no absolute autarchy of the instant".[74] If Descartes' generosity was summoned to think of an act that extends beyond itself, the feedback here also plays on the taking and the taking away:

> each act takes up the past again and encounters it anew; each moral act resists becoming and does not allow itself to be covered over as past; its proactive force is that through which it will always belong to the system of the present, able to be evoked again in its reality, extended, taken up again by an act, later on according to the date, but contemporaneous with the first act according to the dynamic reality of being's becoming.[75]

Photographic writing is not, however, without surprises or hazards: something that could not be seen before in drawing, engraving, lithography, or painting does emerge, and beyond the actual invention of this image, which makes a break in the history of images, there is an unexploited and uncontrollable potential in each shot taken by the camera. If the camera, like any technical object, is a "translation",[76] it is an open system that has never been fully realised.[77]

Simondon basically proposes a theory of photography from the *photographic gesture*, and in this sense an aesthetic re-evaluating the *aesthesis*. We may remember that "what resides in the machines is human reality, human gesture fixed and crystallised into working structures".[78] Since transduction is an operation from near to near, transposed to photography, this means that every photographic image leads to another: the series on the film is at the heart of an endless process. And this process goes beyond the image taken: the irruption of the photograph into the sensitive field is definitive, without return, because it is indeed

---

73   ILNFI, p. 378/ILFI, p. 324.
74   ILNFI, p. 377/ILFI, p. 323.
75   ILNFI, p. 378/ILFI, p. 324.
76   METO, p. 49/MEOT, pp. 46–47.
77   METO, p. 39/MEOT, pp. 35–36: "The technical object is never fully known; for this very reason, it is never completely concrete, unless it happens through a rare chance occurrence".
78   METO, p. 18/MEOT., p. 12.

an "amplifying reticular structure".⁷⁹ It is all the more so because it is transindividual, the multiplied use of this image attests to the fact that a new perceptive form is taking root: it invites itself, imposes itself and circulates. The photographic image is part of the cycle of mental images, it participates in imagination, memory, intellectualisation ... The photographic image-object is materiality and mental, it is both consciousness and object, a place of circulation between the mental and the real. Since the Polaroid does not function without the camera's release, the eye, the hand, the body and the camera match and appropriate each other in the creative interval (*metaxu*). Simondon does not subject us to the image as to an obscure power, it is always up to each individual to go through their genesis as an image-object:

> [A]lmost all objects produced by man are to some extent image-objects; they carry latent meanings, not only cognitive, but also conative and affective-emotional; image-objects are almost organisms, or at least germs capable of reviving and developing in the subject. Even outside the subject, through exchanges and the activity of groups, they multiply, propagate and reproduce themselves in a neotenic state, until they find the opportunity to be reassumed and deployed to the imaginal stage by being reincorporated into a new invention.⁸⁰

The latency here is not that of the 'revelation' on the photosensitive surface, for the latter is without any particular magic. It is the latency of an inventive potential, which can take place only through the artifice of the camera, which has a feedback effect on the mental images.

The gesture is crucial because it is the place where nature and technique meet: it is the act of creating nature, the technical incorporation of the body into the image and of the world into the image:

> [I]n fact, the group of created objects, incorporating more and more "wild" effects, is less and less arbitrary, less and less artificial in each of its elements; nature is recreated as a necessary formalisation and concretisation within the universe of techniques. The more techniques become objects, the more they tend to make nature pass into the created; the progressive evolution of techniques, thanks to the amplifying surplus value of each invention constituting an object, makes natural effects pass into the world of techniques, which results in the fact that techniques progressively become natural.⁸¹

In our opinion, this is one of the places where we can paradoxically understand the homage to Merleau-Ponty written at the beginning of ILNFI. Cézanne invents a painting never before seen, approaching in this way the inhuman, the

---

79   ILNFI, p. 13/ILFI, p. 33.
80   IT, p. 13.
81   IT, p. 292.

void of meaning upon which meaning is based.[82] This is why Cézanne's art is neither imitation nor construction, but expression: "the picture was saturated, linked, drawn, balanced, all at the same time came to maturity (*l'image se saturait, se liait, se dessinait, s'équilibrait, tout à la fois venait à maturité*). The landscape thinks itself in me, he said, and I am its consciousness. [...] Art is a process of expressing".[83] Doesn't the insistence on saturation make sense here in the Simondonian context? Even more profound in our opinion: Cézanne seizes the landscape as a "nascent organism", he incorporates it into his body, while expressing himself through it, he seizes what is in the process of appearing. The picture produced does not merely "join the wandering hands of nature",[84] but

> When it does, the work of art will have joined these separate lives; it will no longer exist in only one of them like a stubborn dream or a persistent delirium, nor will it exist only in space as a colored piece of canvas. It will dwell undivided in several minds, with a claim on every possible mind like a perennial acquisition.[85]

The wildness of invention thus refers to what *The Phenomenology of Perception* calls "the inhuman background",[86] that unthinking background from which meaning is removed, but which does not prevent the white cane from extending the arm of the blind man, from becoming his own, combining as rarely as possible the natural and the artificial.[87] Technical invention being acquired forever and for all, artifice and naturalness combine to save the phenomenal world: "awareness is not enough because organisms do not only have a knowable structure, they tend and develop. It is a philosophical, psychological and social task to save phenomena by reinstalling them in the future, by putting them back into invention, by deepening the image they conceal".[88] Art is inventive, as is the Po-

---

[82] Merleau-Ponty, "Le doute de Cézanne" in *Sens et Non-sens*, Paris, Nagel, 1948, pp. 15–50: Merleau-Ponty insists on the "inhuman character of his painting" (p. 18), a criterion that becomes positive as the article progresses because Cézanne "reveals the background of inhuman nature on which man settles" (p. 30), revealing the base of inhuman nature upon which man has installed himself, p. 16.
[83] Ibid., p. 32.
[84] Ibidem.
[85] Ibid., p. 37.
[86] Merleau-Ponty, *Phenomenology of Perception*, English translation by Colin Smith, London and New York, Routledge Classic, 1958, p. 466; "inhuman gaze" p. 420
[87] Ibid., p. 165: "The blind man's white cane has ceased to be an object for him, and is no longer perceived for itself; its point has become an area of sensitivity, extending the scope and active radius of touch, and providing a parallel to sight"; even better, p. 168: the organist: "He sits on the seat, works the pedals, pulls out the stops, gets the measure of the instrument with his body, incorporates within himself the relevant directions and dimensions, settles into the organ as one settles into a house".
[88] IT, p. 14.

laroid, because both create convergence, against the parasite of use, ignorance, automatism:

> Art is a deep reaction against the loss of meaning and of the attachment to the whole of being in its destiny; it is not or must not be compensation, a reality occurring after the fact, but on the contrary a primitive unity, a preface to a development according to unity; art announces, prefigures, introduces, or completes, but it does not make real: it is the deep and unitary inspiration that begins and consecrates.[89]

However, whereas Merleau-Ponty thinks of the primitive emergence of meaning against a background of non-sense, Simondon substitutes for it, from a philosophy of technique, the dynamism of procedure and insertion.[90] While Merleau-Ponty thinks of the painting as art, Simondon does not think of photography as art, but as technique (that of the gesture of the amateur, the professional). It is indeed because technique, as an operation, liberates, that art will complete.[91]

Invention being rupture by insertion, our reflection ends on the "wild" dimension of the photographic image, a wild dimension inhabiting all invention. As the term comes up several times, it cannot be insignificant.[92] The wildness of the image and the image-object is established in the crossing and reversibility of time:

> [T]his evocation presents ideals, conveys values, and projects itself into the future as an example for other generations to follow: the image-memory wants to reincarnate and perpetuate itself, it brings with it the subjacent of an anticipation, and to a certain extent does violence to the present in order to bring it to open up towards a future of revival. Anticipation, in its turn, takes up old dreams, contains the echo of old aspirations, already materialised in old image-objects.[93]

In a very surprising way, and with almost Benjaminian accents, the wild, the archaic and the obsolescent intermingle: "the object-images – works of art, clothes, machines – enter into obsolescence and become larval memories, ghosts of the past that dwindle along with the vestiges of disappeared civilisations".[94] Reconciling rupture as disengagement and continuity as recovery, Simondon dreams of a profoundly creative archaism of art.[95] Xenakis invented by promot-

---

[89] METO, p. 210/MEOT, p. 200.
[90] METO, p. 195/MEOT, p. 183: "it is indeed this integration (*insertion*) that defines the aesthetic object and not imitation".
[91] I thank Benoît Turquety for his accurate proofreading and discussion of my text, especially of this passage.
[92] IT, p. 284, p. 292; IMIN, p. 181, 182
[93] IMIN, p. 16.
[94] IMIN, p. 14.
[95] IMIN, p. 181: "in accordance with the pattern of this dialectical reversal, the activity of creators in art should be archaising, or at least it could appear to be primitive".

ing the simple and raw whistle against the instrumental sound, Le Corbusier was "futuristic and wild" when he built the convent of l'Arbresle: both recede in order to better rebound, both dilate time and space: "the archaism of wild reality and the local character of the perceptive manifestation of matter, such are the sources of effects that the major artist, that is to say the inventor of created objects, recruits and manifests by dilating them towards the time to come and the universality of a space".[96]

We will conclude with two points that seem particularly salient to us. On the one hand, the wildness of the imagination implies that the development of the Polaroid is in no way an end in itself: there is no closure of the history of photography with this camera, since there is no closure at all of technical evolution as such. Thus, it is possible to think of digital photography as a new bifurcation, a leap, a new moment like the Polaroid may have been .... It is quite likely that this new photographic image pushes to its limit what the text envisaged as a "perpetual unmolding".[97] By considering the photographic image in its technical process of shaping, Simondon avoids *de jure*, even if he could not *de facto* write it himself, the current debates on whether photography is still photography when it leaves the field of the photosensitive emulsion. If the compatibility between the photochemical and the optical-physical was important for silver photography, both at the same time and never one without the other within an interval of suspension (*metaxu*), there residing the indomitable character of its invention, it is possible to consider that other compatibilities are possible, not renouncing the gesture of taking/removing the image, not renouncing living with it, since "Man's presence to machines is a perpetuated invention".[98] If we had to find a work that expanded on Simondon's point, it would be *Zapping Zone. Proposals for an Imaginary Television* by Chris Marker, in which images, both mental and technical, from all horizons (photography, film, computer, video) intermingle, generate each other and respond to each other to question the fluidity, energy and obsolescence of the contemporary regime of seeing, a work that has never ceased to recompose itself over the course of exhibitions.

On the other hand, we must insist on the approach that consists in taking the image from its technical genesis and not from its result: in Simondon's text, we do not contemplate photographic images when we talk about photography. Simondon's text is rather a text of diagrams (on vaults, boilers, types of lamps in *L'invention dans les techniques* ...), there are not many photographic reproductions of the machines analysed, and when there are (for example, in the book of plates that follows METO), they are written on. The place of the hand-drawn diagram reinforces the phenomenological dimension of the gesture, reinforces

---

96   IMIN, p. 182.
97   ILNFI, p. 31/ILFI, p. 47.
98   METO, p. 18/MEOT, p. 12.

through the primacy of the line and the writing not the seizure of the finished and fixed form, but, on the contrary, the process of being made, articulating the sensible and the intelligible. It is no coincidence that Barthes' text opens with a Polaroid of Daniel Boudinet and continues with the contemplation of the photographed image of his mother, and it is even less of a coincidence that Barthes thinks that photography sometimes "annuls itself as a medium", thus as a technical medium, no longer being a sign but the thing itself.[99] The wildness of photography that Barthes also wants to deploy is that of fixed time, a time of loss and catastrophe, the madness of stupor. Barthes certainly insists on the finger that triggers the image, on the mechanism that acts,[100] but not in order to reflect on the technique; rather, he does so to point out the death in the image. Simondon, on the contrary, opens the photographic image to its own technique, quasi opens the image to the camera, and thereby invents a perpetuated meaning, *by* and *through* the camera.

---

[99] R. Barthes, *La chambre claire, op. cit.*, p. 77.
[100] R. Barthes, *La chambre claire, op. cit.*, p. 32: "For me, the organ of the photographer is not the eye (it terrifies me), it is the finger: what is linked to the click of the lens, to the metallic sliding of the plates (when the camera still has them)."

The Problem of Philosophical Style
The Case of Simondon

Sarah Margairaz and Julien Rabachou

Readers and commentators of Gilbert Simondon often emphasise the singularity of his style and his concepts, and struggle to explain his thought by means of a language different from his own. Does this imply that the problems raised by Simondon are merely internal to his way of thinking and writing, and untranscribable into a more traditional language or into another philosophical perspective? And more broadly, should we maintain that any philosophical problem can only be raised within a particular language? If so, it should be concluded that this type of problem is always reducible to the grammar in which it is formulated; thus, there would be no universal problems, which escape the conditions of their elaboration, in philosophy. That is the question we would like to put to the Simondonian style, and to a philosophy which is based entirely both on very specific concepts and on technical and scientific paradigms.

1. The diversity of philosophical styles and the possibility of eternal problems in philosophy

By "philosophical style" – as opposed to "literary style" – we mean the textual result of a triple process. Firstly, the writing of a singular author, such as it is derived not from aesthetic research but from an original work of conceptualisation; secondly and upstream, the singular method of thinking which produces such a conceptualisation; thirdly and lastly, we can suppose it in the opposite way, the influence of the writing itself on the way in which the author's thought is constituted.

But the differences of style, as well as the opposition and the controversies between philosophical schools – formerly the Stoics against the Epicureans, today the Analytics *vs* the Continentals – raise a major problem for the unity of philosophy. These differences appear as a particular obstacle to the universal finality that philosophical thought gives to itself. And if we immediately meet an "epistemological obstacle" which would prevent us from reaching the ideal of philosophy, it seems that style may be responsible for it. The idea of style indeed implies a singularisation of thoughts, but which turns out to be accidental, caused by the contingent way that different individualities have to write and to think, due to their culture, their intellectual development, their encounters, their writing tics or their conceptualisation.

A. Soulez asserts that the history of philosophy begins with Aristotle's reproaching Plato with having "metaphorized" with respect to the theory of ideas;[1] if this is the case, it implies that philosophical language would be distinguished in the first place from poetic language by the refusal, as much as the ever-renewed danger, of metaphor. By "metaphor", one must understand here a singular use of words betraying the universality of thought. But we know that the singular can be the object neither of science nor of systematisation. Consequently, philosophy is unfortunately endowed with a history, which philosophers could have avoided by determining their concepts once and for all. The Vienna Circle inherited this original contradiction in philosophical practice and tried to free itself from it by claiming to establish a "constructional system of concepts",[2] meaning an absolutely rigorous, positive and universal conceptualisation, one that is therefore purely formal and devoid of style. At the beginning of the *Aufbau*, Carnap thus proclaims: "[The] requirement for justification and conclusive foundation of each thesis will eliminate all speculative and poetic work from philosophy".[3] But is it possible to avoid any style at all?

Taking style seriously as an epistemological obstacle invites us, on the contrary, not to try to "eliminate" the history of philosophy too quickly as an unfortunate contingency. G.-G. Granger defines for instance the scientific style as the "modality of integration of the individual into a concrete process which is work".[4] It is true that there is always something singular in philosophy because of the written or oral style of different thinkers, but this singularity only joins in the movement of a collective and processual work which does not harm its unity. According to this hypothesis, the plurality of styles does not mislead the general orientation of the philosophy; however, the antinomy between a universal ideal which would guide philosophical research and a diversity of expressions and concepts relative to historical and cultural variations is not resolved. If scientific progress in general can be nourished by the diversity of contributions, the ideal of universality proper to philosophy remains logically incompatible with a summation of singular points of view.

Furthermore, to take seriously the question of style in philosophy, it is also necessary to oppose the metaphilosophical idea according to which different styles or different positions could be classified in order to give a total panorama

---

1 Antonia Soulez, *Comment écrivent les philosophes?*, Kimé, Paris, 2003, p. 7.
2 According to Carnap's expression.
3 Rudolf Carnap, *The Logical Structure of the World*, transl. Rolf A. George, University of California Press, Berkeley and Los Angeles, 1967, p. xvii.
4 Gilles-Gaston Granger, *Essai d'une philosophie du style*, O. Jacob, Paris, 1988, p. 8 (Our translation).

of philosophical possibilities. This is what J. Vuillemin proposes, starting from the totality of the possible answers given to the dilemma of the Master argument to deduce a "classification of philosophical systems".[5] Vuillemin thus builds a totalising discourse on philosophy through a method of synthesis, but this method has two flaws: first, it grants each philosophical system an arbitrary freedom of choice of its answers; second, and more importantly, it denies the stylistic differences and nuances between the concepts of the different systems by substituting analogies and kinships between the principles.[6] In stronger versions of this metaphilosophical perspective, relativism is even assumed and the possible universality of concepts is definitively refused: each conceptualisation is then conceived only as a particular representation of the world, relative to a culture, a tradition or an individual.[7] Philosophy's aim of being a universal quest becomes quite simply impossible.

We neither want to reduce the history of philosophy to an unfortunate contingency that has to be eliminated in order to reach the universal, nor overcome the differences between philosophers by adopting an overarching perspective that would be systematic and formal, because these two ways of getting rid of the question of style in philosophy seem unsatisfactory. But, in this case, we fall back on our initial antinomy, since the internal ideal of philosophy to reach its ultimate goal remains challenged by the variety of singular styles of philosophers and traditions. This is as much true for the exposition of philosophical doctrines and the answers to fundamental problems brought by thinkers as for the initial formulation of these fundamental problems, so that it is not even certain that such problems really exist outside the singularity of their formulation. We must actually choose between the two branches of the following alternative:

- Either *philosophical problems exist only within a defined style,* and in this case we are faced with a new dilemma. A first attitude invites us to consider that *they are soluble in language* and must be eliminated; the critical task of philosophy is therefore to dissolve such problems. This is how Wittgenstein, whom the Vienna Circle claims belonged to it, treats philosophy as an ever-renewed effort to rid itself of the illusions created by philosophy itself. These illusions are largely produced by the irrepressible desire of men to free themselves from the grammatical rules of their lan-

---

[5] Jules Vuillemin, *Nécessité ou contingence: l'aporie de Diodore et les systèmes philosophiques*, Minuit, Paris, 1997; partially transl. in *Necessity or Contingency: The Master Argument*, CSLI Publications, Stanford, 1996.

[6] Vuillemin, *Nécessité ou contingence, op. cit.*, p. 273: "The synthetic method, in philosophy, cannot be subjected to the inevitable vicissitudes of history. Nor can it limit itself to comparing the individual monuments that the history of philosophy produces under the name of systems ..." (Our translation).

[7] We can recall here the system of the four ontologies of the anthropologist P. Descola.

guage in order to formulate fundamental problems which in reality have no logical meaning. "Philosophy is a battle against the bewitchment of our intelligence by means of language":[8] according to this ambiguous formula, language is at the same time the means of the perversion of our thought, but also the means of recovering mental health. Philosophical therapy forces us to recognise that there are no truly meaningful philosophical problems, and that the endless formulation of problems reveals the temptation of human beings, especially philosophers, to lose themselves in language by "metaphorising". But there is also a second attitude towards the observation that philosophical problems are always inherent to a certain style. This attitude is less radical in appearance, since it recognises the status of philosophical problems as actual problems, but it nevertheless considers that *each problem is individuated by the style in which it is formulated*. For example, Simondon's answer to the problem of individuation cannot refute nor deepen the answer given by Aristotle or by Duns Scotus, insofar as the problem of individuation in Simondon is not at all the same, except by homonymy, as the problem of individuation in Aristotle or in Duns Scotus.

- Or – this is the second branch of the alternative – *problems have their reality independently of the philosophy in which they are expressed*. Philosophical problems are those of every human being universally taken when they face the world and ask themselves questions about themselves or about the world, no matter how they express them. In this case, it is appropriate to grant a new role to style in philosophy: style appears as a fertile operator which allows the same eternal problems to evolve in time, to be refined, to be deepened thanks to the position of additional problems, by producing sometimes happy reformulations which contribute to their resolution. R. Bambrough thus maintains in a famous paper that the same Wittgenstein who calls for the dissipation of philosophical problems also brings a decisive solution to the classic and venerable problem of universals by his remarks on the "family resemblances" between linguistic usages.[9] In short, the differences in style re-form the problems by allowing a history of philosophy, with the possibility that certain formulations produce a happy outcome.

Before undertaking to choose between the two parts of the alternative by relying on the example of Simondon's philosophy, it is useful to add here a criterion of differentiation, undoubtedly vague but easily perceptible: between some philoso-

---

[8] Ludwig Wittgenstein, *Philosophical Investigations*, §109.
[9] Renford Bambrough, "Universals and Family Resemblances", in *Proc. Arist. Soc.*, 1961, pp. 207–222.

phers whose style seems "totalising" or "hermetic", and other philosophers whose thought appears to be clearer, simply expressed and open to debate or exegesis. Thus, some philosophical thoughts would be trapped in the style in which they are constructed and expressed, while other thoughts would manage to reach a kind of "universal style". Here, the case of Simondon seems paradigmatic for the first time, as a clear example of the first category. One can immediately think of the introduction to Simondon's thesis *L'Individuation à la lumière des notions de forme et d'information*, in which the reformulation of the classical problem of individuation is carried out from the start in a very singular and characteristic vocabulary. In four steps and in only a few pages, the most traditional concepts of metaphysics are dismissed and substituted by new notions borrowed from physics. The individual is immediately redefined, against Aristotelian substantialism, as a relative reality, a "phase of being".[10] The common idea of "stability", usually opposed to that of "imbalance" or "instability", is joined by the much more specialised concept of "metastability", obscure if the reader lacks the appropriate scientific culture.[11] Classical logic is frontally questioned by the definition of a regime of being, the "pre-individual", compared to the state of "supersaturation" of a liquid, as "more than unity and more than identity".[12] Finally, Simondon affirms that the "unity of identity" is a false model of being, to which we must substitute the "transductive unity".[13] These reformulations thus immediately raise the problem of the translatability of philosophical concepts, but also, in this particular case, of the use of concepts imported from other fields and that are only destined to be repeated indefinitely by the reader or commentator, for lack of being able to be articulated into another theoretical language. This general impression is reinforced by the fact that Simondon's philosophy is presented as a system closed on itself, which determines, by the same conceptual apparatus – around the notions of "allagmatic" and "transduction" – the reality that it studies and the knowledge that it elaborates about that reality.

The examination of Simondon's style must therefore allow us to answer the double alternative posed by the question of style in philosophy. Does the reformulation of the problem of individuation, for instance, lead to a new problem? Is this new problem still philosophical if it is not expressed in the terms of the tradition, if it does not fit, or fits badly, into the "concrete process which is work" that is philosophy as a whole? Does it even have any sense if it is expressed only through heterogeneous analogies and borrowings? And if such a problem is dependent on the conceptual choices that allow us to formulate it, what kind of solution can we bring to it? Does a solution that is only internal to

---

10   ILNFI, p. 3/ILFI, p. 24.
11   *Ibid.*, p. 5/p. 26.
12   *Ibid.*, p. 6/p. 26.
13   *Ibid.*, p. 12/p. 31.

the system in which the problem is posed have the smallest significance? Would it then be only a stylistic problem whose solution would itself be a stylistic choice? Or would it be an individual problem that would only find an individual solution in the person who poses it in such singular terms? On the contrary, would the translatability of this problem into a style common to the tradition, for example that of Aristotelianism, offer the possibility of a Simondonian solution, of an original insight opening up possible ways of thinking? But then wouldn't it lose everything that makes up the singularity of its reformulation?

A paradox, directly built into Simondonian texts, makes our problem even more complex. The examination that Simondon proposes of the history of philosophy shows indeed that he does not always conceive of his approach as a *tabula rasa* of all previous understandings of individuation; on the contrary, he sometimes considers his thought to be the ultimate outcome of a long history of the problem of the individual, built into philosophy from the beginning. Such is the sense of the long essay "L'Histoire de la notion d'individu", published in 2005 following ILNFI.[14] We should nevertheless specify that this work is not presented as a system, but rather as a chronological and doxographic juxtaposition of notes on the various authors, from the Ionian physiologists to Hölderlin, taking up elements largely borrowed from Bréhier's classic *Histoire de la philosophie*.[15] However, Simondon does not hesitate to give a logical sense to this historical perspective on the problem and to identify coherent ramifications in the development of the doctrines of the individual; but he does so by means of classifications that can appear very subjective, personal and heterodox compared to the classical history of philosophy. In particular he contrasts thinkers who privilege "operations" and those who privilege "structure", by establishing unusual analogies between doctrines, Plato being found for example closer to the Ionians and Aristotle to Parmenides.[16] Simondon also adopts as a methodological principle of reading that "the conception of the individual in reflexive thought was able to be conditioned by the *modi vivendi* and social relations of the thinkers themselves" and, consequently, that "what must be studied is the psycho-social unity formed by the thinker and his audience".[17] It is a particular way of placing each philosophy, his own included, into a single frame of evolution – to which we will return.

The problem raised in our chapter is therefore duplicated. Beyond the general question of style in philosophy, for which Simondon's work seems to be a

---

14   *Ibid.*, pp. 433–650/pp. 339–502.
15   *Ibid.*, p. 546/p. 401: "E. Bréhier posits that there is no Christian philosophy. We will not allow ourselves to contradict the historian of philosophy concerning a point we have followed throughout the whole course of this explication".
16   *Ibid.*, pp. 501–504/pp. 389–391.
17   *Ibid*, p. 521 (translation modified)/p. 404.

paradigmatic example, there is also a second major question, internal to Simondon's thought as it is expressed in a style. The Simondonian style is singular like any philosophical style, but it is all the more singular since it developed in the sociological conditions of individualism in which every author wishes to assert his singularity, and that it borrows resources from conceptualisations outside the history of philosophy. However, Simondon adopts a contradictory attitude of rupture but also of filiation with this history, as if his original formulations made it possible to retrospectively reveal a unity of meaning, thanks to the overcoming of different traditions in a new conceptualisation. We can thus see how the second question determines the first one, since it is by understanding the attitude of the philosopher Simondon in relation to the collective tradition of philosophy and its aporias that we can situate the formulations he proposes from the outside, and perhaps link them to a "concrete process which is work", or even recapture them in the impulsion towards the universal proper to the whole of philosophy. We shall therefore begin by noting certain distinctive features that make it possible to describe the Simondonian philosophical style.

2. The Simondonian style and some of its singularities: outline of a description

At first sight, Simondon's style generates a completely original work, which does not belong to any school or tradition, and which tries to develop itself from technical paradigms (the model of the brick, or that of the motor) or from theoretical physics and information theory (the models of crystallisation, of the amplifying scheme, of information, of the modulation of a strong current by a weak current, etc.). In this sense, one can be tempted at first to bring Simondonian philosophy closer to the work of Bergson, who also tried to elaborate a metaphysics in close relation to the sciences of his time – psychology, neurology, biology and even physics – and to create new notions, supposed to break with the excessively static character of traditional philosophical categories. Bergson goes so far as to affirm clearly that metaphysics "is strictly itself" only "when it frees itself of the inflexible and ready-made concepts and creates others very different from those we usually handle, I mean flexible, mobile, almost fluid representations".[18] However, can one create concepts that are absolutely new but nevertheless understandable and debatable by the metaphysicians' community? It is here that a big difference emerges between the two thinkers: the main concepts of Bergson's philosophy remain close to ordinary language – "duration", "intuition", "image" – and the metaphors he uses speak to common sense – the nail and the coat, the water lilies, the hand in the iron filings – while on the contrary

---

[18] Henri Bergson, *The Creative Mind*, Philosophical Library, Inc., New York, 1946, p. 198.

Simondon imports extremely localised scientific concepts into his philosophical reflection.

The understanding of Simondon's style thus implies at the same time a recognition of the singularity of his philosophical language – which is extremely technical and breaks with the traditional categories of metaphysics – and the singularity of his paradigmatic method, which precisely allows the introduction of such hermetic concepts. It is the very possibility of communication with classical metaphysics that is then put into question through the choice of such uncommon conceptualisations, not even liable to elicit the Bergsonian "fluid representations". A possible explanation could be biographical: Simondon remained a solitary thinker, and the singularity of his style comes from the fact that he did not find direct interlocutors to discuss his system; the problem is however that he himself wanted to be a "thinker of the relation".[19]

In any case, Simondon's desire to introduce into philosophy concepts extrinsic to the traditional philosophical vocabulary proves to be very problematic, as can be clearly shown through two examples among others:

- In the first two chapters of METO, Simondon builds an original conceptualisation of the concretisation of the technical beings, of the unproductive evolution that is the "hypertely", of the analogical naturality of the technical beings and of the geographical and technical environment, by supporting it on examples taken from his time: in particular, the engine of 1956, the evolution of the electronic tube, the Guimbal turbine, the acoustic laboratory. For lack of adequate technical culture, or of having been born at the right time, the principle of these technical objects can only remain obscure to the reader of following generations, who hardly has the possibility of verifying the primary application of this conceptualisation, its place of origin, and thus its general validity. Why can Simondon assert that an engine from 1956 "is a concrete engine, whereas the old engine is an abstract engine"[20] or that "the Coolidge tube is a Crookes tube that is both simplified and concretized"?[21] How can one justify the use of the term "concrete" here? And what does the word "concrete" mean more generally in Simondon's thought, if its definition derives from observations like that of the 1956 engine?
- In ILNFI, the concept of transduction is first illustrated by the famous paradigm of the crystallisation process.[22] But is it legitimate to base a

---

19   Isabelle Stengers, "Pour une mise à l'aventure de la transduction", in Pascal Chabot (ed.), *Simondon*, Vrin, Paris, 2002, pp. 137–138.
20   METO, p. 24/MEOT, p. 27.
21   METO, p. 38/MEOT, p. 40.
22   ILNFI, pp. 68–94/ILFI, pp. 77–97. If "transduction" is not the central concept put forward to describe crystallisation in these pages, it appears as a note as early as (*Ibid.*, p. 69/

general use of the word "transduction" (which allows us not only to think about individuation at all levels of being, including psychosocial individuation, but also the process of knowledge of individuation itself) on the observation of a process as particular as that of the formation of a crystal, and on a science as particular as the thermodynamics of non-equilibrium states? Wouldn't this be a form of physicalism, i.e. a bias linked to a certain singular state of reality, subsequently erected as a universal paradigm? One could thus judge, as I. Stengers, that "the whole of the concepts articulated to the process of crystallisation refer to a really very particular situation from the point of view of a philosophy of nature",[23] and that Simondon's method can therefore be qualified as a "generalized energetics". In other words, the discovery of the fundamental concepts of Simondonian thought would find its fundamental justification in the attempt to adequately describe a singular physical process set up as a model, crystallisation, a description that comes in addition to that of another process put forward previously, the moulding of the clay brick since Greek Antiquity.[24]

These two parts of the work thus illustrate a double difficulty in Simondon, linked to the conceptualisation itself. On the one hand, this conceptualisation stems from paradigms whose specificity and technicality constitute a real obstacle to understanding for the philosopher reader. On the other hand, as a principle it has the extension of these paradigms coming from very particular domains to the whole of the regimes of individuation of the being, an extension whose justification is very problematic. Cannot we indeed suspect a form of arbitrariness linked to the singular culture of the author, which would generate a risk of partial incommunicability of the proposed paradigms and concepts?

First, we have to dissociate the concepts that owe their singularity to the field they come from – such as the concept of "transduction" or "metastability" – from the ones that remain closed to the traditional vocabulary of ontology – for instance the concepts of "pre-individual" or "transindividual". To begin with, the concept of transduction is taken by Simondon from the field of energetics. As we can read in METO,[25] a transducer is "a resistance that can be modulated by an information that is external to the potential energy and to the actual energy". However, Simondon immediately states that "this notion of transduction

---

p. 78): "this gradual propagation constitutes the most primitive and fundamental mode of amplification (amplifying transduction)".
23   Stengers, "Pour une mise à l'aventure de la transduction", *op. cit.*, p. 145 (Our translation).
24   ILNFI, pp. 21–54/ILFI, pp. 39–66.
25   METO, p. 154/MEOT, pp. 197–198.

can be generalized" and that "the human being, and the living being more generally, are essentially transducers". In fact, the individual is conceived by Simondon as an intermediate reality which constantly actualises the potential of a pre-individual reality by resolving tensions and making various dimensions of being appear that don't pre-exist the individuation process. Moreover, transduction is not only considered by Simondon to be a general scheme of intelligibility of the individuation process at the physical, vital and psychosocial level; it is also a scheme of intelligibility to think about the transition between one individuation regime to another. It is the transduction scheme itself that allows a transposition of the same individuation thought pattern from the physical to the psychosocial level without falling into the trap of reductionism. In this sense, the use of the concept of "transduction", which constitutes an absolute novelty, is nevertheless justified insofar as it resolves one of the most common philosophical problems: namely, the articulation between matter, life and spirit.

In fact, the Simondonian ontogenesis aims at thinking about the coexistence of different regimes of individuation by means of an approach that attempts to grasp simultaneously what makes those regimes both identical and distinct; in other words: *analogous*. Contrary to the traditional classificatory approach, which is based on similarities in order to gather several beings under a common genus – and thus involves separating in each being common features and specific differences – the Simondonian analogical thinking process is based on a criterion which allows for the establishment of an identity while simultaneously retaining a difference. According to Simondon, one can find the model for such a classification in Maxwell's electromagnetic theory. The concept of wavelength is indeed based on an analogy between the propagation of light in a vacuum and that of electromagnetic fields. Instead of being premised on a similarity between the phenomena – an identity relationship – such an analogy exhibits a common characteristic to otherwise radically heterogeneous beings, this characteristic having the particularity of being presented in variable form – since there are an infinite number of different propagation speeds. Thus, instead of linking phenomena to a common genus by erasing their specific differences, the classification of phenomena according to their wavelength – from gamma rays to radio waves – is based on a criterion that puts on the same level what distinguishes a phenomenon from others – and makes it an absolutely singular being – and what connects it to them. Each phenomenon is thus specified by the very fact that it is classified, insofar as existing as such a singular wavelength is equivalent to occupying a place on the continuous wavelength spectrum. Moreover, such a classification has the merit of being based on a criterion related to the physical properties of the classified phenomena, and not to extrinsic properties, related to their phenomenal appearance or contingent use. As Simondon writes:

Discontinuities, the limits of pseudo-species, can only be introduced due to vital or technical usages; we can talk about red and violet and we can even talk about visible light; but this is because we introduce the consideration of a living being that perceives.[26]

In the same way, far from improperly equating any individuation process with the process of crystal formation, the analogy established by Simondon between the different regimes of individuation consists in recapturing in each domain of reality the specificity of a process of individuation which is carried out each time according to a particular rhythm and modalities. Indeed, the analogy between the different individuation processes is based on a relational and functional property, which in no way eliminates the heterogeneity of the fields between which it takes place. As soon as the individual is defined as an individuation activity, whose individuality lies in the way it prolongs, in its relation to an environment, the operation of genesis that gave birth to it, there is an identity between the criterion that makes it an individual in general and that which makes it a singular being. It is this conception of analogy that allows Simondon to innovate not only in terms of the concepts he employs, but also to invent a new use of the philosophical concept that breaks with the traditional use.

In fact, if transduction is indeed a general thought pattern of individuation – as a structuring operation that can be extended step by step from the resolution of an initial separation – this operation is however open to an infinite number of variations. If this structuring consists in the case of the crystal in iterative growth, reproducing the same structure each time while keeping its initial orientation, it implies from the level of vital individuation that the internal structures of the individual are modified correlatively to its activity of individuation. It is therefore similar to an inventive activity likely to renew the orientation of the individual in relation to its environment. Viewed in this way, the transduction scheme allows us to distinguish between several regimes of "internal resonance", depending on the way in which the individual retains its initial information – by reproducing or amplifying it – regimes which thus correspond to as many singular "ways" of individuating. In this sense, if the transduction scheme is indeed a general scheme of thought of individuation, it is a functional and processual scheme, whose transposition from one domain of reality to another never goes without a modulation – as Simondon writes, a "composition" – taking into account the specific properties of the domain considered. Thus, far from proceeding to an improper "assimilation" of the whole reality to the particular case of a physical individuation, it is by making itself "transductive" that the Simondonian approach progresses, according to an operating scheme that consists of resolving disparities without eliminating them; in other words, to relate the distinction between apparently heterogeneous realities to a difference in degree of individu-

---

26 ILNFI, p. 117/ILFI, p. 116.

ation, while simultaneously highlighting the irreducible and absolute singularity of each of them.

Simondon bases his entire approach on an analogy established in the first pages of the Introduction to his thesis between the process of individuation and the process of knowledge of individuation. However, such a methodological assumption raises an even more serious problem. Indeed, if it is its transductive nature that prevents Simondon's approach from being qualified as a process of "assimilation", it seems that what saves Simondon from the accusation of energetic reductionism rests precisely on an assimilation that is even more difficult to admit: between the process of thought in itself and the process of transduction resulting from the study of a formation of a crystal. A question then arises: how to interpret the analogy constructed by Simondon between transduction understood as a process of "objective" individuation, and transduction insofar as it designates "the veritable measure of invention, which is neither inductive nor deductive, but transductive, i.e. [which] corresponds to a discovery of the dimensions according to which a problematic can be defined (…)" and finally, as a "a mental procedure, and even much more than a procedure, it is the mind's way of discovering".[27] On the one hand, it seems that Simondon bases the possibility for thought to operate a transduction analogous to the transduction that takes place in being on an essential ontological kinship between subject and object, thought and being. This is suggested in particular by several texts in which Simondon defines thought as "a certain mode of secondary individuation that intervenes after the fundamental individuation that constitutes the subject".[28] Moreover, on several occasions Simondon describes transduction as a form of "intuition", consisting in "following the being in its genesis, in accomplishing the genesis of thought at the same time as the genesis of the object is accomplished".[29] The description he gives of his method thus appears surprisingly close to the Bergsonian conception of intuition, described by Bergson as a tension "to get into greater sympathy with the effort which engenders things", unfolding in an "indefinite series of acts, all doubtless of the same genus, but each one of a very particular species", whose diversity finally "corresponds to the degrees of being".[30] On the other hand, the analogy established between the operations of thought and the operations of individuation outside of thoughts relates only to the "transductive" character of these operations, and constitutes in itself a transduction similar to that operated by Maxwell in his comparison between the propagation of light and that of an electromagnetic field; i.e., a merely operative analogy, which in no way prejudges the ontological kinship of the be-

---

27 ILNFI, p. 14/ILFI, pp. 33–34.
28 Ibid., p. 362/p. 321.
29 Ibid., p. 117/ p. 34.
30 Bergson, *The Creative Mind, op. cit.*, pp. 32 and 212.

ings thus related. This is evidenced by other passages where Simondon specifies that: "What thought transfers is the knowledge of an operative schematism" or that: "The analogical act is the putting into relation of two operations [...]" and "does not suppose the existence of a common ontological ground [...]".[31]

Thus, if there is indeed in the analogical schematism set up by Simondon a transverse use of categories that tends to blur the usual division between the "objective" and the "subjective", such a "blurring" is not so much the sign of a lack of rigor as the result of an attempt to establish a "certain mode of communication"[32] between thought and being by means of an operative analogical paradigm, which does not in itself presuppose any substantial kinship between the beings brought together. A final problem remains, however, with regard to the validity of the Simondonian approach. In fact, there is a kind of *petitio principii* in the way Simondon conceives his method of thought by analogy with the transduction that takes place in a domain of being – that of crystallisation – whereas the latter itself depends on the operation of thought that makes it appear.

3. The justification of paradigms and the axiological vocation of ontology

Indeed, on the one hand, Simondon bases his method on his ontology, admitting that "every theory of knowledge supposes a theory of being", so that "the analogical method is valid if it concerns a world where beings are defined by their operations and not by their structures, by what they do and not by what they are";[33] in other words, the philosopher's singular style finds its validity in the universal order of things. On the other hand, it is only insofar as Simondon relies from the outset on a paradigmatic schematism that he succeeds in highlighting the operative character of the beings considered; in other words, the philosophical perspective adopted is prior to the discovery of unseen ontological processes. There is a kind of methodological circle here, which Simondon seems to assume and even claim, as shown by the answer he addresses, in a lecture given in February 1960 to the Société française de philosophie, to Gabriel Marcel, who questions him precisely about the basis of his analogical reasoning:

> I believe I am legitimating analogy, I believe I am legitimating paradigmatism, and I believe I am legitimating the use of an analogy through the notion of transduction. There is a kind of identity between the method I use and the ontology I assume, which is an ontology of the transductive operation in the taking of form. If the transductive opera-

---

31 ILNFI, pp. 664–666/ILFI, p. 562.
32 *Ibid.*, p. 17/p. 38.
33 *Ibid.*, p. 667/p. 564.

tion of taking form does not exist, analogy is an invalid logical procedure; it is a postulate. The postulate is both ontological and methodological here.[34]

In this sense, Simondon takes full responsibility for a method that he explicitly borrows from the scientific approach, consisting in starting from a hypothesis that cannot be the object of any "justification" in the usual sense of the term, but that takes place within an approach endowed with a "self-justifying" value, as soon as it contributes to the appearance of concrete "effects" that would never have appeared without this initial hypothesis. Simondon explains this clearly in a passage in the Supplements to his main thesis, in which he writes:

> Scientific activity has veritably constituted the concrete based on the abstract, for the concrete that verifies hypotheses is the concrete of a particular space: it is not the concrete of a fact but of an effect that would not exist outside the universe of thought and action created by this very development of science. By constructing its object with the real, we can see in what manner the scientific approach, albeit not logically but nevertheless really, is self-justifying. Our desire would be to follow this second method in order to deal with the problem of the individual.[35]

This is a conception of the role of the hypothesis that could also be compared to Charles Sanders Peirce's conception of "abduction" – also called by the semiotician Umberto Eco the "detective method" – and which finally overlaps with an idea more than widespread in twentieth-century epistemology, according to which there are no real "facts" since the "facts" themselves depend on the theories that make them appear. Once Simondon thus admits and owns the partly arbitrary character of his starting hypothesis, and of the particular paradigms from which he thinks about individuation, we can ask ourselves what is the value of this hypothesis as well as of the way of thinking about individuation that it promotes, and above all, what is its superiority compared to others. Indeed, if Simondon's style and method are in themselves absolutely singular, by what criteria can we evaluate their relevance?

Such a question can be answered on several levels. A first answer is provided by Simondon in the first chapter of the first part of ILNFI, where he proceeds to a detailed critique of the hylomorphic scheme. What he criticises, among other things, of the hylomorphic approach – beyond the fact that it does not take into account the real conditions of possibility of the operation of individuation – is that by conceiving the individual as a substance, it tends to project onto the individual the conception that man has of himself as a subject. As Simondon writes in the Conclusion to his main thesis:

---

34 Our translation.
35 ILNFI, p. 655/ILFI, p. 554.

> The individual is always to a certain extent *thought* as being a *subject*; man is put in the place of what he thinks as an individual; the individual is what could have an interiority, a behavior, volitions, a responsibility, or at least a certain coherent identity. (...) There is an implicit subjectivity to every conception of the individual in contemporary doctrines (...).[36]

Conversely, it is with the aim of discovering criteria of individuality based on the natural properties of beings, and not on an anthropomorphic projection, that Simondon endeavours to construct a scheme of thought of individuation from the observation of the structuring of a domain of being in which physical theory is "rich in well-studied notions", obeying precise criteria of validity. In this sense, there is indeed a form of realism in Simondon, which is confirmed in the conclusion of his thesis:

> The study of individuation [...] can be a source of paradigms only if it is fundamentally (at least in a hypothetical sense) a grasping of real becoming, based upon which the domains of application of the schemata that it unleashes constitute themselves.[37]

However, insofar as this study contains "no prior axiomatics", it enjoins philosophical reflection to take into account data that are *a priori* external to it. This explains and justifies Simondon's abundant use of concepts from physics, biology, developmental theory and Gestalt psychology throughout his work – and thus allows him to respect the singularity of beings in each domain of reality.

Nevertheless, a final objection to the Simondonian approach could be raised. Indeed, the question arises as to whether there would not be also in the assertion of the originally "pre-individual" and "metastable" character of being a form of unjustifiable bias on the part of Simondon, which is akin to a favourable bias towards becoming. In fact, the merit of the pre-individual hypothesis, which means that it is not totally "arbitrary" either, resides for Simondon in the fact that it makes it possible to give a truly creative meaning to becoming, as soon as it allows us to think about individuation, from the physical level, according to a non-teleological schema. Moreover, Simondon specifies in a text that appears as a supplement to his thesis that "a new normativity may be discovered based on this (epistemological) consequence" and that "the principles of a possible axiology will be generated by this examination".[38] This is also confirmed in the last part of the Conclusion of the thesis, where Simondon states that his theory of individuation can serve "to lay down the bases of an ethics, even if it cannot complete the latter due to the inability to present its circumstances".[39] In fact, the only "value" on which such an ethics rests is the affirmation of the relativity

---

36   Ibid., p. 362–363/p. 321.
37   Ibid., p. 366/p. 324.
38   Ibid., p. 654–656/p. 553.
39   Ibid., p. 373/p. 330, translation modified.

of norms, the value of a system of norms being precisely the fact that it carries within itself the possibility of going beyond itself and renewing itself from within. From this point on, the question arises as to whether there is not, from the outset, a normativity inherent in Simondonian research, a normativity that could lead us to suspect Simondon of having anticipated the ethical conclusions of his thought from the very first pages of his ontology of individuation. Conversely, one may wonder whether it is not these values that ultimately justify Simondon's stylistic choices.

In fact, it is the will to reevaluate the inventive and non-teleological character of becoming that justifies the initial hypothetical affirmation of the originally metastable and problematic character of being. This is clearly demonstrated by the formula used by Simondon in a note in the Conclusion, in which he states that "there is no possible definition of becoming as amplification if we do not suppose an initial plurality of the orders of magnitude of reality".[40] In the same way, throughout Simondon's work it is this initial bias in favour of a "self-amplifying" becoming that dictates the corrections he inflicts on notions and thought patterns borrowed from scientific theories, which he claims each time by redefining them in a non-finalist sense, and also explains the constant use he makes of formulas of a normative nature. In this sense, Simondon could be accused of having built his entire ontogenesis on a hypothesis that is itself based on a bias in favour of a certain type of process – which he mostly describes as a process of "amplification". This is what allows him to establish on the ontological level an ethic that could be described as an ethic of "openness", in the sense that it tends to value the indefinitely renewable character of norms. In this respect, Simondon can indeed be blamed for having valued in each domain of being the theories that best put forward the inventive and creative aspect of reality – and it is obvious that the example of crystallisation was certainly not taken randomly. But it is because Simondon accepts the consequences of the fact of having to rely on a paradigm whose choice may seem arbitrary that his thought is distinguished from a self-founding reflective approach. As Simondon writes in ILNFI:

> Every thought, precisely to the extent that it is real, is a *relation*, i.e. includes a historical aspect in its genesis [...], it is *self-justifying*, but not justified before being structured.[41]

However, this tendency to value the inventiveness of becoming in being can also be seen in the light of its aim, which is to give philosophy the scope of a reflection that is capable – well beyond the systematic presentation he gives in his thesis – of tackling the resolution of problems that are apparently outside philosophy. It is in particular in terms of "incompatibility" in METO that Simon-

---

40   *Ibid.*, p. 364/p. 323.
41   *Ibid.*, p. 105/p. 84.

don poses the problem of the articulation between the evolution of techniques and that of culture, the resolution of which aims at giving humanity the means to take charge of its own future, so that the latter can once again have the appearance of progress. This is why this philosophy turns out to be the opposite of a process of "assimilation": a philosophy of the future. Thus, at the end of the book we realise that the final goal of Simondon's entire approach to the technical object is to provide philosophy with a reconsideration of technics, not so much for the sole benefit of philosophical knowledge of technics, but for culture as a whole.[42]

4. Conclusion: Simondon's philosophy or the possibility of a non-naive universalism

We believe we have thus shown, through the case of Simondon, that the variety of styles does not produce a harmful contingency in philosophy which would individualise the problems posed in each author's work by making them false problems; this variety is rather the source of a reformulation of the problems, with a new aim each time determined by cultural goals whose values each style translates. We have also shown that the difficulties posed to philosophy by Simondon's style do not finally derive so much from a biographical originality – leading our author to borrow contingent paradigms from the sciences he knows in order to import them into metaphysics – as from a normative dimension of his thought.

This result should lead us to ask whether the axiological choices that guide Simondon's style of thought can be found in all other philosophical thought or whether they are only a singular characteristic of the Simondonian approach. But we have also seen how Simondon was not only an example or a paradigm for our purpose, but actually a guide. Indeed, he himself develops, in his criticism of Aristotelian hylomorphism, the idea that they are on each occasion paradigms that orient the understanding of the individuation. For example, it is, according to Simondon, the universal paradigm of the living being, inherited from a culture of pastoral origin, that is used to understand the individual in Aristotle.[43] It is also a social and political paradigm, linked to a certain understanding of work – the master-slave model – which produces a conception of the relationship between form and matter that is symptomatic of a misunder-

---

[42] See J. Rogove's introductory Note on METO. This judgment must, however, be tempered, without being reconsidered, by the fact that Simondon, when articulating in the end of METO the genesis of the different forms of human thought, thinks of culture as a movement of convergence leading to philosophical thought itself.
[43] SLΦ, p. 364.

standing of the real processes of taking form and, above all, of an anthropomorphic representation of the operation of taking form – in which one commands and the other obeys – in the hylomorphic way of thinking.

Consequently, our hypothesis is that in philosophy the style obviously does not only represent the artificial and aesthetic framing of a thought whose concepts would refer directly to things, but it constitutes the normed direction that regulates this thought and gives it its cultural dimension. We find here the holistic (and provocative) idea of Quine, when he asserts, at the end of "The Two Dogmas of Empiricism":

> Physical objects are conceptually imported into the situation as convenient intermediaries – not by definition in terms of experience, but simply as irreducible posits comparable, epistemologically, to the gods of Homer.[44]

For Quine, any designation of an entity has something mythical about it, and atoms, for example, are just as mythical as the gods of myths, though simpler to use for an empiricist description of the world; more broadly, any metaphysical choice, any scientific choice, rests on models or metaphors of high cultural significance. Simondon himself understood this, if we think of the way he shows how the valorisation of technical activities is embedded into culture, literature and discourse.[45] Undoubtedly, our consideration of style reveals here a fundamental fact which must be taken into account in order to avoid a naive universalism in philosophy, but without falling into a facile relativism: any philosophical problem, by the very way it is posed, has a cultural aim, which is nevertheless compatible with the maintenance of a non-naive universal aim in philosophy.

Let us finally recall Gilles-Gaston Granger's formula according to which style is a "modality of integration of the individual into a concrete process which is work". One can understand that the individual "integrates" himself into the universality of the philosophical or scientific research by erecting his singularity as exemplarity, and the style is indeed, through the original choices of concepts and paradigms, the main modality of an exemplification of thought. However, we also learned that the formulation of philosophical problems satisfies cultural value requirements and that even metaphysical choices are not alien to cultural issues: Simondon confirms this as much by his assertions as by his metaphysical choices. This is why Simondon's case is heuristic for a renewed understanding of philosophical practice.

---

[44] W.V.O. Quine, "Two Dogmas of Empiricism", in *The Philosophical Review*, Vol. 60, No. 1 (1951), pp. 20–43.
[45] SLΦ, p. 344.

II.

What Is Philosophy about?

On the Mode of Existence of Culture

Jamil Alioui

> Youth animates this culture of enthusiasm for discovery, of the initiatory joy of meeting unknown brothers. And maturity gives structure to this discovered world, organises it and builds it as a network of forces in balance.
>
> Gilbert Simondon (1953)

In this chapter we discuss the evolution of the notion of culture in the published work of Gilbert Simondon. In doing so, we would like to understand why and how the Simondonian determination of culture slowly but surely drifts towards the question of the conditions of possibility of invention.

First, we study some texts from the period before the ILNFI and METO theses, in order to identify a first definition of culture as a "postulation of connection with a universal totality".[1] By defining culture in this way, Simondon circumscribes an ambition; he lays the foundations of a philosophical project which we try to account for. In a second step, by considering the writings of the thesis period, we show how this ambition takes the form of a reflection on symbols and symbolisation and leads to a tension between, on the one hand, a functionalist conception of culture as a dynamic, regulating, and always actual process – identified with the reality that Simondon calls "transindividual" – and, on the other hand, a substantialist conception of culture, as a static basis of meanings and forms that humans may or may not actualise in order to solve problems.[2] In a third step, we examine how the notion of invention informs and thus explains the tension between these two conceptions of culture. By admitting in 1960–1961 that actual and regulating cultural realities cannot be known objectively, Simondon asserts the epistemological impossibility of founding a science or knowledge of culture. The consequence of this impossibility is to transform the relationship between culture and technics: from a problematic situation where technics must enter into culture, Simondon moves to a problematic where culture and technics must find a point of equilibrium where they can meet, with-

---

1 "Cybernétique et philosophie" (1953), in SLΦ, p. 61–62.
2 The distinction between functionalist and substantialist modality of culture is inspired by the distinction between the "particular contents" of culture and its "metaphysical form", which comes from Georg Simmel, *La tragédie de la culture*, French translation by S. Cornille and P. Ivernel, Paris, Payot-Rivages, 1988, p. 185, as well as from Ernst Cassirer, *Substance et fonction*, French translation by P. Caussat, Paris, Minuit, original ed. 1969, 1977.

out which the human world is exposed to a perilous instability, if not to the possibility of its disappearance. Simondon finally locates this point of equilibrium in the object, yet not as a known thing, but as an invented thing.

Our proposal takes advantage of an editorial fact, that of the completeness of Simondon's published works, and shows that a genetic reading of the corpus makes it possible to rethink the individuality of Simondon's thought beyond the problem of the compatibility of the two PhD theses. By considering *de jure* the individuality of Simondon's thought rather chronologically, as a dynamic movement, we offer the means to consider the PhD theses as the problematic moment of a thought that *de facto* spans nearly three decades. Thus, against the usual view of Simondon as a philosopher of technics, we propose to outline Simondon as a philosopher of culture. According to the latter, technics and technicity are only one step in conceiving of the relationship that unites, on the one hand, the ambition of symbolic and ontogenetic continuity that is culture, with, on the other hand, the possibility of non-theoretical objectivation that is invention.

1. The ambition of universality (1953–1958)

Culture first appears in Simondon's texts in 1953, in particular, in a report on an experimental technical initiation conducted at the Lycée Descartes, in Tours, for pupils aged twelve to fourteen. In this report, culture is defined as a *"non-somatic import that the species gives to the individual during the latter's formative phase"*.[3] This definition is ambiguous in that the word "import" does not clearly indicate whether culture is an activity or a content. Moreover, since culture is determined negatively in relation to the body, the expression "non-somatic import" could refer to Merleau-Ponty's use of the term "import" to denote the anthropological and somatic nature of the categories applied by perception to objects.[4] In any case, this "inaugural" ambiguity of the notion of culture prefigures many tensions that we can find in later texts, as well as the intuition that culture is located somewhere other than in the movement of return to oneself, which characterises phenomenology. In the rest of the report the determination of culture becomes clearer. Simondon describes the objectives of the technical initiation experiment he designed:

---

3   "Place d'une initiation technique dans une formation humaine complète" (1953), in SLT, p. 208.
4   It is thanks to the entry "import" in the *Trésor de la Langue Française informatisé* that we became aware of this use of the word by Merleau-Ponty in the *Phenomenology of Perception*.

[this teaching] aims to be a first example of a culture that is not imitative, but constitutive, not symbolic, but real, addressing a continuous society, without internal barriers, whose meaning is no longer the property, but the constitutive activity.⁵

Culture here corresponds more to transmission than to what is transmitted: it is a process of formation. In the preceding pages, we learn that technological education remedies a sociological discontinuity created by the difference between high school education and technical education. In society, this difference corresponds to the difference between those who give orders and those who carry them out. This critique of the cultural predominance of "verbal symbolism"⁶ anticipates a passage in ILNFI where Simondon, considering a sociological situation where "the one who thinks is not the one who works",⁷ relates the hylomorphic form to an "order of fabrication" which is logical and, in this restricted sense, verbal. Simondon thus shows quite well how "verbal symbolism" prevents – or, at least, does not require – an understanding of functioning and operations as performed by those who work. Rather than liberating society from its divisions, this symbolism "prepares the individual to live as a member of a determined social class".⁸ Rather than universalising, it specialises.⁹ Culture then appears as the requirement to "unite in a unitary education intended to form on a new human level the sense of work, the sense of knowledge and the sense of action".¹⁰

Simondon seeks a solution by universalising the problem. Thus, in "Cybernétique et philosophie", social discontinuity takes the form of a distinction between "group" and "society".¹¹ From a specifically sociological and political question, Simondon moves on to a problem formulated in terms of "system states" or "energy modulation". The cybernetic vocabulary comes to the rescue in his attempt to grasp the problem in a broader, more systematic perspective. The year after, in the context of exchanges following the report on technical initiation at the Lycée, Simondon distinguished two different types of pedagogical objectives:

> To adapt a being to a stable society is to specialise it in such a way as to be able to *integrate* it into a row of the vertical structure. To adapt a being to a metastable society is

---

5   "Place d'une initiation technique" (1953), in SLT, p. 207.
6   *Ibid.*, p. 205.
7   ILNFI, p. 43/ILFI, p. 57.
8   SLT., p. 209.
9   This critique presages the critique of "literary culture" found in MEOT.
10 Simondon then conceives of the separation of these "teachings" according to three social classes: "secondary education" is related to the bourgeoisie, "confessional education" is related to the nobility, and "technical primary education" is related to the popular class, *ibid.*, p. 210.
11 "Cybernétique et philosophie" (1953), in SLΦ, p. 57.

to give it an intelligent learning process enabling it to *invent* ways of solving the problems that will arise throughout the surface of horizontal relations.¹²

Against his opponents who argued for a specialisation of education, Simondon relies on a general culture capable of uniting all individuals on an equal footing, without discontinuity, by means of a democratisation of invention and problem-solving skills rather than by integration through adaptation to an established order. It is the thermodynamic lexicon, distinguishing between "stable society" and "metastable society", which is used this time to formulate in a more universal way a problem initially linked to the world of work: a society rich in transformative potential is preferable to a society devoid of such potential, weakened or even exposed to the possibility of its disappearance. This passage prefigures the relationship between the theme of culture and that of invention, which we will find again in various forms later on. For the time being – we have just reached the year 1954 – Simondon is already putting forward the idea that the direction of a technical culture is where we must seek the means to contribute to the establishment of such a society.¹³

In "Cybernétique et philosophie", the formulation of this problem of discontinuity is thus emancipated from the specific question of the division of society into classes or groups, and takes on a more universal form which reveals the relationship between the themes of culture and philosophy:

> philosophical effort is carriage [*apport*] of culture, and culture is a postulation of connection with a universal totality, with the holistic system, imaginary or real, capable of incorporating all existing holistic systems. The philosophical effort [manifesting itself in a particular field] thus brings with it contact with the immense society of systems; it solves a particular problem by integrating it into a general problem, and puts an end to the solitude of problems in order to create the world of problems.¹⁴

Culture as a "postulation of connection with a universal totality" is defined here in terms of the interaction and integration of systems; these are cybernetic terms. It corresponds to the "universal" of the "society of systems" or "world of problems" into which particular systems must be incorporated. It is thus no less a requirement for continuity than before; however, it becomes more general. Exempted from the lexicon of classes and social groups, it now concerns everything that can be categorised as a "system" or "problem". Moreover, culture is defined here as an aspiration, a wish; it is less a present connection with a universal totality than an ambition for such a connection. In order to understand the function of this "postulation", as well as the nature of the relation that culture

---

12 "Prolégomènes à une refonte de l'enseignement" (1954), in SLT, p. 236–237.
13 *Ibid.*, p. 241.
14 "Cybernétique et philosophie", SLΦ, p. 61–62.

actually has to the totality, it is necessary to understand its relation to philosophy.

In the preparatory text "Analysis of the Criteria of Individuality", Simondon says that he finds in Descartes the example of a method that he considers applying in his own philosophical research, which he describes in these terms:

> the initial notional choice is invested with a self-justifying value; it is defined by the operation that constitutes it more than by the reality it objectively seeks, like the cosmogonic hypothesis of vortices, which does not need to be true to be valuable.[15]

The "initial notional choice", i.e. the first postulate of a philosophical system or its "axiomatics", is related to a problem of value rather than a problem of truth. Simondon here revives one of the pre-Aristotelian meanings of ἀξίωμα: the "initial notional choice" is conceived not as a "proposition that commends itself to general acceptance" or "a well-established or universally-conceded principle",[16] but as an operation deemed good and worthy of value. If Simondon speaks of "notional choice" rather than simply of notion, it is because the word "choice" refers less to the static theme of logical formalism than to that of action and operation, which is more efficient and more in continuity with reality. For the same reason, Simondon understands culture not as a postulate but as a postulation.

The difference is small but decisive: it tells us that philosophy is not conceived as a logical discourse, a theoretical posture or even a "verbal symbolism", adequate or inadequate to a contemplated being which would be heterogeneous to it and which, consequently and paradoxically, would be intrinsically discontinuous. On the contrary, philosophy is a set of constructive operations effectively linking what is currently considered incommensurable or incompatible. Actually, philosophy refuses to establish ruptures in being between the mental and the social, or between the physical and the psychic.[17] It constructs its problems in relation to the world in its greatest extension. In other words, if philosophy has a domain, then this domain is what Simondon later calls "complete being"[18] or "the being's whole".[19] The foundation of a philosophy on the election of a preferred – and therefore privileged – domain or notion would imply a

---

15 "Analysis of the Criteria of Individuality", in ILNFI, p. 656/ILFI, p. 524. Amended translation.
16 *Oxford English Dictionary*.
17 For this reason, it chooses "transduction" as its method, i.e. a "physical, biological, mental, or social operation through which an activity propagates incrementally within a domain". ILNFI, p. 13/p. 32.
18 ILNFI, p. 3/ILFI, p. 25.
19 ILNFI, p. 52/ILFI, p. 63.

"methodological egoism" and a "narcissism of thought"[20] that would contradict the "systematic unity"[21] that the philosophy aspires to as it "seek[s] being".[22] Rather than being justified *a priori* in an authoritarian, "defensive", if not arbitrary manner, the "initial notional choice" must be "self-justifying". It must reveal its value in the course of the "philosophical effort", for example when it allows the construction of a system having "epistemological fecundity",[23] in proportion to the number of problems that this system makes it possible to solve, or in relation to the meaning that it brings.[24] Simondon thus suggests the possibility of a measure of philosophical quality or value relative to the continuity that a system is either able to establish or not.

> The [philosophical] system must [...] be studied not as a constituted edifice but as an act of progressive assimilation from a focus which would be the "hot spot" of this interpretive activity. A philosophical system would then be organised according to a gradient, leaving outwardly more and more dark zones, less and less penetrated by meaning.[25]

To assert that philosophical systematicity should not be studied as an edifice is to say that it is not a static structure and that it should not be considered as the finished, substantial result of a construction operation. A philosophical system, precisely because it has been constructed, can be taken up again, modified, extended and reinvented, as much according to the new problems it is called upon to solve as to the initial notional choices on which it is based. In other words, a philosophical system functions; it is organised around a focus, namely a notion that possesses a "self-justifying value" in relation to its power to solve problems, that means in relation to the effectiveness of the system elaborated on and concentrated around the choice of the notion. An "initial notional choice" that allows a large area to be "penetrated by meaning" is more valuable than a choice that "leaves outwardly" large "dark zones".

Thus, the fact that culture is an ambition becomes clearer along with its relation to the totality: as an axiomatic of absolute continuity in being, culture as

---

20 "Recherche sur la philosophie de la nature" (~1955), in SLΦ, p. 30.
21 *Ibid..*, p. 31.
22 This demand for maximum extension can already be found in an early text in which Simondon questions philosophies that claim to be "of" something, as are, for example, the philosophy "of nature" or the philosophy "of Spirit": "A real philosophy cannot first of all define itself as a philosophy *of*; all real philosophy is the instinct to seek being without establishing an initial defensive choice." (*Ibid.*, p. 30).
23 "Réponses aux objections" (1954), in SLT, p. 226.
24 This is expressed by the reference to the "cosmogonic hypothesis of vortices": although it leads to errors in the *Dioptric*, it allows Descartes to "[unify] two asymmetrical notions in a very fruitful association" (these are the notions of frequency and corpuscle). ILNFI, pp. 113–114/ILFI, p. 113.
25 "Recherche sur la philosophie de la nature", SLΦ, p. 32.

a "postulation of connection with a universal totality" is an ambition of the highest possible value to which corresponds the absence of darkness in a compatible world, without discontinuities and without problems.[26] Culture affirms the absurdity of a world divided into heterogeneous substances. It reveals the aberration of a society separated into supposedly independent groups. The latter would imply that certain individuals are paradoxically deprived of a link to the "complete being" within which they nevertheless individuate. Culture is the antithesis of an "initial defensive choice", as are "misoneism" and "xenophobia";[27] it is a welcoming of the diverse and a means of "discover[ing] the foreign or strange as human"[28] as well as "participating in the life of past times and foreign societies in such a way as to make them less past and less foreign".[29] Contrary to substantialism, authoritarianism and arbitrary opinions, culture is the choice to understand all individual systems and particular domains as "phases" of a "complete being". Culture, like philosophy, is related to an "instinct to seek being", to a search for its operativity; there is thus an equivalence between the "philosophical effort" and the "contribution of culture" because both philosophy and culture establish continuity, introduce connection and seek a "universal totality" to which they connect.

2. The problem of culture (1958–1960)

However, grasping the totality of being and solving all current problems are not easy activities. This is why culture operates by means of symbols:

> a stone broken into two halves produces a pair of symbols [...]. The symbol is not what each half is relative to the people who produced it, but each half relative to the other half with which it reconstitutes the whole. The possibility of reconstitution of a whole is not a part of hospitality but an expression of hospitality: it is a sign.[30]

The notion of symbol is used by Simondon in ILNFI to characterise the relationship between the individual and its associated milieu. By analogy, the "complete being" refers to the stone before it is divided into two fragments, corresponding to the individual and the associated milieu, respectively. Thus, the individual "is

---

26   This is even clearer if we remember the opening statement of the "Complementary Note", according to which value, understood as "unlimited complementarity between the individual being and other individual beings", "supposes that there is a way to make all realities complementary". ILNFI, p. 403/p. 331.
27   METO, p. 10/MEOT, p. 16.
28   Ibidem.
29   "Humanisme culturel, humanisme négatif, humanisme nouveau" (1953), in SLΦ, pp. 72–73.
30   ILNFI, p. 52/ILFI, p. 64.

simply the complementary symbol of another real, i.e. the associated milieu".[31] The symbol thus extends the thing of which it is a concrete part, by virtue of the totality – the only reality fully worthy of the name[32] – which it currently forms with it. The symbol is actual; it "has a meaning even for the Gods",[33] which is to say that it is not relative to a certain perspective – for example "relative to the people who produced it" – but to its ontogenetic complement. Conversely, the sign appears as something that is presumed to be a symbol without having the guarantee of it. In the "Complementary Note", this distinction between signs and symbols is formulated more clearly and, in particular, in its relation to culture:

> culture can only be effective if it possesses from the start this capacity of acting on symbols and not on brute realities; the condition for the validity of this action on symbols resides in the symbols' authenticity, i.e. the fact that they are veritably the extension of the realities that they represent and not a simple arbitrary sign artificially linked to the things that it must represent.[34]

The notion of culture retains its relationship to the totality, in accordance with the 1953 definition, but this relationship is now conceived to be mediated by symbolisation.[35] If culture is the search for the coherence and compatibility of the totality of particular individuations, and if each particular can be "manipulated" by symbolising activity – that is, represented by a symbol – then culture, indeed, must produce a coherent "system of symbols".[36] Authentic symbols are thus compatible with each other in a way analogous to the particulars they represent.

It is not surprising, then, to see the sign depreciated in relation to the symbol: it is only an "expression" of a thing, whereas the symbol is a real "part";[37] it is "artificially linked to things" and therefore "arbitrary"[38] where the symbol is

---

31 ILNFI, p. 52/ILFI, p. 63–64.
32 Or, at least, the only reality to which individuation can be attributed as an operation, ILNFI, p. 3/ILFI, p. 25; see further the preamble of *Imagination et invention*, which reformulates this determination even more clearly.
33 Simondon explicitly refers to Plato's *Cratylus*, "Complementary Note", ILNFI, p. 404/ILFI, p. 332.
34 "Complementary Note", ILNFI, p. 404/ILFI, p. 332.
35 Gilbert Hottois rightly defines this symbolisation as "[producing] partial representations of a totality that are at the same time explicitly complementary to each other", Gilbert Hottois, *Simondon et la philosophie de la "culture technique"*, Brussels, De Boeck-Wesmael, 1993, p. 90.
36 "Complementary Note", ILNFI, p. 404/ILFI, p. 332.
37 ILNFI, p. 52/ILFI, p. 64.
38 For without a natural or ontogenetic link to the thing represented, a representation is merely an unjustifiable personal opinion.

"authentic" and a true "extension";[39] elsewhere again, while Simondon explains that philosophy "may wish to be a symbol of being, but not a systematisation of the signs of being",[40] the sign is said to be a degradation of the symbol.

The ontogenetic actuality and effectiveness of symbols is thus opposed to systems of signs artificially linked to reality. In a similar way, Simondon distinguishes two possible modes of existence of culture, which can be found in METO. On the one hand, "complete" or "general" culture is a mode in which culture adequately fulfils its "regulative"[41] function by "allow[ing] for problems to be resolved"[42] as it did "before the great development of technics";[43] culture then appears as "a set of beginnings of action that are endowed with a rich schematism, waiting to be actualised into an action".[44] On the other hand, "unbalanced", "partial", "literary" or "old"[45] culture is problematic insofar as it is "the pure consumerism of means of expression constituted in closed types",[46] preexisting genres in which "reality is absent".[47] It is because this culture, which we call semiotic, only functions in highly specialised, closed environments based on conventions, that it is linked to artificiality.[48] These "closed types" include, for example, "the dryness of grammar exercises",[49] "literature, the art of opinion, advocacy of plausibility, and rhetoric",[50] all of which are semiotic cultural domains insofar as "[t]he symbol is weakened into a mere linguistic turn of phrase".[51]

From a few examples, we would like to suggest that a general form modulates the tension that links these two perspectives. This general form is analogous to the philosophical distinction between substance and function. It thus makes it possible to specify the form of the equivocity of culture and to characterise, by this very equivocity, the moment of Simondon's reflection on culture that corresponds to the theses of 1958. Thus, in the texts of this period, it remains impossible to determine whether culture is a dynamic, actual and regulating process

---

39 "Complementary Note", ILNFI, p. 404/ILFI, p. 332.
40 "Recherche ...", SLΦ, p. 30.
41 METO, p. 20, 21/MEOT, p. 10, 15, 18.
42 "Complementary Note", ILNFI, p. 404/ILFI, p. 332.
43 METO, p. 19/MEOT, p. 15.
44 "Complementary Note", ILNFI, p. 404/ILFI, p. 332.
45 METO, p. 16, 19, 20/MEOT, p. 10, 15.
46 "Complementary Note", ILNFI, p. 405/ILFI, p. 332.
47 METO, p. 20/MEOT, p. 16.
48 There is an analogy between these closed social environments and the greenhouse for the artificial flower or the laboratory for the abstract technical object. METO, p. 49/MEOT, pp. 57–58.
49 "Prolégomènes ..." (1954), in SLT, p. 248.
50 METO, p. 20/MEOT, p. 16.
51 Ibidem.

(functionalist approach) or whether it is relative to the particularities of certain static objects, soliciting actualisation (substantialist approach).

In a particularly difficult part of the main thesis,[52] the problematic takes the form of an insoluble tension between transindividuality and culture. Reading the text too quickly might lead one to believe that culture is conditioned or determined by transindividuality and is therefore distinct from it. *A fortiori* the text explicitly prescribes such a distinction. Transindividuality as "the questioning of the subject by itself" would thus be distinct from culture as a recourse to this questioning. Such a reading, however, must disregard the assertion that the existence of the psychological world implies that of incentive schemes "incorporated in culture". Indeed, it is to culture that the "series of mental schemata and of behaviours" is related: in the "Complementary Note" at least, culture "is a set of beginnings of action that are endowed with a rich schematism, waiting to be actualised into an action".[53] Now, "[t]he notion of the transindividual corresponds to the collective taken as the axiomatic that resolves the psychical problematic".[54] In other words, in Simondon's view, there is no "substantiality of the psychological individual", i.e. no "substantiality of the soul", because "psychological individuality appears to be what is elaborated by elaborating transindividuality".[55] The consistency of psychological individuality must therefore be related to transindividuality understood as "two interconnected dialectics, one of which interiorizes the exterior, the other of which exteriorizes the interior".[56] The psychological world, and with it – for the reasons we have just explained – transindividuality, therefore exist because there is a culture. Thus, the requirement of the subject's self-questioning characterises the transindividual relationship, but this questioning of the subject is linked to culture insofar as it exists "because", writes Simondon, it is "already begun by others". In other words, the reflection leads us to posit the identity of culture and transindividuality; yet the

---

[52] This part is as follows: "the psychological world exists to the extent that each individual finds before it a series of mental schemata and of behaviours already incorporated in culture that compel the individual to pose its particular problems according to a normativity previously elaborated by other individuals. The psychological individual must choose among the values and behaviours from which it receives examples: but not everything is given in culture, and we must distinguish between culture and transindividual reality; culture is neutral in a certain sense; it has to be polarized by the subject that calls itself into question; on the contrary, there is in the transindividual relation a requirement of the subject to be called into question by himself, because this calling into question is already begun by others", ILNFI, p. 312/ILFI, pp. 272–273. The text continues with a distinction between inter-individual and transindividual relationships.

[53] "Complementary Note", ILNFI, p. 404/ILFI, p. 332.

[54] ILNFI, p. 11/ILFI, p. 31, this proposition is highlighted by Simondon.

[55] *Ibid.*, p. 315/p. 273.

[56] *Ibid.*, p. 315/p. 274.

text explicitly asks us to distinguish transindividuality, as that which polarises the subject, from culture, as that which demands to be polarised by the subject, leaving a functionalist determination of culture and its substantialist counterpart face to face.

The notion of culture, as it appears in the context of Simondon's aesthetics in METO, reveals a similar problematic. In the third part of the book, Simondon defines aesthetic thought by the fact that it "seeks totality in thought and aims at recomposing a unity through an analogical relation".[57] He immediately makes it clear that this does not mean characterising "works of art such as they exist in their institutional state in a given civilisation", but rather grasping a "fundamental tendency in the human being" that makes them possible, an "ability to experience the aesthetic impression in certain real and vital circumstances", it being understood that "the work of art above all sustains and preserves the ability to experience aesthetic feeling, just as language sustains the ability to think, without nevertheless itself being identical to thought".[58] On the one hand, there is the functioning of a "fundamental tendency" that is aesthetic impression; on the other hand, the substantiality of the work of art, which needs to be actualised by a new aesthetic experience in order to produce information, that is to make sense. Is culture a fundamental, regulating and operative tendency of the human being as an individual within ontogenesis, or is it a property of the works considered as particular substances?[59]

A similar question arises from various passages in the two theses. For want of an exhaustive enumeration, let us mention two of them very quickly: in METO, culture as regulator or, at least, as selective – insofar as it is what modulates the value of spontaneous and natural aesthetic impressions, conveying them towards what Simondon calls "outstanding points"[60] of the universe – is in tension with culture as the "institutional state in a given civilisation",[61] i.e. as

---

[57] METO, p. 191/MEOT, p. 248.
[58] METO, p. 192/MEOT, p. 248.
[59] Ludovic Duhem clearly shows the distinction between "art" and the "true universality of man's aesthetic attitude"; according to him, culture, by reducing the latter to the former, "reduces to a limited domain that which in reality runs through every human act and that which conceals everything in the world". Ludovic Duhem, "La tache aveugle et le point neutre. Sur le double 'faux départ' de l'esthétique de Simondon", in Jean-Hugues Barthélémy (ed.), *Cahiers Simondon Numéro 1*, Paris, L'Harmattan, 2009, p. 131. Let us specify that here the word "culture" refers to the institutional state rather than to transindividuality.
[60] "Every culture selects the acts and situations that are apt to become outstanding points; but culture is not what creates the aptitude of a situation to become an outstanding point; it only forms a barrage against certain types of situations, leaving narrow straits for aesthetic expression with respect to the spontaneity of the aesthetic impression; culture intervenes as a limit rather than as creator." METO, p. 193/MEOT, p. 249.
[61] METO, p. 193/MEOT, p. 248.

"foundation",⁶² as "basis of significations, of means of expression, of justifications and of forms".⁶³ Finally, in ILNFI, "ancient culture" and "modern culture", whose "pure notion of form"⁶⁴ must be saved, are opposed, by their fixed – and, in this sense, substantial – aspect, to another determination of culture conceived as "[conversion] into signification, [perpetuation] in information",⁶⁵ distinct from the vital as the "implicit" is distinct from the "explicit". This culture is indeed "an individuation in accordance with the collective", i.e. a transindividual reality relative to the "centre of existence" of the individual, in other words, at the top of its operative actuality.

3. From technical culture to perpetuated invention (1961–1976)

This tension between the functionalist and substantialist determinations of culture, which is expressed in different ways in the theses, remained unresolved until 1960, the year of the lecture "Psychosociologie de la technicité", in which Simondon took up the theme of culture in a fresh way.

The tension which characterizes the notion of culture now appears as a "crisis"⁶⁶ of culture. Simondon describes a characteristic incompatibility of our time between, on the one hand, what constitutes the past as a "source of images and archetypes" – the "citadel of culture"⁶⁷ or the "content of culture"⁶⁸ – and, on the other hand, what constitutes the future as a set of actualisable virtualities, i.e. of possible effective actions. If there is a cultural crisis, it is because there is a separation of the ontogenetic totality into, on the one hand, a culture "in the minor sense" – in Simondon's words – claimed by some in the name of all, and, on the other hand, a "civilisation" that is certainly entirely turned towards its future, but in fact always less cultivated.⁶⁹ What defines a cultural reality "in the major sense", i.e. beyond any arbitrary cultural authoritarianism operated by a minority, is the "meaning" that it makes possible. This meaning lies in the synthesis of culture in the minor sense and civilisation; true Culture (with a capital "C") is thus relative to the understanding that culture and civilisation "are recip-

---

62   *Ibid.*, p. 238/p. 315.
63   *Ibid.*, p. 19/p. 15.
64   ILNFI, p. 16/ILFI, p. 35.
65   *Ibid.*, p. 240/p. 216.
66   "Psychosociologie de la technicité" (1960–1961), in SLT, p. 35–36. In METO the problem of culture was still only an "unease" (p. 81/p.102) and not a "crisis".
67   *Ibid.*, p. 37.
68   *Ibid.*, p. 42.
69   The distinction comes from Eliade: "Mircea Eliade opposes the historicity of civilisation to the timelessness of culture" (*Ibid..*, p. 53).

rocal and complementary symbols".[70] In concrete terms, this meaning is made possible by an "overdetermination" of objects, which Simondon conceives as a "power to represent a totality by a single element participating in this totality".[71] We find here the aim of totality which, from the very first writings, characterises the Simondonian notion of culture. However, the distinction between sign and symbol, which earlier allowed us to distinguish between the symbolic actuality of cultural contents and the semiotic inactuality of arbitrary contents, is abandoned. In this text, the realities under consideration are conceived as complex encounters of technicity and sacrality; in other words, they function and are symbolic at the same time, which confers on them their overdetermination, which is also "power to represent". The problem of culture is thus posed more symmetrically in "Psychosociologie de la technicité" than in METO: it is no longer a question of integrating technical reality with symbolic culture or of extending the cultural and symbolic domain to technical reality, but rather of thinking of cultural reality as a mixture of symbolism – i.e. sacrality – and technicity.

Culture in the major sense then appears as a double process that can be described with the words that Simondon reserves, in another text of the same year, to define what he calls "anthropo-technology". The programme of the latter, identical in our opinion to Culture in the major sense, consists in "making technical schemes into contents of culture, and making technology the equivalent of a symbolic logic or an aesthetic".[72] It is then a question of considering a movement of convergence of technics and minor culture, grasped on the one hand from its contents by technology and, on the other, by the theme of symbols. Now, this double movement corresponds quite well to the two dialectics that characterise transindividual reality:[73] on the one hand, technicity, insofar as it is "condensation"[74] and "mobilization of aspects of the world", can be brought closer to the movement which "interiorizes the exterior"; on the other hand, sacrality understood as "infusion of action into space and time" corresponds rather to the one which "exteriorizes the interior".

Thus, we can assert that the relationship between the human and the world is mediated by a third reality – more a relationship than a term – which we call a cultural object or cultural reality, which is both a functioning object and a symbol, at the same time sacred and technical. In this case, Culture in the major sense corresponds quite well to what, in the 1958 theses, is meant by the term "transindividuality". Moreover, the problematic of culture, as it appears in the theses, is lifted: the functionalist determination of culture, ontogenetic, regula-

---

[70] Ibid., p. 35.
[71] Ibid., p. 39.
[72] "Objet technique et conscience moderne" (1961), SLT, p. 364.
[73] ILNFI, p. 315/ILFI, p. 274.
[74] "Psychosociologie de la technicité", SLT, p. 97.

tive and actual, becomes Culture in the major sense, which has the "status of being"[75] and to which corresponds, for this reason, transindividuality; the substantialist determination of culture as sedimented in particular and overdetermined objects is culture in the minor sense, existing only in relation to a solicited actualisation. However, the substitution of this new distribution – where the cultural object, functioning and being a bearer of meaning, is envisaged according to the technical-sacred bipolarity – for the old symbolic-semiotic doublet leads to a new problematic: the impossibility of objectifying the major Culture, currently operative, without distorting it.

Taking up some of the discourses and categories in Eliade's *Images et symboles*, Simondon writes:

> Images, symbols, myths are representations that refer to types of reality that cannot be objectified without losing their real meaning and content. Images, symbols, myths refer to a type of reality of which there can be no fully rational representation, according to the categories of unity and identity.[76]

This non-objectivability goes beyond the framework of "images, symbols [and] myths", which is the framework of sacrality, and concerns technicity as well.[77] A science or knowledge of culture – as an objectifying knowledge of that which, through its double sacred and technical dimension, modulates the relation of the human to the world – can therefore only lead to a desacralisation or an abstraction. Any particular cultural objectivity remains posterior and inferior to actual Culture, which alone has the status of being. This awareness allows Simondon to dispense with the need to establish a criterion capable of differentiating symbolic or functional culture from semiotic or substantial culture; however, it seems to lead back to a pre-critical dogmatic metaphysics according to which there would be a conditioner in itself beyond the reach of the individual: to define culture would be to lose it at once.

The texts from 1961 to 1965 present a series of hesitations which we cannot dwell on in detail due to lack of space.[78] In a word, Simondon hesitates between

---

75   ILNFI, p. 8/ILFI, p. 29.
76   "Psychosociologie de la technicité", SLT, p. 74.
77   "What Mircea Eliade says about images and symbols could be said of that set of technicity that constitutes a network", (*Ibid.*, p. 83). See also the formulation of the same hypothesis on p. 32: "an image or a symbol that is reduced to a univocal objective meaning is desacralized. Similarly, an abstract technical object, a materialized concept, is not a real technical object, but only a pedagogical or scientific set-up."
78   Let us nevertheless mention 1) the ambiguous situation of the notion of "constructivity" in "Psychosociologie de la technicité", a notion that first appears only in relation to technicity before finally being situated in what Simondon calls a "no-man's-land (in English in the text) between sacredness and technicity", SLT, p. 121; 2) the propaedeutic course "Sciences de la nature et sciences de l'homme" given at the University of Poitiers in 1962–1963, in which we

relating the functioning of culture to technicity or relating it to both technicity and sacrality, which is also culture in the minor sense.[79] By opting for the second alternative, Simondon abandons the question of the possibility of knowledge of the regulative functioning. He replaces it with the attempt to grasp, through a different mode of objectification than theoretical knowledge, the relations between actual problems and the inventions as traces.[80] In other words, by admitting that culture is a function involving both a set of technical operations and existing symbolic representations, Simondon relates the problem of culture to the one of invention.

This intellectual movement is not so surprising, if we recall the 1965–1966 General Psychology Course, *Imagination et invention*, in which invention is defined as "the appearance of extrinsic compatibility between the environment and the organism, and of intrinsic compatibility between the subsets of the action".[81] The invention responds to a double problematic situation characterised by the terms "hiatus" and "incompatibility", whose "solutions appear as restorations of continuity authorising the progressiveness of the operating modes, according to a previously invisible path in the structure of the given reality".[82] This problematic situation that invention resolves, through the search for continuity, is analogous, if not identical, to the discontinuity that culture has to solve in early texts. Moreover, invention involves an action of the subject that is mediated by symbols:

---

understand that it is less the "cultural forms" that are problematic than their mode of apprehension as "divine gifts that must be respected and preserved" (SLΦ, p. 265), which allows us to conclude that sacredness is now in Simondon's sights, insofar as it chains culture to an inadequate, theoretical, contemplative, non-participatory conception of its contents (in this same text, Simondon defines the cultural content or object as the "provisional result of an operative genesis that must continue", which signals to the reader a further step in the direction of invention); 3) the text "Culture et technique" of 1965, which manifests a limitation of the content of culture to its minor meaning, as "the basis of the invariance of groups" inadequate to normalise the technical gesture (SLT, pp. 323–324). The end of the text, however, recognises the value of the complementarity of culture and technics in the face of the need to pose the problems properly (p. 329), culture being related to "purely human" problems and technics to "problems of the relationship between man and the milieu" (p. 328).

79   Indeed, in the introduction to the course "Psychosociologie de la technicité", Simondon admits sacrality as a "bedrock of culture" (SLT, p. 31), i.e. - as a "source of images and archetypes" (p. 35) – as culture in the minor sense. Moreover, the third part of the course, entitled "Technicity and sacrality", is announced at the end of the second part as a study of the "structures of culture and technicity" (p. 73), indicating that Simondon identifies culture in the minor sense with sacrality.

80   Much could be said about the relationship between invention and its traces; in the meantime, see the 1975–1976 course, "Invention et créativité", in RP, p. 207.

81   IMIN, p. 139.

82   *Ibidem.*

The souvenir, in its most condensed form, that of the symbol, is only a moment in the cycle of the image, which has as much functional meaning in relation to the action to be undertaken after the invention as in relation to the action already accomplished.[83]

In the framework of Simondon's theory of the image, we again find this connection between symbols and the "beginnings of action"[84] through which, already in the "Complementary Note", culture finds a determination. We thus move from images to symbols, then from symbols to invented realities, which can in turn serve as technical and symbolic conditions, new images figuring in what Simondon, rightly, refers to as an "auto-kinetic" cycle.[85]

Simondon thus proceeds to an extension of the notion of invention that can be found elsewhere, for example in a 1972[86] text in which, while questioning the distinction between the provisional and the permanent in technical matters, Simondon asks what is at the origin of the "durable part" of the arts. Cultural realities are what the author is talking about – works of art and texts – even if the mere occurrence of the cultural theme appears problematic, if not negative, since it concerns the barriers that the object must cross. Moreover, in order to achieve this crossing, the "work", which is the result of a "construction", must, Simondon writes, "contain invention"; invention is therefore indeed extended to cultural realities, it is not limited to exclusively technical ones.

Later in the same text, while looking for an example of a work capable of being both rapidly realised and inventive, Simondon turns to Descartes and recalls the role of the choice of French, rather than Latin, as a means of communication which conditions the accessibility and success of the discourse. Here, philosophy serves as an example of construction and invention, as we saw earlier.[87] This example illustrates once again the extension of the notion of invention to cultural realities; the choice of a language can be understood as both a technical and symbolic decision, contributing to the internal structuring as well as the social success of a cultural reality.

An investigation into the extension of the notion of invention brings us to the conclusion of another general psychology course, that of 1976 entitled "Invention et créativité":

---

[83] Ibid., p. 138.
[84] "Complementary Note", ILNFI, p. 404/ILFI, p. 332.
[85] IMIN, p. 191.
[86] "Technique et eschatologie" (1972), in SLT, p. 332.
[87] Similarly, in the 1976 lecture, Simondon very explicitly brings philosophy closer to technical thought: "philosophy must be considered as a mode of thought capable of real inventions, in the manner of technical thought, according to the rhythm in three phases: syncretic, analytical and finally synthetic.", "Invention et créativité" (1976), in RP, p. 203.

[The] second postulate of this course is the assertion that there can be transindividual psychic processes, passing from one subject to another from generation to generation, transmitted by written documents, graphics, or by the objects themselves, in the form of monuments, engines, information machines. The transmission can also take place through living examples (from master to disciple).[88]

The reappearance of the theme of transindividuality, almost twenty years after the theses, is remarkable. Whereas METO was only interested in the transindividual relationship through the technical object,[89] the 1976 course includes in the category of "media [*supports*] and symbols of transindividuality" a whole range of things: "written documents, graphics" but also "objects themselves, in the form of monuments, engines, information machines". Although METO implies that technical objects are not necessarily the only realities that can occupy this cultural function,[90] no connection between engines and written documents seems to be as obvious. Graphic design is thematised only in relation to its role in perpetuated invention or concretisation[91] and "literary culture" is depreciated, qualified on several occasions as "old".[92] In the 1976 course, the set of realities worthy of mediating and symbolising transindividuality is not limited to objective technical realities: it also includes the means of inventing which contribute, in the same way as "living examples", to the transmission of psychic processes between subjects and between generations. The content of the notion of culture is clarified and modified insofar as the problematisation of the conditions of technical objectivity as a medium [*support*] and symbol of transindividuality is enriched and becomes a problematisation of invention as a condition of possibility of transindividual reality. This more general problematisation has two complementary aspects: the first, functional, is that of invention as a process linked

---

88   *Ibid.*, p. 255.
89   "The technical object taken according to its essence, which is to say the technical object insofar as it has been invented, thought and willed, and taken up [*assumé*] by a human subject, becomes the medium [*le support*] and symbol of this relationship, which we would like to name *transindividual.*", METO, p. 252/MEOT, p. 335.
90   Simondon seems to hesitate: he posits that technical activity "is the model of the collective relationship" insofar as it is neither exclusively psychological nor exclusively sociological, but then he immediately adds that it "it is not the only mode and the only content of the collective", *Ibid.*, p. 250/p. 332.
91   The encyclopaedia's plates are valuable in Simondon's eyes, particularly because "the information in them is complete enough to constitute a useable practical documentation, such that anyone who owns the book would be capable of building the described machine or of further advancing the state reached by technics in that domain through an invention, and to begin his research where that of others who preceded him leaves off", *Ibid.*, p. 110/p. 133.
92   In particular, Simondon asserts that "[t]here is more authentic culture in the gesture of a child who reinvents a technical device, than in a text where Chateaubriand describes the 'terrifying genius' of Blaise Pascal.", see METO, pp. 19–20, 123, 124/MEOT, pp. 15–16, 151, 153.

to the imagination (in the 1965–1966 course); the second (in the 1976 course), substantial, is constructed rather from the "traces left by invention".[93] It is the complementarity of these two aspects that gives the open problem of invention its resolving function in the problem of culture.

4. Conclusion

From this journey, it emerges that it is ultimately invention, as a functional and non-theoretical mode of objectification, that responds to the problematic of culture as a requirement of continuity and ontogenetic compatibility. It opens up the ethical question of the conditions of possibility of invention, which is crucial insofar as this notion covers the effectiveness of the acculturation process and guarantees the reality of the relationship between humans and the world. The possibility of creating a functioning thing is therefore not simply a faculty of the subject; it is a relationship between, on the one hand, the theme of action, freedom and human ends, and, on the other, that of physical legality, cosmological determination, or ontogenesis.

It is the refusal of the theoretical posture that, in our opinion, particularises the Simondonian solution; and this refusal can be explained immanently, starting from culture as a requirement of continuity: because the theoretical posture itself presupposes a discontinuity between object and method, if not between object and subject; because it distributes value according to a point of view; because, like substantialism, it is incapable of avoiding authoritarianism and arbitrariness; because, confined to representation, it struggles to grasp its own operativity without alienating it.

Non-theoretical objectification remains a challenge for philosophical thought. At least, it enjoins the latter to look for the possibility of an exit from the theoretical. Thus, we could imagine thinking such a thing on the model of what Étienne Souriau called the "mode of existence of the work to be done".[94] This proposal is still only a track to interrogate in a transcendental way the Simondonian idea of a philosophy as a non-theoretical operation of invention. Conversely, at the crossroads of symbols and technicality, philosophical writing – to which this thought of culture, which is very classical on this point, owes all or part of its possibility – is certainly not without function in the constitution of the Simondonian notion of invention. In this case, everything leads us to believe that it is the very possibility of inventing new ways of doing philosophy that Simondon seems to have released.

---

93 "Invention et créativité" (1976), in RP, p. 254.
94 Étienne Souriau, *Les différents modes d'existence*, Paris, PUF, orig. ed. 1943, 2009, p. 195.

Science and Philosophy in Gilbert Simondon's Work[1]

Jean-Yves Chateau

The main possible mistakes about Gilbert Simondon's work, and namely ILNFI,[2] generally originate in the fact that insufficient consideration is given to his very project, as exposed in the very first lines of his introduction: this is a research intended to be first and foremost a *philosophical* research (and in particular not "scientific", even though science and science history play an important role), on the subject of *individuation* (and in particular not on the subject of "the individual"). This research feeds itself from the analysis of *some examples* ("paradigms"), moving from one to another, step by step, according to a method that he calls a transductive, analogical method. It is not about constructing a concept that could be uniformly and extensively applied to everything potentially relevant to individuation within science, following a thinking by genus and species, as if the intention was to build an "encyclopaedia" (according to the unlikely thesis of a commentator). This lack of understanding sometimes leads to idle discussions and arguments. And yet, on the three points above, enunciation, clarification and caution are clearly present: there is a clear enunciation of the research object in the introduction's very first sentences, and a warningly figuring prominently in the last paragraph, a high point of the introduction, warning concluding this introduction and drawing its full consequence. Simondon concludes here the long analysis of his project by a very precise and explicit indication: for reasons of principle, it is excluded that his theory be a *knowledge, a science* of individuation, even if this theory has to take into account everything that scientific knowledge can teach. It is strongly emphasised that individuation can only be grasped through a philosophical approach.

This warning was admittedly justified (the intention is to elaborate a *philosophy* of individuation, not a knowledge or a science), even if it was obviously not sufficient to provide complete clarity at this early stage of research and characterise the rapport between philosophy and science that would be found in ILNFI and more generally in Simondon's work, so great is the diversity of ways philosophers profess to deal with science. It will then be necessary to specify the difference between science and philosophy that Simondon establishes mainly in

---

1 Translation by Dominique Simondon
2 The translation of quotes referring to other authors, namely Bergson, Canguilhem, Ruyer, are our own.

the last paragraph of ILNFI introduction, and the usage he effectively makes of science in his philosophy.

On the other hand, *individuation*, as Simondon intends to study it, is not the individual, nor the property of what is individual, something "individuality criteria" could allow to identify – even if it was once the starting point of his reflection; but he abandoned very early this starting point for profound reasons that are at the heart of what he has carefully elaborated and definitively established in his thesis, as published[3] – even if studying *individuation* allows to determine what can justifiably address most of the questions on *individual and individuality*. But what justifies the necessity to study individuation rather than the individual is closely linked to the fact that an objective, scientific knowledge of individual and individuation cannot exist: the individual barely exists, being constantly between its advent and its transcendence,[4] it only really exists in its individuating becoming, its individuation. But precisely, what only essentially exists as becoming is not, as such, an object of scientific knowledge but of intuition, of philosophy. We will come back on what could be seen as Bergsonian in this way of thinking, something claimed by Simondon[5].

---

3   In the current ILNFI edition, manuscripts corresponding to drafts and essays not kept by Simondon and to which he sometimes comes back quite distinctly (such as the decisive substitution of individuation problematic to that of individuality) have been included. Unfortunately this may have led some readers to make as if everything written by Simondon had the same consistency and importance, because they seem to be more at ease with the sometimes more conventional discourse of his early research, that was later abandoned. This means refusing a mind to search, wander, try and finally decide about what to think and write. It could only correspond to the genesis of a thought which would happen through simple accumulation, leaving no room, in the research phase, for backward steps, discussion, rebuttal, resolving of contradiction, all this being far from Simondon's conception. Let's recall that texts in brackets in the current ILNFI edition were withdrawn by himself in the 1964 thesis edition, without us knowing if it was to shorten the text or because he was reluctant to publish what had been written very early (who did not correct their thesis in view of publication?). These texts were re-introduced after his death, with a view to providing elements on his research evolution, to allow to observe how he initiated and drafted his project and to identify what had not been conserved or taken up as such; but it was not claimed that what is said in these drafts is fully identical to the final thesis. Every time a passage is quoted by a commentator, and particularly in the case of two of the 'Supplements' (Analysis of the criteria of individuality and Allagmatics), it would be sensible to take into account the very clear editor's notes (namely in 2013) indicating their origin and status, and to verify that what is found here is consistent with the rest of the text Simondon wrote, approved and published.

4   A brick is a simple example of what could lead to the idea of a reality subsisting materially: "the veritable individual exists for a mere instant during the technical operation: it lasts as long as the form-taking" (ILNFI, p. 49/ILFI, p. 61).

5   See for instance METO, p. 242/MEOT p. 321.

Neglecting the decidedly reflexive (and not scientific) ILNFI project, which deals with individuation rather than individuality, could be the reason for some readers to over evaluate the meaning of transduction and analogy as claimed by Simondon, and their value in knowledge, as well as to give an erroneous meaning of normative model to what Simondon understands by "paradigm"; or, on the contrary, it could possibly be the desire to see ILNFI as a positive discourse with scientific ambitions that would lead some readers to understand it as a purely analogical thought, based upon an arbitrary and debatable paradigm (understood as model or reference for thought), which makes it easier to challenge. As a matter of fact, these three ways of misunderstanding or bending Simondon's thought tend to combine among certain readers.

1. Philosophy and science on the subject of individuation, according to the *ILNFI's* Introduction

With a radicalism that sometimes disconcerted some readers, Simondon is eager to stress that ILNFI is an individuation theory that does not claim to be scientific, to be a *science* of individuation, not even a *knowledge* of individuation, but a philosophical, "reflexive" theory, as he likes to describe it; in the last paragraph of the ILNFI introduction[6] he explicitly and insistently distinguishes it from any form of knowledge, and not only from scientific knowledge, in order to avoid any misinterpretation of his work: "we cannot have an immediate knowledge or a mediated knowledge of individuation". Individuation, studied in ILNFI, cannot be grasped by a knowledge (be it mediated or immediate). However, a number of individuation cases are studied in ILNFI through explicit and precise references to scientific, physical, biological, or social science analyses. Scientific references play an important part in ILNFI, and it is important to say what is the precise rapport of philosophy to diverse sciences (it is not the same in all cases). Moreover there are not so many cases and it cannot be said that ILNFI's goal would be to try and present what science (physics, biology, social science) could have to say about individuation, as a science historian or an epistemologist would do on a theme extracted from scientific work (like Canguilhem studying cellular theory or the concept of reflex). First, because through these few cases (well selected for Simondon's project, we will see this), numerous areas of knowledge are not covered; then, more radically, because there is no real scientific discourse on individuation, no explicit, unified, univocal, demonstrated, shared discourse, neither in science in general nor in any science, "be it biology" as Canguilhem says, since "all sciences can and should make their contribution

---

[6] ILNFI, p. 17/ILFI, p. 36.

to this clarification".[7] No science *in its own right* can say what individual or individuation would be, even within an area restricted to its expertise. This does not mean that the scholar cannot think for himself (privately, not as a scholar) the reality being the object of his work as an individual, even if he does not elaborate explicitly this reality as such; but in general, his scientific work properly speaking does not require him to elaborate the individuality status of his object, or to take sides on this point. Indeed it can happen that some people develop theoretical reflections on this subject, as for example the biologist Rabaud in a philosophical review, shortly before World War II;[8] but this does not commit science as such, and this discourse is not less "reflexive" (as opposed to properly scientific) because this reflection originates from a science person. Besides, nothing warrants that when science deals with what would be individual, it would use this term[9] or would elaborate the concept in an explicit, distinct and determined way; when, in science like quantum physics, theory seems to be necessarily led to use and define the notion, it seems impossible to align the most prominent scientists on what should be understood by "individual", beyond what is established and agreed upon. This precise point is thoroughly examined in ILNFI; science, sometimes, seems unable to dispense with thinking in terms of individual or in reference to the notion of individual, but nevertheless cannot succeed in leading beyond *thoughts,* on the basis of which one can discuss without reaching an agreement comparable to what is usually the case for scientific matters, thoughts that can be considered as *knowledge* "in the usual sense of the word". Moreover, even if every reality could be thought in terms of individual, issues arising in different domains would not be the same, they would vary from one scientific domain to another, even if some of them could coincide; and verifying the consistency of these different approaches would remain to be done in full. Science itself does not provide an explicit teaching on what should be understood by individual that history and philosophy would just have to collect and gather.

This is the reason why an individuation theory, even as connected as possible to proven scientific knowledge, cannot be itself scientific nor fall under an objective and positive science history (which would only have had to gather what is explicitly formulated in it) but cannot have anything else than a philosophical, "reflexive" status, in the best possible case. "We cannot *know individuation* in the ordinary sense of the term"[10]. We should not say that we can

---

7 Georges Canguilhem, *La Connaissance de la vie*, Vrin, 1971, p. 78
8 Etienne Rabaud, "L'interdépendance générale des organismes", in *Revue philosophique de la France et de l'Etranger*, vol. 119, 1934.
9 "Under the name of cell, this is biological individuality that is discussed" says Canguilhem, *ibid.*, p. 78.
10 ILNFI, p. 17/ILFI, p. 36.

"know" individuation, even though we consider everything science can teach us, we should say that we can "grasp" it.

How does Simondon explain this? Only the subject's individuation, the subject's thought individuation is possible, and this is opposed to the impossible knowledge of an object individuation, object external to the subject: all we can do is "only individuate, be individuated and individuate within ourselves" but we cannot know the individuation of what is external to ourselves, to our thought. "Only the individuation of thought", "the analogical individuation of the subject's knowledge" can allow grasping the individuation of the real external to the subject, "by accompanying it":[11] "The individuation of knowledge" is not (only) this knowledge becoming, its formation, its learning, its growing, its improvement as knowledge, but it is what *transforms this knowledge into thought*, into an object of thought.[12] It is by becoming thought that knowledge must individuate to become a means to grasp the individuation of an object external to thought. It is necessary to transform the knowledge of an object into thought, in order to be able to grasp (analogically) its individuation. Through this understanding of the individuation of knowledge, losing the externality of any knowledge in relation to its object allows knowledge to individuate in the subject's thought, in such a way that the individuation of its object can be diluted in the individuation of the subject's thought, be analogically conflated with it. In these conditions, thought can act in itself as the object of individuation and allows it to play a role, object that has become its object proper, in short like an actor acting in the theatre and as if thought invented individuation (whereas inventing is not knowing, in principle).[13]

A being, Simondon says, can be known, even scientifically known; but the *individuation of a being* cannot be known but only *grasped*, intuitively grasped; this intuition is direct, since the subject grasps the individuation of its own

---

11 Ibid.
12 Those used to a positive form of epistemology and science history, and preferring not to take Simondon's position seriously, represent for themselves "the individuation of knowledge" in the subject as the establishment or even the growth of this knowledge. What makes this understanding impossible is that "individuation of knowledge" is only used in brief in the last lines when it is about opposing "individuation of knowledge" to "knowledge only", and correlatively opposing "knowledge" as "knowledge of beings" to "grasping of beings' individuation". Simondon's words are then deprived of their sense if one understands "individuation of knowledge" only as establishment or growth of this knowledge. For his words to make sense, this individuation of knowledge must be transformed in thought, by thought, into something different from simple knowledge; this is what has been stated at the beginning: "by being accomplished, only the individuation of thought can accompany the individuation of beings other than thought"; this subject's thought must be other than any knowledge, mediated or immediate, even if it reflects on knowledge.
13 See METO p. 59/MEOT, p. 70.

thought. This thought is analogical, insofar as it is the thought of the individuation of a reality external to the subject "consisting in following the being in its genesis, in accomplishing the genesis of thought at the same time as the genesis of the object is accomplished"[14]. Indeed this is a certain individuation, in the subject's reflection, of the knowledge of beings external to the subject which can give rise to an intuitive analogical grasping of the being's individuation, based upon scientific knowledge: the part of knowledge that individuates then in the subject's reflection may appear to it as analogical to the individuation of beings, which may strike it as *grasping* but that it cannot know. "In the margin of knowledge properly speaking" (as knowledge can apply to beings but not to the individuation of beings), the subject's reflection can allow to grasp this analogy between the real external to it, only known to it, and the thought that individuates in itself, this thought being the only thing that the subject can grasp by direct intuition insofar as it is entirely homogeneous to the whole of its thought: through this analogy, this reflection can assign to the real outside an individuation that cannot be an object of knowledge, but rather, should we say, an object of analogical intuition, "a certain mode of communication".[15]

What Simondon formulates in the last sentences of the ILNFI introduction has been analytically explained and built in previous pages[16]. In terms of "logic of thought", grasping individuation is a work of "transduction". Transduction is the reasoning of the mind, a mode of *thought* allowing to grasp a domain of reality as the place for a transductive operation, i.e. an individuation: "The possibility of using an analogical transduction to *think* (underlined) a domain of reality indicates that this domain is effectively the groundwork of a transductive structuration. Transduction corresponds to this existence of rapports that takes hold when pre-individual being individuates; it expresses individuation and allows for individuation to be thought"[17]. "This a notion that is both metaphysical and logical, insofar as *"it applies to ontogenesis and is ontogenesis itself"*,[18] but this is not a scientific notion, precisely because the difference and distance between subject and object, that are conditions of objective knowledge, tend to fade away in it, as expressed in this formulation of transduction. Ontogenesis, individuation are not objective and objectivable properties of the real, but what can be applied analogically to reality only after having been thought, even if thought is aware of anything science can teach, not being however conflated with it. Transduction, then, being "a notion that is both metaphysical and logical" should not be mistaken for a scientific method (even if a scientific approach can

---

14   ILNFI, p. 14/ILFI, p. 34.
15   ILFNI, p. 17/ILFI, p. 36.
16   *Ibid.*
17   *Ibid.*
18   *Ibid.*

be transductive), nor for "a logical procedure having a proof value"[19]; this is a "mental procedure", rather than "a logical procedure in the ordinary sense of the term", and it would even be more accurate to say that this is a *reasoning of the mind* rather than a procedure: "the mind's way of discovering"; a way of thinking which, without technicality or prepared method, "consists in following the being in its genesis, in accomplishing the genesis of thought at the same time as the genesis of the object is accomplished".[20] Of course, in order "to follow the being in its genesis",[21] nothing of what science can know and teach should be excluded, but this is not sufficient to allow for the grasping of the being's genesis, of ontogenesis, of individuation, and here again, the (analogical) relation is not properly from *knowledge* to the being's genesis, but from *thought* (with everything science can contribute to) to the being's genesis. Only *transductive thought* is capable of grasping this ontogenesis, this genesis of the being as such, individuating, i.e. coming from pre-individual. This is different from an empirical genesis objectively known, which gives information on all successive known states of the system, on the relations between them and the factors allowing to calculate the system, but which does not make it appear as the individuation of a being. This is why transductive thought, an analogical thought, is more than "the reasoning of the mind", this expression being too related to an exclusively discursive model of thought: "it is also intuition", it sees, it touches, it is that through which something "appears".[22] *This is not a knowledge but a thought, but a thought that is an intuition, a thought that allows to see and touch, to put in contact, to coincide with a becoming, that is accompanying a becoming.*

1.1. Knowledge, a vital function among others

Moreover, when one presents the nature of the relation of the intuitive grasping of individuation to scientific knowledge, it is important to situate it in the general framework of the ensemble of the rapports of man to the world. Simonond's thought, taken in its entirety, reveals that the individuation of the being is a general function of existence, and is not only grasped on the basis of science and objective knowledge, but also on the basis of each of the vital and psychosocial functions: movement, imagination, perception, thought, desire and affective-emotionality, action and production, and, generally, everything related to its psychosocial existence.[23] "Individuation" designates the fact to become individuated

---

19 Ibid.
20 Ibid.
21 Ibid.
22 Ibid., p. 15/p. 35.
23 Psychosocial realities whose individuation is discussed in the third part of ILNFI (perception, affectivity, emotion, social relations) are also a part of the conditions to grasp individ-

(to become an individual), as well as the fact to individuate, i.e. to make an individual, to tend to make an individual, to refer to something as an individual; Simondon's conception allows to establish the real unity or the continuity of both significations; individuation is not an objective property of the real, it exists only insofar as the real is individuated by a subject, which tends to make it an individual; the subject only tends to make it an individual by becoming individuated itself, by individuating in itself the thought through which it grasps the real, by individuating its relation to it. "The individuation of objects is not entirely independent from the existence of man"[24]: the individuation of reality external to the subject is not entirely independent from the subjectivity of the subject. However, this does not mean that the individuation of reality external to the subject depends entirely on the subject and is reduced to its subjective signification. "It should not lead to the conclusion that individuation does not exist and does not correspond to anything". "However, it cannot be arbitrary, there must be a support that justifies and receives it".[25] All vital functions of the individual put it in relation with individuating realities, but this does not assume in all cases the same rapport to objectivity (to perceive, imagine, dream, fabricate, desire, consume, know, all these functions imply the individuation of their object but according to a varying rapport to objectivity and subjectivity); conversely, in all cases a convenient support must be found for each individuation, a support able to "justify and receive it". The individuating activity of the subject grasping the individuation of an external reality cannot be entirely and rigorously separated from the individuation of this reality, and neither can be separated from what would be relevant to the objective individuation of this reality and what would be relevant to the subjectivity related to it, since this is by individuating in itself its grasping of the object that the subject analogically grasps the individuation of the object external to it. To this extent Simondon's theory expressly escapes the classical alternative of idealism or realism that some commentators were trying to link him to. This appears clearly in Simondon's theory, whichever function relating the subject to the external reality is considered: this is true for functions in which subjectivity is most radical, but it is also true for knowledge, that on its own cannot establish objectively what an individuation would be. Most scientific and objective knowledge cannot establish in the real anything other than what its theoretical and experimental apparatus allows it to reach. In all cases, each

---

uation in all realities. Through all vital, psychological and psycho-sociological functions, a course such as *Imagination and Invention* presents the continuity between objective and subjective individuating factors, by starting image in movement (even before perception) and by making this image a dimension of all psychical and cognitive activity, and studying its becoming object in the fabricating realisation.

24   ILNFI, p. 47/ILFI, p. 60.
25   *Ibid.*

vital function, including knowledge, establishes a relation and, rigorously speaking, this relation is individuated, not only one of the terms of the relation, even if one is interested in this one only, for instance because it is linked to the objectivity pole, as when one is particularly concerned with objective scientific knowledge.

ILNFI grants a prominent role to science in the study of individuation, but knowledge, be it scientific, is not the only domain, the only vital function from which man could grasp the individuation of the real. To a certain extent, ILNFI, in its own way, and considerably expanding it, revisits this idea that Canguilhem had placed at the start of his book *Knowledge of Life*, in such a way that this idea be liberated from a philosophy dealing exclusively with operations of knowledge, and forgetting about its primary vital sense. Recalling that science is first of all a vital function of man, is in no way denying science the autonomy to build its own norms. In Simondon's work, the scope develops in a vaster dimension, extending explicitly to any knowledge, scientific or not, related to all domains and not only to biology, and raising knowledge to the level of the main functions of the living. A study of individuation cannot dispense with carefully taking into account everything scientific knowledge can establish, despite the principal inability of the latter to provide alone sufficient knowledge and conception of individuation; but it should not be forgotten that men, even scholars, do not grasp the being and its individuation (that is not, let's recall, the whole of the being) exclusively on the basis of this scientific knowledge. Most scientific knowledge remains a knowledge, and is one among other vital functions, we should bear it in mind when investigating how science can contribute to the grasping of the being's individuation. We will have to come back to this point and precisely see how Simondon effectively deals with science in ILNFI. However, this relativity of knowledge as vital function does not preclude that scientific knowledge be the only source of objectivity for man: science grasps the being (the individual), even if it does not grasp the individuation of the being; a reflexive elaboration is required to proceed from science to the grasping of the being's individuation. Through some well selected examples, ILNFI shows how this reflection can be performed, reflection starting from scientific knowledge, and able to allow the grasping as an individuation of the being known by science. This grasping is not, however, scientific but reflexive: Simondon warns us that it does not constitute a knowledge, a knowledge that could complete or modify science – even if, assuming that the grasping of individuation is of ontological and psychological importance (knowledge psychology), possibly of importance also for scholars and researchers, such reflections and issues raised could lead, as the case may be, researchers to rethink a way of thinking, of formulating, of postulating, of representing themselves, in this area of scientific activity which cannot be easily separated from common existence, which precedes scientific work and that scientific work cannot validate directly, as can be expected generally about established knowledge. ILNFI is a reflection on scientific knowledge, this reflection does not claim to be knowledge, nor a knowledge of scientific knowledge susceptible to constitute a justification or a questioning, even if it could contribute to revealing the nature of scientific work on some points (epistemology and science history), and, possibly, if appropriate, on certain scientific issues. Everything is written as reflection, hypothesis, interrogation, and is never presented as something that could be exempted from the task of elaborating properly scientific and verifiable hypotheses – for example as if, for Simondon, and as some readers seem to think, transductive and analogical thought could constitute an alternative to science, whereas it is at the basis of reflective thought, including in the case of scientific thought and invention.

Science commentary cannot be of the same order as science, whatever its nature and the sense it gives itself. Contrary to many people who do not disagree with him, Simondon does not forget to state this, and he insists on what distinguishes his position from those, more common, that could be confused with it. On the other hand, his position is not shared by some people, who imagine the sense and the limits of the whole of their own work as providing a knowledge of science as being objective as possible, or even as accounting for the way science represents its own work under the form of an unsurpassable norm for reason and objectivity. Nothing surprising here; but on the other hand, isn't it surprising that Simondon's effort to support and detail this thesis is not noticed at least by those who do not agree with it, and that some people act as if this thesis was mingled with what it insistently refuses? If the aim of the last paragraph was finally to present the knowledge of individuation as knowledge and not as thought, what sense could there be to insist throughout this paragraph on the difference between thought and any knowledge, be it mediated or immediate? How can such a clarification be neglected or considered as negligible? In order to ascertain the importance of this fundamental thesis, we will compare it to the position of three authors very important for Simondon and in reference to whom his thought takes its sense – before examining how this reflection effectively proceeds in ILNFI, and how it is different from what is generally the purpose of science historians but also from certain science "metaphysics".

2. Comparisons: Kant, Bergson, Canguilhem

Without referring explicitly to Kant, Simondon reexamines to a certain extent the fundamental Kantian distinction between knowledge (whose model is science) and thought, as common evidence that can only impose itself. For Kant, philosophical reflection has nothing to contribute to science, has no lesson to give, neither to challenge it nor to found or complete it, but it can only try and understand how science is possible. This not Simondon's problematic. Moreover, Simondon achieves an apparently non-Kantian result insofar as, for him, reflection on scientific knowledge can lead to *intuition*, whereas for Kant, there can be no valid intuition in the intellectual domain, and this is only in the aesthetic and artistic domain – and precisely this point should be noticed – that *reflection*, the reflexive judgment, with a free play of the representative faculties, can generate something like *intuition*. However, with Simondon, resorting to intuition is intimately linked to the subtle and precise distinction established between knowledge and thought, and, to appreciate it fully, it is instructive to situate his position, proximity and difference, in relation to Bergson's, on the subject of the relation between philosophy, science and intuition.

Intuition as a method proper to philosophy, namely when it deals with a true becoming, intuition as a method to obtain a direct grasping of the thing considered and a sort of participation ("the direct vision of mind by mind"[26]), as a method different in nature from a scientific approach but requiring an effort of thought, a tension of reflection aiming at coinciding with the true becoming of reality, – all this can be found in Bergson's work. However, mainly at the beginning of his life and work, Bergson consequently reserves intuition, a properly philosophical method, to what is becoming, what is linked to life and consciousness. Science, on the other hand, should deal with what is inert material and space. Simondon, for his part, differs from Bergson[27] in thinking that there is no reason to exclude applying intuition to the material domain: everything that is, is in becoming, and this is still partly Bergsonian.[28]

---

26 Bergson, *La Pensée et le Mouvant*, Introduction, Pt. 2., in Bergson, *Œuvres*, Paris, Presses universitaires de France, Edition du centenaire, p. 1271.
27 See METO, p. 242/MEOT, p. 321.
28 It is true that this exclusion is mainly present at the beginning of Bergson's work, but is progressively softened in *La pensée et le mouvant*. Intuition deals primarily and very effectively with self-consciousness and duration, but, in the second introduction to *La pensée et le mouvant*, Bergson, while stating that he maintains his doctrine, strives to demonstrate that intuition can be progressively extended beyond the limits he had given, and which remain those of its proper domain; intuition can be extended by degrees to what is apart from it, under the condition that duration be involved, one way or another.
1- "Intuition we are discussing deals before all with internal duration. It grasps a succession which is not a juxtaposition, an internal growth, the uninterrupted continuation of the past in a present that infringes on future. This is the direct vision of the mind by the mind. Nothing left in between [...] Intuition then means first consciousness, but immediate consciousness, a vision barely distinguishable from the object seen, a knowledge in contact and even coincidence", Bergson, *Ibid.*, p. 1272–1273.
But from this priority given to internal duration as the object of intuition, the remainder of the text establishes four other possibilities for applying intuition, on different levels:
2- "Next, this is consciousness extended", *ibid.*, p. 1273, to what is called the unconscious,
3- "Isn't it going further? Is it only intuition of ourselves?", *ibid.* Through sympathy, intuition deals with other consciousnesses,

As to the relation of philosophy to science, Simondon is close enough to Bergson for their differences to be significant. Both have a profound and admirable respect for and knowledge of science; to both of them, science is of utmost importance for philosophical work. Simondon knows Bergson extremely well and when he determines the difference between philosophical and intuitive thought and knowledge, it is clear that he has in mind Bergson's position, that he then corrects on this point.

Because Bergson considers philosophy (with intuition) and science as "two ways of knowing"[29]. He thinks it necessary to implement a sharing between these "two ways of knowing: philosophy and science" insofar as it corresponds to a difference in method as well as in object. This difference is not only related to two different ways of approaching reality (the same reality, the whole of the reality), but it is founded on the acknowledgment of the existence of two domains of reality, different in nature, and whose nature calls for different approaches to knowledge: on the one hand the domain of positive science (physical science essentially), dealing with inert material and juxtaposed, repeatable and measurable facts, and on the other hand the domain of philosophy, which is that of mind and duration, where everything is reciprocal penetration and that is refractory to measure. In both domains, each of them, science or philosophy, is alone knowing and thinking, and cannot be improved, completed or intensified by the other. In these conditions, there is no question "to make philosophy an ensemble of generalities exceeding scientific generality"[30]; for philosophy, there is no question either, to "move further than science in the same direction: in truth, strange pretence! How philosophical trade could confer to the one practicing it the power to move further than science in the same direction?"[31]: and when philosophy

---

4- "But are we only sympathetic with consciousnesses?", *ibid*. There are also living beings in general, insofar as the living is becoming, development, duration, "If any living being is born, grows, dies, if life is an evolution and if duration is here a reality, isn't there also an intuition of the living and consequently a metaphysics of life which will extend the science of the living"?, *ibid.*

5- "Let's go even further. Beyond organization, unorganized matter probably appears as something that could be broken down in systems on which time glides without penetrating them, systems related to science and to which understanding applies. But the material universe, globally, *keeps* our consciousness *waiting*; it waits itself. It lasts, or else it is supportive of our duration", *ibid.*, p, 1272–1274.

Thus Simondon keeps from Bergson his fundamental initial idea of intuition and, by proposing to extend it to the whole of the real, he systematises a move shyly sketched by Bergson in his late publications.

29 Bergson, "L'Intuition philosophique" (1911), in *Idem, La pensée et le mouvant, op. cit.*, p. 1361.
30 *Ibid.*, p. 1360.
31 *Ibid.*, p. 1359.

deals with "objects in which science is concerned" it cannot be by "intensifying science".

> Truth is that philosophy is not a synthesis of particular sciences and that if it is often present on science ground, if it embraces sometimes in a simpler vision objects in which science is concerned, it is not by intensifying science, by raising its results to a higher generality level. There would be no room for two ways of knowing, philosophy and science, if experience was not presented to us under two different aspects, on one side under the form of facts juxtaposing facts, more or less repeating themselves, more or less measurable, developing in the direction of distinct multiplicity and spatiality, and on the other side, under the form of a reciprocal penetration that is pure duration, refractory to law and measure.[32]

But how to apply this Bergsonian division of competences? In the domain of physical science, there is nothing to complain about nor to add to science, it can be only repeated, whatever way it is presented:

> At first glance, it could look cautious to leave to positive science the consideration of facts. Physics and chemistry will deal with raw material, biological and social science will study the manifestations of life. Philosopher's task is then clearly circumscribed. From scholars, philosophers receive facts and laws, and either they try to go beyond them to reach deep causes, or they believe it impossible to move further and they prove it through an analysis of scientific knowledge itself; in both cases, they respect facts and relations as transmitted by science, as one respects a judged cause.[33]

But the situation is more complicated in the domain in which duration and mind are decisive, i.e. in biological and psychological sciences, and a positivist good will is not enough:

> But how isn't one able to see that this alleged work sharing comes back to blurring and confusing everything? The critique or metaphysics that the philosopher reserves the right to do, they will be given to him ready made by positive science, already contained in descriptions and analyses left to the scholars to be concerned with. Not having wanted to intervene from the beginning in questions of facts, the philosopher is narrowed down to purely and simply formulate in more precise terms, for questions of principle, unconscious and therefore inconsistent metaphysics and critique sketched by the science attitude toward reality.[34]

The critique of science is not a veritable alternative to the obedient repetition of the scientific discourse. "From this moment, philosophy is done. The philosopher is left with no other choice than dogmatism or metaphysical skepticism,

---

[32] Ibid., p. 1360–1361.
[33] Bergson, L'évolution créatrice, in Idem, Oeuvres, op. cit. pp. 487–809 (p. 660).
[34] Ibid.

both being finally founded on the same postulate ..."[35]. Philosophy should be given authority and finally priority. Indeed, what sense could be given to an activity that examines and finally judges results' validity once they have been established and documented? Isn't it too late then? It would be preferable for it to become involved all along the elaboration of research. Independently of this so called "interventionist"[36] position in the relation of philosophy to science, of the issues that it can raise, and of its properly Bergsonian origin, that Simondon will revisit, shouldn't we acknowledge that Bergson is particularly clear and lucid in enunciating a fundamental problem, in terms in relation to which Simondon's position makes sense?

For Simondon, revisiting in his own way the Kantian distinction between knowledge and thought-reflection, the Bergsonian separation between two domains of reality, one reserved by nature to scientific knowledge, the other to intuition and philosophy, does not correspond to his idea of the real: thus there can be *a science* of everything which exists, including in the domain that Bergson calls "the mind" (Simondon was himself, by the way, a professor and researcher in psychology), and nothing excludes in parallel the possibility and even the necessity of reflecting on any scientific domain, as long as it is about grasping individuation, under the condition that the one dealing with this is sufficiently knowledgeable and repeats with a sufficient accuracy what science has established. In truth the question raised by Bergson remains (and revisited by Canguilhem's interrogation at the beginning of *Knowledge of Life*): what goal, what limits, what sense can be attributed to such an activity of re-evaluation and reflection? Could it be anything else at best than repeating strictly the results of science, with no foreign addition, if one remains within scientific as well as philosophical legitimacy (and even the sense of ridicule). But again in this case what sense could it have for a philosopher?

The originality of the object that Simondon assigns to philosophical research, at least to his own research, individuation, creates a certain ambiguity in his rapport to Bergson: on the one hand, it can be said that insofar as individuation is not and cannot be a scientific notion, philosophy could appear as a complement to or a transcendence of science, and from this viewpoint, Simondon would show how the limit assigned by Bergson to philosophy can be exceeded; on the other hand, for the same reason, it can be said that here, it is not about a complement or a *scientific* transcendence of science: Simondon's philosophy of individuation does not claim to "move further than science in the same direc-

---

[35] *Ibid.*, p. 662.
[36] Jean Gayon, "Bergson entre science et métaphysique/ Bergson between science and metaphysics" in *Annales bergsoniennes, III, Bergson et la science*, PUF, 2007, p. 178: "This interventionist attitude" would be "characterized by him through two key words, cooperation and confrontation".

tion"; by making sure, in the final part of the ILNFI introduction, to exclude the possibility of *knowing* individuation, and by making it an object of *reflective thought* only, i.e. of philosophy, he finally remains partially in agreement with Bergson's warning, at least with the reasons for it. But whereas Bergson separates science and philosophy as dealing with two different domains, Simondon separates them on the subject of the whole of the real, with each of them being totally concerned with it: on any object studied by science, philosophy, by reflecting on its individuation, raises a question that is not scientific insofar as by itself no science (or ensemble of sciences) can provide an answer, but the philosophical answer to this question requires to call for everything science can contribute.

This position, on the other hand, is in full agreement with Canguilhem's, who acknowledges the difficulties to award a scientific status to individuality, a position formulated in a passage already quoted:[37] "Under the name of cell, this is biological individuality that is discussed. Is the individual a reality? An illusion? An ideal? No science, be it biology, can address this question. And if *all* sciences can and should make their contribution to this clarification, it is doubtful that this question be properly scientific, in the usual sense of the word". This last sentence, which is being commented, reminding us of the one used by Simondon in the last part of the ILNFI introduction ("we cannot *know individuation* in the ordinary sense of the term"[38]), probably indicates that at the time of writing, he has in mind not only the Bergsonian position, which he does not align with, but also this Canguilhemian expression that he almost exactly takes up. Canguilhem's agreement with this thesis is even more explicitly ensured by the 1971 edition note, referring to the last word of the preceding quote, acknowledging Simondon's contribution to the question of individuation: "since these lines were written, Gilbert Simondon's thesis: *The individual and its physical-biological genesis* (1964, Paris, PUF) has fortunately contributed to clarifying these questions".[39]

3. What does Simondon do with science?

3.1. Neither simple obedient repetition nor poetic metaphysics

However, Canguilhem's deep agreement on the general ILNFI thesis does not allow yet to sufficiently characterise the way Simondon effectively relates himself

---

[37] Georges Canguilhem, *La Connaissance de la vie*, Vrin, 1971, p. 78.
[38] ILNFI, p. 17/ILFI, p. 60.
[39] This approval is all the more significant because Canguilhem was not known for complimenting easily, and that it probably comes from a very careful reading of ILNFI. Is it necessary to recall that Canguilhem was one of two Simondon's thesis directors?

to science, a way certainly not similar to Canguilhem's. Let's see how Simondon deals with science and, first of all, to what extent does what he is trying to achieve and how he does it differ from what science historians and epistemologists usually do, exposing and analysing what is presented as science or what they think is validated science.

To assert that individuation is not accessible to knowledge alone, be it scientific, but only to reflection, excludes science from being unquestionable and complete knowledge, but also that reflection susceptible to apply to it be considered as a knowledge that would complete or correct science, and could be dogmatically seen as a superior truth. The Simondonian commentary about science is reflexive, it seeks in science what can make us think, think beyond it, think what is problematic in it; but this commentary never presents this reflection as a positive knowledge, as a knowledge going beyond science, as anything other than hypotheses, suggestions for postulates whose validity could be explored but that in no case could elude being elaborated and verified scientifically.

To start with, there is obviously no risk of confusing Simondon, despite his passionate and erudite interest in science, with positivists or members of the Vienna circle who think that philosophy should defer to "the scientific conception of the world", to science, which only can know. Simondon had no sympathy for logical positivism[40] that he sometimes scratches and compares to North American pragmatism[41]. As noted by Dominique Lecourt[42], the emerging "encyclopedic aim" linked to a "conquering and anti-metaphysical tone" can only be wrongly seen as being close to the ILNFI project. There is nothing positivist in Simondon's passion for science.

3.2. The sense of science

But in ILNFI this is also not about satisfying oneself with an epistemological work, understood as "a rigorous analysis of scientific discourse, in order to examine the modes of reasoning implemented and to describe the formal structure of its theory"[43], a work performed by researchers who, as Lecourt notes, "concentrating on the knowledge approach, very often exclude reflecting on its sense". This is a reference to Canguilhem's notorious theme at the beginning of the introduction to *Knowledge of Life*, already mentioned above:

---

[40] ILNFI, p. 77/ILFI, p. 83.
[41] See for instance ILNFI p. 77/ILFI, p. 83, SLΦ, p. 79, and SLΨ, p. 42.
[42] Dominique Lecourt, *La philosophie des sciences*, Presses universitaires de France, Coll. "Que sais-je?", 2018, p. 34.
[43] Ibid., p. 17.

One of the characteristics of any philosophy concerned with the question of knowledge is that the attention dedicated to the operations of knowledge leads to a diversion from the sense of knowledge. At best, it happens that this latter question is addressed by an affirmation of sufficiency and purity of knowledge. And yet, knowledge for knowledge does not really make more sense than eating for eating, killing for killing or laughing for laughing, because it is both admitting that knowledge must have a sense and refusing to find another sense than itself.[44]

The profundity of this text corresponds in a certain way to the magnitude of Simondon's very project in ILNFI, and to his way of achieving it, even if Canguilhem's and Simondon's ways are quite different. Passages of properly epistemological reflection are doubtless present in ILNFI, and are sometimes presented as such through a subtitle (for example, p. 88: "Epistemological consequences"); however, these are precisely consequences, and not the core of the theme. But it is certain that ILNFI cannot be suspected not to take an interest in the *sense* of the operation of knowledge, and first of all in its vital dimension, as Canguilhem thought it, – it may be what certain commentators do not notice sufficiently clearly.

Regarding science history, it seems almost constantly present, but as an object of analysis and an occasion to raise problems rather than as a reference allowing to definitively ascertain a scientific thesis. Specific and established theses on individuation will not be found in science, theses that could be gathered and exposed as objectively as possible, as science historians and epistemologists usually do; at best problems, opportunities to raise interrogations, to discuss, to reflect: everything remains to be explained, and even, in most cases, to be constructed. Because if individuation is not established by science, one can nevertheless find sometimes a more or less explicit and determined reference to the individual, as if science, without establishing it, could not do without it, or would find it easier to seemingly assume its existence, as this is the case, although differently, in microphysics or biology. Simondon does not claim to expose synthetically what science says in such or such a domain, as some science history studies do; nor does he claim to juxtapose everything these studies could say about it; he is content with a few analysis objects in each of the three reality domains selected. We will see why his project and his method did not call for anything else (in any case, his work is in nothing an encyclopaedic project, contrary to what is claimed by an unlikely thesis despite all evidence).[45]

---

44 Canguilhem, *La Connaissance de la vie, op. cit.*, p. 9.
45 See: J-H. Barthélémy, *Simondon ou l'encyclopédisme génétique*, Paris, PUF, 2008.

3.3. Neither complement to science nor rectification. A theory of individuation that learns from the sciences without being confused with them

Simondon is also not seeking to complete or rectify science, but to *show how one can reflect* on it, or rather on such or such an example, in the perspective of constructing a theory of individuation. It can be noticed that insofar as this is not the kind of question science is raising in general, Simondon consequently avoids, in principle and with few exceptions, to be in the situation to have to criticise science – even in the case of microphysics and quantum theory in which researchers themselves sometimes step into and seem to complete science by reflections exceeding what science can establish in a consensual manner. Here the difference with Bergson's statements can be seen, for instance, related to "the biological facts and the psychological facts" ("there is no reason for philosophy to 'abandon' them to positive science alone, as it has rightfully done so for physical facts"[46], or with Ruyer's position (in a certain continuity on this point with the early Bergson) considering that science indeed objectively accounts for the real, but cannot account for its intelligibility, for its why, for its formation, this being particularly clear in the study of the morphogenesis of living forms.[47] This is what leads him, in order to account for the formations that science can observe, to assume the existence of something like a world other than the known world, where forms 'trans-spatially' form themselves through a consciousness of themselves, an 'auto-overflying', auto-finalised consciousness that knows everything about itself and "conforms to a general theme dominating constitutive elements" of its formation[48]. In other words, for Ruyer, at a certain point in time a non-scientific type of reality and of explaining principles should be substituted each time in view of the intelligibility of what science describes.[49] We see the difference with Simondon's approach, who disputes nothing in principle about science, and does not suppose that it is possible to objectively explain phenomena differently to how science does, but only remarks that science does not raise the question of individuation, in general, for structural reasons, and when it does, cannot address this question. This is precisely this flaw that allows philosophy to exist, that makes it necessary for philosophy to exist, but necessarily "in the margin of knowledge", even if it is very close to and starting from it, when an objective knowledge can exist[50].

---

46   Bergson, *L'Evolution créatrice*, op. cit., p. 662.
47   Raymond Ruyer, *La Genèse des formes vivantes*, Flammarion, 1958, p. 8.
48   *Ibid.*, p. 240, p. 248.
49   Raymond Ruyer, *Paradoxes de la conscience et limites de l'automatisme*, Albin Michel, 1966, p. 167.
50   ILNFI, p. 256/ILFI, p. 228.

By doing so, Simondon places himself in the situation of not having to simply repeat the content of science, since the object of his philosophy is not completely the same, although so close that it could not be elaborated without taking carefully into account what science teaches about this object. Thus Simondon solves in his own way the problem that constitutes, for a philosopher, the tension between the need to always take into account science in its evolution and its actuality, and the need to keep the philosophical work autonomous in principle (do not make philosophy a servant of science after it ceased to be one of theology). This is a possible illustration of the attitude toward science claimed by Canguilhem, against Bachelard, in one of the articles he wrote to commemorate Bachelard's death in 1963,[51] therefore in a perspective free of any controversy, and this underlines the importance for him of this characterisation of Bachelard's philosophy, that he presents as "a difficulty"[52]. "On the one hand, Bachelard is apart from positivism. He does not describe his scientific philosophy as philosophical science". However, in contradiction with Bachelard's frequent statements against positivism, it should be noticed that

> on the other hand, he does not depart from science when it comes to describing and legitimating its approach. For him there is no distinction nor distance between science and reason. Reason is not founded on divine truth or on the demand for unity in the rules of understanding. From reason, this rationalism requests no genealogical title, no other justification for exercise than science in its history.

Science alone would say what reason is and would pilot its evolution. "Bachelard professes that science only is constituent, that science only defines norms for using categories". On the previous page, Canguilhem summarised Bachelard's position in *La Philosophie du non* by saying that "it is up to science to order philosophy"[53]. Indeed, Bachelard[54] writes: "The sense of the philosophical evolution of scientific notions is so clear that we should conclude that scientific knowledge orders thought, that science orders philosophy itself". Here, says Dominique Lecourt, a very knowledgeable admirer of Bachelard as well as of Canguilhem, Canguilhem "distances himself explicitly from one of Bachelard's major theses": for Canguilhem, who clearly agreed with a 'reconciliation' between philosophical reflection and science", "this formulation actually 'reconciliates' Bachelard with positivism".[55] This 1962 Bachelardian lesson about philoso-

---

51 "Dialectique et philosophie du non chez Gaston Bachelard", in Georges Canguilhem, *Etudes d'histoire et de philosophie des sciences*, Vrin, 1970 (p. 196 f.).
52 *Ibid.*, p. 200.
53 *Ibid.*, p. 199.
54 Gaston Bachelard, *La Philosophie du non*, Paris, PUF, 1962, p. 22.
55 Dominique Lecourt, *Georges Canguilhem*, Paris, Presses Universitaires de France, 2008, p. 66.

phy's obedience to science continues the one already found in *Le Nouvel esprit scientifique* in 1934, right from introduction: "It would be beneficial, this is our belief, to take scientific philosophy in itself, to judge it without preconceived ideas, even outside of the too strict obligations of the traditional philosophical vocabulary. Indeed science creates philosophy. The philosopher therefore must alter his language to translate contemporary thought in its flexibility and mobility".[56]

Simondon is certainly much closer to Canguilhem on this decisive point, including in Canguilhem's opinion, than to Bachelard, insofar as his passionate interest for science and for its actuality does not lead him however to follow the Bachelardian way: in a way, if it can be a good thing for science to have a formative influence on philosophy, it would be desirable that the reverse be possible to a certain extent,[57] and in all cases the philosopher's proper task cannot be reduced to a positivist work of repeating science, but consists in seeking, starting from scientific objectivity, how beings' individuation can be grasped and represented. This is what Simondon says in the last lines of the ILNFI part related to vital individuation, in words confirming the statement of the last paragraph of the introduction:

> an axiomatic of ontogenesis remains to be discovered, at least if this axiomatic is definable. It could be that ontogenesis is not able to be axiomatised, which would explain the existence of philosophical thought as perpetually marginal with respect to all other studies, since philosophical thought is what is driven by the implicit or explicit research of ontogenesis in all orders of reality.[58]

Having chosen to study individuation, Simondon not only gives a masterful demonstration of what can be a way for philosophy to study science in detail without submitting to it, as if science was in charge of ultimately regulating reason and the path to thought and being, but he also advises the principle behind: *the thought of individuation*, object proper to philosophical reflection, "in the margin of knowledge", and at the same time very close to it.[59]

---

56 Gaston Bachelard, *Le Nouvel esprit scientifique*, Paris, Presses Universitaires de France, 1934, p. 3.
57 This is more or less as stated in an early text: "Cybernetics and philosophy" in *Sur la Philosophie*, PUF, 2016, pp. 35–36.
58 ILNFI, p. 256/ILFI, p. 228.
59 One can appreciate here, despite the distortions of sometimes Bachelardising presentations of Simondon's philosophy, the way Simondon distances himself from the general orientation of Bachelardian thought. Simondon had once contemplated taking Bachelard as thesis director; it can be understood why he quickly changed his mind. The 1955 first drafts already exhibit a very different orientation compared to Bachelard's to thinking the relation between philosophy and science. The idea of reciprocal acceptance and critique is no longer current at

the time of the thesis in 1958 (it is no longer requested). The philosopher elaborates a theory of individuation that learns from the sciences without being confused with them.

Ontogenesis and Finitude
Remarks on the Marginality of Philosophical Thought in Simondon

Michaël Crevoisier

1. Introduction

Gilbert Simondon's position regarding the ambition of his theory of individuation is ambivalent. On the one hand, his discourse is cautious, presented in the form of hypotheses and postulates;[1] on the other hand, it is formalised by means of a universal theory of operations that he calls allagmatic[2] and seems to aim for a new philosophical axiomatic.[3] This ambivalence can be explained by the nature of what he seeks to know, ontogenesis, that is to say, being insofar as what it is is not reducible to what is individuated but also consists in the process of individuation of beings. Indeed, the aim of his *magnum opus*, *Individuation*, is to grasp being from the point of view of the genesis of individuals; his hypothesis is that the theory of allagmatics provides the means to do so because this theory developed a formalisation of the relationship between structure (the individuated being) and operation (the individuation). His idea is therefore to think that it is through the study of individuation that the theory of ontogenesis can be elaborated.[4] In the first pages of *Individuation*, Simondon shows that philosophers

---

1   See: Jean-Yves Château, "Analogie, science et philosophie chez Simondon", in *Canal-U*, 2019, https://www.canal-u.tv/82307 (22.01.2022).
2   Simondon summarises this theory in a few pages in a preparatory document to *Individuation* published in the "Supplemental texts", in ILNFI, pp. 663–673/ILFI, pp. 559–566. In another preparatory document, he states explicitly that it is an "universal allagmatic" ("Épistémologie de la cybernétique" (1953), in SLΦ, p. 185).
3   This exposition of Simondon's position calls for a clarification. We agree with Château's assertion that *Individuation* does not fulfil the programme of the axiomatised theory of allagmatics (see "Science and philosophy in Gilbert Simondon's work" in this volume). Nevertheless, we think that it is still relevant to question their relationship because it explicitly appears that Simondon continues to want to carry out a systematic reform of philosophical conceptuality. In what way is this systematic reform aimed at developing a theory of individuation that is not axiomatic? Why would he refuse or give up this axiomatic ambition? There is an ambivalence in his work that could be interesting in itself because we wish to show that the Simondon's meaning of philosophy depends on it.
4   "[I]t is possible to consider individuation as what must be known beforehand about being", ILNFI, p. 17/ILFI, p. 35.

have never been consistent with the idea of individuation. A true knowledge of individuation requires "a reform of fundamental philosophical notions".[5]

This is why the study of individuation implies a major ambition: a new discourse on being, a theory of ontogenesis whose outcome should be the uncovering of a new scheme of intelligibility of reality, implying a new philosophical axiomatic.[6] However, he points out that "we cannot *know individuation* in the ordinary sense of the term",[7] so it is not certain that this new kind of "knowledge" can lead to a new philosophical "science".[8] So, the theory of ontogenesis is thus a reform of the metaphysical ambition of philosophy: the discourse on being is no longer *a priori* a science of being, an ontology, but an ontogenesis. Because of this distinction, the status of the theory of ontogenesis is ambivalent: Simondon aims to establish a new structure of philosophical conceptuality in order to provide the means to think differently about being, but at the same time, he affirms that this new thought of being will not be scientific because: "It could be that ontogenesis is not able to be axiomatized".[9] We will aim to clarify this doubt of Simondon: why can ontogenesis not be axiomatised? Is it because individuation can only be known in a particular sense?

Commentators have already highlighted the particularity of this "knowledge" of individuation.[10] This particularity is explained by the coherence of Simondon's thought concerning individuation: a theory of knowledge of individuation implies thinking about knowledge from the point of view of individuation, and thus taking into consideration the fact that knowledge individuates itself.[11] However, asserting that knowledge individuates itself implies the idea that the knowing subject individuates itself by knowing. In other words, knowledge is an operation that modifies the subject. But, if the subject is no longer the same before and after the operation of knowledge, this raises a problem concerning the

---

5   *Ibid.*
6   The result of this conceptual reform lies mainly in the possibility of a way out from what Simondon calls the hylomorphic scheme, thanks to the development of new concepts, in particular those of metastability, internal resonance, causal recurrence, modulation and a new method based on the notion of transduction.
7   ILNFI, p. 17/ILFI, p. 36.
8   However, there is an ambivalence because Simondon states in the first sentence of the "Allagmatic" (ILNFI, p. 663/ILFI, p. 559) that the allagmatic theory, thanks to which the study of individuation should make it possible to elaborate the ontogenesis theory, belongs to the order of sciences.
9   ILNFI, p. 256/ILFI, p. 228.
10 See: Jean-Hugues Barthélémy, *Penser la connaissance et la technique après Simondon*, Paris, L'Harmattan, 2005.
11 Strictly speaking, this means that Simondon must elaborate an ontogenesis theory based on new concepts that are themselves the result of the individuation of Simondon's thought based on his reflection on what his study of the notion of individuation allows him to discover.

foundation of knowledge which should remain the same in order to guarantee the necessity of knowledge. More precisely, this is necessary in a Kantian perspective, but Simondon seems to adopt this perspective since he defends the idea that the validity of knowledge presupposes the identification of a universal subjective foundation, i.e. the *a priori* structure of a "transcendental subject".[12] But the theory of individuation seems to be contradictory with the search for such a foundation. We want to question this apparent contradiction by examining the ontogenesis theory of the knowing subject developed by Simondon. From the point of view of ontogenesis, the subject is never adequate to itself, and we will show that it is for this reason it cannot truly know individuation, and consequently Simondon (insofar as he is a subject too) cannot complete the axiomatisation of ontogenesis. The subject can grasp individuation because he is individuating too but, for the same reason, some parts of individuation necessarily escapes it. Our aim will be to make this limitation of the knowing subject explicit by emphasising the ontogenetic "finitude" of the subject that Simondon thematises. In this way we can understand the function he attributes to philosophical thought: "perpetually marginal".[13]

We will begin by explaining why Simondon wishes to axiomatise the theory of ontogenesis, and then we will show that an ontogenetic conception of the subject allows us to understand why this is impossible. Finally, we will note that such an impossibility determines the meaning of philosophical thought.

2. Ontogenesis theory and axiomatic ontology

First of all, we need to understand why the axiomatisation of the theory of ontogeny is not obvious in Simondon's work. At first glance, wanting to produce an ontology that consists in formalising a discourse on being in a coherent set of axioms does not seem specifically problematic. Simondon would not be the first to do so. However, from the point of view of the question of individuation, that becomes a problem. That is the reason why he clearly distinguishes ontogenesis theory and ontology.

Indeed, the contribution of the question of individuation consists of leaving a structural conception of being. Being is not reducible to what is individuated, and being is not only individuals as results of individuation. From the theory of ontogenesis' point of view, it is a question of affirming that, in reality, being consists primarily of individuation operations, i.e. what makes individuals individuate. On the other hand, it is not a question of going back to the principle of

---

12 ILNFI, p. 293/ILFI, p. 258.
13 *Ibid.*, p. 256/p. 228.

all individuation, because such a principle would itself be external to individuation. Simondon's idea is to remain with the immanence of individuation:

> We would like to show that it is necessary to reverse the search for the principle of individuation by considering the operation of individuation as primordial, on the basis of which the individual comes to exist and the unfolding regimes and modalities of which the individual reflects in its characteristics.[14]

The challenge of the ontogenesis theory is therefore neither to analyse the structure of being by establishing a list of categories, nor to identify the principle that precedes and commands individuation, but to formalise a theory of the operations of individuation. Thus, the ontogenesis theory sets itself the task of analysing the different modalities of individuation (physical, living being, psychical and collective) and the phases of being (pre-individual, individuated, transindividual).

The ontogenesis theory is thus a discourse on being insofar as there is individuation, i.e. "through which the being becomes insofar as it is, qua being".[15] In this way, Simondon does seek to know being, but from individuation theory's point of view, this involves newly questioning what is called "being". It also involves a new questioning of what is called "knowing". This is why Simondon's ontogenetic questioning presupposes that the reflection is situated beforehand of ontology, i.e. without presupposing either the meaning nor the possibility of an adequation between being and knowing.

> According to this perspective, ontogenesis would become the starting point for philosophical thought; it would really be first philosophy, anterior to the theory of knowledge and to an ontology that would follow this theory.[16]

This is why Simondon carefully avoid saying that the ontogenesis theory is about knowing being, but rather about "following" or "grasping"[17] individuation.

However, the purpose of this "grasping" is to produce adequate new concepts to an ontogenetic understanding of individuals. And these new concepts are interesting because they allow us to develop new axiomatics. For example, Simondon insists on the concept of field, whose ontogenetic meaning he grasps by following its individuation in physical sciences, in Maxwell, then in psychology (*Gestalttheorie*), sociology and finally cybernetics. He defends the idea that the field concept makes it possible to unify the human sciences into a single ax-

---

14 *Ibid.*, p. 3/p. 24.
15 *Ibid*, p. 4/p. 25.
16 *Ibid.*, p. 319/p. 278.
17 "Beings can be known through the knowledge of the subject, but the individuation of beings can only be grasped through the individuation of the subject's knowledge", *Ibid.*, p. 17/p. 36.

iomatic, revealing the continuity of the psychosocial domain, in accordance with the unity of psychological and collective individuation.[18] But more broadly, some concepts cross all the modalities of individuation and thus seem to belong to the universal domain of ontogenesis. These transversal concepts are therefore not relative to a specific field of object, to a particular science, but they are the concepts that structure the ontogenesis theory that Simondon seeks to establish. We must therefore distinguish between scientific concepts, relative to a specific individuation domain, and ontogenetic concepts whose domain of validity is ontogenesis itself, i.e. the domain of being totalising all the modalities of individuation. Then, why is the ontogenetic domain not scientific?

Scientific concepts are knowledge insofar as their meaning is stable. So, these concepts must be individuated in the same way in the minds of scientists and must serve as a structure of thought for the development of new knowledge. Therefore, ontogenesis concepts could be knowledge if it were possible for the discourse on being to also meet a criterion of stability.[19] It is on this point that Simondon seems to have some doubts. We can hypothesise that, on the one hand, ontology can be formalised to the point of consisting of an axiomatic, i.e. a coherent conceptual structure from which all the concepts of a philosophical system can be deduced. But, on the other hand, there is a major difference between the structuring of scientific discourse and the structuring of philosophical discourse because the conceptual structure of a philosophy is usually the product of a single philosopher. However, Simondon notices there are intelligibility schemes that cross philosophical systems, and thus determines a common individuation foundation: he highlights this point with the notion of hylomorphism. But, the hylomorphic scheme is an *a posteriori* construction produced by Simondon, and not an explicitly structuring concept of ontological discourse in general. This scheme allows us to identify a certain stability in the discourse on being, but it would be an exaggeration to say that there is an axiomatic of hylomorphism shared by philosophers, as there was, for example, an axiomatic of Newtonian physics. Philosophy thus has a different status than sciences, even if it is possible that certain concepts cross different philosophical systems (more or less implicitly structuring philosophical discourse in general). In short, for Simondon, ontogenesis theory may have the ambition to develop a new scheme of intelligibility to replace hylomorphism, but this possibility is not comparable to the structuring of scientific knowledge. This is the reason why Simondon remains cautious and he does not set out ontogenesis theory as if this were a knowledge of being understood as a primary science.

---

18   See: Xavier Guchet, "Merleau-Ponty, Simondon et le problème d'une "axiomatique des sciences humaines". L'exemple de l'histoire et de la sociologie", in *Chiasmi International* 3, 2001, pp. 103–127.
19   ILNFI, pp. 76–77/ILFI, p. 84.

Nevertheless, we insist on the ambivalence of Simondon's position: on the one hand, it is clear that the ontogenesis theory does not aim to produce a scientific knowledge; on the other hand, the ambition of this theory is to replace hylomorphism by producing concepts of universal value, i.e. concepts whose individuation would have no limit and thus, from one to the other, would make it possible to establish a continuity between the different domains of individuation. In accordance with this, the concepts from ontogenesis theory are not knowledge, "in the usual sense of the term" as Simondon states, but it would be an exaggeration to say that they are not knowledge at all. Let us not forget that allagmatic theory has a universalist ambition: the ambition to build a new universal domain thanks in particular to the concept of transduction. Transduction is both an epistemological concept that allows us to grasp the way in which new domains of continuity have been established in sciences,[20] and a gnoseological concept that allows us to think *de jure* of a universal domain of continuity, discovered by transductive thought as a method based on analogy.

At first, the universal value of transduction is based on an epistemological postulate,[21] but it is as ontogenetic concepts individuate by transduction from one domain to another that the concept of transduction acquires its stability and thus its universal value. In this sense, the individuation of the concept involves a constructivism that Simondon claims.[22] In short, in the first stage, ontogenesis theory understood as a theory of individuation has an exploratory function, it is a question of following the individuation of knowledge in the different scientific domains in order to identify the new concepts corresponding to new representations of the reality of the individuation modalities. In the second stage there is a reflexive phase; it is a matter of recapturing these concepts from a philosophical point of view and, thanks to the analogical method, of transferring them from one field to another in order to see if they correspond to a new field of continuity. In this way, philosophical thought can seek to construct a domain of universal continuity in which new concepts, but also new methods, can investigate the totality of reality and thus reform philosophical thought in order to establish a new axiomatic for its fundamental problem, which is to think being in its becoming.

---

20 See for example the analysis of the "domain of transductivity [...] of electromagnetic waves", ILNFI, p. 120/ILFI, p. 118.
21 "*The epistemological postulate of this study is that the relation between two relations is itself a relation.*", Ibid., p. 76/p. 83.
22 Simondon explains this aspect of his method at the end of "Analysis of the Criteria of Individuality" (published in the supplements to *Individuation*). This text was supposed to introduce the book, but Simondon abandoned it because, in this first draft of his reflection, he had not yet reached the radicality of the questioning of individuation. This is why the way he writes seems less cautious.

In sum, for Simondon, philosophical thought consists of constructing new conceptual structures that allow individuation to be grasped: "philosophy intervenes as a power of structuration, as a capacity for the invention of the structures that resolve problems of coming-into-being".[23] This "grasping" is not scientific knowledge because what matters is less stability of the concepts in the community of philosophers than the universality of the domain of individuation that their transduction allows to think. However, this conceptual structure, which makes it possible to think about individuation in general, does involve the ambition of an axiomatisation of ontogenesis. In this case, why does Simondon remain cautious? Why does he assert that: "[i]t may be that ontogenesis is not axiomatizable"? We understood that the questioning of individuation, that Simondon develops, presupposes a precaution: before seeking to know being (ontology), we must ask ourselves what is the relation between being and knowing from individuation's point of view. This precaution means that we must first reflect concepts that allow us to grasp physical and living being's individuations, in order to transfer these concepts to psychic and collective individuations, to think about the individuation of knowledge in the subject. Indeed, strictly speaking, there must be a continuity between the different modalities of individuation. So, concepts through which we grasp the individuation of physical beings must also allow us to grasp the individuation of psychic and collective beings and thus to develop ontogenesis theory of the subject. In this way, it should be possible to examine the co-individuation relation between things and subjects, between what is to be known and the knowing subject. Our hypothesis is that it is in the ontogenesis theory of the knowing subject that we find the reason of the gnoseological precautions shown by Simondon. He discovers the knowing subject finitude by questioning the nature of this knowing subject from the individuation point of view. We will show that this finitude is the reason why the subject cannot claim to know being, and why the subject can only follow its individuation.

3. Ontogenesis theory of the knowing subject

Before understanding how Simondon defines the subject's finitude, we need to outline his knowing subject theory. Simondon locates the *de jure* foundation of the universality of knowledge in subject's psychic structure, what he calls the "individuated being" of the subject, which he identifies as a "transcendental subject".[24] A subject must be something absolutely fixed in order to remain the same and to be able to reflect the structure that it is. Simondon does not explicitly state this, but the concepts he uses to think about the legal necessity of knowl-

---

23 ILNFI, p. 244/ILFI, p. 323.
24 *Ibid.*, p. 293/p. 258.

edge possibility refer to the Kantian theory of knowledge and the idea of subject's apperception. Now, the theory of individuation requires to think at the same time about the transcendental structure of the knowing subject (the individuated being of the subject which is "conditions of possibility of knowledge") and that knowing involves to continue to individuate itself (the "individualization" of the subject). Simondon develops a theory of the "complete subject",[25] in order to think the articulation between these different levels of the subject. The knowledge possibility is no longer to be considered only from the subject as a result of individuation, but also as a way for the subject to continue individuating itself as a knowing subject. The subject is thus both an *a priori* structure ("a milieu of *a prioris*") and what individuates itself. We will show that the tension between these two aspects of the subject brings into crisis the subject's apperceptive unity, and this is the reason why Simondon thinks it is not certain that the subject may know itself. We assume that this finitude of the subject's reflexivity explains the impossibility of axiomatising ontogenesis.

Firstly, in decisive pages about psychical individuation Simondon sets up the foundation of the theory that he will later call the "complete subject".[26] This foundation consists of thinking the very subject reality as a relation between two modalities of individuation: living being individuation and psychical and collective individuation. Regarding the knowing subject, this means that knowing must be understood from the fact that there is a life of the subject that evolves from the biological reality of the relationship to the environment through which the conditions of its existence are structured, to the social reality which conditions its insertion in the world. The subject's activity is caught between these two conditions: the fixed structure of its biological existence which conditions its *de jure* possibility of experience (the subject's individuated being) and the structure of the social world which conditions its *de facto* possibilities of realising experiences (the individualisation of the subject).

However, the articulation of these two levels between which the subject individuates itself is not so easy to analyse. The (empirical) subject makes experiences which are not simply actualisations of what he can do according to the structure of its individuated being (transcendental). Simondon insists on that point. In some particular experiences, the subject feels its own structure as a problem, it feels "phase-shifted", this experience is "overflowing", so that its own existence may appear as impossible, incompatible with what it is as a living being. This is the reason why, while continuing to individuate psychically and collectively, the subject discovers within itself a tension between what it is and what it becomes. This tension is not an accidental difficulty that would be resolved in the normal course of existence, but rather a tension that fundamentally charac-

---

25   *Ibid.*, p. 348/p. 310.
26   *Ibid.*, pp. 257–260/pp. 192–194.

terises the subject as a problem: "the transcendental subject is that through which there is a problem".[27] The subject is this individual who is aware that it is more than what it recognises itself to be when it reflects on itself. It feels its psychical and collective life overflows its biological life. Now, this subject's overflowing has gnoseological consequences.

Secondly, Simondon insists on this idea: knowledge is individuation of knowledge, i.e. operation, and from this point of view, it is necessary to understand why the subject seeks to know, before critically analysing limits of its power of knowledge. The subject's overflow explains why it seeks to know. Indeed, Simondon's answer seems to start from an observation: everything happens as if the subject (unlike an individual which was simply a living being), was looking for itself. But why does the subject seek to know itself? This search does not correspond to a vital need, its problem is no longer to explore the world in order to find the means to live, but nor does it correspond to a metaphysical need that would be inscribed in the nature of human reason. Rather, the subject discovers the meaning of the world for its existence to make sense. Simondon discovers that the experiences of the subject can lead it to be more than it is. Indeed, having experiences is not only to actualise possibilities of being but also to invent new ones. The subject then understands it is not identical to itself, its relations to the world participate in what it is.[28] This is the reason why the subject experiences itself as a problematic being: when it reflects on itself it does not discover the synthetic unity of a being whose possible experiences are adequate to the structural conditions of what it can be, but it discovers a problematic difference between the structure that conditions its individualisation (the transcendental schemes of its mind) and what it actually becomes (its empirical characteristic). The subject is phase-shifted with itself. This phase-shift, this internal difference, is not secondary but already given because it is the principle of its reflexivity: the subject reflects itself because its being is problematic.[29]

---

27   Ibid., p. 293/p. 265.
28   From the individuation point of view, the definition of the individual explains this definition of the complete subject: "the individual is not considered identical to the being; the being is richer, more durable, and larger than the individual: the individual *is individual of the being, individual taken out of the being, not the primordial and elementary constituent of the being*; it is a manner of the being, or rather a moment of the being", Ibid., p. 361/p. 310.
29   The subject is called into question for two different reasons. 1) This kind of self-questioning comes from the outside, that starts from sensation, that is to say from the objective orientation given by the environment: "the problematic that exists on the level of sensation is a problematic of orientation according to an axis that is already given". Therefore "there is a manner in which the being is called into question by the world that is anterior to any consistency of the object", Ibid., p. 286–287/p. 258. 2) A self-questioning which comes from within: it is the subject's affectivity, the subject's relationship with itself, that is at stake. It is no longer a question of orienting oneself in space, but in becoming. The problem is no longer knowing where to go,

Thus, the transcendental subject as a problem does consist of a dynamic: the empirical subject becoming aware of its psychical existence. This dynamic shatters the subject's apperception. Indeed, the phase-shifting is primary. In the order of the individuation's level, the subject appears when it individuates psychically, that is to say when it begins to live in relation to a world of meanings constructed by others and itself. But, in a sense, it is already too late, it has already begun to construct itself in excess of what it is and can no longer find itself in what it does. Its subject is doomed to live itself psychically, and therefore to know itself as a problematic being. The world invites it, at every moment, to exist beyond its condition, to become what no one has ever been, to give new meaning to the fact of living, as it risks, by existing beyond what it can live, to reach such a degree of incompatibility that it would die. In short, Simondon's theory of individuation develops a new explanation for the desire to know: the subject seeks to know because it is never itself. By seeking to know itself, the subject discovers a structure, what it is, an individual, but this structure is problematic because overwhelmed by the world through which the subject becomes other than what this structure determined it to be: "the subject is individual and other than individual; it is incompatible with itself".[30] And the more the subject explores the world, the more it digs into the internal difference of the selfness. Existence is a forever unsolved problem, which means that the life we lead is merely the endless construction of a solution to an unsolvable problem: Simondon writes that the subject is a "self-constitutive dynamism" "that constructs itself and conditions itself", that poses "a problematic without a solution [...] given in experience".[31]

Therefore, the subject is problematic because what it does overflows what it is. This problematic characteristic means that the subject's apperception is just substantialism abstraction; in reality, it is impossible, it cannot know the synthetic unity of its being, nevertheless it can grasp this problematic tension between what it is and what it can become. In this sense, Simondon's contribution is to consider this problematic characteristic of the subject not as a difficulty to be solved, but as a reality to be thematised. Despite the "anxiety",[32] the point is

---

the solution is no longer exploration, but knowing what to become, how to be in the future: "this being is polarized in accordance with the world on the one hand in accordance with becoming on the other", *Ibid.*, p. 289/p. 260.

30   *Ibid.*, p. 280/p. 248.
31   *Ibid.*, pp. 309–310/pp. 270–271.
32   " [I]n anxiety, the subject feels as if it exists as a problem posed to itself, and it feels its division into pre-individual nature and individuated being; the individuated being is *here and now*, and this *here and now* prevent an infinity of other *here and nows* from coming into existence: the subject becomes conscious of itself as nature, as undetermined (ἄπειρον) [apeiron], and as something it will never be able to actualize into a *here and now*, that it will never be able to live", *Ibid.*, pp. 282–283/pp. 250.

to admit internal difference of the individual, rather than trying to think about its resolution. This difference is problematic, but this problematic is the complete subject as a relation between two phases of being: individuated being (structure) and individuating being (operation). The ontogenetic theory's stake is to reflect on its problematic in order to construct a new understanding of the subject in the continuity of the conceptual structure that the study of physical and vital individuations has begun to establish.

The stake of the subject's self-reflexivity is no longer to find in the subject a fundamental synthetic unity in order to solve the problem of apperceptive identity, but to grasp this gap, this internal difference of the subject as a problematic that characterises the dynamics of its activity.[33] This point seems crucial to us because it designates the transformation that Simondon makes in relation to the Kantian subject or, more broadly, to the paradigm of the *cogito*, i.e. of a subject defined as identical to itself. This transformation does not invalidate the legal foundation of knowledge because the subject remains, partly, an individuated being, the given result of a vital individuation. But this is only one aspect of the subject: the individual subject is only a *"moment of the being"*[34] of the complete subject. In other words, the subject can know itself only when it seeks a fixed structure, an eternal form. In this sense, a structural conception of the subject allows to think of a continuity between the knowledge produced by the sciences of structures and philosophical reflection. But, by focusing on the recent appearance of certain sciences of operations, Simondon highlights a discontinuity with the state of philosophical reflections and the need for a reform of the subject theory.[35] Now, by completing the subject theory through taking into consideration the operations of individuation that characterise it, the subject appears problematic, i.e. as a structure that is perpetually phase-shifted. Therefore, the point is to understand that our psychosocial life leads us to experiences that go beyond what we are. The subject's life is worth living insofar as it individuates

---

[33] J.-H. Barthélémy emphasises this point in his reading of Simondon. He shows his originality (in relation to Kant and Husserl) is to succeed, thanks to the concept of phase-shifting, in thinking the subject's temporal being not as a subjective form, but as a dimension of an individuation that is not centrally subjective: the subject being caught in the temporality of the individuation of being. Therefore, J.-H. Barthélémy develops the notion of "décentrement" to explains the Simondonian subject concept and he concludes to a new philosophical position, which he calls "Philosophical Relativity", Barthélémy, *op. cit.*, p. 46.

[34] *Ibid.*, p. 360/p. 310.

[35] This delay of the philosophy of the subject appears clearly at the end of the "History of the Notion of the Individual", *Ibid.*, p. 650 f./p. 499 f. Simondon shows how in the German Romantics (in particular Fichte, Schelling and Hölderlin) the concepts of field and recursivity are already transforming what philosophy in general has still not taken into account.

itself beyond any resolution, in the direction of a perpetual individuation.[36] In other words, the solution must not be a resolution, but an overflowing towards another problematic.

The subject's overflowing must therefore be understood as a possibility of overcoming. For Simondon, the subject's existence consists in overcoming the problematic that it is by constructing itself, as a "personality", beyond (and through) the internal difference that undermines it. It is not a matter of cancelling this difference because, for Simondon, the overcoming is not dialectical in the sense of Hegel. The difference persists as an internal tension of the subject, but the subject maintains itself in spite of this difference by overcoming (in a specific sense) the tension through the structuring of its problematic being. Indeed, the subject's own characteristic is to be able to overcome the problematic of its being by considering it not as the end of a unity but on the contrary as what constitutes it structurally. In sum, the subject has experiences that reveal the problematicity of its being, but these experiences at the same time overflow it and structure itself as personality, i.e. as a singular individual: "The individualised being tends toward singularity and incorporates the accidental as singularity".[37] In other words, the problematicity of the individuated being must be understood according to an internal dynamism of overcoming which means that subject's crises are some moments of refoundation.

> The individual problematic is beyond the relationship between the being and its environment; this problematic requires solutions by overcoming, not by reducing a gap between a result and a goal. The individual problematic must only be solved by constructions, by increasing information according to a divergent determinism [...] the individual is a being in which the accomplishment of the operation reacts on the axiomatic, by intense crises which are a refounding of the being.[38]

---

36   Simondon's subject theory is also an ethical theory because he considers the question of knowledge should not be parted from action, and therefore an "axiontology" should be developed. From this point of view "ethics is that through which the subject remains subject [...] Ethics expresses the meaning of perpetuated individuation", *Ibid.*, p. 380/p. 335.
37   *Ibid.*, p. 294/p. 258.
38   "Note complémentaire sur les conséquences de la notion d'individuation", in ILFI, p. 346 (our translation). In this passage, Simondon distinguishes the living being from the machine. The characteristic of the living being lies in the effect of its operations on the structure. This exchange (between operation and structure) is central to the allagmatic theory. In METO, Simondon takes up this distinction by emphasising the "plasticity" of memory in the living being and he summarises his thought in one sentence: "the *a posteriori* becomes *a priori*", METO, p. 138/MEOT, p. 172. This point has often been commented on (see: Baptiste Morizot, *Pour une théorie de la rencontre. Hasard et individuation chez Gilbert Simondon*, Paris, Vrin, 2016, p. 130; and Yuk Hui, *Recursivity and Contingency*, London, Rowman & Littlefield, 2019, p. 194). These readings are right to emphasise the originality of this plastic conception of the *a priori*, but tend to apply this definition of the living being to the subject. Of course, Simondon

In other words, the subject constructs itself by determining its problematic's structure. We also understand this structuring is a "refoundation of being", i.e. a new way of determining who the subject is as a psychical and social person. This point is important because Simondon indicates it corresponds to the axiomatics of the subject. So, the subject's axiomatisation means that by reflecting itself the subject is not condemned to be collapsed into the anxiety of being problematic, but it can "incorporate" what overflows it. This "incorporation" means that these overflowing experiences are then no longer understood as accidental, contingent, but constitutive of what it is insofar as it is also in relation with the world, i.e. living with others in a given situation. Thus, axiomatisation is the result of the subject's reflection on this operation of incorporation: the awareness of the structure of the problematic that characterises its existence.

However, it would be too quick to conclude the subject constructs or transforms its axiomatics itself, because that would be to give too much power to reflection. However, the subject's axiomatic is not given *a priori*, it is not discovering what it already is.[39] In order to understand why Simondon asserts more generally that ontogenesis is not axiomatisable, we have to go into detail about the status he gives to the axiomatisation operation. The difficulty is that axiomatics has both an ontological reality (the structure that conditions the individual being's possibilities) and a gnoseological validity (the concepts through which it is possible to represent the individual being). Simondon's constructivism does not consist in confusing these two aspects, the reflection is not autopoietic, but it is nevertheless necessary to think their articulation. This is the reason why Simondon distinguishes between implicit axiomatics (present in being) and reflected axiomatics (knowledge of being).

> Thought comprises clear, separate structures, such as representations, images, certain memories, and certain perceptions. All these elements, however, participate in a ground that gives them a direction, a homeostatic unity, and which acts as a vehicle for informed

---

moves away from the anthropological cut between animal and man, nevertheless we think the subject is not reducible to a living being insofar as it is a knowing subject. There is a transcendental moment of the living subject that implies thinking about the fixity of the *a priori*, without which its axiomatics would be too plastic and could not be considered as a foundation of knowledge. In this sense, our reading of the Simondonian concept of the *a priori* takes the opposite view to that proposed by J.-H. Barthélémy, who sees in it an exit from Kantian fixity (Barthélémy, *op. cit.*, p. 52 f.).

39 In some texts, Simondon states axiomatics is "discovery", but we understand that this discovery is at the same time a process of incorporation, in other words that this discovery is not a simple revelation, it is also what brings about a structuring: "The individuation that is life is conceived as the discovery in a conflictual situation of a new axiomatic that incorporates and unifies all the elements of this situation into a system that contains the individual", ILNFI, p. 10/ILFI, p. 30.

energy from one to the other and among all of them. One could say that the ground is the implicit axiomatic; in it new systems of forms are elaborated. Without the ground of thought, there would be no thinking being, but rather an unrelated series of discontinuous representations. This ground is the mental milieu associated with the forms.[40]

We understand that the axiomatic is already implicitly in the matter of thought, i.e. in the pre-individual reality of the subject's complete being. The pre-individual is never absolutely indeterminate because in reality it is always relative to the individuation of a structure. Therefore, an individual cannot structure itself into everything. The experiences of the subject overflow it and so transform it, but these transformations are not absolutely free, they are conditioned by what these experiences newly give to know. In other words, the subject's pre-individual reality already forms a system with what the subject does not yet know. Hence the overflowing experiences, through which he will newly know, are oriented: "this implicit axiomatic is constituted by the relation that exists between the reality to be known and the knowing subject, i.e., by the primary status of the reality to be known".[41]

The concept of "implicit axiomatics" helps us to understand that the solution is actually already in the subject who discovers itself as a problematic being. This solution is not a resolution of its problematic being, which will persist, but is its overcoming towards a new structuring of this problem.[42] In other words, from a gnoseological point of view, the transcendental subject always remains a moment of the subject's being. But this must be understood by distinguishing between the subject's problematic and its axiomatisation. The transcendental subject is this kind of structure which appears problematic for the subject itself, because the subject is aware that its experiences are overflowing that which it is. Whereas axiomatics is the determination of this structure that the knowing subject wishes to establish in order to elucidate the universal subjective foundation of knowledge. So, self-knowledge as a problem consists in the elucidation of a

---

40   METO, p. 62/MEOT, p. 74.
41   METO, p. 240/MEOT, p. 318.
42   We can specify that the subject is double: on the one hand it is the problem, on the other hand, through its reflective activity, it carries the solution. Reflection makes it possible to elucidate the problem's structure, but Simondon adds that this elucidation is at the same time a determination of this problem. By reflecting itself, the subject determines itself as a particular problem. "[T]he individual exists the moment that a reflexive becoming-conscious of the posed problems has allowed the particular being to introduce its idiosyncrasy and its activity (including that of its thought) into the solution; the proper characteristic of the solution on the level of the individual resides in the fact that the individual plays a double role, on the one hand as an element of the data and on the other hand as an element of the solution; the individual intervenes twice in its problematic, and it is through this double role that it calls itself into question", ILNFI, p. 310/ILFI, p. 271.

new axiomatics. But why cannot the axiomatisation be achieved? Why cannot the subject completely elucidate its structure and thus know itself adequately?

> The individual can live with the problem, but he can only elucidate it by solving it; it is the *supplement of being* discovered and created in the form of action that allows consciousness afterwards to define the terms in which the problem was posed.[43]

We can therefore add that the subject always elucidates the problem afterwards. Then, the axiomatic that the subject discovers in self-reflection is never anything other than what it has been, it is only the past problem on account of which it has reflected. Axiomatisation is always axiomatisation of a past problem. By axiomatising it, the subject constructs a theory of the conditions of possibility of his new existence, but he also participates in the production of meanings for a new world. This new world is the source of new experiences that already problematise the structure that the axiomatisation discovers.[44] In this sense, axiomatisation always lags behind individuation.

4. Ontogenetic finitude of the philosophising subject

Axiomatisation is an act of the knowing subject, but axiomatics also refer to reality, a structure's reality. The difficulty of Simondon's reflection lies in this ambivalence of the status of axiomatics: epistemic and ontological. We have seen that his constructivist position clarifies the meaning of axiomatics as part of the

---

[43] "Note complémentaire sur les conséquences de la notion d'individuation", ILFI, p. 334 (our translation).
[44] Simondon's developments on technique clarify this idea: the world is renewed for the subject. In reality it is not the world that is the source of renewal but the relation between the subject and the world, i.e. the technique. This is the reason why, at the bottom (but we will not develop this point here), it should be said that it is the evolution of technical systems that characterises the problematisation's dynamic: "We can therefore be assumed that the most fundamental relationship in which a human group is engaged is the source of the basic problematic by which the philosophical thought of every age and every society has conceived individual reality. [...] it is in the most constant way relation to the world as humanity lives integrated in a world. Technique in its deepest and most universal sense is this relation; *technè* signifies means and technique is the set of all mediations through which this relation is established. We can therefore posit that the state of technology is the source of the relationship grasped by the various philosophies as the foundation of the individual problematic", "Introduction" (1955), SLΦ, p. 24 (our translation). In another text, Simondon states the link between technique and thought's transformation: "Through the intermediary of allagmatics, and even cybernetics as it exists today, it seems that new patterns are being developed in the relationship between the machine and man, and that man's thinking is being transformed as a result.", "L'objet technique comme paradigm d'intelligibilité universelle" (1956), SLΦ, p. 420 (our translation).

theory of the subject: axiomatisation is a determination of the problem's structure that the subject is, it is the overcoming of the problem towards another structuring of the conditions of possibility of experience and of thought in general. So, there is a circularity between the problematic and the axiomatic, i.e. between the fact that a subject remains problematic to itself and the fact that it seeks to make the axiomatics of this problem explicit. The subject can reflect on itself in order to make explicit the axiomatics of its being (and of being in general), but Simondon retains a distinction between being and knowing: the subject can axiomatise being, but it is not certain that being, understood ontogenetically, is totally axiomatisable. Indeed, Simondon's theory of ontogenesis is based on an idea that is difficult to grasp because it is circular: 1) being is on the one hand a problematic whose structure the subject can reflect upon and make explicit, and on the other hand 2) being is that which overflows the *a priori* conditions of the knowing subject and consequently renders it problematic to itself; furthermore 3) it is because of its problematic being that the subject reflects on itself and desires to know. Simondon explains this circularity between the problematic and the axiomatic: the subject is always behind the problem it seeks to axiomatise because it is behind itself. This is the reason why the subject can only know itself afterward and therefore inadequately. But why should this impossible self-knowledge involve the impossibility of an axiomatisation of ontogenesis in general? It is this point that remains to be clarified.

In both cases (axiomatising ontogenesis in general or axiomatising one's own problematic being) the subject must reflect on the individuation of the being that it grasps analogically, i.e. on the individuation of its own thought. In a Bergsonian perspective, it is within oneself that the subject finds the outside of being. And what he finds is an overflow of itself: the pre-individual. Indeed, we have understood that being overflows the subject and this is why the subject on the one hand seeks to reflect it (to contain it, to incorporate it) and on the other hand seeks to know it insofar as it is such an overflow, i.e. from an ontogenesis point of view, as being in becoming. But it seems that this overflowing of being is both what invites the subject to know ontogenesis (to elucidate the axiomatics of the problem that is this overflowing) and what prevents it from knowing it (because of this overflowing the subject can only ever reflect itself afterward). So, it seems it is for the same reason that axiomatics appears and that ontogeny cannot be axiomatised. In a sense, the condition of possibility of knowledge is at the same time a condition of impossibility. Simondon identifies the ambivalence of this *a priori* condition of knowledge with the finitude of the subject.[45] It is therefore by deepening our understanding of the ontogenetic finitude of the sub-

---

45 "[T]he axiomatic of every human problem can only appear to the extent that the individual exists, i.e. establishes a finitude within itself that confers a recurrent circularity onto the problem of which it becomes conscious", ILNFI, p. 310/ILFI, p. 271.

ject that we will be able to understand: 1) why the subject can reach being by reflecting itself; 2) the reason why ontogenesis cannot be axiomatised.

Firstly, the subject must reflect itself in order to grasp within itself the movement of individuation in which it participates, but in reflecting itself he overflows itself. This finitude of reflection is both what limits its possible knowledge and what allows it to discover the problematic of being, i.e. being is what overflows its own structure. Thus, ambivalence is inscribed in the structure of the act of reflection.[46] But, more specifically, Simondon situates the ultimate reason for this double structure of possibility/impossibility of knowledge in the subject's existence.

> If the individual were posited as eternal, none of the problems that appear to it could receive a solution, because the problem could never be dissociated from the subjectivity that the individual confers on it by figuring among the data and elements of the solution; the problem must be able to be freed from its inherence to individuality, and this requires that the individual only intervene provisionally in the question that it poses.[47]

The subject is finite, in the sense that it is going to die, that is the reason why problems appear to it. "[I]t is only what dies that is alive"[48] said Jankélévitch, this means in particular that there is a life of thought in the subject because the subject knows itself to be alive, and it knows itself to be alive because it knows that it is going to die.[49] Here Simondon interprets this thanatological character

---

[46] In another text, Simondon explains that the condition of reflection is twofold: subjective insofar as this incompleteness involves "internal tensions of the reflecting subject" ("Introduction" (1955), SLΦ, p. 22 (our translations)), and objective insofar as reflection is related to an "original reflexive field" (*ibid.*, p. 21). In this way, Simondon reforms the notion of reflection: reflection at the intersection of these two conditions, a double problematic, objective and subjective. Reflection is both an introspective act, the subject's return on itself to stabilise its own structure, and an act that passes through the exterior and brings with it the causes of its overflow, its destabilisation. The reflecting subject is both upstream and downstream of its own stability, in prey to the metastable nature of its being, which it soothes and stimulates, reasons and anguishes: "neither *a priori* nor *a posteriori*, but *a praesenti*; it [reflexive thinking] returns on itself in such a way as to be at once prior and posterior to itself" (*ibid.*, p. 20). Reflection, as an act, is thus this individuating relation at the active centre of individuation of complete subject, where the movements of problematisation and resolution constitutive of the phases of its being intersect: "reflection is a particular case of a relation between a problematic and the different operations by which it can be resolved thanks to the presence of an already constituted but still incompletely balanced subject" (*ibid.*, p. 23).
[47] ILNFI, p. 310/ILFI, p. 271.
[48] Vladimir Jankélévitch, *La mort*, Paris, Flammarion, 2017, p. 666.
[49] Ludovic Duhem comments on this passage and summarises: "The criterion of individuality is thus the living being insofar as it dies" (Ludovic Duhem, "L'idée d' "individu pur" dans la pensée de Simondon", in *Appareil* 2, 2008, http://journals.openedition.org/appareil/583

of the life of thought to explain the existential reason for the finitude of knowledge. The existence of the subject is the resolution of the problem of being, but this resolution just a "moment" of the being. The subject structures itself and by reflecting itself axiomatises its being, but this does not involve the resolution of the problem of being in general. For the problem of existence is its own, but we have seen that the solutions he can bring to it by existing, by constructing itself as a person, they do not cancel the problem.

So, secondly, it is this persistence of the problem of being that reveals to the subject that it is a problem beyond him. The problem of the individual is not only psychological or existential, it is ontological.

> [T]he individual exists to the extent that it poses and resolves a problem, but the problem only exists to the extent that it forces the individual to recognize its temporally and spatially limited nature.[50]

By reflecting on itself, the subject discovers a problem greater than itself and thus recognises its own finitude. From the gnoseological point of view, this makes it possible to understand that it is because of its finitude, i.e. because the subject is limited to its empirical individuality, that the subject can grasp the gap between what he can become and individuation in general, i.e. the potentiality of being. In this sense, the subject can construct its own structures, but the subject's life is a testimony of a permanent individuation problem that goes beyond it. The subject can grasp this problem which exceeds him, but what it constructs to grasp it will necessarily be a "moment", commensurate with its individuality, and therefore incomplete.

Simondon defines philosophical thought by this subject's reflection on itself who discovers a problem that exceeds its own individuality. In a sense, the individual is a solution to the ontogenesis problem, but this problem is the finitude of the individual, as "death is both the means of living and the impediment to living".[51] This is what explains why, from a gnoseological point of view, Simondon doubts that ontogenesis is axiomatisable: it is a problem that goes beyond the individual. Philosophy is the name of the thought that poses and seeks to deal with such a problem. In this sense, philosophy is clearly distinct from science. The objects of science appear axiomatisable because they are given *a priori* as objects, i.e. as individuals to be known. New individuals may appear (we have given the electromagnetic field example), but the region of being (e.g. the physical individual) remains the same, as if it were a structure of being itself. Philosophical thought questions the individual in its universality, and therefore

---

(30.07.2020), §20 (our translation). He also notices the importance of the reference to Jankélévitch.

50   ILNFI, p. 310/p. 271.
51   Jankélévitch, *op. cit.*, p. 666.

without an *a priori* region. Of course, Simondon inherits a thought's structure,[52] which gives him an order of analysis, but his aim is to identify the continuity which, in the end, concerns not the genesis of such and such a type of individual, but the universality of ontogenesis.

> It could be that ontogenesis is not able to be axiomatized, which would explain the existence of philosophical thought as perpetually marginal with respect to all other studies, since philosophical thought is what is driven by the implicit or explicit research of ontogenesis in all orders of reality.[53]

Philosophical thought is marginal because what it is interested in is not a particular object. Even if the philosopher gives himself an object, the way he questions it confronts him with the impossibility of guaranteeing its stability. It happens that philosophy believes that it succeeds in obtaining this guarantee, in structuring its representation of being, and this certainly remains its goal. This is the reason why Simondon adds that it is "perpetually" marginal, in the sense that this structuring is only a "moment" of the philosophical thought individuation. The world changes, what a subject is changes, because being changes. Philosophical questioning has to do with change, which is why philosophical thought is aware of its finitude. With the allagmatics theory Simondon believes he has found a way to structure thought on ontogenesis, and his major contribution is certainly to have grasped the importance of the appearance of the sciences of operations to operate this structuring. But we have shown that the ontogenesis theory enables him to carry out a reflection on the subject that reveals its finitude. This ontogenetic finitude of the subject involves a limitation of possible knowledge (the impossibility of a complete axiomatisation of being) and at the same time this finitude is the reason for the possibility of knowledge (the subject seeks to know because it is finite). The philosophical thought's function is to recall this structure of possibility/impossibility that subject's finitude explains. But this time, and we think this is Simondon's bravura piece, allagmatics shifts the relaunch of reflection because it enables us to grasp the circularity of the problematic and the axiomatic.

In other words, Simondon explores new margins of thought and being, he brings to life the thought of being, by proposing a new conception of the articulation between problem and solution, operation and structure. As an individual, the subject has a universal structure, which is why it can know, but it has a universal structure because its ontogenesis proceeds from a universal problem. The subject can reflect this structure and make explicit the axiomatics of this problem, but this elucidation is a particular determination of the problem because it is relative to its structuring as a knowing subject solving the problematic of its

---

[52] See: Maurice Merleau-Ponty, *La structure du comportement*, Paris, PUF, 2013.
[53] ILNFI, p. 256/ILFI, p. 228.

own being. This is the reason why there is perhaps a kind of universal allagmatics structure, but it is only a "moment", the one relative to the Simondon subject, relative to the resolution of the being problem that goes beyond him.⁵⁴

5. Conclusion

We summarise our point by applying to Simondon's theory of knowledge what the ontogenesis theory of finitude has allowed us to understand about the philosophy theory. It is impossible to know individuation because to grasp the operation of a being involves that this operation takes place in the subject's mind, and this risks modifying more or less profoundly the thought schemas through which he can know. In short, "grasping" involves modifying oneself, whereas knowing involves remaining the same, without which the edifice of knowledge would never be stable. The risk of grasping (intuition) is that the subject will drift, will be overflowed by the adventure of the concept. This is the reason why he must, at the same time, take himself again, i.e. reflect on what is happening to him (reflection). But this "at the same time" is impossible: reflection can only take place afterward, after that operation has taken place in him. Intuition and reflection are two operations that are themselves in tension, so that the awareness of the individuation of knowledge in itself always lags behind the individuation of knowledge: when the subject reflects on it, the being of knowledge has already become something else; when Simondon reflects on the current state of scientific knowledge, it has already changed, and by the time the structuring of a new domain of continuity takes place philosophically, i.e. reflexively, a new shift, a new gap from the scientific domain has already opened up.

However, the ontogenesis axiomatisation is not useless. Without this perpetual invention of unified representations of the world, subjects would find themselves overflows, and so unable to make their orientation in the world compatible with the state of the world. Yet, in order to exist, subjects must structure themselves. At the same time, this perpetual delay is the driving force of reflection, which pushes the subject to get hold of itself in order to newly elucidate the problem of its existence in relation to the world in which it has to participate. Therefore, the adventure of philosophical thought must assume to follow this line, in tension between the finalist will to complete the construction of a total

---

54 Andrea Bardin crucially shows that the non-axiomatisable characteristic of ontogenesis involves a persistence of the transcendental problem: "we consider that ontogenesis as theorised by Simondon is the place where the transcendental problematic, eliminated (but not solved) as a problem of the *a priori*, comes back again and again", Andrea Bardin, "Simondon: transcendantal et individuation", in Rametta Gaetano (ed.), *Les métamorphoses du transcendantal. Parcours multiples de Kant à Deleuze*, Hildesheim, Georg Olms Verlag, 2009, pp. 209–210 (our translation).

representation of the world, and the impossibility of anticipating the scientific discoveries from which the objective conditions of reflection will change. Positive science is not the basis of reflection, but its discoveries are the cause of a phase-shifting that destabilises the subject's internal relationship when it reflects on what it teaches it about the world and nature.

In this sense, knowledge individuation is doubly conditioning for the philosophical subject: both a condition of possibility and of impossibility of the philosophical task. On the one hand, by grasping the objectivity of the world insofar as it is scientifically known, and on the other hand by reflecting on the conditions of possibility of scientific objectivity, the philosopher finds himself condemned to this aporia: he must try to recapture what is known within him in order to universalise knowledge, but by such a recapture what he becomes already escapes him. In short, axiomatisation is necessary but its completion is pointless; the adventure of transductive thought is an endless twilight, and reflexive re-grasping is the dawn of a past world. The noon of thought is never more than the midnight of being.

"Un avènement analogue"
Philosophy and "Its" Objects

Sacha Loeve

1. Introduction

> Reflection responds to a need of the object subjected to reflection and brings it a complement of being without which this object would remain incomplete. [...] Reflection, this exceptional treatment of objects, is thus a certain moment of the becoming of the object, but a moment which marks an advent of being, without this advent being able to take place from the outside. An "analogous advent" (*un avènement analogue*), such would be the name given to this activity by which an object is augmented, made more itself than it was before, without this advent of being entailing a corresponding alienation.[1]

This "exceptional treatment of objects" is perhaps what most distinguishes the philosophical attitude of Gilbert Simondon. Not only is such deference to objects rare in philosophy, but philosophy itself, as Simondon practises and conceives it, seems to be characterised by the instauration of a very special relationship to objects.

Simondon has long been touted as a "philosopher of technics", and his "philosophy of technics" as first and foremost a "philosophy of the technical object". However, as we shall see, Simondon denies any "philosophy of". While endorsing the idea that, to some extent, the *technical* object provides Simondon with the paradigm[2] of the object for philosophy, I will argue that the centrality of objects can be given a wider significance in Simondon's philosophy,[3] and, at the end of this chapter, that the technical object's privileged status is due to the fact that it provides above all the paradigm of *analogical thinking* and the condition *sine qua non* of the validity of the analogical method for a diversity of objects.

"Objects" here, are meant intentionally in a broad and indeterminate sense: they may indeed be technical objects, but also scientific, aesthetical, symbolic, socio-economic ones; or they may even be philosophy's own "objects" (philosophical concepts, systems, threads and lineages), so that questioning the rela-

---

1 "Introduction (note sur l'attitude réflexive)" (*c*.1955), in SLΦ, p. 21.
2 In the pre-Kuhnian meaning of typical example or analogical model in which Simondon uses it.
3 In addition to the now "classical" work published during the author's lifetime – mostly his doctoral writings ILNFI and METO – my contribution relies largely on the preparatory writings for the thesis, dating from the early 1950s and published only recently in SLΨ.

tionship of philosophy to "its" objects is inseparable from questioning the nature of philosophy itself. This prior indeterminacy says precisely what is at stake: to understand the relation between the non-philosophical object and the philosophical object, and thus the becoming-philosophical of the object (as well as the becoming *of philosophy* regarding the object).

There is no doubt that philosophy has covered considerable paper addressing the relationship between the subject and the object. However, it has not said much on how objects become objects *for* philosophy or *of* philosophy, in what sense of appropriateness they become "proper" philosophical objects, and how this impinges on the becoming of objects as much as on the ways of doing philosophy. What relationship, then, does philosophy have to its *realia*? Where and when is the object for philosophical thinking? Is it intrinsic or extrinsic to philosophy? And what, then, would be the "in-between", the common *mi-lieu* that both separates and links philosophy and "its" objects?

These questions may seem unusual, weird, if not meaningless. But that's just it: as this contribution will argue, the originality of Simondon's philosophy lies in the fact that it does address these unusual questions and does provide even more unusual answers to them. This is in particular the case of the early – and rather intriguing – statement quoted above, that philosophical reflection "responds to a need of the object", and qualifies as an "advent of being", analogous to the becoming of the object.[4] Therefore, it seems that the question is not only that of the role and the status of the object *for philosophy*; it is also that of the role and the status of philosophy *regarding the object*; and ultimately, to ask what philosophy can and cannot be so that these strange questions become legitimate philosophical problems.

2. Reflexive *versus* speculative philosophy

Objects, first of all, "need" philosophy: they require philosophy to be something more than just an autotelic activity, practised for its own sake.

The first requirement that the objects impose on philosophy is to take an entirely *reflexive interest* in them. Such an interest towards objects provides the touchstone for distinguishing the style of *reflexive philosophy* that Simondon embraces and fully claims,[5] from another one, which, although close in appearance, does clearly not suit the philosophical attitude of Simondon, namely *speculative philosophy*.

The claim for a reflexive philosophy may seem at first sight very classical, but this is because it is usually articulated on the side of the subject, whereas

---

4   Ibid.
5   See "Introduction (Note sur l'attitude réflexive)" (*c.*1955), in SLΦ, pp. 19–25.

Simondon articulates it on the side of the objects. As Frederic Worms rightly notices, Simondon's main works, ILNFI and METO, are thoroughly works of reflexive philosophy although they are centred on specific objects (i.e. the individual and its principle of individuation, technical objects and technicity). According to Worms, this is because "contrary to what one might think, reflexive philosophy is the one that can least speak of itself, since it only makes sense to speak and think in the light of something else, in relation to its objects".[6] To put it simply, philosophy needs objects in order to be reflexive.

This co-implication between reflexivity and the primacy of the object explains many singular if not disconcerting features of Simondon's work: for instance, the beginning of the first part of ILNFI, "Physical Individuation", which opens the critique of hylomorphism as a scheme of (self)understanding of the individual with a dozen pages dedicated to the attentive meditation of the moulding of a brick.[7] More broadly, it makes sense with the choice of "the individual" (traditionally identified with the reflexive subject) as a central philosophical object, insofar as its process of genesis exceeds any principle given before its individuation; the individual's reflexivity will have to be brought by its genesis as an aspect among others, opening to a reflexivity which is "more than individual"[8] (i.e. transindividual). It also sheds light on the link of "the individual" with Simondon's other main terrain of reflection, "technical objects": both give rise to a refusal to posit a speculative principle prior to their genesis *qua realia*.

On the contrary, speculative philosophy would claim to thrive without objects (or at best, with pure and unconditioned ideas of objects). It starts with the inaugural gesture of setting its point of departure beyond the condition of finitude in which particular objects exist and entertain concrete relationships between themselves and ourselves, a "farewell to objects".

It is worth noticing that "reflexive" and "speculative" share the same etymology, which refers to the operation of a particular object: the reflection of the mirror, the *speculum* in Latin. However, this etymological kinship does not undermine the distinction and allows for specifying it: rather than the presence or absence of reflection, it is the reflection *orientation*, and the way such orientation shapes the notion of reflexivity, that distinguishes the reflexive from the speculative attitude.

Indeed, *reflection* for Simondon is always a function of an activity; biologically anchored, it is linked to a fundamental situation in which an activity takes place and where the living being defines an "internal systematics" to resolve its "problematic". "Reflexive intention finds its source in the incompleteness

---

[6] Frédéric Worms, "Présentation", in SLΦ, 2016, p. 7.
[7] ILNFI, pp. 22–36/ILFI, pp. 39–51.
[8] *Ibid.*, p. 344/p. 307.

(*inachèvement*) of non-reflexive life".⁹ This situation is also a *condition*. The problematic situation *conditions* the living being to invent beyond the living. Reflection arises with the object, and the object arises as a problem for the living being at the threshold of reflexive life. This is why both the reflection and the object can only be stabilised as complementary symbols in a larger order of reality that Simondon names the collective, and which, according to him, is the "condition of signification".¹⁰ Contrary to the inaugural gesture that all speculative philosophy suggests, reflection can never be originative: "Thought brings reflection, but it does not create information out of nothingness".¹¹ This is why truly reflexive philosophy must think "*in the light*" of objects, i.e. not only to cast light *on them*, but to host, reflect and amplify *their* light.¹² Contrastingly, in speculative philosophy, reflection absorbs the light from objects and keeps it confined by looping back and closing upon itself, as if it were its own – original – light. Reflexivity flows back into the subject.

Yet *reflexivity* – this allegedly distinctive capacity of the humanities researcher, and supremely so, of the philosopher – if we read Simondon close enough, it is not described as an internal cognitive competence of the research subject, a quality of thought of the philosopher or of her philosophy (her "thought"). The cognitive side of reflexivity is only the conscious form of that what Simondon describes as a *reflexive situation*.¹³ It is a situation such that an "energetic exchange" takes place, marking "the continuity between the reflexive terrain and the reflection itself." Reflexivity is "the situation of a being that can be transformed by the intervention of reflection".¹⁴ Reflexivity even refers, here, to the situation of a *non-subject* being since "the subject", in the next lines, is described as the one who "operates" this transformation while "seeking himself a higher accomplishment".¹⁵ Surely reflexivity remains, quite classically, the capacity of treating one's own reflection on a problem as an element of the problem.

---

9   "Introduction (Note sur l'attitude réflexive)" (*c*.1955), in SLΦ, p. 20.
10 ILNFI, pp. 344–355/ILFI, pp. 307–315.
11 "Point de méthode (Note sur Individuation et Histoire de la pensée)" (*c*.1955), in SLΦ, p. 27.
12 Worms, *op. cit.*, p. 6.
13 An "exceptional situation" Simondon adds: it cannot happen every day. Compare with his evocation of the "psychical situations" of animals in ILNFI, p. 417, note 7/ILFI, p. 165, note 6.
14 "Introduction (Note sur l'attitude réflexive)" (*c*.1955), in SLΨ, p. 21.
15 *Ibid.*, pp. 21–22. This conception is reminiscent of an ancient alchemical motif according to which the alchemist transforms and elevates his soul by transforming and elevating material substances such as metals, perfumes or drugs – an operation of both care and cure by which substances are brought higher up the ladder of perfection and saved from corruption. See Bernard Joly, "Prolonger la vie: les attrayantes promesses des alchimistes", in *Astérion. Philosophie, histoire des idées, pensée politique*, vol. 8, 2011, https://doi.org/10.4000/asterion.1993.

However, to put it bluntly, reflexivity is not something enclosed in the head of the philosopher[16] or deposed in the books of philosophy (although they both take part in it): it entails a collective situation[17] (while speculative philosophy fosters a rather individualist, if not narcissist, style[18]). Reflexivity marks the quality of a reciprocal and transformative relationship between the activity of reflection and its objectual field. Reflexivity is the internal resonance of the system formed by reflection – in this case philosophical reflection – and its objects.

This is why, when Simondon, in *Les limites du progrès humain*,[19] finally concludes that reflexive thinking, equated with philosophical thought, is the only true vector of human progress, he does not simply succumb to a form of academic idealism that would praise philosophy for itself as an autotelic activity. In fact, he sticks to his conception of reflexivity by recalling that "this internal resonance of the ensemble formed by the objective concretisation and the human is

---

16 See ILNFI, p. 311/ILFI, p. 278, "The Problematic of Reflexivity in Individuation": "The psychological detour is not an abandonment of life but an act through which psychological reality becomes decentered relative to biological reality to be able to grasp in its problematic the rapport of the world and of the ego [...]. The direct communication of the world and of the ego is not yet psychological; for psychological reality to appear, the implicit link between the world and the ego must be broken and then reconstructed solely through this complex act of two mediations that suppose one another and are mutually called into question in reflexive self-consciousness."

17 See ILNFI, p. 179/ILFI, p. 166: "The living cannot borrow the potentials that produce a new individuation [i.e. a psychical individuation] from the associated nature without entering into an order of reality that makes it participate in an ensemble of psychical reality which surpasses the limits of the living; psychical reality is not self-enclosed. The psychical problematic cannot be resolved in an intra-individual way. [...] [It] leads to the level of the transindividual", i.e., to the collective.

18 It is true of course that Simondon's style is, in its own manner, strongly, and even sometimes obsessively, "individuated". However, regarding the *writing style*, his semantic choices are not so rigid and definitive as they might seem. For instance, "reading the introduction [of the thesis] can give the feeling that the idea of a 'principle of individuation' does not correspond to anything and that one can say that individuation is without principle, or that it is itself the principle of everything, so much that, within the framework of a rigorous definition of Simondon's vocabulary, one would have to say that there is no principle of individuation, that it is an illusion. Then, we discover that we can speak of the principle of individuation positively, that what counts is to understand that [...] 'the principle of individuation is the complete system in which the genesis of the individual takes place', etc." Jean-Yves Chateau, *Le vocabulaire de Simondon*, Ellipses, Paris, 2008, pp. 8–9. As Jean-Yves Chateau points out, Simondon is wary of the purely verbal definitions of the traditional school culture. Now, regarding the *philosophical style*, i.e. the conceptual gestures operated by his philosophy, the style *must* individuate itself in order to be faithful to Simondon's own method, according to which "the individuation of beings can only be grasped through the individuation of the subject's knowledge". ILNFI, p. 17/ILFI, p. 36.

19 "Les limites du progrès humain" (1959), in SLT, pp. 269–278.

thinking" and reciprocally, that "the reflexivity of thought is the conscious form of the internal resonance of the ensemble formed by the human and the objective concretisation", i.e. language, religion, technics.[20]

In this sense, speculative philosophy, by presenting itself as a liberal, autotelic, self-generative and self-contained activity, lacks genuine reflexivity, i.e. open, relational, collective, and situated reflexivity (even if such situatedness can extend, in Simondon's case, to considering the historical situation of human culture in general). Going back to the etymology of the *speculum*, one might say that genuine reflexive philosophy symbolises the *operation* of the mirror, while speculative philosophy reflects the *representation* in the mirror, and thus tends or pretends to become, quite absurdly so, a self-sufficient mirror. Speculative philosophy does not "maintain the integrity of its relation to an originative reflexive field", while "a reflexive philosophy contemporary of its originative terrain must be able to give an account of its path (*cheminement*) by incorporating into this path all the dynamisms contained in the terrain which is the basis of the reflection".[21]

To use one of Simondon's recurrent distinctions, it could be said that speculative philosophy tends to become a system of *"signs* of being", i.e. of abstract and self-sufficient representations, rather than a *"symbol* of being",[22] i.e. a complementary reality preserving the memory and the potential of re-actualisation of the relation. To understand this, one must recall how Simondon accounts for *symbolism* (the use of symbols) as an operation of thought analogous to the operation of a thing: the symbol in the primitive sense, that of a gathering stone.

> The joining to obtain a complete functional being has been able to provide a scheme of intelligibility from ancient institutions: the foundation of a relation of hospitality, in the Greek antiquity, was marked by the breaking of a stone in two complementary parts; the bringing together of these two parts, giving back the complete stone, would authenticate, sometimes several centuries later, the relation contracted one day. The two parts of the stone were symbols, things that could be completely brought together.[23]

The symbol symbolises hospitality. The notion of a symbol is itself symbolic, self-reflexive, insofar, paradoxically, as its primitive meaning is material (the gathering stone) and its operation is kept vivid. Otherwise, the usual fate of the symbol is to become a *sign*: its meaning is abstracted from its primary situation and mode of existence of an object.

> The symbol became all that serves as a *sign* of recognition or constitutes a convention. But generally the word of symbol keeps something of its primitive meaning; it is a thing,

---

20   Ibid., p. 278.
21   "Introduction (Note sur l'attitude réflexive)" (c.1955), in SLΦ, p. 21.
22   "Recherche sur la philosophie de la nature" (c.1955), in SLΦ, p. 30.
23   "The Use of Symbols in Reflexive Thinking", in RP, p. 121.

a reality that, despite its simplicity and materiality, refers to an order of reality that is more complex by matching with it.[24]

Yet such a fate – the becoming-sign of the symbol – is usually what happens with human *language*. The operative meanings of symbols are occulted and overlaid by the second-order materiality of language that the symbols nevertheless contribute to produce at a collective level.[25]

In this respect, the symbol partakes to an "institution" in the sense of Maurice Merleau-Ponty[26]: a process that implies at the same time the unlimited fecundity of a singularity, which opens an infinite field of resumptions, revivals, and transformations, and the oblivion of its concrete origins. As such, the symbol conditions both the reactivation of the "institutive" operations and the seemingly independent life of the "instituted" signs – their speculative existence.

3. The continuing relevance of metaphysics

To avoid any misunderstanding, one must specify that this rejection of speculation should not be confused with that of *metaphysics*. As an approach that refuses to reduce the knowledge of *realia* to the perception (logical or phenomenal) we have of them, metaphysics is not rejected by Simondon.[27] Neither is *ontology*, insofar as it is *genesic* ontology,[28] ontogenesis. What Simondon rejects in the speculative gesture is the abstraction of objects from their constitutive processes of genesis, existence, and knowledge. His rejection of speculation is, in a sense, that of an epistemologist, but whose epistemology includes metaphysics as a necessary component of both philosophy and science, as his critical reading of Comte indicates.[29]

---

24   *Ibid.*, pp. 121–122, my emphasis.
25   Hence the criticism, often misunderstood, that Simondon makes of the philosophies that pretend to ground signification on language: "it is absolutely insufficient to say that language is what allows man to access significations; if there were no significations to sustain language, there would be no language; language is not what creates signification; [...] Signification is a rapport of beings, not a pure expression; signification is relational, collective, transindividual, and it cannot be provided by the encounter of expression and the subject". ILNFI, p. 344–345/ ILFI, p. 307.
26   Maurice Merleau-Ponty, *L'institution – La passivité – Notes de cours au Collège de France (1954–1955)*. Belin, Paris, 2003.
27   The process of transduction, for instance, is said to be "both metaphysical and logical". ILNFI, p. 14/p. 33.
28   I use "genesic" to translate Simondon's adjective *"génétique"*, which refers to the processes of genesis, in order to avoid any confusion with the biological use of the term.
29   See "Epistémologie de la cybernétique" (1953), in in SLΦ, pp. 177–181.

Comte, indeed, is well known for having rejected metaphysics as the adolescence of the mind, the obstinate quest for the absolute behind the relative. Metaphysics is the pretence of knowledge to go beyond phenomena by grounding them on abstract *substrata* and hidden *causes* (the Cartesian *res extensa*, the Spinozist substance, the Leibnizian monads, the Newtonian atoms and forces, the sensitive matter of Diderot …). Instead, the "positive mind" contents itself with the relative structure of phenomena, i.e., their constant *rapports* accessible to us under the form of mathematical *laws* without the need of postulating substrates (*"rapports sans supports"* says the Positivist formula). Positivism – be it Comte's historical positivism or the logical positivism of the Vienna Circle – is defined first of all as the rejection of a metaphysical foundation of physics, and by derivation, of all other sciences. To Simondon on the contrary,

> every theory of knowledge supposes a theory of being [...]. The first question of the theory of knowledge is therefore metaphysical: what is the relation of operation and of structure in *being*? If the answer [to the question what is primordial in being] is structure, we end up with the *phenomenalist objectivism* of Kant and Auguste Comte; knowledge then necessarily remains relative and becomes indefinitely extensible through scientific progress.[30]

Yet scientific progress is precisely one of these instances in which positivism, as a "monism of the structure [...] re-creates over the course of its development the term that it had initially excluded [i.e. the operation].[31] Structural positivism reintroduces the notion of hierarchy, whether vital or energetic,[32] and thus reintroduces a pure dynamism independent of all structure, since it produces structure".[33]

Simondon characterises positivism as structural objectivism coordinated by the epistemological dynamism of scientific law-making activity. Only the mathematical representation and the epistemological reflection escape the field of phenomenal objectivity. As means of expression and coordination of the "positive methods" of the various sciences, mathematics and epistemology belong to the

---

[30] ILNFI, p. 667/ILFI, p. 564. The other branch of the alternative reads: "If the answer is operation, we end up with the *dynamic intuitionism* of Bergson; knowledge is absolute and immediate but does not necessarily reach all objects: the inert term, like matter, can only be known as a degradation of vital dynamism, and the knowledge of the static is an intuition that degrades and disintegrates". ILNFI, pp. 667–668/ILFI, p. 564.

[31] And symmetrically, in Bergson, "The operative dynamism of life produces a systematics of immobility: via dynamism, structure is reintroduced into knowledge as a dishonored, dismissed, and second-class intuition". ILNFI, p. 668/ILFI, p. 564.

[32] As Simondon also points out "the invasion of positivist rationalism by principles that are irreducible to phenomenal laws such as thermodynamics defines them or biology utilizes them", ILNFI, p. 668/ILFI, p. 564.

[33] *Ibid.*

operative term: their operations define the subjects of positive knowledge in front of its objects of positive knowledge while these later are reduced to the phenomenal *relata* of the nomological structure (i.e. the scientific laws as constant "*rapports sans supports*"). But neither the subjects nor the objects of positive knowledge, nor their interrelations, are self-sufficient. By therefore refusing ontology, the discourse on being, positivism posits a supreme being. Indeed,

> humanity is not a phenomenon among the phenomena, simple term of the relation: humanity is a being, and a privileged being, source of the knowing and acting subject that is every individual: as real as the whole order of the known and unknown phenomena, more real than every phenomenon, it is also more active, more dynamic, richer in normativity than any individual-subject: this being is beyond every *subject* and every *phenomenon*: Thus is founded, at the top of the hierarchy of the sciences, the reflexivity of the thought which discovers a being more objective than any phenomenon and more charged of operative dynamism than any *subject*, since any subject draws its origin from it. This reflexivity discovers thus, in the synthesis of the *operation* proper to the subject and of the *structure* proper to the objective phenomena, the unique principle of an absolute *normativity*. Thus, positivism separates the operative domain from the structural domain as deeply as it can in order to reunite them in a unique being, humanity, which then becomes the absolute principle of normativity.[34]

In short, what's bred in the bone will come out in the flesh, *chassez la métaphysique, elle revient au galop!* Simondon takes thus the risk to grant metaphysics an important role and relevance (which was rather rare in the 1950s).

One could wonder, however, if metaphysics, once revaluated in a Simondonian context, should not be understood differently: not in the traditional sense of the search for what lies "beyond physics" and thus *grounds* the sciences, nor in the contemporary sense of that which *ignores* them, but as that which is "amid physics", *between* the various sciences or *across* them, and not amenable to a supreme genre of science. As Simondon asserts it for cybernetics, Norbert Wiener's "no man's land between the sciences", is not a science itself: the interscience is of *technical* nature,[35] and this is why technology is as much the ally of metaphysics as is philosophy of nature.

---

[34] "Epistémologie de la cybernétique" (1953), in SLΦ, p. 179.
[35] *Ibid.*, pp. 186–189.

4. The hosting function of philosophy

As the symbol of the "symbol" testifies, there is, furthermore, some sort of *ethics of hospitality* that plays out in Simondon's conception and practice of philosophy with regard to objects. This is what he refers to as a "hosting function" (*fonction d'accueil*), which he holds to be the "prime function" of philosophy.[36]

According to him, the philosopher's reflective consciousness must first establish itself as the hosting milieu of an extra-philosophical field[37] containing a "spontaneous issue (*problématique spontanée*)",[38] a "pre-reflexive terrain (*terrain pré-réflexif*)"[39] or "paradigm".[40] Technics, for instance, is "not considered as a substructure ..." (by difference to thinking as a superstructure in the Marxist doctrine) "... but as a paradigm," i.e. as technology in the sense of technical *thinking*, even if it is pre-reflexively embedded in technical objects.[41]

Yet the choice of such a pre-reflexive terrain from which the reflective consciousness is put in motion is all-determining as it "must contain in the form of internal tension a potential of information large enough" and sufficiently "plurivalent"[42] for, after the "long detour" of philosophical reflection, this consciousness to arrive at a reflexive notion without loss of information, or with having even *increased* the information initially contained in the pre-reflexive terrain under the form of potential. So the terrain where the reflection starts must *hold* this potential, just as much as the philosopher must be sensitive to it. It is "the enlightening field, the κύριος, the pilot-field".[43]

We can see in these early formulations the way Simondon chooses his objects (i.e. the individuation of physical, living, psychological beings, the teleological systems of cybernetics), and that the choice of the objectual field dramatically informs the method since it commands the use of concepts – such as those of information, individuation and transduction – borrowed from the "pre-reflex-

---

36 "Cybernétique et philosophie" (1953), in in SLΦ, p. 36.
37 In "Point de méthode (Note sur Individuation et Histoire de la pensée)" (*c.*1955), in SLΦ, pp. 27–28. Simondon refers to the physical, biological and psychological processes of individuation and their scientific formulations.
38 "Cybernétique et philosophie" (1953), in in SLΦ, p. 36.
39 "Point de méthode", SLΦ, p. 27.
40 "Recherche sur la philosophie de la nature", SLΦ, pp. 30–31.
41 "Introduction (Note sur l'attitude réflexive)", SLΦ, p. 24.
42 "Point de méthode", SLΦ, p. 27; "Recherche sur la philosophie de la nature", SLΦ, pp. 31–32. "The paradigm is transposable because it is, originally, plurivalent" (*Ibid.*, p. 32).
43 "Recherche sur la philosophie de la nature", SLΦ, p. 31. Very interestingly, the κύριος (*kurios*) provides the common etymology for the curious (eager for knowledge), the curator (who cures and takes care), the master (who exerts dominion, including masculine supremacy in Greek society), and the helm of the ship's pilot, the *kubernetes*, on which Norbert Wiener has forged the word "cybernetics".

ive" terrains in question. In this respect, Simondon recognises and even explicitly assumes the *relativity of the method*, in the sense that the method is relative to the object, and thus inseparable from it.[44]

Simondon does theorise and justify this inseparability of the method from the objectal field. He does this, in particular, by questioning the divide he attributes to Kantian criticism and then to Comtian positivism between the structural axiomatics of objective phenomena and the operative axiomatics of the knowing subject's "methods".[45] As seen above, this divide making the cognitive law prevail over the object, it leads to the reduction of the latter to a pure term of an external rapport, "the phenomenon". The object is therein reduced to pure *relata* of a cognitive (and to Comte, to a pragmatic) relation and operation: "the scientific law". The method, i.e. the operation of thought, remains thus untainted by any "thingly" contamination (e.g. the Kantian divide between the thing-in-itself and the phenomena; the Comtian rejection of metaphysics). Conversely, the upper meeting of the operation (proper to the knowing and acting subject) and the structure (proper to objective phenomena) provides the point of absolute normativity hierarchising the whole system: the moral law in Kant, the religion of humanity in Comte.

Simondon certainly admired these philosophical systems whose construction schemes he deciphers so brilliantly. This, by the way, is one – and not the least – of the specificities and qualities of Simondon as a historian of philosophy: that of developing a history of philosophical schemes through their operations rather than a hermeneutics of infinite commentary. But he must all the more decode the workings of previous philosophical systems if he wants to get his own enterprise out of them and accomplish this, once again, not to directly edify his own system, in the individualistic style so typical of speculative philosophy. In the case of the early text referred to here,[46] Simondon's critique of Kant's and Comte's "phenomenalist objectivism" serves rather to detect and to host the specific lights of cybernetics as a field that reshuffles the traditional distribution of roles of the knowing subject and the known object and thereby redefines scientific truth:

> The emergence of Cybernetics imposes a choice on the epistemologist: to condemn herself to consider Cybernetics as an aesthetical daydream on scientific topics, or to modify the axiomatics of *phenomenalist objectivism*. If Cybernetics is a science, one must admit that the object does not manifest only a *structure* in the deterministic chain of phenome-

---

44 See ILNFI, p. 653/ILFI, p. 553: "The object of this study is inseparable from its method. A relation of reciprocal conditions in fact links the reality of its object to the validity of the approach undertaken".
45 "Epistémologie de la cybernétique", SLΦ, pp. 178–180.
46 "Epistémologie de la cybernétique" was written to serve as a basis for the establishment of an interdisciplinary collective on the matter.

na, but that it really holds, in itself, a certain number of *operations*. [...] Cybernetics, as the science of objective operations, would then no more involve a knowing subject *inventor of operations* (as the mathematical operation for Kant or Auguste Comte), but a knowing subject *inventor of structures* that would allow theorizing the objective operations by converting them into structures.[47]

Cybernetics qualifies thereby as an "inter-scientific technique" that defines the "operative interdependence" of the different sciences devoted to the structure of various objective phenomena.

> From then on, the very notion of scientific truth is transformed and completed: the inter-scientific technique holds a truth complementary to the knowledge of particular objective truths.[48]

The epistemology of cybernetics was one of Simondon's central projects in the early 1950s. At that time, he was trying to launch an interdisciplinary research group on cybernetics based at the École Normale. In those early works, Simondon's epistemology of cybernetics leads to the definition and to the project of the instauration of a "general allagmatics"[49] which seeks to be a "universal Cybernetics",[50] and whose challenge, Simondon writes, is "of metaphysical order".[51] General allagmatics is meant to be a philosophico-scientific synthesis of analytical science (i.e. knowing objective structures through cognitive operations) and analogical science (i.e. knowing operations through inventing structures). It also seems to crown *History of the Notion of Individual* as it entirely takes up its conceptual economy (i.e. the couple structure/operation). The project of allagmatics plays a pivotal role in the shift from "the individual" to "individuation". It precedes and prepares the reformulation of the problem of individuation, which will eventually become the object of his principal thesis, where allagmatics intervenes only in the background and is used mostly as an adjective ("allagmatic relation", " - operation"). A nice illustration of a "long detour", which, far from being superfluous, seems all the more necessary as it allows the philosophical choices of priority to change, the thought to individuate itself among its objects.

---

47 "Épistémologie de la cybernétique", SLΦ, pp. 180–181.
48 *Ibid.*, p. 187.
49 From the Greek ἄλλαγμα, "change" (*Ibid.*, p. 197).
50 ILNFI, p. 663/ILFI, p. 561.
51 "Épistémologie de la cybernétique", SLΦ, p. 197.

5. A risky and restless enterprise

As seen above, philosophy is – or ought to be – "the symbol of being" and the symbol symbolises hospitality. Philosophy must thus take care of such a hosting function in order to take care of itself. However, a philosophical ethics of hospitality towards objects suggests not only that philosophy must host the objects, but that it should use such a hosting function with particular care.

Indeed, while Simondon recognises the *relativity* of all philosophical method because it is bound to its pilot-domain, he recognises at the same time and for that very same reason the *decisive importance* of the method: "a philosophy is capable of what its paradigms are capable of".[52] This is why the choice of the object and its pre-reflexive ground turns out to be highly risky.

On this regard, it would be interesting to compare and contrast Simondon's philosophical attitude of hospitality towards extra-philosophical objects with that of his doctoral supervisor for his complementary thesis on technical objects, Georges Canguilhem, when he famously declared, in order to assert the philosophical value of studying medical practices and modes of reasoning, "Philosophy is a reflection for which all foreign material is good, and we would gladly say, for which all good material must be foreign".[53]

Simondon does walk in the footsteps of Canguilhem in that he too refuses the preconception that there are naturally "good" objects for philosophy, philosophy's "native" objects, so to say. However, Simondon's restless attitude contrasts with the bonhomie of his former thesis director. Indeed, as generous as it is, the hosting function of philosophy is no less *selective* because the choice of the pre-reflexive terrain is decisive.

In this respect, Simondon stands in stark contrast with the thread of Speculative realism of the years 2000–2010s. For instance, in the Object-Oriented Ontology of Graham Harman, the objects allegedly put back in the foreground as the prime characters of philosophy can be *anything whatsoever*.[54] On the con-

---

52 "Recherche sur la philosophie de la nature", SLΦ, p. 31.
53 Georges Canguilhem, *Essai sur quelques problèmes concernant le normal et le pathologique*, La Montagne, Clermont-Ferrand, 1943; trans. Carolyn R. Fawcett, *The Normal and the Pathological*, Zone Books, New York, 2007, p. 33 (translation modified).
54 Graham Harman, *The Quadruple Object*. Zero Books, Winchester/Washington DC, 2011. It is Tristan Garcia, however, who proposed a contribution to Speculative realism in which the object is precisely *not* anything whatsoever (Tristan Garcia, *Forme et objet. Un traité des choses*, Presses universitaires de France, Paris, 2011; transl. Mark A. Ohm & John Cogburn, *Form and Object. A Treatise on Things*, Edinburgh University Press, Edinburgh, 2014). Garcia distinguishes the *object* from the *thing*, not like Heidegger does (i.e. the recalcitrant *Gegenstand* vs. the good old *Ding* that gathers the qualities of the world), but as two opposite and complementary views on ontology: the formal and the objectal. He posits a world of things without values or hierarchies; it is the reign of indeterminacy and indifference, an ontologically flat world

trary, to Simondon, not every object lends itself to a fully philosophical exercise of reflexive thought. There are conditions for this, such as their plurivalence, the richness of spontaneous information, the variety of sub-domains, and the ability of their schemes to be analogically transposed and to radiate onto other separate fields across disciplinary or socio-cultural boundaries.

However, there is no aristocratic contempt for objects unworthy of philosophy here: some objects lend themselves to other forms of attitude, notably aesthetic, techno-aesthetics or design, which are far from being dismissed by Simondon.[55] Through the detour and mediation of practices other than philosophy – such as art, design, and even marketing![56] – all objects can be philosophically thought about, without having to serve as paradigms for reflexive thinking, and without philosophy having the pretension to appropriate them entirely.[57]

---

where everything is equal and where anything is something; the thing is anything whatsoever. An idea, even absurd, a God or a nail clipping are equally things; they have nothing to do with one another. Things are indeterminate, unrelated, non-relational, alone in the world; each one of them exists separately in the world, which Garcia defines as the "form", the contour or "negative" of every thing. The "formal" is the world of indeterminate things. But it is quite different with objects: the object is a thing into another thing; it always already embedded in exchanges, norms, values, temporalities. The object is the togetherness of things, even if "formally", the object remains a thing, which constitutes its "chance" – that of becoming something else, and thereby of escaping any essentialist definition. In this respect, Garcia's "object" provides an analogy with Simondon's individuation: it is always a relation and a difference between what the thing is intrinsically (the things that it contains in itself), and its extrinsic situation (its relation to other things). Of course, there is nothing in Simondon that corresponds to Garcia's "formal ontology". However, quite like Simondon's preindividual, the "thing" is both nothing and anything if it is not tensely engaged into an individuation.

55 See Simondon's "Réflexions sur la techno-esthétique" (1982), in SLT, pp. 379–396; Sacha Loeve, "Du récit au design, et retour: des modes de résolution du problème de l'unité de la technologie chez Simondon", in Vincent Bontems (ed.), *Gilbert Simondon ou l'invention du futur. Colloque de Cerisy*, Klincksieck, Langres, 2016, pp. 113–124; Victor Petit & Timothée Deldicque, "La recherche en design avant la 'recherche en design'", in *Cahiers COSTECH*, 1, 2017, http://www.costech.utc.fr/CahiersCOSTECH/spip.php?article16.

56 "L'effet de halo en matière technique: vers une stratégie de la publicité" (1960), in SLT, pp. 279–292.

57 See for instance Simondon's surprising considerations on the "*jument de retour*", i.e., a mare in heat, and by extension, an insult qualifying someone incorrigible, persisting in wrong deeds: "Can there be an entelechy of the 'returning mare', this being so downgraded that the expression that designates it can be used as an insult? Yes, undoubtedly, in the same way that there can be beautiful old people". "Réflexions sur la techno-esthétique" (1982), in SLT, p. 393. From the "techno-esthetic" viewpoint he adopts here, Simondon manifests even more openness than Etienne Souriau when he states that "there is no being – a single cloud, the smallest flower, the smallest bird, a rock, a mountain, a wave of the sea – which does not draw, as well as man, a possible sublime state above itself, and hence, that hasn't a say in the rights it has on

Simondon's philosophical attitude is more radical than the one suggested by Canguilhem's "foreign material" statement reported above. Objects, to Simondon, are not merely "materials" that philosophy should appropriate to itself; it could be said they are also *milieux* that radically *situate* and *disappropriate* philosophy from itself, to the point of making philosophy foreign and even *alien* to itself, in order, finally, to force philosophy to reinvent itself and to become what it is, i.e. to discover its normative function for *culture* and the permanent revitalisation of *humanism*, a humanism that each epoch must reinvent, and which Simondon defines by borrowing Terence's words, "*humani nil a me alienum puto*" – literally: "that nothing human be *alienated* from me."[58]

It is here that the link between the relation of philosophy to objects and the history of philosophy begins to be seen: this link is nothing other than the *issue of human progress*. As indeed "human progress cannot be identified with any crisis of progress according to language, religion, or pure technics, but only to what, from each of these crises of progress, can be passed under the form of reflexive thought, to other crises of progress", namely "philosophical thought".[59] Simondon does not mean that the history of philosophy is likely of progress (for example, that Kant would mark as progress compared to Descartes), but that philosophical thought, in the reflexive continuity that it institutes between the various phases and crises of progress of the objective concretisations (language, religion, techniques), is the only one able to establish a *commensurability* between them: "it is this thinking that assures the continuity between the successive phases of progress, and it is it alone that can maintain the preoccupation of totality, and to make so that the decentring of the human, parallel to the alienation of the objective concretisation, does not take place".[60]

It is thus the common struggle against the reciprocal alienation of the human subject and the "non-inhuman" objects (the objective concretisations) that moves in the same gesture the philosophical concern for contemporary objects and the permanent re-actualisation, and thus the study, of the history of philosophy.

---

man as this latter posits himself as responsible for the accomplishment of the world". Etienne Souriau, "Du mode d'existence de l'oeuvre à faire", 1956, reed. in *Les différents modes d'existence*, Presses Universitaires de France, Paris, 2009, pp. 195–217, p. 216. Indeed Souriau limits his enumeration to "beautiful" things here whereas Simondon goes on to consider the technoesthetics of "ugly" or "bad" things.

58   Simondon's reformulation reads: "humanism [...] means the will to return the status of freedom to what has been alienated in man, so that nothing human should be foreign to man." METO, p. 117/MEOT p. 101.
59   "Les limites du progrès humain", SLT, p. 278.
60   Ibid.

6. Philosophy as the individuation of thinking

As stated above, the hosting function of philosophy is pushed so far that it impinges upon the method of study of the object. In order not to be artificially imposed, the method must allow itself to be altered, contaminated – polarised, Simondon suggests[61] – by the objectal paradigm in which it takes its source. The method, once again, must establish itself as the "symbol" of the studied being (i.e. its complementary reality) rather than a "system of signs" of the being (i.e. a secondary translation in a system submitting being to thinking). This second attitude, which I identified above with the speculative mode of philosophising, but which concerns more broadly any philosophy that sets up its method as truth, is castigated by Simondon as a "methodological egoism, a true narcissism of thought".[62] To him, "the only obligation of the philosophical program is the opening of the reflexive system",[63] i.e. the capacity to let itself be affected, altered, ramified, contaminated, polarised by its objects, while instituting itself reflexively as the historical awareness of this alteration. This condition, thanks to which objectual philosophy converges with the history of philosophy, is essential because

> the shift to reflexivity *cannot* be done, in a closed field of spontaneity, with the only forces, data or structures which the situation comprises; but it [philosophical thought] brings the memory of the past challenges it was able to carry out, it brings a relatively universal [sic] load of schemes, concepts and "philosophical gestures" which take a particular meaning in the new situation.[64]

We can then recognise individuation, in its strict definition of an act of two mediations that suppose one another in a mutually constitutive relation between a rapport to otherness (here with an objectual field external to philosophy) and a rapport to oneself (here with the history of philosophy). Philosophy is therefore and very exactly determined as an *individuation of thought*. This is the reason why Simondon can state that

> One should not consider the appearance in the consciousness of a new field of research as a new "influence" that reflexive thought undergoes. In fact, if philosophical thought is really reflexive, the emergence of a new field is a crucial fact both for the previously spontaneous elements of this field and for the reflexive thought that comes to turn towards it.[65]

---

61 "Recherche sur la philosophie de la nature", SLΦ, pp. 32–33.
62 *Ibid*, p. 30.
63 "Cybernétique et philosophie", SLΦ, p. 36.
64 "Recherche sur la philosophie de la nature", SLΦ, p. 37.
65 *Ibid*, p. 36.

In other terms, the encounter with the objectual field does not simply affect philosophy from the outside; it acts as a germ of individuation. Philosophy, thus defined as an individuation of thinking, is not the pursuit of "thinking for its own sake": it is the joint transformation of meaning and of the subject constituted by this meaning.[66]

7. History of philosophy as the transindividuation of philosophical thinking

Thus, even when philosophy takes its own concepts, systems, authors, threads and lineages as objects of study, Simondon refuses the *academic* closure of the history of philosophy upon itself as much as he refuses the *speculative* closure of philosophy upon itself. But this is, paradoxically, not because he would reject the history of philosophy, but precisely *because* of his (non-academic) "philosophy of the history of philosophy",[67] as well as *because* of his (non-speculative) philosophy of philosophical thought.

As Jean-Hugues Barthélémy argues, most philosophers act as if they – or their thought – were originary.[68] Thus philosophy often posits itself as an activity in which the originary and radical genesis of thinking coincides with itself (as the instituting act of the Cartesian *cogito*), resumes and accomplishes itself (as in the Hegelian *Aufhebung*), or is authentically listened to (as in the Heideggerian history of being). Yet this self-positioning of the philosophical subject as a thinking subject attending its own genesis is castigated by Simondon as a form of substantialisation of the subject – as if the subject[69] wanted to absorb all the relations that constitute it by establishing itself as an "absolute term":

---

[66] In a way that might be found quite close, after all, to what Jean-Hugues Barthélémy proposes, even though he intends to distance himself from the view of ontology as a prime philosophy that he discerns in Simondon, in order to start from the "pluridimensionality of meaning", of which "ontological information" is only one of the dimensions. See Jean-Hugues Barthélémy, *La société de l'invention. Pour une architectonique philosophique de l'âge écologique*, Matériologiques, Paris, 2018; *Ego Alter. Dialogues pour l'avenir de la Terre*, Matériologiques, Paris, 2021.
[67] On Simondon's philosophy of the history of philosophy see ILNFI, pp. 433–434/p. 339; Ludovic Duhem, "*Apeiron et physis*. Simondon transducteur des présocratiques", in *Cahiers Simondon*, 4, L'harmattan, Paris, 2012, pp. 33–66.
[68] Barthélémy, *op. cit.*
[69] Let us recall that the subject differs from the individual in Simondon's philosophy. "[T]he subject is more than individual". ILNFI, p. 344/ILFI, p. 307. It is the ensemble formed by the physico-biologically individuated individual and its pre-individual "charge of nature", which synthesis occurs in the psycho-collective constitution of the transindividual.

the substantialization of the subject as a term is a facility that thought grants itself to be able to witness the genesis and justification of itself; thought seeks to be identified with the subject, i.e. to be identified with its condition of existence so as not to lag behind itself. (…) The subject is *substantialized by thought* so that *thought can coincide with the subject*. Yet the subject's substantialization, which supposes that the subject can be taken as a term of relation, gives it the status of an absolute term; substance is like *the relational term become absolute*, having absorbed into it everything that was the being of relation.[70]

Thought, for Simondon, is a secondary mode of individuation; it occurs *after*, *with* and *within* other modes of individuation (physical, biological, technical, collective) that are both constitutive of the thinking – but never *only* thinking – subject, and of its non-subjective conditions of existence – which are in turn never *devoid* of what Simondon calls "signification".[71]

> Thought is a certain mode of secondary individuation that intervenes after the fundamental individuation that constitutes the subject; thought is not necessarily capable of thinking being in its totality; it is second relative to the subject's condition of existence; but this condition of the existence of the subject is not isolated and unique, for the subject is not an isolated term with the capacity to constitute itself.[72]

"Secondary", here, does not mean "less important" (than physical, biological and technical individuation) but "non-originary".[73] Thought is *not originary*; neither is philosophy. Philosophy alone is not the origin of thought as much as thought alone is not the origin of philosophy.

The history of philosophical thought, in turn, is a process that cannot be separated from the other processes of individuation.[74] It is an individuation of thinking that presupposes previous individuations of thinking – lineages of philosophy – and that transindividuates with them by implicating those past individuations of thinking in new problematic situations that collectively integrate

---

[70] ILNFI, p. 362/ILFI, p. 321.
[71] Through attempting "to save information as signification from *the technological theory of information*", the "goal", Simondon states, is nothing less than "to discover the inherence of significations to *being*". ILNFI, p. 17/p. 35. And later: "There is no difference between discovering a signification and existing collectively with the being relative to which the signification is discovered, since signification is not of the being but between beings, or rather across beings: it is transindividual". ILNFI, p. 344/ILFI, p. 307.
[72] ILNFI, p. 362/ILFI, p. 321.
[73] On "non-originarity" after and beyond Simondon see Barthélémy (2018; 2021). Note that other individuations are not fully originary either, as "the *physical* individuation and the *biological* individuation are modes of resolution; they are not absolute starting points" (Simondon, 1964, 320).
[74] "Point de méthode (Note sur Individuation et Histoire de la pensée", SLΦ, pp. 27–28.

new objects, paradigms, and so forth. The history of philosophy is thus to be understood as the *transindividuation of philosophical thought.*

8. A direct and free reflection

We have seen so far why Simondon refuses the academic closure of the history of philosophy upon itself just as he refuses the speculative closure of philosophy upon itself: the posture, if not imposture, of "philosophy for its own sake". To him, philosophy must "lead to the discovery of a certain number of solutions" which are "not purely conceptual but real solutions, i. e. that can give rise to an action and thus constitute the basis of an ethics".[75]

But to the refusal of "philosophy for its own sake" are added, paradoxically, two other refusals that may seem antithetical to the former: that of "philosophy for" or *activist philosophy* and of "philosophy of" or *applied philosophy*. Concerning the first, Simondon deplores the fact that

> the recent evolution of the currents of ideas has made reflexive philosophy almost entirely disappear in favor of a certain number of thoughts that present themselves as philosophies but that are rather, in fact, uses of customs of thought acquired in philosophical thought for the benefit of a cause already defined before the moment when thought begins to be exercised.[76]

What Simondon has in mind here, in the French post-war context, is the competition for philosophical primacy between Marxist, Christian, and phenomenological streams of thought. To him, philosophy must refuse such initial determinations that negate its very nature of "a direct and free reflection".[77] Of course philosophy is never a neutral enterprise: it is always polarised by its pilot-domain, and is, in this sense, concerned, implicated, and engaged, as Simondon's struggle for recognising the cultural status of technical objects left no doubt.[78] However, the authenticity and concreteness of the philosophical engagement lies in "the authenticity of the transposition", not in the authenticity of a *telos* that would be known in advance, in a "desperate" quest for "success at any cost".[79] Faithful in this respect to the Socratic ideal, philosophy does not own but must *research* and (in the best case) discover its destination, and not act as if it knew

---

75 "Introduction (Note sur l'attitude réflexive)", SLΦ, p. 25.
76 *Ibid.*, p. 19.
77 *Ibid.*
78 "Awareness of the modes of existence of technical objects must be brought about through philosophical thought, which must fulfill a duty through this work analogous to the one it fulfilled for the abolition of slavery and the affirmation of the value of the human person." METO, p. 15/MEOT, p. 9.
79 "Introduction (Note sur l'attitude réflexive)", SLΦ, p. 20.

it from the start. Instead of defending this or that "spiritual interest",[80] philosophy can only seek humanism at the end of a "long detour", like Ulysses accomplishing his odyssey.[81] For instance, the long detour of philosophy is needed for human thought to "establish an egalitarian relation, without privilege, between technics and man",[82] as well as the long detour of technology (the study of technical objects and technicity) is needed for philosophy to uncover its cultural and humanist destination. And although humanism can be defined as the claim that "nothing human should be foreign to man", no one knows in advance what can participate in the human reality, for "it is because there is no human nature definable once for all that any event and any singularity can be part of humanity".[83]

Finally, a truly reflexive philosophy being neither "philosophy for its own sake", nor "philosophy for", it must also not be defined as a "philosophy *of*" (e.g. of mind, of perception, of nature, of technics).[84] It cannot simply apply a predefined method to an object delimited once and for all for a determined end. This is accurate because any "philosophy of" is based on a paradigm that is anterior to the activity of thought as *research* and not contemporary with it. Yet philosophical reflection as genuine research should for Simondon be considered as a genesic and transformative activity – as the individuation of thought – that is analogous to the genesis of the *realia* in which it participates. It is a mode of thinking that is "neither *a priori* nor *a posteriori*, but *a praesente*; it comes back on itself in a way to be both anterior and posterior in relation to itself".[85]

Furthermore, a "philosophy *of* an object" institutes itself as the *representation* of an object, reduced to a *vis-à-vis* of the philosophical subject. While drawing its original impetus from the reflective potential of the object, it can only degrade into a system of signs as soon as it moves away from its "hot spot," and this all the more as it sees itself as *applied* philosophy and does not recognise that it is the object that moves its thinking. By contrast in the "paradigmatic reflection" in which philosophy consists for Simondon, "the act of reflection apprehends itself in the course of its development as being analogous to the object submitted to reflection".[86] Thinking and being are parallel to each other in a symbolic relation and not facing each other in a representative relation.

Two notions are of prime importance here: participation and analogy. The notion of participation plays out at the heart of the discussion of Platonic, Neo-

---

80   Ibid.
81   "Humanisme culturel, humanisme négatif, humanisme nouveau", SLΦ, pp. 72–73.
82   METO, p. 125/MEOT, p. 87.
83   "Humanisme culturel, humanisme négatif, humanisme nouveau", SLΦ, p. 72.
84   "Recherche sur la philosophie de la nature", SLΦ, pp. 30–31.
85   "Introduction (Note sur l'attitude réflexive)", SLΦ, p. 20.
86   Ibid.., p. 25.

platonic and Christian philosophies that Simondon undertakes in *History of the Notion of Individual*,[87] where one can read between the lines the outline of his own conception. In the principal thesis, participation is "the relation interior and exterior to the individual", "the fact of being an element in a vaster individuation" and the "condition of the individuation of the collective".[88] It is that by which "individuation does not merely occur in the individual and for it; it also occurs around it and above it." Although the detailed examination of this notion and of its philosophical genesis would exceed the limits of this contribution, Simondon's conception of it can be stated simply as follows: participation is not mereological (the parts participate in the whole) but rather *analogical* (the activity of the individual participates, through its pre-individual potential, in the individuation of a higher order of reality). Participation institutes analogies between orders of magnitudes, be such participation physical, affective, symbolic, political, or philosophical participation. As analogical participation of thinking to being, philosophy institutes itself as an individuation of thinking analogous to the individuation of the object, and ultimately, at the collective order of magnitude of the history of philosophy, as a transindividuation of thought analogous to the transindividuation of culture. For the common *milieu* of philosophy and "its" objects is *culture*, in both the two meanings of *mi-lieu:*[89] their dynamical in-between and the larger reality into which they are included and in which they participate. And for the reason that philosophy is invested with the task of revitalising humanistic culture, its objects are both extrinsic and intrinsic to it: they individuate philosophy in relation to otherness as well as in relation to itself and to its own history; they allow philosophy to apprehend "oneself as another".

Now concerning analogy, as this notion carries with it a long philosophical history, I will limit myself here to underlining a key aspect of this notion in Simondon, namely, that the validity of analogy has no other basis than the existence of concrete technical objects: the technical individual is the paradigm of real analogy.

---

[87] ILNFI, pp. 447–557/ILFI, pp. 349–430.
[88] *Ibid.*, pp. 8–9/p. 29.
[89] Victor Petit, *Histoire et philosophie du concept de "Milieu": individuation et médiation*. PhD dissertation, University of Paris 7 Denis Diderot, 2009.

9. Technical objects as paradigms of analogical thinking / technology as paradigm of analogical metaphysics

"The word analogy seems to have taken on a pejorative meaning in epistemological thought", Simondon notices.[90] Indeed, Bachelard for instance, sees analogy as an epistemological obstacle, an "escape of thought" prone to justify anything whatsoever.[91] Simondon sees the source of this disgrace in the confusion between metaphor, which is based on resemblance, and genuine analogy, which he defines as

> an identity of rapports and not a rapport of identity. The transductive progress of thought effectively consists in establishing the identities of rapports. These identities of rapports strictly are not at all based on resemblances but are instead based on differences, and their goal is to explain the latter: they tend toward logical differentiation and do not at all tend toward assimilation or identification.[92]
>
> But it must be specified that these identities of rapports are identities of operative rapports, not identities of structural rapports. This is how the opposition between analogy and resemblance is revealed: resemblance consists of structural rapports. Pseudo-scientific thought mainly utilizes resemblance and sometimes even the resemblance of vocabulary, but it does not make use of analogy.[93]

However, the epistemological justification of analogy is a very tricky matter. For Simondon, in order to be valid or "logical", an analogy must be a relation between two operations, a logical operation (stating a rapport between one being and an analogous being) and an ontological operation (the operative schema of the known being), and thus a relation between two relations (the individuation of thinking, and the individuation of being). "If it were a simple transfer of modalities of thought by which one contemplates a being, the analogy to another being would be merely an association of ideas".[94] The analogy in thought must reproduce the real analogy in being, i.e. the relationships between the terms articulated by its constitutive operations, its operative schema. But how is such an operative schema known, if not by analogy?

This is why, even if analogies are distinguished from metaphors, their justification remains aporetic within the strict limits of the theory of knowledge. Because analogy puts the relation at the heart of its procedures, it cannot find a definitive term that serves as its foundation. Any epistemological justification of the analogy is thus circular and without ending because it sends us back indefinitely to the relations. It amounts to an attempt at grounding the relation *be-*

---

90 ILNFI, p. 107/ILFI, p. 108.
91 Gaston Bachelard, *La formation de l'esprit scientifique*. Paris, Vrin [1938], 2004 p. 88.
92 ILNFI, p. 107/ILFI, p. 108.
93 ILNFI p. 666/ILFI, p. 563.
94 *Ibid.*, p. 666/p. 562.

tween thought and reality on a relation *in* reality, but such attempts can receive no demonstrable foundation because it is always thought that points to a relation in reality ... unless we leave the epistemological register to consider that these relations may be already embedded in concrete functionings even before being possible and thinkable. Yet this characterises the mode of existence of concrete technical objects: they are "testimony to a certain mode of functioning and compatibility that exists in fact and has been built before having been planned";[95] they are real before being possible. The problem of the epistemological justification of analogy is thus moved away from the epistemology of sciences to the epistemology of technics, or to technology.

For it is only in the domain of technology that analogy finds its primary justification (and a derived justification in the other domains). Indeed, the essence of technical objects is constituted by their scheme of functioning or operative scheme, and this scheme is also the vector of analogy: it is at the same time what makes the object function (the real relations which are established in it, by it and through it) and that by which the object can be known. It is thus the facticity of the very existence of individualised technical objects that justifies the use of analogy and its ability to be "logical". For a concrete technical object presents itself as an effective and coherent case of relation between a relation in thought and a relation working in reality.

In this respect, technical objects are the *hidden symbols* of metaphysics: symbols because their very existence gathers what metaphysics has always striven to make compatible: being and thought; hidden, because the academic history of metaphysics is built on the denial of such a status to be granted to technical objects. It remains traditionally blind to, or at best secretly acquiescent to it.[96] Hence we can see in negative what is technical culture and what could be the general culture integrating technics "in the form of knowledge and in the form of a sense of values"[97] that Simondon calls of his wishes: it would be less a scientific expertise and an analytical knowledge of the technical artifacts, than a de-occultation – including a *critical* de-occultation – of the constitutive role of technical schemes as symbols and vectors of the analogies that support and amplify the participation to the diverse forms of otherness of which culture is made.

Of course, founding analogy on technology does not clarify the conceptual structure of the analogy (for technical objects "are never entirely known"[98]). This even leads to holding any purely conceptual justification of analogy as im-

---

[95] METO p. 50/MEOT p. 48.
[96] On philosophy and technology as "intimate enemies", see François-David Sebbah, "The Philosopher and (his) Techniques: From the Work of Pierre Ducassé", in *Diacritics*, vol. 42, issue 1, 2014 pp. 6–21.
[97] METO p. 15/MEOT p. 9.
[98] *Ibid.* p. 39/p. 35.

possible. But this inserts analogical thought in a larger system of reality, in which it participates, and which justifies it while exceeding it, while obliging it to become – to individuate itself, that is to say, to *invent*. This is how we can understand Simondon's famous formula according to which

> The individuation of the real, exterior to the subject, is grasped by the subject due to the analogical individuation of knowledge within the subject; but it is *through the individuation of knowledge* and not through knowledge alone that the individuation of non-subject beings is grasped.[99]

10. Conclusion

The attention to objects commands a very demanding conception of philosophy that is radical in its own way, but also *unquiet*, preventing any quietude that philosophy could provide as an activity exercised for its own sake.

To summarise, the question what is philosophy with regard to "its" objects has been examined in the light of three refusals: i) *speculative* philosophy as "philosophy for its own sake"; ii) *activist* philosophy or "philosophy for"; iii) *applied* philosophy or "philosophy of". To put it in more positive terms, it could be argued that the mode of philosophising proposed by Simondon is: *reflexive* rather than *speculative*; and *participatory* rather than *applicative*. Concerning the former, reflexive philosophy only makes sense in the light of objects. Concerning the later, philosophy is not "applied" to an object but *participates in* the object's individuation, making it "more itself than it was before".[100]

Finally, such an attitude towards objects pleads for a *fieldwork philosophy* or "*philosophy of terrain*" that would not be an "*applied* philosophy" but rather an "*implied* philosophy." A practice of philosophy that would engage with the hottest contemporary issues without being a prisoner of actuality, and that would draw the best from the history of philosophy without fetishising it – or, to use Simondon's term, a practice of philosophy that would not be *a priori* or *a posteriori*, but a *a præsenti*, and this, not to coincide with itself in pure actuality but rather "to be both anterior and posterior in relation to itself" and to regain thereby an untimely character.

---

[99] ILNFI, p. 17/ILFI, p. 36.
[100] "Introduction (note sur l'attitude réflexive)", SLΦ, p. 21.

Philosophy of/as Information

Ashley Woodward

In this chapter I will explore the nature and function of philosophy in Simondon from a single perspective, that of information. The recent development of a branch of philosophy named "Philosophy of Information" allows the framing of this perspective: it permits us to take a retrospective look at Simondon's work from our current situation, and to appreciate what, in this remarkable work, continues to speak to us with great force and urgency today.[1] Simondon, of course, who died at the end of the 1980s, did not see the recent fruits of the information revolution, but his writings were deeply inspired by cybernetics and the theory of information at its heart. Accordingly, we can readily see Simondon as one of the earliest philosophers of information, who reformed philosophy on the basis of the notion of information in multiple key areas. In what follows, after a first discussion of Simondon's notion of information and its place in his thought, I will focus on reforms in two main areas: a new *image* of philosophy (thought as individuation), and a new *task* for philosophy (the integration of philosophy and culture). Throughout, what I wish to emphasise – as my title indicates – is that for Simondon, information is not simply an object for philosophical study, but a notion that comes to reform what philosophy itself is and how it is done. In other words, for Simondon, philosophy *of* information is also philosophy *as* information.

1. Why information?

It is remarkable that information has long remained one of the more opaque notions in the developing understanding of Simondon. Its centrality in his work can hardly be denied, and is indeed glaring; it is one of the main terms in the

---

1   The most influential of current philosophers of information is Luciano Floridi, who has mapped out new understandings of key philosophical coordinates inspired by information technologies as they have been taking shape since the 1990s. See for example Luciano Floridi, *The Philosophy of Information*, Oxford, Oxford University Press, 2011 and Idem, *The Fourth Revolution*, Oxford, Oxford University Press, 2014. In situating Simondon with Floridi and contemporary philosophy of information, I follow Andrew J. Iliadis, "Informational Ontology: The Meaning of Gilbert Simondon's Concept of Individuation", in: *Communication+1*, vol. 2, issue 1, 2013, Article 5 and and Jean-Hugues Barthélémy, "Gilbert Simondon and the Philosophy of Information. Jean-Hughes Barthélémy interviewed by Andrew Iliadis", in: *Journal of French and Francophone Philosophy*, vol. 23, issue 1, 2015, pp. 102–112.

title of his major thesis: *Individuation in Light of Notions of Form and Information*. Yet it was not taken up sympathetically by either Deleuze or Stiegler, the two most prominent philosophers inspired by his work, and early commentators in Simondon's posthumous reception also largely passed it over, or displayed some fundamental misunderstandings. For example, Muriel Combes's influential study, so astutely perceptive on so many points, barely mentions the concept of information, and Thomas LaMare, in his preface to his English translation of this book, suggests that "Simondon's concept of information has nothing in common with Information Theory in the usual sense of transmitted data (or in the cybernetic sense, for that matter)."[2] Yet these approaches to Simondon are untenable, and omit the notion which Simondon himself presented as central to his work of conceptual reform, and which, although modified, was drawn from and continues to work alongside cybernetic Information Theory. More recently, many scholars have rightly begun to pay more attention to the notion of information in Simondon's work.[3] This current chapter aims to contribute to this deepening understanding of the nature and role of information in Simondon's thought by drawing out its implications for his unique conception of philosophy.

While Simondon reformed the notion of information, it is clear from his early studies of cybernetics that he was deeply inspired by this new science and the centrality of information to it.[4] Moreover, he also makes it clear that his own ontological notion of information is not supposed to challenge or be incompati-

---

2 In Muriel Combes, *Gilbert Simondon and the Philosophy of the Transindividual*, transl. Thomas LaMarre, Cambridge, MA, MIT Press, 2012, p. xv.
3 See Jean-Hugues Barthélémy, *Penser l'individuation. Simondon et la philosophie de la nature*, Paris, L'Harmattan, 2005 (chapter 3); Jean-Yves Chateau, "Presentation: Communication et Information dans L'œuvre de Gilbert Simondon" in: *Communication et information*, Paris, Presses universitaires de France, 2015; Iliadis, "Informational Ontology", *op. cit.*; Kane X. Foucher, *Metastasis and Metastability: A Deleuzean Approach to Information*, Rotterdam, Sense, 2013; Andrea Bardin, *Epistemology and Political Philosophy in Gilbert Simondon: Individuation, Technics, Social System*, New York, Springer, 2014 (chapter 2); Yuk Hui, "Simondon et la question de l'information", in: Jean-Hugues Barthélémy (ed.), *Cahiers Simondon* 6, 2015, pp. 29–47; Simon Mills, *Gilbert Simondon: Information, Technology and Media*, London and New York, Rowman & Littlefield International, 2016; Juho Rantala, "The Notion of Information in Early Cybernetics and in Gilbert Simondon's Philosophy", Paper presented at Doctoral Congress in Philosophy 22, University of Tampere, Finland, 2018. (Available online: https://www.researchgate.net/publication/337670231_The_Notion_of_information_in_early_cybernetics_and_in_Gilbert_Simondon%27s_philosophy). An early exception to the rule is Jacques Garelli, "Transduction et information" in: Gilles Châtelet (ed.), *Gilbert Simondon – Une Pensée de l'individuation et de la technique*, Paris, Albin Michel, 1994, pp. 55–68. Recent interest in this topic is also indicated by the symposium "Simondon and the Concept of Information," organised by Giovanni Menegalle, held at King's College London, 13 May 2019.
4 "Cybernétique et philosophie" and "Épistémologie de la cybernétique," both manuscripts dating from 1953, first published in 2016 in SLΦ.

ble with technical Information Theory, but to extend and modify it to provide a properly ontogenetic dimension, on the basis of which it – along with so many other things – might be better understood.[5] First, then, let us note what Simondon saw in information that he found so compelling. In his 1953 text "Épistémologie de la cybernétique," he writes:

> [T]he theory of information studies how a specified structure – for example, that of words constituting a message – is transformed by a specified operation into another structure equivalent to the first, or into a more basic level of information (that is, one incapable of fully retransforming itself back into the first structure) – for example, a temporal series of telegraphic signals. The theory of information thus does not directly have for its aim the study of information, but the particular *operations* which transform information into another type of information: coding, ciphering, deciphering, modulation, demodulation, the theory of background noise, or the conversion of a sinusoidal signal into a pulse signal. It invents a hypothesis on the nature of these operations, which really transform a type of information into another type of information.[6]

Already we see here, then, Simondon's move away from the communication of content – the message – between already-constituted positions (sender and receiver), in favour of the *operational* and *transformational* aspects of information, which make it suitable for the philosophy of individuation and ontogenesis that he will shortly develop. The theory of information, initially developed for engineering problems, was extended in cybernetics to model how systems of all kinds become ordered and structured through processes that are communication-like. Simondon takes this up, but emphasises the genetic aspect of these processes, rather than assuming already individuated forms that would communicate information. What Simondon centralises in information is in fact *transformation*, the communicative operation which gives form and changes form. While to my knowledge Simondon himself never expresses this in such a pithy formula, I would suggest that for him, *information is transformation*. It is notable that Simondon already saw this aspect *in* the technical and cybernetic theories of information, since it adds historical (or genetic) weight to the important corrective to the view that his notion of information is completely different to these theories.

For Simondon, then, Information Theory is a theory of *operations*, of *transformations* (and thus an *allagmatics*, in Simondon's terms). An important aspect of the value of the notion of information is that it is *general* enough to apply to any domain. In Information Theory, information content is independent of its support, meaning that the same message can be carried by different supports (or media). This independence of specific support would also seem to apply to

---

5   See ILNFI, p. 31 note 10/p. 384 note 12.
6   SLΦ, pp. 181–182. Translations from French texts are mine.

the transformative capacity of information: the same kind of transformative operation can be seen in different domains, regardless of the "substances" that are being transformed. This gives information a paradigmatic and transductive power, meaning that the notion can be applied in any domain of reality, as well as between different domains. Moreover, information also seems to have both *quantitative* and *qualitative* dimensions, increasing its capacity to work in different domains, from the physical to the psychosocial. Raymond Ruyer highlights the way that Information Theory arose from precursor theories such as behaviourism and linguistic pragmatics, which focus on the *effects* communication has, rather than on semantic meaning.[7] In this way, information seems to connect the pragmatic, effective dimensions of *operation* and *transformation* with the more usual or common sense notion of information as meaningful semantic content, or *signification*.

Indeed, it is this connection between the non-meaningful and meaningful aspects of reality (to put it crudely) that Simondon further indicates as being important to the notion of information as a *reform* of the notion of *form*. Simondon presents information as the latest and best development in a genealogy of the notion of form, and states that "we actually uncover the same goal at work in the successive theories of hylomorphism, good form, and then information: the goal that seeks to discover the inherence of significations to *being*."[8] This implies the connection, as I put it above, of the non-meaningful and meaningful aspects of reality, or of how meaning "emerges" from the non-meaningful – or as Simondon expresses this here, "the inherence of significations to *being*." And, he adds, "it is precisely this inherence that we would like to discover in the operation of individuation."[9] Placed in this lineage, then, information appears for Simondon as a way of thinking form itself in its role as *ontogenesis*, which the notions of form in hylomorphism, and in the Gestaltists' notion of 'good form' did not manage to do (because the former understood form as a fixed pre-existent term, and the latter as a stable equilibrium).

This, then, is the promise that Simondon sees in the cybernetic theory of information. But he also believes that the notion needs to be reformed in order to take it out of the relatively narrow technical confines of its cybernetic application, in order that it may have truly encyclopaedic, paradigmatic power.

---

[7] Raymond Ruyer, *La Cybernétique et l'origine de l'information*, Paris, Flammarion, 1954, pp. 7–8.
[8] ILNFI, p. 17/ILFI, p. 35.
[9] ILNFI, p. 17/ILFI, p. 35.

2. Simondon information

The various technical theories of information are sometimes called after their inventors – for example, "Fisher information," "Shannon information," "Kolmogorov information," etc. In a similar fashion, we might talk of "Simondon information."[10] Simondon information is what he at one point calls "first" or "primary" information, in relation to technical information. This occurs in the important note in which he indicates the complementarity of technical theories and his own ontological theory of information. After affirming the importance of the latter, he notes:

> This affirmation does not lead to contesting the validity of the quantitative theories of information and the measures of complexity, but it does suppose a fundamental state (that of pre-individual being) anterior to any duality of emitter and receiver and therefore to any transmitted message. What remains of this fundamental state in the classical case of information transmitted as a message is not the source of information but the primordial condition without which there is no effect of information and therefore no information: this condition is the metastability of the receiver, whether it be a technical being or the living individual. This information can be called "first information."[11]

As we noted above, "information" is for Simondon the name of the transformative operation in general. In this sense, perhaps his best general description of information, as he understands it, is to be found in the essay "L'Amplification dans les processus d'information," which he presented at the conference he organised at Royaumont in 1962 on The Concept of Information in Contemporary Science. Here we read the following:

> *To be or not to be* information does not depend solely on the internal characteristics of a structure; information is not a thing, but the operation of a thing arriving in a system and producing a transformation in it. Information cannot define itself outside of this action of transformative effect [*incidence*] and the operation of reception.
>
> ... the *local* reality, the receiver, is *modified in its becoming* by the *incident* [*incidente*] reality, and it is this modification of the local reality by the incident reality that is the function of information.[12]

---

10   A precedent in this is Foucher, *Metastasis and Metastability, op. cit.* (chapter 2).
11   ILNFI, p. 384, note 12/ILFI, p. 31, note 10. Taylor Adkins, whose recently published translation of *Individuation* I quote from here and throughout, and which should now be taken as the standard reference in English, renders "*information première*" as "first information." However, I prefer to follow previous translators who have rendered it as "primary information," since "first" seems to more strongly imply a temporal order, while "primary" can better suggest a temporally neutral *order of priority*, which I think better expresses the ontological nature of this idea, with its attendant temporal paradoxes (since temporality is itself generated by the primary information processes involved in individuation).
12   CI, p. 159.

Information as transformative operation is difficult to "locate" definitively in any specific stage of the transformative or form-taking process that Simondon describes, since he states that it is never a term but is always a relation of tension;[13] because time itself is generated by the process of individuation as one of its dimensions (such that information does not exist at one point in a time that would pre-exist and envelop it, but which it itself generates); and because, in practice, Simondon locates it in multiple times and places in the processes he describes: information is both the seed for individuation (the message) and the metastable system that individuates (the receiver), but more properly perhaps it is the tension that is set up and is resolved in the communication between them. Moreover, information is what is resolved by signification, and it is also this signification that resolves. As Simon Mills explains,

> information is descriptive of the process by which individuation occurs and as such is often used by Simondon as a description of different aspects of that process. [...] As such, for Simondon, *information* is the term used to describe the individuation process from a number of different perspectives.[14]

In tracking the various ways in which Simondon uses the term "information" in his writings, we might seem to run into logical contradictions: how can it be both this, *and* that? This however should not be unexpected, since Simondon does in fact insist that concepts do not seem adequate for the thought of individuation, and asserts that the laws of classical logic, such as the principles of identity and excluded middle, are appropriate only to individuated beings, and not to the thought of being in its genesis. If "information is the formula of individuation,"[15] it should not be surprising then that Simondon's elaboration of information seems to run afoul of classical logic. In sum, "information" is the most basic and general term for what in a metastable system establishes a communication between disparate orders of potentials and produces an internal resonance, and the resolution of the problematic so generated such that a transductive operation of individuation results and a signification is produced. The *link* between "primary information" and the technical information described by cybernetics and Information Theory is given in the cultural relevance of information technologies, as described in *On the Mode of Existence of Technical Objects*, as we shall see in the section on the new *task* Simondon sets for philosophy, below.

---

13   ILNFI, p. 11/ILFI, p. 31.
14   Mills, *Gilbert Simondon, op. cit.*, p. 44.
15   ILNFI, p. 12/ILFI, p. 31.

3. A new *image* of philosophy: thought as individuation

Taking inspiration from chapter three of Deleuze's *Difference and Repetition*, I want to suggest that Simondon gives us a new image of thought. The character of this thought is *individuation*. I will begin with a general description of this image, then show how Simondon's early studies of cybernetics reveal an informational inspiration and character of this image of thought. One of the fundamental roles of philosophy for Simondon is to provide a knowledge of individuation (an ontology, or ontogenesis), and he announces in the Introduction of *Individuation* that knowledge of individuation must take the form of individuation of knowledge:

> by being accomplished, only the individuation of thought can accompany the individuation of beings other than thought; we therefore cannot have an immediate knowledge or a mediated knowledge of individuation, but we can have a knowledge that is an operation parallel to the operation known [...] this apprehension is [...] an analogy between two operations, an analogy that is a certain mode of communication. The individuation of the real, exterior to the subject, is grasped by the subject due to the analogical individuation of knowledge within the subject; but it is *through the individuation of knowledge* and not through knowledge alone that the individuation of non-subject beings is grasped. Beings can be known through the knowledge of the subject, but the individuation of beings can only be grasped through the individuation of the subject's knowledge.[16]

While other modes of thought can have knowledge of individuated things, it is philosophy's task to think ontogenesis through the individuation of knowledge. This requires a new image of thought: thought itself must be understood as individuation, which becomes adequate to what it thinks through an analogical relation with it, in which both subject and object co-individuate.

Simondon elaborates this later on in *Individuation*, stating that "*[t]he epistemological postulate of this study is that the relation between two relations is itself a relation.*"[17] We need then to understand ontogenetic knowledge as involving three relations which all have an individuating character, which combine in the individuation of knowledge. First, there is the relation in the domain of the object which individuates the object of study. The nature of these relations in the different domains is what is studied throughout *Individuation*, starting with the basic paradigm of physical individuation, crystallisation, with the relation between the seed and the supersaturated solution. Second, there is individuation in the realm of the subject, that of thought. Simondon explains this as a historical genesis of thought: "every thought, precisely to the extent that it is real, is a *relation*, i.e. includes a historical aspect in its genesis."[18] Thoughts appear in relation

---

16 ILNFI, p. 17/ILFI, p. 36.
17 ILNFI, p. 76/ILFI, p. 83.
18 ILNFI, p. 77/ILFI, p. 84.

to past thoughts. And thirdly, there is the analogical relation between the subjective and objective relations, which itself has an individuating power, and produces knowledge of individuation.

The *informational* aspect of this image of thought is more clearly revealed in a note only recently published in *Sur la philosophie*. This note is explicitly related to the abandoned second part of Simondon's major thesis, on "The History of the Notion of the Individual," and so cannot be taken at face value in terms of its consistency with the completed thesis. Nevertheless, we can see the basic structure of an analogy between the process to be studied and the process of thought that studies it, and a specification of the origin of this image of thought in Information Theory:

> We will employ [...] a postulate conforming to the theory of information, which states that for reflective consciousness, the prereflexive ground from which this consciousness emerges must contain, in the form of internal tensions, a potential of information large enough for this consciousness to be capable of defining a reflective notion possessing the same quantity of information as the very prereflexive ground from which it emerged. The thought provides the reflection, but it does not create the information by taking it from nothing.[19]

Moreover, Simondon understands the two terms – objective reality and the thought which thinks it – in a co-constitutive relation. The metastable state of the object to be thought contains in itself an incompletion which is partially fulfilled by the knowing subject, and the subject itself desires to know the object because of its own incompletion. He explains:

> Reflection is a particular case of the relation between a problematic and the different operations by which it can be resolved thanks to the presence of a subject that is already constituted, but still incomplete in its equilibrium. A perfectly completed subject which would not have in itself any lack of unity would find itself incapable of thinking and reflecting.[20]

As such, we can see the idea of information as a *transforming operation* between two orders – which, we saw above, Simondon emphasises as the most important aspect of Information Theory – as operative in the image of thought as the individuation of knowledge. Knowledge is a communication of information between the subject and the object, each individuating the other. In the relation that is knowledge, thought and its object are both modified, their metastable states taking on greater stability.

---

19 "'Point de méthode' (Note sur Individuation et Histoire de la pensée, autour de 1955)", in SLΦ, p. 27.
20 "'Introduction' (Note sur l'attitude refléxive, autour de 1955)", in SLΦ, pp. 23–24.

When Simondon describes a "simple" process of individuation, involving a single relation or relations in a single order, he emphasises that there is *no loss* of information, but rather a *conservation of information*.[21] When it is a matter of two different orders of individuation communicating and producing a new individuation, however, it is a matter of greater complexity, and Simondon describes this as the production of a *higher level or degree of information*. In the preparatory study "Point de méthode," he explains:

> the postulate of this method is that the access to the reflexivity of a form of individuation can perform like the condition of the appearance of a form possessing a higher level of information. [...]
>
> One can call this necessity "ontological necessity" or "allagmatic necessity", because it combines the foundation of two other necessities [logical and physical]; one can formulate it thus: information does not create itself *ex nihilo*, but is produced by successive stages of conversions of operation into structure and of structure into operation. Each conversion integrates, in a quantum manner, a higher degree of information, which is produced by this act of conversion itself. The act of conversion includes some supplementary information in its result, which creates a difference of level between the initial state and the final state: this act achieves a decrease of the initial number of operations or structures, to the profit of the level of information of the resulting operations or structures; it is a creator of synthesis.[22]

What this means for knowledge is this: the order of thought is informed by the order of the object it studies, and there is a transfer of information between these orders which enables an individuation which produces knowledge as a "higher level" of information than that of either the object or subject alone before they come into communication.

In the 1953 draft "Cybernétique et philosophie," Simondon further indicates the cybernetic inspiration for the model of philosophical thought he is developing, highlighting in particular the way that thought contributes to the domain that it studies by enabling the resolution of a problematic state already contained in the domain itself, which it could not resolve on its own:

> In terms of this investigation, we see that the philosophical effort can think itself cybernetically: the philosophical effort, which manifests itself in a domain, is a becoming conscious of a certain problematic which up to that point existed in a spontaneous fashion and would not be able to resolve itself solely on the basis of the structural characteristics of the holistic system in which it manifests itself; the philosophical effort transforms the structure of the holistic system [...] it brings reflexivity, in addition to spontaneous functions, which creates a new internal resonance.[23]

---

21 ILNFI, p. 15/ILFI, p. 34.
22 "'Point de Méthode", SLΦ, p. 28.
23 "Cybernétique et philosophie", SLΦ, pp. 61–62.

Simondon further compares the relation of thought to its object to the physical paradigm of individuation, thus underlining the image of thought *as* individuation:

> This situation of a being which can be transformed by the intervention of reflection is comparable to that of a system in a state of over-tension [*surtension*], like, for example, a supersaturated solution such as it is studied by physics. But it is also necessary that the subject capable of operating the transformation of the over-tense state is such because it tries to find a higher completion itself. It is in this way that the seed of the crystal is able to operate the resolution of a state bearing a certain number of internal tensions. It is in the same way that the subject capable of reflecting a specified given must be animated by a certain number of internal tensions capable of provoking the structuration of a field, of an operational field, itself incomplete and in a state of tension.[24]

In sum then, we can see from these early studies that the image of philosophical thought as individuation is inspired by cybernetics and Information Theory: Simondon proposes to think knowledge as a kind of cybernetic system, in which metastable states communicate and resolve problems through processes which are informational in the sense that they involve operations of transformation. The resolution of the tension between two states of incompletion, the subject and the object, produces knowledge which can be understood as a level of information higher than that which either of the two states alone contained. This would seem to correspond to the general intuition that knowledge is a gain in information.

4. A new *task* for philosophy: the integration of technics and culture

In *On the Mode of Existence of Technical Objects*, Simondon gives philosophy a specific task: to overcome alienation by accomplishing the integration of technics and culture. The general features of this task have become well known in the secondary literature, but an overlooked aspect of it I wish to emphasise here is the role of information. In fact, and crucially for our interests here, Simondon writes that "the notion of information is the most suitable for accomplishing the integration of culture with a representative and axiological content adequate to technical reality envisaged in its essence [...]."[25] Let us briefly rehearse Simondon's account of the problem of alienation and the challenge of overcom-

---

24 "'Introduction", SLΦ, pp. 21–22.
25 METO, p. xiii. This comment is found in the "Summary of *On the Mode of Existence of Technical Objects*" included at the end of Nathalie Simondon's Note in the English translation, and does not appear in the French edition.

ing it through integrating technics and culture, before highlighting the role of information in this new philosophical task.

Simondon proposes that, at a deeper level than the alienation proposed by Marx (which he interprets as functioning on an economic level), in contemporary culture there is an alienation between the human and technical objects. This alienation is based on a split between culture, which deals with human representations, and technics, which are considered to be different in essence from the human, and are treated as objects with an exclusive function of utility. According to Simondon's innovative thesis, however, this is an illegitimate exclusion of technics from culture, based on an artificial divide. In fact, technics contain an aspect of humanity just as "cultural" products do, because they are creations of human beings and express a possible relation between the human and the world. Our experience of technical objects produces a feeling of alienation, because the objects themselves are alienated from human culture. There is a general dimension to this alienation which, in a speculative genealogy presented in the third section of *Mode*, Simondon traces to a phase shift from the "primitive magical unity" to the two modes of human relation to the world that are religion and technics. However, there is also a more specific dimension of technical alienation which devolves from the fact that the representations of technologies that do circulate in culture lag behind the reality of current technological developments: we maintain ideas of artisanal or industrial technologies, while our current technologies are post-industrial (that is, informational).[26]

To overcome our alienated relation to technical objects, Simondon proposes that such objects need to be understood by studying them in their *genesis*; by understanding how notions of *progress* shape the human relation to technics; and by understanding the *essence* of technicity, which is a broader reality than individual technical objects, and indicates a mode of the relation between human being and the world. Each of these tasks corresponds to each of the three main sections of *Mode*. As elaborated in the final chapter of the book, philosophy has a privileged role as the only type of thought able to accomplish the integration of culture and technics.

The key role of information in the first two of the three parts of *Mode* is clearly explained in the Prospectus of the book. The place of information in the evolution of technical objects is indicated as follows:

> There is something like a redundancy of information in the technical object having become concrete. [...] This notion of information allows the general evolution of technical objects to be interpreted via the succession of elements, of individuals and of ensembles,

---

26   "Post-industrial" is a term not used in METO, but Simondon uses it in some later writings, for example, "Technical Mentality" (trans. Arne de Boever in: Arne de Boever, Alex Murray, Jon Roffe, and Ashley Woodward (eds.), *Gilbert Simondon: Being and Technology*, Edinburgh, Edinburgh University Press, 2012, pp. 1–15).

according to the law of conservation of technicity. [...] there is a preservation throughout the successive cycles of evolution of technicity as information.[27]

I will not pursue this issue of the evolution of technical objects further here, other than to note that Simondon indicates that ensembles – to which we will return below – are more evolved, and have a higher degree of technicity, because they have a greater openness to information.

Corresponding to the second section of *Mode*, the role of information in the notion of *progress* which regulates the rapport between man and technical objects is explained as follows:

> [W]hat remains to be elaborated is a new notion of progress corresponding to the discovery of technics at the level of the ensembles of our epoch, by virtue of a deepening of the theory of information and communication: [...] man [...] is the agent and translator of information from machine to machine, intervening within the margin of indeterminacy harbored by the open machine's way of functioning, which is capable of receiving information. Man constructs the signification of the exchanges of information between machines.[28]

The *value* of information as a paradigm of progress is that it is related to *regulation*, in contrast to the paradigm drawn from thermodynamic machines, which, Simondon says, are symbols of power, and give rise to the danger of a controlling technocratism. The key difference between the technologies of the thermodynamic age and the information age, Simondon tells us, is that the former involve the same channels for energy supply and for regulation, while the latter separate these channels.[29] This separation allows the idea of regulation to emerge as an independent technical schema, and a series of values to develop on the basis of the study of information channels. Simondon explains:

> [I]n machines, the advent of the use of information-channels that are distinct from energy channels caused a very profound change in the philosophy of technics. [...] Beyond the dimensions defined by thermodynamics, a new category of physical dimensions emerges that makes it possible to classify information channels and compare them. This elaboration of new concepts has a particular sense for philosophical thought because it provides the example of new values which, until this day, made no sense in technics, though they made sense in human thought and behaviour.[30]

The related ideas of information channels and regulation thus present a close link between technics and human culture. Regulation is a highly "suitable" technical schema for incorporation into culture, because culture itself, for

---

27 METO, p. xv/MEOT, p. 362.
28 METO, p. xvi/MEOT, pp. 362–363.
29 METO, p. 143/MEOT, pp. 179–180.
30 METO, pp. 143–144/MEOT, pp. 180–181.

Simondon, has the role of regulating human behaviour, including relations between human beings and the world, and thus also the relation between the human and the machine. Information machines thus seem to supply a technical schema which has the special characteristic (regulation) of being more suitable to overcoming technical alienation than the schemas of the technics of previous paradigms.

Moreover, information technologies have a specific relevance to the third type of technical objects in their evolution, *ensembles*. Simondon writes:

> the birth of a technical philosophy at the level of ensembles is possible only through an in-depth study of regulations, which is to say of information. True technical ensembles are not the ones that use technical individuals, but those that form a fabric of technical individuals through a relation of interconnection. Any philosophy of technics that starts from the reality of ensembles using technical individuals without putting them into a relation of information remains a philosophy of human power through technics, not a philosophy of technics.[31]

Simondon presents us, then, with a convergence of several qualities and tendencies attendant to information technologies which make them – and the technical schema of information – especially suitable for an overcoming of alienation.

However, in section 2 of *Mode*, Simondon moves from establishing the paradigmatic superiority of Information Theory over thermodynamics to then marking some definite *limits* to the *technical* theory of information, and sketching a non-technical or extra-technical theory of information as a necessary supplement. This move coincides with a critique of cybernetics, as well as the idea of the automaton, and an argument for a necessary relation of humans *with* machines. This intriguing section[32] is extremely important in understanding Simondon's philosophy of information, since it allows insight into the relationship between the *technical* notion of information, as developed in Information Theory and cybernetics, and Simondon's original, ontological notion of "primary information."

The *limit* of the technological notion of information is that it does not allow us to understand the necessity of the human as mediator between machines. The physical analogy between humans and machines which predominated in cybernetics did not acknowledge a qualitative difference between the ways human beings and machines process information, but Simondon believes this difference is essential.[33] He introduces this limit and this difference by pointing out the

---

31 METO, p. 141/MEOT, p. 176.
32 METO, pp. 147–159/MEOT, pp. 185–203.
33 Raymond Ruyer had mounted a similar argument in his 1954 book *La cybernétique et l'origine de l'information*. Jean-Hugues Barthélémy reports that Simondon read this book, and calls it an "indispensable" [incontournable] source for his own work on cybernetics and Information Theory (Barthélémy, *Penser l'individuation, op. cit.*, p. 21). However, it is a largely hidden source, as Simondon's references to Ruyer in his writings are extremely rare, the only

nonunivocal nature of information, its paradoxical quality as lying between "stereotypy"[34] and "contingency." In Information Theory, information is understood as a measure of surprise – if the receiver receives something it already knows, it is not information. Information thus needs to involve a dimension of contingency, of the chance event. However, the receiver must also be so constituted that it can make some sense of the message, so must bear a degree of similarity or "stereotypy" in relation to the message, or as Simondon puts it, it must contain some common forms. He states that

> [t]his opposition represents a technical antinomy that poses a problem for philosophical thought: information is *like* the chance event, but it nevertheless distinguishes itself from it. An absolute stereotypy, excluding all novelty, also excludes all information.[35]

This "technical antinomy" in information then points to the necessity of *a margin of indeterminacy* in information machines. This is the open space of possibility of a machine to be in different states or to serve different functions. Mechanically, a reduction of indeterminacy – a choice between possibilities – is effectuated by a transducer. Yet the technical transducer is only a very inferior version of the transducer which is a living being. Simondon suggests that ultimately, the decisions and choices which *inform* machines must be supplied by living beings, which contain a capacity of information *within* them, as machines do not. We can understand this to mean that human beings are needed to make the choices which inform the operations of machines, which programme them and which feed them new information. In *Mode*, Simondon distinguishes be-

---

substantial engagement being his essay "Les Limites du progrès humain" (SLT, pp. 412–427), a response to Ruyer's identically titled essay ("Les Limites du progrès humain", in: *Revue de métaphysique et de morale*, vol. 63, issue 4, October–December 1958, pp. 412–427). On this exchange, see Philippe Gagnon, "Ruyer and Simondon on Technological Inventiveness and Form Outlasting Its Medium", in: *Deleuze Studies*, vol. 11, issue 4, 2017, pp. 538–554. The relations between Ruyer and Simondon on the issues of information and cybernetics need to be reconstructed. See Barthélémy's efforts in this direction, *op. cit.*, pp. 125–130. I would note that several arguments Ruyer develops bear a strong similarity to those Simondon mounts. For example Ruyer's argument concerning the "perpetual motion" of information machines as an absurdity to which the cybernetic theory seems to lead, with the example of telephones in circuit talking amongst themselves. His argument that machines are only capable of relations of causality in the dimension of actuality, whereas the creation of information requires a virtuality that can only be supplied by a human mind, are also close to the terms of Simondon's arguments in section 2 of METO. Barthélémy rightly notes, however, that the metaphysics which frames Ruyer's approach is too "vitalist" and "spiritualist" for Simondon's taste (*op. cit.*, 128).

34 I here follow Malaspina and Rogove's translation of *stéréotypie*, but I would suggest that "standardisation" or "conventionality" would perhaps more clearly translate the antonym of contingency indicated in this context.

35 METO, p. 149/MEOT, p. 189.

tween *forms*, which are what machines can work with, and what in this context he calls simply *information*. The descriptions Simondon gives here of the information that humans need to provide are closely reminiscent of the descriptions of "primary information" in *Individuation*, indicating a resolution of problems and an actualisation of potentials. In *Mode*, Simondon identifies this type of information with *signification*,[36] the meaning or sense which humans are capable of creating and understanding, and machines are not. This then is why the *technical* understanding of information is limited, and why machines need human beings: they need the level of signification to translate between the operations of different machines, uniting them through meaning and purpose. We could translate Simondon's claims into the language of contemporary philosophy of information by saying that what machines operate with is *the syntax of data transmission*, while human beings are exclusively capable of supplying the *semantics* of information.[37]

Simondon thus proposes Information Theory as the current, and the best – provided it undergoes the modifications he specifies – paradigm for the incorporation of technical schemas into culture. In this regard, he supports Norbert Wiener's basic proposal of the link between information and values, writing:

> [I]nformation is opposed to background noise in the same way that negative entropy is opposed to entropy as defined by thermodynamics. [...] this opposition contains within itself an entire method for the discovery and for the definition of a set of values that are implied in technical ways of functioning and in the concepts by means of which one can think them.[38]

Social regulation can thus be understood in terms of the positive value of information and communication, and the negative value of noise. Simondon explains:

> [T]hermodynamic energeticism is replaced by information theory, whose content is normative and eminently regulative and stabilizing: the development of technics appears to be a guarantee of stability. The machine, as an element of the technical ensemble, becomes that which increases the quantity of information, increases negentropy, and opposes the degradation of energy: the machine, being a work of organization and information, is, like life itself and together with life, that which is opposed to disorder, to the leveling of all things tending to deprive the universe of the power of change.[39]

---

36 While in *Individuation* signification is more clearly identified as one type of information, or information from a certain perspective. See the section "From Information to Signification," ILNFI, pp. 244–250/ILFI, pp. 219–223.
37 See for example Floridi, *The Philosophy of Information*, op. cit., chapter 6.
38 METO, p. 161 /MEOT, pp. 205–206.
39 METO, p. 21/MEOT, pp. 17–18.

Again, however, while being deeply influenced by cybernetics, Simondon critiques and departs from it by suggesting that Wiener's applications of these values to culture need to be modified in the following ways. First, while Wiener puts the emphasis on individual leaders as best being able to instantiate such values for social regulation (Platonic philosopher-kings, as Simondon has it), Simondon puts the emphasis on *culture*. Second – and crucially, in my view – Simondon suggests, in opposition to Wiener, that *homeostasis* should not be an absolute social value, and points also to the social and political values of "advent," or change, as also important and consistent with the model of social regulation drawn from cybernetic and informatic principles. Finally, Simondon suggests that technicity cannot solve *all* problems, as cybernetics seems to imply – instead, technicity needs to be placed in rapport with other modes of relation between the human and the world, such as religion and aesthetics. It is precisely *philosophy* which has the role of doing this.

The third part of *Mode*, on the essence of technicity, which explains this role of philosophy, falls strangely silent with regard to information. Here, beyond the letter of Simondon's text, I want to suggest that we can develop this aspect by drawing a link back to the *informational* nature of philosophy, as developed in *Individuation* and early notes, and outlined above.

5. Conclusion: philosophical thought as information process

In the last section of *Mode*, Simondon presents a speculative genealogy of the relation between human being and the world, proposing that an original magical unity phase shifts into religion and technics, which each then phase shift into theoretical and practical aspects. Alienation is due to the division of these various phases, especially the divorce of the technical from the others. What gives philosophy the special power to overcome alienation is precisely its "neutrality" with respect to any particular phase or mode of relation to the world; its ability to understand any domain of reality by following the processes of individuation as they unfold, and to integrate them by charting the transductive relations between them. Philosophy thus has a unifying function, effectuating the relations between different domains, individuals, and problems, and realising a transductive unity in being, reminiscent of the primitive magical unity.

This function of philosophical thought recalls the new image of thought as individuation, and the inspirations from Information Theory in composing this new image, as we saw above. Simondon writes here that "philosophical thought reintegrates itself into genetic coming-into-being in order to fulfil it,"[40] a descrip-

---

[40] METO, p. 244/MEOT, p. 323.

tion reminiscent of his early studies concerning the way that two types of information transform and complete each other in the relation that is knowledge. Broadly speaking, then, while Simondon is silent on this particular issue in *Mode*, we might propose that thought is capable of overcoming alienation because of its informational character.

More specifically, I want to suggest that the image of philosophical thought as information process plays an essential role in the accomplishment of the task of integrating culture and technics. Elaborating the general problem of overcoming alienation, Simondon writes: "The philosophical effort thus finds itself faced with a unique task to be accomplished: the search for unity among the technical and non-technical modes of thought."[41] The foundation of this task, and an essential step in its accomplishment, is the integration of the technical and the non-technical in the image of philosophy itself. This is crucial, because philosophical thought (along with poetry, art, and other exemplars of human culture) has often been held up as itself a paragon of non-technical thought. The integration of these different modes, I would argue, thus needs to begin with a changed image of philosophy, one which better conforms to the ideal "neutrality" with respect to different phases and domains of being Simondon points to, and this is in fact what he provides us with through the notion of information.

In short, Simondon's complex notion of information allows an integration – through a nonreductive, transductive relation – of the technical and of what has been thought to be exclusive to human culture – that is, reflective thought or philosophy. The notion of information performs this integrating function because it proposes a single idea – information – with two extreme poles, technical information and primary information, with a transductive relation between them.

This particular, Simondonian image of thought as information process lies between two popular extreme images of thought which both fail to overcome alienation. On the one hand, there is the reduction of thought to technical information processing, as cybernetics seemed to imply, and as many more recent views, such as functionalism, computationalism, and cognitive science have continued to suggest in various ways. On the other hand, there is the belief in an absolute difference between technical information on the one hand, and philosophical thought and human culture on the other, a view dominant in most continental philosophical traditions of the twentieth century, and most canonically expressed by Heidegger, whose critiques of cybernetics and Information Theory, while brief and schematic, were well known and widely influential.

Simondon's informational image of philosophy thus sails between the Scylla and Charybdis of these equally alienating positions, presenting an idea of thought which is inspired by technical information, which exceeds it to encompass the hu-

---

41 METO, p. 225/MEOT, p. 296.

man, cultural dimension, and which envelops and maintains a connection with technical information, presenting a transductive unity of technical and primary information. The reform of philosophy's image is then itself a part of philosophy's task of integrating culture and technics: it is a philosophy of information which embodies "humanistic needs," and connects them with information technologies: philosophy becomes informational; information becomes philosophical.

III.

Philosophy as Ethics and Politics

Gilbert Simondon's Grammars of Value

Matthieu Amat

This chapter starts from an observation: the Simondonian use of the concept of value has been little considered by commentators, although this concept plays a central role in several crucial texts – the manuscripts on cybernetics of 1953, the introduction to the METO, and above all the conclusion of ILNFI, where Simondon's speculative effort culminates. We want to show that value belongs to the "fundamental philosophical notions" which Simondon undertakes to "reform", including being, the form, and the individual.[1]

The notion of value, which may seem common or even trivial, is thus only a recent subject in philosophy. Not until the second half of the 19th century, first in Germany, was value thematised as a philosophical concept, in the wake of the Kantian approach to objectivity in terms of validity (Lotze), of the critique of economics (Marx) and of Nietzsche's philosophy of life. In French-speaking philosophy, value imposes itself, from the 1930s to the end of the 1950s, as one of the centres of gravity of the philosophical field, under the particular influence of neo-Kantianism, of the phenomenology of values, and of Nietzsche.[2] In 1950, Émile Bréhier speaks of a "sudden and smashing development" of the "theory of values" in French philosophy.[3] In this context, value is substantivised: evaluations and "value judgments" are less interesting than *the* value(s), which become the *sui generis* object of a philosophy conceived as "value theory" or "axiology".[4]

One must keep this in mind when reading Simondon's developments on value(s). In addition to the significant allusions to a supposed "doctrine of val-

---

1   ILFI, p. 35/p. 17
2   Let me mention in particular: René le Senne, *Obstacle et valeur*, Paris, Aubier, 1934; Alfred Stern, *La Philosophie des valeurs. Regard sur ses tendances en Allemagne*, 2 vol., Paris, Hermann, 1936; Eugène Dupréel, *Esquisse d'une philosophie des valeurs*, Paris, Alcan, 1939; Raymond Polin, *La création des valeurs: recherches sur le fondement de l'objectivité axiologique*, Paris, PUF, 1944; Raymond Ruyer, *Le monde des valeurs*, Paris, Aubier, 1948, and *Philosophie de la valeur*, Paris, Armand Colin, 1952; Louis Lavelle, *Traité des valeurs*, 2 vol., Paris, PUF, 1951, 1955; Paul Césari, *La valeur*, Paris, PUF, 1957. In 1955, the PUF published Max Scheler's phenomenology of values, translated by Maurice de Gandillac: *Le formalisme en éthique et l'éthique matériale des valeurs*.
3   Émile Bréhier, *Transformation de la philosophie française*, Paris, Flammarion, 1950, p. 65; see also: É. Bréhier, "Doutes sur la philosophie de la valeur", in *Revue de Métaphysique et de Morale*, Juillet 1939, vol. 46, No. 3, pp. 399–414 and É. Bréhier, *Les thèmes actuels de la philosophie*, Paris, PUF, 1951, chap. X: "Les valeurs".
4   *Ibid.*, p. 67–70.

ues" or the "phenomenology of values", the expressions, common in Simondon's text, of "table of value" and above all of "axiology" unambiguously inscribe him in these debates and indicates his intention to take a clear position. However, Simondon's writings raise the question as to whether the language he uses is borrowed in order to open up a dialogue with his contemporaries. Does this language merely make his thought more communicable, or does it end up twisting his thought, or even constituting an obstacle or a dead end for the author himself? We will support this thesis in selected points relating to the grammar of value mobilised in METO. But above all, we want to show how Simondon, aware of a certain discourse on value, sought to reform its aporias by differentiating between various axiological regimes and by proposing a novel determination of value as "action due to which there can be complementarity" and the "transductive expansiveness" of an act.[5]

The contemporary debates in the philosophy of values revolved around four main problems: 1) to know whether there is monism or pluralism of values;[6] 2) to determine in what sense value is transcendent;[7] 3) to determine the relation between being and value, ontology and axiology;[8] 4) to conceive of the individual relation to values as objective: "what seems to me most novel in the contemporary theory of values in France," wrote Bréhier in 1951, "is what could be called the problem of the individualization of values".[9] It would be a stretch to see this as an early formulation of the Simondonian programme. Nevertheless, the formula is suggestive. We will see Simondon position himself, implicitly or explicitly, in each of these problematic fields. In so doing, this immanent analysis of Simondon's grammars of value will also help to better situate his work in a history of contemporary philosophy. It also aspires to offer some conceptual resources in a context where value is, once again, at the centre of discussions in philosophy and in the human and social sciences.

This study will show how it is possible to recognise value as a variable quantity without falling into axiological reductionism or relativism. Starting from the 1953 manuscripts on cybernetics, I will show that it implies 1) dismiss-

---

[5] INLFI, p. 402, p. 378/ILFI, p. 331, p. 324.

[6] Bréhier starts from this problem: *Transformation de la philosophie française, op. cit.*, p. 128–147.

[7] For example, as an absolute metaphysical value for René le Senne, as an ideal entity object of a specific intuition in Max Scheler, as self-transcendence of existence for Raymond Polin, or as a social institution in Eugène Dupréel.

[8] Bréhier explains the rise of reflection on values by "the need to seek a guide of conduct and a rule of appreciation apart from the reality that we are" (É. Bréhier, *ibid.*, p. 67). Value is the Good separated from the Being, the good which *is* not anymore, but which *has worth* (Herbert Schnädelbach, *Philosophie in Deutschland. 1831–1933*, Frankfurt M., Suhrkamp, 1983, pp. 197–200).

[9] Bréhier, *ibid.*, p. 66.

ing the neo-Kantian separation of ontology and axiology. I will then consider 2) the limits of the conception of culture as a table of values, as presented in the METO. By relying on ILNFI and its "Complementary Note", I will finally show 3) that it is more broadly the grammar of value oppositions that we have to dismiss in order to defend a unipolar axiology based on an ontology of individuation.

One word on the title: To clarify the status and functions of the concept of value in Simondon, I prefer to speak of "grammars of value" in the plural than of "philosophy" or "theory of value". The Simondonian text does not really offer a stabilised conceptual systematics for what concerns value, but rather an instability and a plurality of uses, which mobilises distinct conceptual and metaphorical networks. Being attentive to this variety of "grammars", rather than attempting a systematic reconstruction, allows value to be approached as a philosophical concept, that is to say as a problem. This will not prevent us, in a last step, from attempting to articulate these different grammars to approach what we could call a Simondonian philosophy of value.

1. The writings on cybernetics of 1953. The project of an axiontology

Two early texts suggest that the question of value constitutes a potential point of departure into Simondon's work: "Cybernétique et philosophie" and especially "Épistémologie de la cybernétique", both written (but never published) in 1953.[10] Simondon's proposal is to universalise cybernetics to make it an "interscientific technique": "universal cybernetics" would identify the "common operations" of the different sciences in order to promote their interconnection. Assuming a "functional equivalence [of] operations", it would propose, for example, an "operative analogy" between the "inversions of polarities" observed in certain pathological psychological disorders (from the manic state to the depressive state) and the self-oscillation of an amplifier.[11] This analogy being admitted, could not self-oscillation and mental disorder "be stopped by functionally equivalent processes"?[12] In fact, the voltage drop that decreases the gain of the amplifier and the lobotomy that reduces the exchanges between the parts of the brain present a form of functional equivalence. It follows that "from the operative analogy comes a normative idea that has a scientific value".[13]

---

10 On these texts: SLΦ, p. 35, n. 1.
11 SLΦ, p. 191.
12 Ibid.
13 Ibid., p. 191; my emphasis.

The normativity in question here is implied by the concept of functioning, as a concept of finality. From then on, the information theorist could judge that the drop in voltage, although it reduces self-oscillation, is undesirable, because it "denies the internal purpose of the amplifying mechanism". He will then look for another solution, such as "changing the phase of the reaction". In the same way, "if the psychiatrist can discover a curative method which, contrary to lobotomy, does not consist in denying the internal finality of the living being [...] he will judge it preferable": for example, psychoanalysis, which aims at "a new adjustment of the mind which does not destroy its finality".[14] Among the operations that can transform dysfunctional structures into more functional ones, some are preferable from the point of view of internal purpose. "The cybernetic method thus leads to a doctrine of values".[15]

What does this mean? Simondon immediately speaks of a "scientific doctrine of values". The expression is surprising, as it blurs the usual distinction between fact and value. It is indeed the task of the philosophically reflected cybernetics: "criticism or the positivism cannot lead to a scientific doctrine of the values, because one cannot pass from the object, seized as phenomenon (...) to the dynamic interiority of a norm".[16] For these two objectivisms, which brings face to face "the being-subject" and the "the being-object", "the meeting of a spontaneity [which poses or recognises values] and an objectivity is exceptional": we find it, for example, in respect to the Kantian sense (by which reason recognises in its very activity the normativity which justifies it).[17] In contrast, "in cybernetic theory, normativity is omnipresent", since the object is not an "inert term", but an operation oriented by a certain finality.[18] In this sense cybernetics is a science of (physical, biological or psychic) values. It is at least a horizon: "*it is possible* to foresee as an extension of cybernetics a unipolar axiology" (we will come back to this unipolarity later); "cybernetics *would be* a universal axiology and would become an instrument for the unity of knowledge and action".[19]

This presents great difficulties and a risk of misunderstanding. Does the evaluation of an operation according to a functional purpose really imply a "universal axiology"? It is then certain that one refuses "an absolute jump from the domain of being to the domain of having to be"?[20] But is it really this functionalism that Simondon would like to extend to all axiological problems? Certainly not, as is shown by a critical assessment of Norbert Wiener's use of the notion of

---

14   Ibid., p. 192.
15   Ibid.
16   Ibid., p. 180.
17   Ibid., pp. 179–180.
18   Ibid., p. 192.
19   Ibid., p. 192; my emphasis.
20   Ibid.

value. Wiener identifies normativity and "homeostatic finality", recognising in homeostasis and negentropy "two possible sources of value".[21] However, explains Simondon, "neither homeostasis nor negentropy are models of values in themselves, but only functions, teleological mechanisms"; they are at best "relative values".[22] Such is the case with the ideal of social cohesiveness, which reduces any evaluation of a social phenomenon to its integrative function for the social body. The link between functional teleology and the doctrine of values is therefore not as simple as it seems.

Should we therefore recognise "values in themselves"? This anti-reductionist lexicon brings Simondon closer to the theories of value mentioned in the introduction. In fact, the conclusion of the text evokes the contribution of the "phenomenology of values" as a "negation of an ontological deductivism of norms".[23] Simondon does not elaborate; he means probably that phenomenology promotes, on the one hand, the suspension of any metaphysical claim on the difference of being and value; and, on the other, the description of value as the object of intuition in the life of the consciousness, no less consistent than the constitutive essences of sensible phenomena – whereas both positivism and criticism, after abstractly separating fact and value, are suspended so that any axiology is deduced from a fundamental norm, supposedly universally recognised (practical pure reason) or institutionally posed (legal positivism).

Simondon then adds that the "dialectical test of passage by phenomenology" was for philosophy what "the dialectical test of passage by cybernetics" is for science.[24] But this instructive parallel cannot be Simondon's last word, because it juxtaposes science and philosophy. Yet "axiontological synthetic knowledge" is supposed to make an end of "the long detour by which scientific thought and reflexive thought, the doctrine of being and the doctrine of values, diverged from each other".[25] There are two competing discourses on value. On the one hand, the "scientific doctrine of values" of cybernetics, for which "the only valid axiology is an axiontology",[26] but which proceeds to a reductionist identification of value with the immanent finality of an operation. On the other hand, the "phenomenology of values", which by its intuitionism and its "material" conception of value, makes credible the seizure of "values in themselves" but threatens to constitute a form of axiological substantialism.

Axiontology will thus be realised beyond cybernetics: "cybernetics [...] does not give reflexive criteria clear enough to build a [true] axiontological theo-

---

21 "Cybernétique et philosophie", SLΦ, p. 62.
22 *Ibid.*, pp. 62–63; my emphasis.
23 "Épistémologie de la cybernétique", SLΦ, p. 199.
24 *Ibid.*
25 "Épistémologie de la cybernétique", SLΦ, p. 199.
26 "Cybernétique et philosophie", SLΦ, p. 62.

ry", because of its "abstract pragmatism".[27] It is pragmatic in the sense that it conceives value in terms of efficiency, and abstract because "[its] normativity has no point of application":[28] its objects are formal systems such as "the" society or "the" psyche. But "an axiology without beings is like an ontology without values". On what condition can we concretely link ontology and axiology? Simondon says it clearly without yet providing justification:

> As long as Aristotle's definition remains true: "there is no science of individual being", ontology and axiology will remain separate: it is not a formulation of the structural system or a definition of an operative schematism that will bring ontology and axiology together.[29]

Before being the attribute of a science or a method, the "axiontological" is a state: the "syncretic state of being", a "state of indivision which characterizes individuality", upstream of its differentiation between operation and structure.[30] A non-reductionist axiontology will be possible only if philosophy is able to know and reflect this syncretic state and the genesis of the distinction between operation and structure.[31]

2. Axiontology prevented: The grammar of the "Table of Values"

It is in the thesis on individuation that this non-reductionist axiontology will unfold. In order to better understand what is at stake, we must first consider the grammar of value mobilised in METO. The notion of value occupies a central place in the position of the problem and the intention of work:

> The most powerful cause of alienation in the contemporary world resides in this misunderstanding of the machine, which is not an alienation caused by the machine, but by the non-knowledge of its nature and its essence, by way of its absence from the world of significations, and its omission from the table of values and concepts that make up culture.[32]

These eloquent formulas are often quoted. But are they so clear? Without a doubt, Simondon is very convincing when arguing that the technique, or rather the technicity, as the relation of the man to the world, must integrate a cultural

---

27 Ibid.
28 Ibid., p. 198
29 Ibid.
30 Ibid., p. 199
31 Ibid.
32 METO, p. 16/MEOT, p. 10.

symbolisation that has too often repressed it, by rigidifying itself in the forms of a traditional or literary culture. This philosophical project has been the object of compelling comments.[33] It does not follow that the exact necessity and function of the lexicon of value are thereby fully clarified. Are we even able, at the end of METO, to designate these technical "new values"[34] that must enrich culture?

In the introduction of METO, "value" is immediately linked to "culture" and to the "human": culture appears as a set of values (always in the plural) whose focus is an idea of humanity. Just as the abolition of slavery implied recognising "the value of the human person", so it is necessary to recognise, in the technical object, something human that became "misunderstood", "foreign", "alienated".[35] One recognises a humanist *topos*: "humanism (...) means the will to return the status of freedom to what has been alienated in man, so that nothing human should be foreign to man".[36] The link between this humanist rhetoric and the lexicon of value remains tenuous, however, even conventional.

The theme of alienation and strangeness also has Marxian echoes, of course. But looking to "values" as a remedy contradicts, at least in its letter, the Marxian critique of economy, which sees in the objectification of value the very expression of the "commodity form", as Marx shows in the famous section of *Das Kapital* on the "Fetishism of Commodities".[37] One finds traces of the Marxian critique in the care taken by Simondon to distinguish between "economic value" and "technical value".[38] But Marx does not call for defending or opposing values against others, not even for "use value" as opposed to "exchange value", since this very duality characterises the "form-value" of the commodity,[39] which is a symptom of our alienation. Furthermore, Marx forges the tools of a "critique of the value" as a critique of the economy; and consequently, a critique of the philosophies of values.[40]

As to the expressions "table of values" and "new values", they are typically Nietzschean. However, the comparison can also be misleading: Nietzsche's "critique of value" – as described, in particular, in the foreword to *Genealogy of*

---

33   See in particular Gilbert Hottois, *Simondon et la philosophie de la culture technique*, Brussels, De Boeck, 1993 and Xavier Guchet, *Pour un humanisme technologique*, Paris, PUF, 2010, pp. 231–255.
34   METO, p. 181/MEOT, p. 144.
35   *Ibid.*, p. 16, p. 119/p. 10, p. 145.
36   *Ibid.*, p. 144/p. 117. On this point: Jean-Hugues Barthélémy, "What new Humanism today?", trans. C. Turner, in *Cultural Politics*, vol. 6, 2/2010, pp. 237–252.
37   Marx, *Capital*. eds. Ernest Mandel and New Left Review, trans. Ben Fowles. London: Penguin Classics, 1990, pp. 166–167.
38   METO, p. 76/MEOT, p. 94.
39   Marx, *Capital, op. cit.*, pp. 152–153.
40   Starting with Herbert Marcuse's article: "Über den affirmativen Charakter der Kultur", in *Zeitschrift für Sozialforschung*, vol. 6, 1/1937, pp. 54–94.

Morals – attacks precisely this objectification of values, considered as a metaphysical operation and a symptom of a devaluation of life. The genealogy brings back the values, abstractly objectified, to the evaluations they express, so that the reversal of values consists less in replacing some values by others than in changing the very meaning of the term of value, in particular, by making a form of individualising the value conceivable.[41] On this last point, Simondon's enterprise has undeniable affinities with Nietzsche's, but the grammar of value used in METO diverges considerably.

In 1950, Émile Bréhier recalled that in France, "at the beginning of the century, we studied less the values themselves than the value judgments or the appreciations, which we opposed to the existence judgments", in a psychological or sociological perspective. In contrast,

> The current philosophy of values, in the very diverse forms it has taken, is opposed to this subjectivism. It looks for the value less on the side of the subject who appreciates it than on the side of the object that embodies it, and it looks for how this value is present in this object, how it has acquired it.[42]

The axiological relativism borne by psychology, sociology and historical sciences is succeeded by a philosophical resumption of the question of value, paying attention to what resists the genetic approach in the claim to validity. This objective orientation does not commit to a Platonising idealism; it does not exclude attention to the conditions of the emergence of value.

> No value exists for us, writes Bréhier, without a technique that realizes it in a work or in an operation; as there is a technique of beauty, so there is a technique of health, truth, justice, charity.[43]

Value "exists" only at the end of a genesis whose determinations are multiple, but its validity does not disappear in the relativity of these determinations. This philosophy of values, in its various forms (neo-Kantian, phenomenological or existentialist), breaks with the "immanentism" of the philosophies of the turn of the century (above all, Bergson): "on all sides the continuum is attacked", it is up to "human existence to 'transcend' itself". The "theories of value" take charge of this discontinuity.[44]

The grammar of value mobilised in METO seems to participate in this paradigm. To integrate the "technical object" into the "table of values" of culture

---

41   See Arnaud François, "Pourquoi inverser les valeurs, ce n'est pas mettre de nouvelles valeurs à la place des anciennes", in Yannick Souladié (ed.), *Nietzsche – L'inversion des valeurs*, OLMS, 2007, p. 133–167.
42   Bréhier, *Les thèmes actuels, op. cit.*, pp. 70–71.
43   *Ibid.*, p. 72.
44   Bréhier, *Transformation, op. cit.*, pp. 65–66.

is to recognise it as the bearer of a *sui generis* validity, and this in two senses. First of all, it is to apprehend it as a carrier of specific values, distinct from those that we attribute, for example, to the "aesthetic object" or to the "sacred object".[45] In this we are close to the neo-Kantian philosophy of culture: culture is specified in domains of objectivity carrying distinct axiological requirements (aesthetic, religious, technical, etc.). Then, attributing a value to the technical object is to refuse to treat it as a simple means, and to reject it "into a structureless world of things that have no signification but only a use, a utility function".[46] One must recognise in technicity "the inherence of values surpassing utility".[47] Certainly, values participate in a process of culture, so that aesthetic, religious or technical values can become "political and social value[s]" or "cultural value[s]".[48] But to become cultural, the value must first be objective: "to see the technical relation functioning in an objective way is the prime condition for the incorporation of the knowledge of technical reality and of the values implied by its existence into culture".[49] That value is objective does not mean that it resides in the isolated object. The "machine's schemas of functioning", describing a "correlative existence of men and machine", are what "imply" values.[50] Thus, it is necessary to "intervene as a mediator in this relation between machines" to feel a "respect" and a "responsibility towards them" that is quite distinct from the utilitarian position of the owner who owns them or the worker who operates them.[51]

The "technical reality", as the concrete relation between men and machines, is the source whence "technical values" must be drawn. An incomplete table of values is a cultural symbolisation in which "reality is absent".[52] But what "technical values" are supposed to be drawn from the technical reality? It seems that they must be sought by means of substituting the thermodynamic paradigm for the informational paradigm. The former evaluates the machine in terms of "energy efficiency", as "productive capital". The technicity is then subjected to a "finality external to the operating system [regime] of machines which is that of productivity".[53] But no more than the economic value do "the values of work" (increase in power, the submission of nature to human finalities …) correspond to technical values: "The foundation of the norms and of law in the industrial domain is neither labour nor property, but technicity".[54] In the age of "technical

---

45 METO, p. 16/MEOT, p. 10.
46 Ibid.
47 Ibid., p. 230/p. 303.
48 Ibid., p. 16, 235/p. 10, 311.
49 Ibid., p. 159/p. 203.
50 Ibid., p. 20/p. 16,
51 Ibid., p. 159/pp. 203–204.
52 Ibid., p. 20/p.16.
53 Ibid., p. 204/p. 160.
54 Ibid., p. 257/ p. 342.

ensembles" that link machine and man, technicity is better described in terms of "relation of information", conceived not as signal but as meaning. "The human individual thus appears to have to convert the forms deposited into machines into information".[55] The information-based approach operates an "inter-individual coupling between man and machine" and institutes a "relation of equality, of reciprocity of exchanges: a kind of social relation".[56] Thus becomes conceivable a "technical wisdom in men who feel their responsibility toward technical realities".[57]

We do have new concepts, new virtues and prospects for educational, social and political reforms (see, in particular, the theme of leaving the state of minority vis-à-vis technology).[58] In short, there is no lack of material to feed a discourse on values, in the current and trivial sense of the term. But what exactly can be classified under the category of technical value? Simondon does not say.[59] This is not a matter for substantive objection, except perhaps with regard to the way in which the problem was initially formulated. For it is this grammar of values that really poses a problem. Justified by its pedagogical virtue – indeed, it offers the least difficult and favourite access to Simondon's work – it becomes equivocal as soon as we try to determine its precise meaning. The truth is that Simondon himself warns us when he explains that thinking in terms of a "table of values" is characteristic of the disjunction between the theoretical and the practical. The "pluralistic table of values of practical morality" is the expression of a "practical thought that is not integrated within the real", but simply contents itself in listing "*optatives*, freed from their application to the technical gesture".[60] Thus, for example, with the so-called values of "simplicity" or "efficiency": "such values must have been experienced and lived through an action integrated with-

---

[55] Ibid., p. 150/pp. 190–191.
[56] Ibid., p. 135, 105/p. 168, 127.
[57] Ibid., p. 159/p. 204.
[58] Ibid., pp. 104–127/pp. 123–158.
[59] One finds in truth an unambiguous thesis: the value of a technical ensemble is measured by its concretisation, i.e., the level of the "reciprocal causality" or "internal resonance" – that is also to say the level of "individualisation" – of each of its sub-ensembles. "This criterion has an *axiological value*, the coherence of a technical ensemble is at its maximum when this ensemble is constituted by sub-ensembles with the same level of relative individualisation" (METO, p. 64/MEOT, p. 77; Simondon's emphasis). This statement is found in Part I: "Genesis and Evolution of Technical Objects". We have here a formula for technical validity, but one which does not yet integrate the relation with the agent necessary to speak about cultural value – we have validity without value. Part II, "Man and the Technical Object", does not contain such a precise and univocal statement about the axiological value of the technical relation. The necessary link between value and individualisation (or, rather, individuation) will only really be clarified in ILNFI.
[60] METO, pp. 216–217/MEOT, p. 283.

in the world, before being grouped and systematized". It is afterwards and by abstraction that these values are objectified. Moreover, "they cannot be completely systematized, because they lead to a plurality of different values, just as inductive theoretical knowledge leads to a plurality of properties of things and laws of the real".[61] One cannot say, for example, "why there is one value for an action to be simple and easily accomplished, and why there is another value for its efficiency".[62] The grammar of the table of values, with its afterthought abstractions, only appears to be clear.

As for "experienced and lived" values, are they really values before being objectified as such? Not, in any case, in the sense that they could appear in a table of values. The objectification of value appears as an expression of an abstract or even reactive relationship, in the sense of Nietzsche, to the axiological question. If "culture has constituted itself as a defence system against technics",[63] as Simondon deplores it, is it not precisely because culture believed that it could define itself from a definitive and closed system or table of values? Blind to the processes of individuation carried by the technical ensembles, traditional culture does not see that "the machine, being a work of organisation and information, is, like life itself and together with life, that which is opposed (...) to the levelling of all things".[64] It is not by establishing lists of values that we will fight against a levelling culture, but precisely by situating the requirements of value within concrete "living" processes, in this case, technical relations. This is what Simondon tries to do in METO, but with a partially inadequate grammar, which condemns technical value to ambivalence: to defend and determine it, it must be proclaimed and objectified, but this very gesture of objectification threatens to make the value an abstraction separated from life and, in this sense, without value.

3. Axiontology realised: The value of the individuating act

The clearest expression of Simondon's axiontology, and thus of its position regarding the legitimate use of the notion of value, is found in ILNFI. The question of value seemed so important to Simondon that he followed the conclusion of his dissertation with a long "Complementary Note" which opened, in its first draft, with the question "What can we understand by value?" Deleted before the thesis defence, this note was reinstated, according to the author's wish, in the 1989 edition. The first chapter is entitled "Values and the Search for Objectivity", and the note as a whole was first entitled "The Objective Foundations of the

---

61 Ibid.
62 Ibid.
63 Ibid., p. 15/p. 9.
64 Ibid., p. 21/p. 18.

Transindividual". That is to say, the clarification of "what (…) we understand by value" is a way to approach the concept of transindividuality.

The interest of ILNFI and of this note lies first of all in the differentiation of the grammars of value, through which the equivocity and ambivalence of a certain discourse on value is exposed and explained. We can identify in ILNFI three main uses of the notion of value, which I shall call sociological, ethical and physico-mathematical. "Sociological" is understood here in a rather pejorative way, according to the Simondonian usage: as a common discourse on values as cultural references, which are, in part, imposed on the individual – as "a normativity previously elaborated by other individuals" – and, in part, presented as an object of choice: "The psychological individual must choose among the values and behaviors from which it receives examples".[65] Simondon occasionally uses the term "value" in this sense, but he also criticises it. The "ethical" or "moral" approach, properly philosophical, is exposed in the conclusion of the work. The value becomes a "power of transductivity" related to the "being's dynamic".[66] Finally, a third use articulates values, variables and distributions, to describe, for example, the "properties with highly variable values" of crystals, or to question the theories of electricity, according to whether they suppose a "finite number of values" or a "continuous infinity of values".[67] At first sight, this quantitative determination of value may seem very far from the ethical perspective, which is necessarily qualitative. But we shall see that the latter could not have found its formulation without a reflexive resumption of this physico-mathematical grammar.

3.1. Community and society, or the bipolarity and unipolarity of values

The first chapter of the "Complementary Notes" is structured by the tension between the sociological and the ethical sense of value, which covers the distinction between community and society. Let us start from there. "Community" designates the social group as a "whole", as protecting itself from "a transindividual relation, going from individual to individual" that is characteristic of "society". In the community – more precisely, to the extent that the social group is a community rather than a society – individuals "communicate indirectly and without a precise awareness of their individuality". Their relations are reduced to their function within the whole.[68] Community thus involves a "valorisation of the

---

[65] ILNFI, p. 312/ILFI, p. 273.
[66] Ibid., pp. 377–379/pp. 323–325.
[67] Ibid., p. 265, p. 125/p. 235, p. 122.
[68] Ibid., pp. 413–414/p. 342.

stereotypy of behaviours'": "the average characteristic becomes superior in a community wherein values have a statistical sense".⁶⁹ This is not to say that the awareness of values disappears into the behaviour's regularity and everyday nature. On the contrary, "communal integration" requires that some values be defended, proclaimed and objectivated: the community is "hypertelic" and "elaborate[s] a code of values that is meant to prevent changes of structure and avoid the position of problems".⁷⁰ This hypertelia is merely the flip side of a reductionist functionalism. The code of values, in its formal transcendence, "conditions the functional value of an individual in the community", preventing individuals from interrogating the group functioning.⁷¹ Just as it devalues what is individual, the community reduces the "technical being" to a "utensil", giving it "a use value that is foreign to its own dynamic essence" and repelling the inventive power of which this being is the expression. Thus considered, the technical being "no longer has meaning for the individual".⁷² As a result, the community is essentially defensive and functions through the opposition of values. "Exterior communities" are "thought to be bad" and threatening, so that "out of these primitive categories of inclusion and exclusion (...) there develop annexed categories of purity and impurity, kindness and harmfulness, which are the social roots of the notions of good and evil." Consequently, the community can be recognised by its "bipolarity of values". In that sense, the community is "biological": it extends the "bipolar opposition of the dangerous and the assimilable" that is characteristic of the living individual.⁷³

In contrast, as a "synergistic group[ing] of individuals", society undergoes an "immediate relation between individuals" that is beyond the "code of extrinsic obligations" that is specific to the community:⁷⁴ society is transindividual collectivity. It problematises its functioning, and solves its problems notably by means of technical invention, in which it discovers an "intrinsic and absolute" normativity that cannot be reduced to "social normativity": The technical object is either valid or not according to its internal characteristics, which express the schematism "inherent in the effort by which it is constituted".⁷⁵ The group is society insofar as it integrates this normativity without reducing it:

> Technical normativity modifies the code of values of a closed society, because there is a systematic of values, and by admitting a new technics, every closed society that intro-

---

69 Ibid., p. 422/p. 348.
70 Ibid., p. 420/p. 347.
71 Ibid.
72 Ibid., p. 416/p. 344.
73 Ibid., p. 409/p. 337.
74 Ibid., p. 413/341.
75 Ibid., pp. 412–413/p. 341.

duces values inherent to this technics thereby carries out a new structuration of its code of values.⁷⁶

If the word "table" is replaced by the word "code", one finds the METO's lexicon. However, this description is provisional. What Simondon calls the "systematic of values" is not a "code of values". Indeed, "technical activity does not introduce a bipolarity of values in the same way as biological activity": "for a being who constructs, there is no good or bad, but the indifferent and the constructive, the neutral and the positive".⁷⁷ The technical individuation process supporting the formation of a transindividual collective cannot be evaluated in terms of value oppositions, but as a degree or an intensity: "the positivity of value stands out from a background of neutrality". The axiological system becomes one of "unipolarity of values" in an ethical rather than biological mode.⁷⁸

INLFI's conclusion offers a further determination of this unipolar ethics of values and its function in the overall philosophical intention. Before examining it, let us consider the definition of value proposed at the beginning of the "Complementary Note": "value is the action due to which there can be complementarity", that is to say, "unlimited complementarity between the individual being and other individual beings".⁷⁹ The strangeness of this definition, which makes value not a reference *for*, nor a quality *of* an action, but *the* action itself, must be noted. Simondon introduces a distinction that preserves this more conventional usage, while ordering it to this new determination of value as action: the distinction between *relative* and *absolute* value. Relative value is assigned to the organic or technical "conditions" of complementarity; this is, for example, "the value of the remedy that cures", and contributes to restoring the complementarity between the biological individual and its milieu. "[T]his value is linked to the very thing (...), but it nevertheless does not reside in this thing": the remedy is valuable, but is not a value.⁸⁰ The absolute value is "the value that makes relation possible", not as a condition, but as "the beginning or initiation of the reaction that makes this activity possible" (that is to say, the activity that links, that makes compatible). "Culture can be ranked among these values, since it is a set of beginnings of action that are endowed with a rich schematism, waiting to be actualised into an action" – not as mere formal possibilities, but as real virtualities.⁸¹ The value of culture, or rather culture as (absolute) value, does not lie in a table or code of objectifiable values, but in a real process. Certainly, culture is a "capacity of acting on symbols and not on brute realities". It therefore requires as a

---

76 *Ibid.*, p. 413/p. 341.
77 *Ibid.*, p. 409/p. 337.
78 *Ibid.*, p. 409/pp. 336–337.
79 *Ibid.*, pp. 401–402/p. 331.
80 *Ibid.*, p. 402/p. 332.
81 *Ibid.*

condition objects and actions with a relative value.[82] But symbolic activity, precisely, does not concern an autonomous, abstract object domain, opposed to or external to the being:

> [T]he condition for the *validity* of this action on symbols resides in the symbols' authenticity, i.e. the fact that they are veritably the extension of the realities that they represent and not a simple, arbitrary sign artificially linked to the things that it must represent.[83]

The real symbol is to the arbitrary sign what the value of culture is to culture as a "code of values". It is clear that describing culture in terms of tables or codes of values is an *a posteriori* objectification, pedagogically justifiable but philosophically non-rigorous and typical of a community attitude. Culture as community is a supposedly given table of values; culture as society or transindividuality is the value of actually or virtually operating acts – particularly, for example, through the intermediary of the technical object as "crystallization of creative human action [that] perpetuates it in being".[84]

3.2. Norms and values

The "Complementary Note" starts from a definition of value and remains largely on the level of axiology. In contrast, the conclusion of ILNFI starts from a thesis on being – as "polyphasic" and in "reserve of becoming"[85] – to end on a thesis of value. It tries to expose the axiontology to which the writings of 1953 aspired. Since we cannot explain here the ontological presuppositions of the thesis, let us start again from the problem of complementarity. In general ethical terms, this problem can be formulated as follows: Can "the plurality of systems of norms (…) be envisioned otherwise than *as a contradiction*"?[86] The sage's theoretical and contemplative ethics and the practical ethics of action, for example, "define norms that provide incompatible directions".[87] A decisionist approach, like that of Max Weber, would speak here of a "polytheism of values": there are ultimately irreconcilable "value positions".[88] It is a widely shared thesis, of which we find

---

82 *Ibid.*
83 *Ibid.*, my emphasis.
84 *Ibid.*, p. 411/p. 340.
85 *Ibid.*, p. 358/pp. 307–308.
86 *Ibid.*, p. 376/p. 322; Simondon's emphasis.
87 *Ibid.*, p. 374/p. 320.
88 M. Weber, "Science as Vocation", in H. H. Gerth and C. Wright Mills (translated and edited), *From Max Weber: Essays in Sociology*, New York, Oxford University Press, 1946, pp. 129–156 (145–150).

versions in various works that Simondon could have had at hand.[89] But this axiological aporia relies on an insufficient distinction between norm and value (the norm would be merely the objectification of a position of value) and, more fundamentally, on the dissociation of the ontological and the ethical levels: the incompatibility between pure ethics and ethics of the action, before being contradiction between norms, is incompatibility in thought between "the theoretical substantiality of the individuated being" and the "perpetual evolution of the ever-moving being".[90]

> [N]orms could be conceived as expressing a definite individuation and consequently as having a structural and functional meaning on the level of individuated beings. On the contrary, values can be conceived as linked to the very birth of norms, which expresses the fact that norms emerge with an individuation and last as long as this individuation exists as an actual state.[91]

The norm is proper to an individuated functional structure, be it biological, psychic or social; the value is attributed to acts participating in a process of individuation, in relation to which the formation of norms is second in the genetic order. From then on, the contradiction of the norms is relativised: "There is no contradiction arising from the *multiplicity of norms*, except if one makes of the individual an absolute and not the *expression of an individuation* that creates a merely provisional and metastable state".[92] Considered in isolation, norms are incompatible functional structures. From a genetic point of view, they are relatively stable structures (metastable), subject to transformations, according to the problems affecting the system of psychic or social individuation that they momentarily stabilise. Norms are functional, "but their system is more than functional, and this is why it is value".[93] This circumstantial identification between system and value must guard against the temptation to interpret too simply the idea that value is at the origin of the norm; it is rather what persists in the succession of norms.

This persistence is described in energetic and semantic terms. The value is a "guiding force that is not lost", it is the continuity of an energy that supports individuation. But it is not blind: "values are (...) norms led to the state of information: they are what is conserved from one state to another".[94] Value is information, while "the reduction to norms is identical to the reduction to

---

89 See for example E. Dupréel, *Esquisse d'une philosophie des valeurs, op. cit.*, pp. 233–235 or Raymond Polin, *La création des valeurs, op. cit.*, pp. 98–101.
90 ILNFI, p. 373–374/ILFI, pp. 320–321.
91 *Ibid.*, p. 376/p. 322.
92 *Ibid.*, p. 376/pp. 322–323; Simondon's emphasis.
93 *Ibid.*, p. 375/p. 321.
94 *Ibid.*

forms".⁹⁵ Norm and value are the counterparts, in ethical terms, of the notions of form and information. The form can well indicate constituted and individualised structures, but it is not "significative form", or only in the narrow sense of a sign system. Information is the truly significative form, the one that makes sense, because it is not a given, univocal signification, but "the signification that emerges from a disparation", the signification as a problem, that "maintains the energetic level of the system, conserves its potentials by making them compatible", but without abolishing their tension.⁹⁶ It is in very similar terms that the question of value was approached in "Cybernetics and Philosophy", against a cybernetics identifying value as a norm of social regulation.

> For there to be value, there must be a problematic, that is, the presence of a thanatological element in a holistic system. The value is what, for a holistic system that has reached a state of problematic incompatibility, is capable of making a new structure of compatibility appear.⁹⁷

Then followed the example of "awareness" which, in psychoanalysis, is supposed to lead to a reorganisation of the "psychic structure".⁹⁸

Just as the notion of information completes and subverts the philosophies of form, so this determination of value reforms a philosophy that makes the norm the transcendental element of any ethical question. But let there be no mistake: it is not a question of defending an ethics of value against an ethics of norms, in the way Bergson defends open morals against closed morals, or in the way the philosophy of life, according to Nietzsche, defends the mobility of a life positing its own values against the danger of petrification of forms. It is precisely the refusal of such an alternative which is in play, since ethics, as "the meaning of the synergy of successive individuations" is also "the meaning according to which in each act there is both movement to go further and the schema that will integrate into other schemata".⁹⁹ The ethical act overflows the forms in which it is taken, without being hostile in principle towards any form – as a characteristic fantasy of the "crazed act".¹⁰⁰ Well-understood ethics (at the bottom of ontogenesis) refuses the abstract separation between life which evaluates and the norms to which it is subjected, but without abolishing their tension: "Norms and values are the extreme terms of the being's dynamic".¹⁰¹

---

95 *Ibid.*, p. 378/p. 323.
96 *Ibid.*, p. 35/p. 16.
97 "Cybernétique et philosophie", SLΦ, p. 63.
98 *Ibid.*
99 ILNFI, p. 377/ILFI, p. 323.
100 *Ibid.*, p. 379/ p. 325.
101 *Ibid.*, p. 377/p. 323.

3.3. Value as breadth of an act. A physico-mathematical analogy

We can now return to the thesis of the "unipolarity of values". Once the bipolarity of the community is excluded, value can still be understood in two ways as a "pole". On the one hand, value is a term of an "indefinite, unidimensional and bipolar dyad", the other term of which is the norm. This bipolar axis distributes the degrees of "opening and closing", of potential becoming and of normative structuring, proper to the "state of a civilization", more largely, to a system individuating itself.[102] This bipolarity could not be suppressed, since the process of individuation could not do without the individuated being. On the other hand, as it expresses a transindividual collective, value is understood, as we have seen, as a "positivity" that "stands out from a background of neutrality", a significant form standing out against an amorphous background. These two dualities – the value and the norm, the value and the indifference – belong to points of view and problems that we must distinguish, all the more so as Simondon imperceptibly slips, in the last pages of ILNFI, from the problem of the norm-value bipolarity to that of the neutrality-value unipolarity.

In both cases, value is not an identifiable ideal entity, but an intensive quantity. What has worth, is worth more or less, without being able to be worth negatively – only in a regime of biological individuation can one speak strictly of negative value. According to the bipolar axis norm/value, value measures an emancipation from inherited normative schemes, a capacity for invention, even revolution. However, this degree has an upper threshold: value and norm form a dyad, such that the disappearance of the norm would also be that of value. According to the unipolar axis emerging from the background of neutrality or indifference, the measure of value does not seem, in contrast, to have to know a maximum threshold. "The value of an act is not its universalisable nature according to the norm that it implies, but the effective reality of its integration in a network of acts that becoming is".[103] The value of the act resides in its power of concrete universalisation, by transindividual extension and intensification. The acts arouse and call each other, in proportion to their value. We find here the humanist theme of *exempla*, underlined by the idea of a contemporaneity of the valuable acts. The value of an act is its communicative power, and this cannot *a priori* know a maximum threshold. "There is only a *centre* of the act, there are no *limits* of the act. Each act is centred but infinite; the value of an act is its breadth, its capacity of transductive expansiveness."[104] While transduction suggests the convertibility of value into norms, here Simondon emphasises its dimension of propagation rather than of structuring.

---

102 *Ibid.*, p. 377/p. 323.
103 *Ibid.*
104 *Ibid.*, p. 378/p. 323.

What does the "breadth" or "expansiveness" of an act mean? Simondon resorts to a spectroscopic analogy: "The relation between acts does not pass through the abstract level of norms, but it goes from one act to other acts just as one goes from yellow-green to green and yellow by increasing the bandwidth of frequencies."[105] Does this mean that the network of acts can be rendered as a spectrum of distribution of possible acts, the value of each one being comparable to the position of each colour in the spectrum, that is to say, to the value of the variables determining the wavelength of the light? We would then have a scheme of continuous distribution of values (to be distinguished from the discontinuity of the norms), but we do not see in what this quantitative determination, although continuous, would be properly qualitative. Here there is an infinity of values, but not yet a value susceptible of infinite variations. But the analogy goes further. We must see the relations between acts as similar to the resonance between waves: the value of the act resides in its capacity to "spread out, phase-shift into lateral acts". An act without value is an act "which does not radiate outward and that has no lateral bands", so that it does not allow the "resonance of the acts with respect to one another".[106] The value then measures a certain level of resonance between acts whose network constitutes the becoming, resonance thought by analogy to exchanges of energy and movement between the parts of a system. Developing the analogy even further, one could say that the "non-moral act", which Simondon says that it is "lost within itself", is the act incapable of entering into resonance with the others, indifferent, while the "immoral act" would expressly hinder or destroy the phenomena of resonance.[107]

The analogy suggests yet another determination of the measure of value: I have said that the value of an act, according to this unipolar logic, knows no maximum. One could, however, wonder whether it might know an optimum that would correspond to the most fertile level of resonance for the system. The value of the act would have something of the excellence of the virtuous act as a middle ground, in the sense of Aristotle, a middle ground which is precisely not an average but an optimum, not only because it is at an equal distance from two vicious acts, but above all, because it constitutes the fairest intervention in a complex situation, which includes the whole of the agents, of their acts and of their objects.[108] It seems possible to reconcile these two determinations of the value of the act as an intensive quantity: it is likely to grow indefinitely if we consider the network of acts as an open system of becoming, but it must be conceived as an optimal value if it is considered within a finite system of acts. The value of an act is a quantity that is determined without being fixed. It varies

---

[105] Ibid., p. 378/p. 324.
[106] Ibid., pp. 377–378/pp. 323–324.
[107] Ibid., p. 379/p. 324.
[108] Aristotle, *The Nicomachean Ethics*, 1106 a–b.

according to the point of view of the evaluation. This is not to say that it is relative in the sense of arbitrariness or subjectivity, and thus finally of the absence of value; its relativity expresses an "objectively", or rather concretely determined, relationality. As the resolution of a problem in a situation, the value of the act is conceived as optimum. But insofar as its effects go beyond the context of its first effectivity, it has worth in a potentially unlimited way.

4. Conclusive remarks: "Sense of Value" and "Value of Being"

Thus, the axiontology announced in the writings on cybernetics takes shape, but by means of an analogy borrowed from a physico-mathematical grammar of value. To make this solution possible, it was necessary to start from individuation rather than from the individuated structures. The reformed grammar of value dismisses abstract axiological objectivism to bring back value in the being, but without reducing it to the efficiency of a functioning. Intensive in magnitude, the value measures in the individuating act not its conservative or adaptive scope according to the given criteria of a normativity, but precisely what of the act exceeds this normativity, in a problematic context that this given normativity does not allow to be solved. In order to have value, however, this act that deviates from the norm must be universalisable, recognised as a virtual carrier of a new normativity (e.g., as inspiration for a new artistic style or a new political constitution). This solution to the problem of the ambivalence of the value has affinities with that of Nietzsche and that of the contemporary existentialism of Simondon, for example in Raymond Polin: it refuses the split of the being and the value by conceiving it as a form of the self-transcendence of the being (of life or existence). It seems superior to these two solutions, however. To the first one, because it avoids the confusion with a biological axiology by situating from the start the value in the domain of culture or, better, of the senses. To the second, because through its realism it escapes the formalism of an existentialism inherited from the philosophies of the subject: "A sense of value is what prevents us from having to confront the problems of choice; the problem of choice appears when all that remains is the empty form of action".[109] Simondon's philosophy vigorously rejects any decisionism: "The sense of values is the refusal of an incompatibility in the domain of culture". In fact, the presupposition of such incompatibility condemns the value to ambivalence, to be valid for one and not for the other, and to have no validity in truth.

---

[109] ILNFI, p. 406/ILFI, pp. 335–336.

There remains a strange, insistent formula which we have ignored: "relation has the value of being",[110] with its variations: "operation has the value of being", "the relational operation [has] the value of being".[111] By a kind of chiasmus, the problematic order from which we usually consider the relation between being and value is reversed. It is no longer a question of knowing whether it is possible to base value on being, but of suggesting – the formula remains ambiguous – that being itself is a value, or even the value. Being is value as an act of perpetuated individuation, in the "mutual convertibility of structures into operations and of operations into structures".[112] It is necessary to hear, in "value of being", the subtly provocative watchword and, let us say it, the metaphysical ambition of a philosophy which refuses to stick to an analytical, formalist or transcendental perspective. Indeed, here there is something like a decision or a proclamation of value. To proclaim a "value of being" is to load with the weight of the "real" what philosophers, by critical prudence or formalism, refuse to consider otherwise than as concepts, forms or functions. Thus, of a knowledge whose dynamic scheme is analogous to that of the object that it knows, of a participative knowledge, Simondon can say: "this relation that is knowledge is founded on the being; it has the value of being".[113] Although he still uses the Kantian lexicon of the validity, Simondon breaks strongly with a neo-Kantian philosophy of the values whose starting point is to complete the ontology by an axiology that is based on a formal subject.[114]

---

110   Ibid., e.g., p. 131, 138, 151, 405, 423/p. 127, 132, 143, 334, 349.
111   Ibid., pp. 556–557/p. 447, 291.
112   Ibid., p. 334/p. 291.
113   Ibid., p. 531/p. 429.
114   See, e.g., Wilhelm Windelband, *Einleitung in die Philosophie*, Tübingen, Mohr, 1914, p. 244.

Simondon's "Right Technology"

Eco-technology, Scalability and Negative Progress[1]

Vincent Bontems

> *A deepened technology must learn not only to invent the new, but also to reinsert the old and update it into the present under the call of the future.*
>
> Gilbert Simondon, "Trois perspectives pour une réflexion sur l'éthique de la technique", 1983.

As humankind reached a sufficient technological level and managed to gather enough energy resources, they sent a spaceship to colonise a distant exoplanet. The colony prospered but lost contact with their home planet and decided to send the spaceship back to Earth. After a long journey, some emissaries from the colonies returned to Earth and were stunned. They imagined arriving in a far more advanced civilisation with powerful technologies, but they discovered a network of farming communities working with low-techs. Thus, when one of them is injured they believe he will die for lack of proper medical care, but their hosts unearth a high-tech device, and a peasant turns out to be an accomplished surgeon. "We don't despise technology, we still do research and learn how to use new technologies, but we only use them when it is *right*", they are told. The emissaries understand how wrong they were in assuming that the Earthlings have regressed. On the contrary, they made great progress: they developed a philosophy of "Right-Tech" that prevented them from destroying their ecosystem.

This is the pitch of a science fiction novella,[2] but it may be somehow close to what Gilbert Simondon had in mind when he was pleading for a deepened technology that would not only invent the new but update the old in view of the future. A rightful use of technology depends not only on performance, but also on its scale. Originating from the field of information and communication technologies, "scalability" means the capability of a material or digital object to change the order of magnitude, whether in terms of production or operation.

---

[1] This text is adapted from Vincent Bontems, "Écotechnologie: entre exo-transcendance et retro-scalabilité. Le principe de moindre puissance d'après Simondon" in Jean-Hugues Barthélémy & Ludovic Duhem (eds.), *Écologie et Technologie*, Paris, Matériologiques, 2021, pp. 17–39.

[2] Marion Zimmer Bradley, "The Climbing Wave", *The Magazine of Fantasy and Science Fiction*, February 1955.

Long before this word was coined, Simondon pointed that the main purpose of technologies is to establish communication between disparate orders of magnitude and to change the scale of application of human activities: "Of all the transductive aspects of technology, the fact that it allows for the change of order of magnitude, and consequently mobilization, in-temporalization, potentiation, is without doubt the most important".[3] The hot issue with scalability is whether this process is, by nature, out of control. Our late friend Bernard Stiegler thought that technology is an "exo-transcendence",[4] the emergence of an irreversible trend of disorder within individuation due to the technical amplification of human activities, and that this change of order of magnitude implies the increasing of "anthropy" (entropy in human individuation). We will challenge this thesis in the perspective of a Simondonian eco-technology for the analysis of the integration of technical reality in nature, claiming that their joint evolutions do not imply any transcendence.

1. Eco-technology in Simondon's philosophy of technology

The eco-technological issue runs through the whole of Simondon's philosophy of technics. The introduction of *The Mode of Existence of Technical Objects* (METO) proposes a teleological definition of the machine as meant to maintain the homeostasis of the universe:

> The machine, as an element of the technical ensemble, becomes that which increases the quantity of information, increases negentropy, and opposes the degradation of energy: the machine, being a work of organization, of information, is, like life itself and together with life, that which is opposed to disorder, to the leveling of all things tending to deprive the universe of its powers of change. The machine is that through which man opposes the death of the universe; it slows down the degradation of energy, as life does, and becomes a stabilizer of the world.[5]

Progress is a deceleration of entropy, a preservation of the condition of the vital individuation. However, this characterization of technical progress in METO seems paradoxical with regard to this definition insofar as it claims to form an alliance with the living but, at the same time, does not integrate respect for any ecosystem. The process of concretisation tends to increase the circular causality

---

3   "Naissance de la technologie" (1970), in SLT, p. 136. Our translation.
4   Bernard Stiegler, *Qu'appelle-t-on panser? Tome 2: La leçon de Greta Thunberg*, Paris, Les liens qui libèrent, 2020, p. 303: "The *order of the technique*, [...] such as it allows the change of order of magnitude, as say Simondon and Bontems who tries after him to theorize the relations of scales, it is what constitutes an exo-transcendance."
5   METO, p. 21/MEOT, p. 18. Translation amended by us.

between "the technical individual" (the machine) and its "associated environment",[6] which is only "that through which the technical being conditions itself in its functioning".[7] The machine contributes to the homeostasis of an artificial environment based solely on the requirements of its own existence, and the progress of its technical lineage takes place without the slightest consideration for the preservation of a natural balance, which would guarantee the persistence of the conditions of existence of living beings on Earth.

Furthermore, the adaptation of the technical object to pre-existing environments would not constitute a factor of progress but of over-adaptation ("hypertélie"), which increases the performance at the cost of a dependence on a particular environment and a loss of genericity. This means that all the historical evolutions of techniques towards performance are not necessarily progress, but at the same time, it reserves the qualification of progress for the evolution of the machine towards an autocorrelation and a self-regulation from which results a transcendence vis-à-vis the environment and its changes. Concretisation is an adaptation to Nature conceived as a set of physical constraints and not resources for living beings.

Has Simondon ignored (or endorsed) the fact that technical evolution threatens the biosphere with irreversible destruction? Yet, he expressed an acute awareness of the ethical responsibilities of humankind towards all living beings.[8] In the introduction of METO, he even underlined the ravages of technical progress during its industrialisation phase: "To this phase corresponds a dramatic and passionate notion of progress, becoming the rape of nature, conquest of the world, harnessing of energies".[9] If this declaration, which dates from 1958, seems to suggest that this phase is over, nothing prevents to think that corrections, or the stopping, of the operation of certain machines are necessary in view of ecological considerations. However, what remains paradoxical is the apparent closure of the notion of progress as concretisation through its characterisation as self-adaptation, namely an increasing of circular causality between the machine and its own associated environment. Why would Simondon have defined technical progress by making any reference to the conditions of vital individuation impossible?

In order to understand the apparent lack of relationship between technical progress and the joint individuation of living things and their environment, we shall underline that it would be wrong, according to Simondon, to stick to a static confrontation of the artificial environment and the ecosystem as if they

---

6   Here and after we translate "milieu associé" by "associated environment" because we want to stress that the "milieu associé" is not a separate reality from the global environment.
7   METO, p. 59/MEOT, p. 70. Translation amended by us.
8   Simondon, *Deux Leçons sur l'animal et l'homme*, Paris, Ellipses, 2004.
9   METO, p. 21/MEOT, p. 17.

were two separate domains. Certainly, the ecological effects of the tidal power plant of la Rance could have reflected on the laudatory judgment of Simondon on the bulb-group invented by the engineer Jean Guimbal, but such an analysis leads above all to a dynamic conception of the relations between this device and the ecosystem. From this dynamic point of view on the combined evolution of the artificialisation of the associate environment and of the evolution of the environmental conditions of vital individuations, technical progress appears as an adaptation not simply by the machine to the associated environment, but also by humankind (bearing the ethical responsibility for the survival of all living things) to its whole environment through the mediation of a technical network. Technical invention then no longer aims to achieve only technical progress but a "supernature".[10]

During the 1970s, Simondon reformulated the concept of invention and developed a more complex conception of technical evolution as a *double adaptation*. Invention consists in an adaptation to the environment, which is not a hypertely, when its result integrates the conditions of insertion of the machine ingeniously (promoting the reception of information provided by the environment) and sparingly (taking resources without depleting the environment). The diversity of solutions discovered by different cultures to the same technical problem may most often be explained by such an adaptation to the constraints and resources of their environment as the state of their culture (and scientific knowledge) enabled them to understand it. This is why invention constitutes not a single but a double adaptation. On the one hand, it meets "the requirement of auto-correlation which makes the process or the object viable, non-destructive with respect to itself", on the other hand, it integrates "the terminal adaptations, which allow it to fit into the environment and to be directed by an operator or by the information that he receives or that he takes".[11] This duality has always existed, however the balance between these two adaptations evolves according to historically variable "conditions of atmosphere" ("*ambiance*"). If the atmosphere changed in the 1970s, it is because information on the effects of the technique was no longer collected only at the local level of the individual but considered according to several relations of scale.

A second point to be noted in Simondon's perspective is indeed that the invention of an eco-technology supposes an analysis of scale relativity. What explains the contradiction, in METO, between progress at the level of individuals (within technical lineages) and ecological considerations, is above all the change of scale between the associated local environment and the global environment.

---

10   METO, p. 171/MEOT, p. 218: "Technicity becomes oversaturated by once again incorporating the reality of the world to which it applies." Translation amended by us.
11   "L'Invention dans les techniques" (1971), in IT, p. 230. Our translation.

After having read Jacques Lafitte's book *Réflexions sur la science des machines*[12] (in 1968), Simondon adopted the distinction between passive, active and reflexive types of machines (the latter type being extended to all information machines) and analysed the relations between the structure of the object, its microstructure and the higher scales with which it interacts. This elucidates the paradox: the machine may be organised and organising matter, which creates negentropy on its own scale, and, as the same time, a cause of entropy at the scale of the global environment because of the combined effect of the functioning of all the machines. In addition to concretisation, we should hence consider a second dimension of technical evolution: scalabilisation.

The emergence of global phenomena, such as climate change, chemical pollution and the collapse of entire ecosystems are the results of scalabilisation. Does that mean that it is an "exo-transcendence"? Since technical progress has not only abolished natural selection in favour of an artificial selection of individuals and species (which was already established by Charles Darwin as by André Leroi-Gourhan), but also seems an immanent and irreversible tendency emerging from biological evolution, it may lead inexorably to the destruction of the conditions of life by the living being turned technician. Stiegler feared that the progress of technique was such a self-destructive tendency. He pointed to manifestations of this tendency at the level of psychosocial individuation, and paid homage to Greta Thunberg's parrhesia.[13] Yet Simondon's philosophy, precisely because it involves the analysis of scale relations, escapes this tragic slope without eluding the danger towards which technological civilisation is moving. In the 1980s, Simondon insisted on the destructive effects of technology: "Man lives in a natural environment into which he has inserted himself by devastating it in various ways, by plundering resources, by devoting certain species to destruction."[14] However, Simondon grants technical progress a vocation to "recover" the destruction induced by pollution.

Simondon knew the limits of the dilution of pollution in the oceans and the atmosphere. Some externalities were not, and still are not, recoverable, but only dispersible until they compromise homeostasis on a larger scale. In return, the technical amplification of human activities threatens most of the local ecosystems:

> With the proliferation of humans on the surface of the Earth and the expansion of their habitat, as well as the development of industry, the coupling is gradually becoming closer and closer; currently, the fate of nature depends closely on the turn that human civilizations will take; there is a community of destinies; the intensive exploitation of natural

---

12 Jacques Lafitte, *Réflexions sur la science des machines*, Paris, Vrin, 1972.
13 Stiegler, *op. cit.*, pp. 13-51.
14 "Trois perspectives pour une réflexion sur l'éthique et la technique" (1983), in SLT, p. 341.

resources in terms of energy and material, initiated with the use of fire and metallurgy, threatens natural resources with exhaustion and forces the use of forms of energy that compromise the distant future, by polluting nature and changing climates.[15]

Moving from pure technological analysis (disregarding any ecological consideration) to ethical thinking, which is immediately placed under the aegis of scientific ecology, through a study of socio-cultural adaptations of invention, Simondon looked further into eco-technological evaluation and radically changed his point of view. This transition is not a political conversion nor in rectification of the method, but rather a change of scale of the analysis. Unlike Stiegler, Simondon did not consider the destructive tendency of scalabilisation as evidence for the self-destructive nature of technical progress as exo-transcendence. Rather, he established a second distinction, this time no longer between concretisation (progress at the level of the technical individual) and scalabilisation (progress between different levels of organisation of technicity), but between progress (efficiency) and growth (productivity). This can be evidenced by the analysis of the energy consequences of industrialisation.

The industrial phase of technical evolution corresponds to a scalabilisation maximising power, for chemical as well as for thermodynamic industry. Nevertheless, industrialisation has been, and remains, a phase of technical progress insofar as it is based on the improvement of efficiency. To stabilise humankind's relationship to the environment, this progress in active performance should compensate for the effects of population growth on aggregate energy consumption: by improving the efficiency of converters, it becomes possible to benefit more people with the same amount of energy. However, this progress is generally achieved during crises of growth of the technical system, and the progress of the efficiency of the system does not compensate the effect of its growth: being more powerful, it produces more externalities. Industrial concentration improves energy efficiency, but this efficiency is not used to decrease the energy consumption but for an intensification of productivity.[16]

This scalabilisation predates the appearance of thermodynamic machines, since concentration and intensification of production in agriculture or mining had already been a factor of growth in the past. Just as he dissociates technical progress and the increase in performance of technical lineages, Simondon does

---

15 "Art et nature (La maîtrise technique de la nature)" (1980), in SLT, pp. 197–198.
16 André Gorz, *Capitalisme, Socialisme, Écologie*, Paris, Galilée, 1991, p. 91: "Ecological rationality consists in satisfying material needs as well as possible, with as little as possible with the smallest possible quantity of goods with a high use value and durability, thus with a minimum of capital and natural resources. The search for the maximum economic return, on the other hand, consists in selling with a profit as high as possible a maximum of productions realised with a maximum efficiency, which requires a maximisation of consumption and needs." Our translation.

not confuse progress and growth during the phases of scalabilisation: progress of technicity between scales should induce a reorganisation of the technical system towards a decrease in consumption of materials, energy and time (psychosocial attention). This *retro-scalable* progress (based on negative feedback from upper scales) escapes the dilemma between growth and regression because eco-technological regulation consists of setting up technical networks reducing the ecological footprint of humankind by limiting the use of too powerful techniques compared to global homeostasis. We must therefore stop equating progress with the growth of the technical system.

2. Eco-technological analyses

2.1. The paradigm of the Guimbal turbine

In order to proceed to an eco-technological evaluation, it is necessary to distinguish, within technical evolution, the effects of three distinct processes: technical progress, the search for performance and the growth of the technical ensemble. It is also necessary to analyse these effects in terms of scalability. In METO, the invention of the Guimbal turbine illustrates the self-adaptation aspect of concretisation: "the insertion of the generator in the conduit *renders itself possible* by simultaneously authorising an energetic cooling by water".[17] Simondon underlines that "the only environment in relation to which there exists a non hypertelic adaptation is the environment created by the adaptation itself."[18] Thus, there can be technical progress only through the establishment of a relative indifference of the operation with respect to the pre-existing environment and its variations. As Xavier Guchet underlines, "there is indeed a relation to nature implied in the Guimbal turbine, nevertheless this relation is interior to the technical object itself, it is in the operative coordination which defines its organisation, in the functional systematics which governs its functioning."[19]

This level of analysis remains insufficient, however, in that it does not take into account the multiplicity of scale relations that determine the "functional systematics" of the technical individual. The relation of the associated environment to the natural environment as an ecosystem does not necessarily appear at the scale of the technical object. Simondon pointed out, in passing, that turbines of the same type "equip bulb groups of the new French tidal power plants."[20] He

---

17   METO, p. 57/MEOT, p. 67.
18   METO, p. 57/MEOT, p. 67. Translation amended by us.
19   Xavier Guchet, "Évolution technique et objectivité technique chez Leroi-Gourhan et Simondon ", in: *Appareil*, vol. 2, 2008, online, accessed 19 October 2020, url: http://journals.openedition.org/appareil/58. Our translation.
20   METO, p. 57/MEOT, p. 66. Translation amended by us.

should have expressed himself in the future tense, since he was anticipating the realisation of these plants by mentioning the prospects of application of the patent filed by the engineer Jean Guimbal in 1953. In reality, only one tidal power plant was built, that of La Rance, in 1966, and this final realisation did not correspond to the invention celebrated by Simondon, for, as Paul Naegel has pointed out,[21] the bubble groups were precisely not immersed in oil.

More importantly from our perspective, Simondon could not have guessed the environmental consequences of the implementation of the tidal plant of La Rance. These were assessed afterwards and judged to be catastrophic: the cessation of the cyclical variation of the water level in the estuary, its desalination and silting up, have destroyed the pre-existing ecosystem. However, after a few years, some opportunistic species, such as mussels for example, took advantage of the "artificialization of the Rance estuary".[22] Then attracted by this resource, cephalopods and dolphins managed to circulate through the artificial barrier when the sluices open and, in 1976, studies showed the stabilisation of a new ecosystem, different but not necessarily less rich than the previous one (this depends on the eco-diversity index used). Nothing prevents us from extending Simondon's analysis by integrating the triple geo-*bio*-technical dimension of the associated environment. The final considerations of METO on the role played by aesthetic thought in guiding the harmonious insertion of the works of art in nature, or on the beauty of the tractor "when it is at work ploughing, leaning into the furrow while the soil is turned over",[23] already showed Simondon's particular sensibility towards the artificial balance between man, nature and technology ("terroirs").[24] It is then obvious that the result of the eco-technological analysis of the transition from nature to supernature depends on the spatio-temporal scale considered.

Considerations of different scales are also necessary because the Rance tidal power plant is a "green" energy source. If there were no other tidal plants, it was not for ecological but for economic reasons. A Simondonian methodology challenges economic reductionism: the eco-technological evaluation of the effects of the tidal plant of La Rance should above all take into account the relativity of the effects caused by multiple levels of technical organisation on the physical, biological and psychosocial individualisations taking place at different orders of mag-

---

21 Paul Naegel, "Une première mondiale énergétique française: l'usine marémotrice de la Rance", HAL, online, 2012, accessed 19 October 2020, url: https://halshs.archives-ouvertes.fr/halshs-00746910/document. Our translation.
22 Hermine Durand and Anouch Missirian, "L'usine marémotrice de la rance", Département Géographie et Territoire / ENS Paris [online], 2009–2010, accessed 19 October 2020, url: http://www.geographie.ens.fr/Les-mecanismes-a-l-origine-d-une.html.
23 METO, p. 197/MEOT, p. 255.
24 Élie Chevignard, *Qu'est-ce qu'un terroir?*, Beaune, Le souci de soi, 2019.

nitude. In the present case, the tension lies between the indifference or ignorance of engineers and decision-makers as to the effects of the device on the local ecosystem and their political responsibility towards the global environment in the name of future generations (and other factors that will be neglected here). The same machine, whose operation is locally and/or transiently harmful to vital individuation, can be considered highly negentropic on a larger scale, and therefore favourable to the persistence of life in the universe. This tension between the scale of the associated environment and that of the global environment means that the integration of ecological considerations must not be carried out only at the immediate local level, within the "compromise" between the natural and technical environments. The design process must be overdetermined by an eco-technological reflection integrating the analysis of entropic effects at all scales of the scalabilisation of the technical individual: should we build, as Simondon hoped in his time, other tidal plants?

2.2. The sense of adaptation

In the course "L'invention dans les techniques" (1971), the invention is no longer exclusively oriented towards the self-adaptation of the technical individual to its associated environment. It constitutes a compromise between this objective and another one, which is the insertion of the object into the psychosocial environment subject to the filter of culture. The arbitration between these two goals results from the historical atmosphere ("*ambiance*"): "this ambiance being essentially defined by the state of the technique and the science serving as a basis for the activity of invention".[25] The balance established between the requirement of circular causality with the associated environment and the requirements of a socialisation of machines varies according to the technical and scientific culture of the society where the invention originates. In the 1970s, the atmosphere had changed: the knowledge acquired by scientific ecology as well as climatology challenged the concept of progress, understood as self-adaptation, but the idea of dual adaptation elaborates on evolutionary trends already identified within the process of concretisation.

After reading Lafitte's *La Science des machines*, which prompted him to integrate into his analysis the distinction between "passive", "active" and "information" types in the course "L'invention et le développement des techniques", Simondon crosses this typology with the analysis of the scale relations between the structure of the object, its microstructure and the environment. The solidity of the wheel is a structural adaptation to the state of the roads, the choice of materials for building constitutes a reciprocal adaptation of the structure and the

---

25 "L'Invention dans les techniques", in IT, p. 230. Our translation.

microstructure, and the vault – whose stability depends on its structure, materials and insertion in the world through interactions with disturbances at other scales (weather, floods, earthquakes, etc.) – corresponds to the highest degree of passive performance, which takes into account all scales.

Adaptation to material conditions is not limited to bridges and buildings. It dominates the handicraft and pre-scientific phase of technical progress: "The pre-scientific inventions developed especially adaptations about tools, vehicles, constructions, roads; they operated a reorganization of the environment allowing these adaptations, and generally provided intermediate terms between the Man and the World".[26] These adaptations privilege solidity, uniformity and stability, all performances specific to passive machines, but which one finds in the majority of the artisanal creations. For example, the craftsman judges his tool as much by its efficiency as by the fact that it is an assembly so well adjusted that it will wear out slowly and in solidarity: "It is a little like the carriage of an English poet that Norbert Wiener quotes, saying: '… in it everything was worn out at the same moment and everything collapsed'".[27] This solidarity in the face of wear and tear represents an optimal artisanal solution for ensuring the durability of objects. This concept of craft industry is transhistorical and Leroi-Gourhan's analysis of the progress of lithic tools, which is marked by the precision of the gesture and the reduction in the amount of material used, can still be applied to the quality of today's custom-made products made "by hand".

Adaptation also concerns the active performances. The case of the internal combustion engine with a cooling circuit highlighted that the process of concretisation establishes an equilibrium that is no longer stable but dynamic and maintained by energy exchanges aimed at compensating for the self-destructive effects of the machine's operation. The progress of contemporary active techniques (often thermodynamic) consists in mastering an increased power by taking more and more energetic resources, in particular carbonaceous, and by contributing therefore more and more to the entropy and also, most of the time, to the greenhouse effect. The temptation is to identify this form of self-adaptive progress of active performances with a factor of environmental destruction. However, before being a search for power, industrial inventions are mediations between distant orders of magnitude and, more often than not, energy converters are intended to provide the best performance by saving energy: "systems of transformation of one or more forms of energy where self-correlation is provided by the rigor of the sequence and the conservation of energy during the transformations".[28] The progress of active machines, including thermodynamic ones, aims at extracting energy at other scales, elsewhere than in the bodies of the

---

26 *Ibid.*, p. 232. Our translation.
27 "Entretien sur la mécanologie" (1968), in SLT, p. 411. Our translation.
28 "L'Invention dans les techniques", in IT, p. 232. Our translation.

living beings. As counter-intuitive as it has become for us, because of the awareness of externalities, the progress of machines consists first of all in not mobilising the energy of living beings. Industry, and the use of motors in particular, corresponds to "the conquest of energy supplied by nature [at other scales], whereas until then it was supplied by man and animals."[29]

Finally, the informational adaptation increases negentropy within technical ensembles: the circulation of information allows the regulation of technical ensembles according to the information on larger scales, for example, according to the anticipation of global catastrophes:

> The third group of inventions, forsaking the inertia of the engines, deals mainly with the transmission of the signals and their amplification, as well as their combination in the form of calculations. In this way, thanks to a superior speed of forecast and diffusion of information, a new kind of adaptations arises, the random events and the variations of the course of nature, instead of being only stopped by the stability of the human constructions, are foreseen and announced; they are almost not events anymore; a cyclone detected by the satellites, announced by radio, can be made less deadly by the implementation of the industrial means.[30]

Like Jean-Hugues Barthélémy, one shall emphasise that the era of informational ensembles opens up the possibility of a new "society of invention",[31] adding that eco-technology, based on information about the large-scale evolution of the coupling between the environment and the humanity-machines system, determines the conditions for the invention of future technologies. The climate simulations of the IPCC change the scale of forecasting so that the extreme weather events that manifest climate change can no longer be considered the result of chance.

There is an axiological coherence between the different dimensions of progress. Material and energetic adaptations, which can be seen primarily in the progress of passive and active machines (crafts and industry), correspond to an eco-technological trend, insofar as they have always aimed to perfect efficiency in order to save matter and energy, and thus to optimise the use of natural resources. Their long history explains the development of what Thorstein Veblen calls "the craftmanship instinct",[32] i.e. the taste of beautiful work and the contempt of waste and useless destruction, which is opposed to the "predatory instinct", which expresses using techniques as weapons to dominate other living beings.

---

29 *Ibid.*, p. 272. Our translation.
30 *Ibidem.* Our translation.
31 Jean-Hugues Barthélémy, *La Société de l'invention. Pour une architectonique philosophique de l'âge écologique*, Paris, Éditions Matériologiques, 2018, pp. 123–130.
32 Thorstein Veblen, *Théorie de la classe de loisir*, Paris, Gallimard, 1970, p. 12.

Simondon points out, however, that, due to lack of knowledge, artisanal production does not fill all the conditions of self-adaptation. The optimisation of matter that prevails in the artisanal era does not provide in itself a solution to the contemporary eco-technological problematic. If artisanal activity is evoked with nostalgia by defenders of the environment, it is because of the assumption of a possible balance with the renewal of natural resources. This equilibrium used to exist because of the relative scarcity of resources on the local scale. The imaginary of the artisanal activity is associated with a remote period where the modesty of the human hold on the environment left to Nature the capacity to compensate, on a large scale, the effects of technicised activities. An eco-technological transition could set itself the goal of making such a balance available again locally.

In the meantime, the model of stable equilibrium is insufficient and outdated to think about the modalities of the eco-technological transition, even if it indicates the orientation of a retro-scalable progress with techniques that are not concentrated, not very powerful and remain under the control of human individuals. Symmetrically, the dynamic equilibrium model of the industrial machine is mostly rejected by ecological thinkers because of its scalabilisation modalities: the concentration of intensive means of production, the increase in power and the neglect of externalities. However, these modalities would not, in themselves, be wrong if developed below the damping threshold of the global system. The concentration of nuisances is an acceptable strategy for mass production. Energy efficiency and efficiency control characterise progress in terms of active performance, which allows the use of the smallest possible power to achieve a given effect. The industrial concentration coupled with the networks of circulation, supply and communication, can be a "Right Technology" if it is the most effective organisation in terms of eco-technological regulation.

This would not, however, be sufficient to guarantee human progress. In his essay on "The limits of human progress", Simondon underlines that the exploitation of natural resources can represent human progress only through an equitable democratisation of access to energy, which does not exclude in particular the populations living where the resources are extracted.[33] Conversely, decrease, like growth, can serve human progress or the will to power. As André Gorz pointed out, an ecological regulation may take an eco-socialist form as well as a techno-fascist form;[34] it does not, in itself, provide a universal formula for human progress.

---

[33] "Les limites du progrès humain" (1959), in SLT, p. 277.
[34] André Gorz, *Écologica*, Paris, Galilée, 2008, pp. 43–69.

2.3. The design of "negative progress"

Compared to previous spiritual movements expressing a sympathy towards Nature, the contemporary ecological movement is characterised by its awareness of scientific information on the large-scale effects (spatial and temporal) of the technical activity:

> The ecological tendency is not new, but this tendency is based nowadays on scientific information on biological order aware that resources, on Earth, are necessarily limited, whereas population growth and the consumption of energy and raw material follow an exponential law.[35]

The particular futurological value of ecological thought results from what it "considers at one glance, technically and scientifically, man, the living beings and the environment, geographical and cosmic, as a single organized whole".[36] An eco-technology must manage the operation but also the design, the maintenance and the recycling of machines according to a feedback anticipating the entropic consequences of amplification onto other scales, that is to say of scalability. The technological feedback on the process of invention transforms this into an activity of design, which integrates the double adaptation of the object to the natural environment and to the cultural environment in view of its diffusion. This design should not be confused with what Simondon denounced as the cultural acceleration of obsolescence: "Obsolescence does not reach only things, furniture, clothes, but sometimes even household equipment or industrial material, because of a difference of 'design', varying from year to year."[37] This venal design is over-historicity, while the eco-design of Right-Tech is what defines the historicity of technical value according to the contemporary scientific ambient conditions: an object is "outdated" neither because it looks obsolete nor because it is old or bad, but *because it has no future with regard to the requirements of human adaptation to the changes in the global environment.* Many current innovations can be already considered outdated. An eco-technological evaluation must not confuse "Right Technology" with innovations endowed with a halo of futuristic images, because these, in reality, often represent a dead end. There are, around us, a lot of "zombie technologies"[38] that persist even though they are

---

[35] "Trois perspectives pour une réflexion sur l'éthique et la technique" (1983), in SLT, p. 343.
[36] "Art et nature (La maîtrise technique de la nature)" (1980), in SLT, pp. 196–197.
[37] "Trois perspectives pour une réflexion sur l'éthique et la technique", in SLT, p. 346.
[38] José Halloy and Alexandre Nova "Au-delà du low-tech: technologies zombies, soutenabilité et inventions. Interview croisée de José Halloy et Nicolas Nova par Alexandre Monnin" in Isabelle Attard et al. (eds.), *Low Tech: face au tout numérique, se réapproprier les technologies*, Paris, Passerelle, 2020, pp. 120–128, online, accessed 14 January 2021, url: https://www.ritimo.org/Au-dela-du-low-tech-technologies-zombies-soutenabilite-et-inventions.

incompatible with the persistence of living conditions on Earth, while techniques that would still be useful have disappeared, and other scalable eco-technological devices are yet to be invented. Simondon learns to reinvent progress by no longer identifying it with the course of technical evolution: "Deepened technology must learn not only to invent the new, but to reinsert the old and reactualize it and make a present under the call of the future."[39] This undoubtedly implies a number of heartbreaking choices with respect to our current lifestyles and consumption patterns. Here again, Gorz helps us to understand the implications of eco-technological reasoning when he defends an existentialist ethic according to which no one should consume something whose aggregate consumption at the global level is capable of destroying the world. Hence the feedback of scalability supports this criterion of concrete universalisation of the eco-socio-existentialist ethic. It is not limited to it, however, and liberal thought also provides points of comparison. If innovation designates the "creative destruction" of the economic value for Joseph Alois Schumpeter, one could say, by analogy, that *negative progress* designates, for Simondon, a creative destruction of the technical value of existing techniques. It is necessary to underline the primacy of the negative aspect of progress: Right Technologies will emerge only if cultural obsolescence is put to the service of the reorganisation of the technical system towards decreasing energetic consumption, which implies the abolition of certain economically viable technologies. This supposes a deallocation and reallocation of economic resources by a system of large-scale political regulation of which there are hardly any examples.

In general, the eco-technological problematic offers itself to a plurality of political resolutions (that is to say, to transformative visions of society) because it is more profound than the problematic of political organisation: it points to the survival of the species. Humankind will provoke its own doom (as if confronted with an exo-transcendence) if it does not operate a radical redefinition of technical progress as negative progress oriented in the sense of an eco-technological retro-scalability. It is no longer a lack of knowledge, nor a deficiency of the communication networks, that oppose this redefinition of progress, nor even the absence of geopolitical consensus among the principal economic agents (even if this factor is, of course, to be taken into account), but the global alienation of the "civilization of productivity".[40] While efficiency improvement remains a value of progress, always opening the possibility of doing the same work with less energy and time, the norm of productivity is profoundly enslaving for machines and humans (or other living beings) forming a system with them. In his time, Simondon underlined that liberal capitalism, Soviet communism and

---

39 "Trois perspectives pour une réflexion sur l'éthique et la technique", in SLT, p. 351.
40 "Note complémentaire sur les conséquences de la notion d'individuation", in ILFI, p. 355. Our translation.

Nazism represented three variants of the alienation to power: the first one justifying this alienation by the increase in individual standard of living, the second by an invocation of collective good, the third by the exaltation of domination over other peoples.[41]

The improvement of efficiency is the progress of a technical value, while productivism is a social norm overdetermined by a cultural value that can take on different faces (profit, the construction of a classless society, the conquest of vital space, etc.) but that ultimately comes down to the "will to power", power being taken in its scientific sense: power = energy / time. Not only does humankind seek to express its power over machines treated as slaves, and, through them, over all people, living beings and Nature, but also this norm of maximum productivity corresponds to the most powerful uses of technology, i.e. those that consume the most energy in the shortest time, the destructive uses. As long as the technical system is subject to this will to power, it will be impossible to correct the trajectory of the technical system without resorting to "negativity, that is to say [to] war".[42] On this point Simondon agrees with Schumpeter's conclusions: when creative destruction does not play its role, the situation drifts towards the outbreak of pure destruction. The great difference lies in the fact that Schumpeter's mechanism of innovation was intended to maintain the permanent growth of the economic system, whereas Simondon's negative progress is intended to break this solidarity between technological renewal and growth. Right-Tech gives a completely different meaning to innovation as the shift from zombie technologies to the technologies that makes possible a sustainable future for humankind and the living.

3. Conclusion: The 3Rs of Right-Tech: Recovery, Regulation and Recycling

Simondon helps us to design Right-Tech according to an eco-technological evaluation by accomplishing a triple operation:

a. the shift from a static analysis to a dynamic analysis of the relation between the artificialisation of the environment and the management of ecosystems;
b. a deepening of technology such that the effects of technical concretisation are assessed on all the scales of the associated environment rather than only on the scale of the local associated "milieu";

---

41   METO, p. 231/MEOT, p. 304–305.
42   Simondon, "Le progrès, rythmes et modalités", in: *Critique*, no. 816, May 2015, pp. 384–400 (397).

c. a radical revocation of the linear representation of progress as a march forward or growth in favour of a "negative progress" that integrates transitions to less power and feedbacks between scales, updating technologies from the past as well as present ones.

In order to escape an increasingly dark and ephemeral future, technical progress can no longer be conceived simply as a march forward, nor as acceleration,[43] and its assessment cannot be reduced to the sole criterion of the concretisation of technical lineages. Technicity operates on several scales. Its scalabilisation becomes a factor of human progress only when it metastabilises culture by opening it up to a transformation of the norms of the system formed by humankind, machines and the rest of the living world, capable of counteracting the entropic effects of the technical system. Between METO (1958) and Simondon's last published text, "Trois perspective pour une réflexion sur l'éthique des techniques" (1983), a change of scale occurs: Simondon treats the eco-technological problematic from the point of view of large-scale consequences and implicitly takes as its stake retro-scalability, that is to say the feedback of this point of view on the whole technical life cycle, from design to recycling. He then suggests ways of reformulating the criteria of progress from three perspectives: the recovery of externalities, the regulation of energy consumption, and technological "recycling". These three approaches diverge from the linear conception of progress: recovery presupposes the crossing of thresholds in the most advanced techniques (for example, the development of nuclear fusion to recover the externalities of nuclear fission); regulation implies the limitation of the growth, or even the decrease, of the technical system; recycling lends a second life to objects and techniques from the past, and therefore seems to tend towards regression since it invites returns to older techniques (it involves less materials than technical schemes).

There is however no contradiction between these three orientations, because progress is not confused either with technical evolution towards performance, nor with system growth. It unfolds in the dimension of scales through the retro-scalability that pushes the abandonment of technologies with too large an ecological footprint. It is therefore important to symmetrise the analysis: if progress is not synonymous with growth, neither is decrease synonymous with regression. Very enlightening in this respect is the comparison between the description that Simondon gives of the crisis between culture and civilisation at the beginning of the 20th century,[44] when culture was unable to assimilate the progress of the growing technological civilisation, and the crisis at the end of the 20th

---

43   Hartmut Rosa, *Aliénation et Accélération. Vers une critique de la modernité tardive*, Paris, La Découverte, 2014.
44   "Psychosociologie de la technicité", in SLT, p. 391.

century, when a reorganisation of technological civilisation was needed because it could no longer function with the cultural norms set up during its growth. In the first case, culture had to learn to grow in order not to become alienated, in the second case, technological civilisation had to learn to decrease without regressing, that is to say, culture had to invent a "negative progress":

> [...] crises of reorganization, crises of aging, which are quite comparable to growth cycles, but in the opposite direction. And if these crises are not possible, the degradation becomes much more pronounced, leading to a pronounced and lamentable disorganization. Reductions in the level of activity must be seen in this light.[45]

In both cases, Simondon relies on the example of the reorganisation of the camp of Publius Quinctilius Varus, but in the first case, he underlines the analogy with madness, while in the second, he emphasises that "the essence of progress can be present within the processes of degradation". This negative progress presupposes that some elements are left aside to allow for reorganisation, but they are not lost. The enemy is not technical progress but the absence of retro-scalable regulation.

As utopian as it may seem, in the Right-Tech perspective airships probably have more future value than airplanes, bicycles than automobiles, and sailboats than oil tankers, but it will be necessary to decide to do without the latter in order to rediscover the former or to favour the emergence of as yet unknown technologies. What principle will orient our negative progress towards "Right Technology", i.e. will organise recovery, regulation and recycling?

A principle emerges from Simondon's eco-technological analyses that makes it possible to assess the future value of technologies depending on the relationships of scale between their life cycles, their performance in their associated environment, and their global entropic effects – *"what I call"* (we use this expression in homage to Bernard Stiegler) the "Principle of Least Power". We must privilege technologies whose impact on the environment is the least powerful. This includes decarbonised energy sources that do not contribute to the greenhouse effect, low power operations that consume little energy per unit of time, and all technologies whose scalability reduces the externality of the technical system as a whole. This requires a political (cyber-democratic) invention of which Right-Tech is only one dimension.

---

45   Simondon, "Le progrès", *op. cit.*, p. 391.

Humanism, Technology and Care in Simondon

Xavier Guchet

Introduction

In the past years, care has increasingly outflanked the domain of those activities – medicine, nursing, etc. – which focus on vulnerable people (children; the sick, elderly or dying people). Indeed, it is widely admitted that from now on, care should dramatically pervade our general relationships to social institutions, to living beings and to the whole of nature. Fischer and Tronto's famous definition of care echoes this extension of care: according to them, care is

> a species activity that includes everything that we do to maintain, continue, and repair our world so that we can live in it as well as possible. That world includes our bodies, ourselves, and our environment, all of which we seek to interweave in a complex, life-sustaining web.[1]

In this respect, it could be expected that technology become a core issue in contemporary philosophical reflections on care. Is not technology always requested in order "to maintain, continue and repair our world"? However, on the whole, the ethics and philosophy of care generally pay little attention to technology. To be more precise, it is commonly recognised that care cannot be conceived without technology, but technology can mainly be split into a couple of categories to which opposite values are attached: skilful technical gestures can be put in the service of care, but care and technology are usually considered incompatible when the latter refers to complex high-tech machines or industrial products (chemistry, biotechnology etc.). However, the opposition between "cold" technologies and "warm" care is still generally accepted as obvious – a situation that is definitely unsatisfactory, insofar as the line between both categories is never clear-cut. In view of several philosophical studies of the last decade which evidence, on the contrary, the close intertwining of technology, including high-tech devices, and care (see in particular Mol[2] and Pols[3]), this diagnosis could undoubtedly be qualified.

---

[1] Joan Tronto, *Moral Boundaries. A Political Argument for an Ethic of Care*, Routledge, New York and London, 1993, p. 103.
[2] Annemarie Mol et al. (eds.), *Care in Practice. On Tinkering in Clinics, Homes and Farms*, transcript Verlag, Bielefeld, 2010.
[3] Jeannette Pols, *Care at a Distance. On the Closeness of Technology*, Amsterdam University Press, Amsterdam, 2012.

Is it possible to better articulate technology and care in a philosophical perspective that would refuse any divide between supposedly "good" (that is to say artisanal) and "bad" (that is to say industrial) technologies? The main characteristic of Gilbert Simondon's philosophical analysis of technology is precisely the refusal of such a divide. Simondon never ceased to castigate the injustice caused to technology, in particular industrial machines, by culture: placing technology outside the realm of what is culturally valuable in human life results in cutting humans off from their own reality – in "alienating" them. This analysis echoes what has been extensively commented on by specialists of Simondon's thought, namely his conception of humanism.[4][5] A true humanism, Simondon argues, must take into account technology from three perspectives: knowledge, aesthetics and ethics. The last perspective claims to value technical objects for they are carriers of human inventiveness and constructive efforts. Simondon suggests that we should show respect and even courtesy toward technical objects: we are committed to highly prizing them, to cherishing them and to taking care of them. In this respect, Simondon considers that any kind of beings, including technological beings, should not be considered according to crude oppositions (e.g. technology versus culture) and classificatory categories (e.g. good or bad), but according to their potential refinement and optimisation, in line with previous efforts made to improve them.

However, an additional point has not been sufficiently underlined until now: according to Simondon, technology, far from being antinomic to respectful relationships to nature (including industrial machines), allows humans and nature to more intensively intertwine, and in a more constructive way, in comparison to humans equipped with mere tools. As he emphasises,

> Humanity by itself creates much devastation. A highly technologised humanity, intelligently technologised through a network, which has a geographical sense, is much less dangerous for nature than humanity by itself.[6] [author's translation]

This quite enigmatic and counterintuitive sentence asserts that technology is not only something we should take care of, for it carries human values; it is also what makes us able to better care for nature.

The chapter is devoted to explaining how Simondon links his technological humanism to care for nature. The first part returns to Simondon's humanism and explains its specificity in relation to classical humanisms, namely both Plato's humanism and the humanism of the Enlightenment. The second part of the chapter positions Simondon's conception of technology in relation to the

---

[4] Xavier Guchet, *Pour un humanisme technologique. Culture, technique et société dans la philosophie de Gilbert Simondon*, Presses Universitaires de France, Paris, 2010.
[5] Jean-Hugues Barthélémy, *Simondon*, Les Belles Lettres, Paris, 2014.
[6] SLT, p. 443.

three philosophical approaches to technology that have inspired most of the philosophy of technology in the last century, namely Marx, Heidegger and Bergson. The third part details the nature of Simondon's technological humanism: linking human beings to nature. The fourth part of the chapter explains how human beings, because they are technologically equipped, are made responsible for nature. It concludes that in this respect, Simondon may be considered a major contributor to current philosophical reflections on care for nature, even though he did not explicitly address the issue of care in his writings.

1. Humanism adapted to our times

Simondon's philosophical project includes, among other things, the requirement of a new form of humanism, which is defined according to Terence's well-known formula: "the will to return the status of freedom to what has been alienated in man, so that nothing human should be foreign to man".[7] If we need a new form of humanism today, it is because humanism, as well as the danger of alienation that it intends to overcome, is a historical concept.

> Humanism can never be a doctrine or even an attitude capable of being defined once and for all; each epoch must discover its humanism, by orienting itself toward the main danger of alienation.[8]

Both the ancient world and the Age of Enlightenment developed their respective forms of humanism in order to respond to the specific danger of alienation that threatened them.

Simondon explains that a strange law seems to govern history, according to which the solution invented at a time to overcome the danger of alienation with which it is confronted, constitutes the ferment of what shapes alienation in the following period. What is "a means of liberation and rediscovery of man, becomes through its historical evolution an instrument that turns against its liberation and enslaves man by limiting him".[9] This historical understanding of the couple alienation/humanism allows us to cast a retrospective glance on the relationship of previous times to technology.

The ancient Greeks had an ambiguous relationship with *technai*. Plato expresses this ambiguity very precisely. On the one hand, he considers craftsmen as demiurges, participating in the vast field of creative activities. In this sense, Plato is still close to the Homeric hymn to Hephaestus, celebrating craftsmen

---

7   METO, p. 117/MEOT, p. 101.
8   METO, p. 118/MEOT, p. 102.
9   METO, p. 118/MEOT, p. 102.

alongside the poets, the aedes – that is to say, all those who are creators.[10] On the other hand, because they are creators, craftsmen represent a danger in the city: they have the power to vary indefinitely the forms they give to things, according to their good will if nothing comes to limit them. They therefore have the power to destabilise the world – a serious danger according to the Greeks. The human being is indeed conceived as a living being struggling with hostile nature against which he counts for very little. His own power is out of all proportion to that of the *physis*. His life can only flourish in a world that blocks the power of Nature. The human world must be solid and durable.[11]

Plato's response to this danger of destabilisation of the world by the form-creating power of artisans is well known: it lies in his metaphysics. It is not up to the craftsman to decide on what the forms should be. The form of a thing is fixed for eternity by its *eidos*, the craftsman only realises it in the matter, as faithfully as possible. Plato's craftsman is anything but an inventor, he is even the opposite of an inventor: he must not invent, he must imitate. The good craftsman is not the one who possesses manual dexterity, skilful know-how: he is above all the one who shapes the materials he deals with while keeping his gaze fixed on the *eidos* of what he is making.

> The creation itself, the *poiema*, which is the goal of his work, is beyond him [...] Whether it was a house, shoe, flute, or shield, the product answered a specific natural need. It was not seen as something artificial, in the true sense of the term. It was an *eidos*, a Form laid down in advance, as was the case for natural objects. The artisan did not invent it, nor could he alter it [...] Form is superior to the workman and to his *techné*, and it directs and controls the work that brings it into being. It gives this work its goal, fixes its limits, defines its framework and its means.[12]

Moreover, the craftsman himself is fixed in an unchanging nature: being a shoemaker requires an apprenticeship, of course, but the man who becomes a shoemaker possesses shoemaking as "a gift granted and fixed once and for all".[13] He is only one thing, a shoemaker and not a carpenter or a joiner. *Techné* is thus above all a form of knowledge – the knowledge of the *eidos* and of the outcomes. Plato refuses to call "art" those activities which are unable to give a rational explanation of their outcomes. They are only routines and irrational activities. Those who cannot account for what they do, and the effects they produce, like the cook, are deprived of any *techné*.

10   Richard Sennett, *The Craftsman*, Yale University Press, New Haven, London, 2008.
11   Hannah Arendt, *The Human Condition*, The University of Chicago Press, Chicago, 1958.
12   Jean-Pierre Vernant, *Myth and Thought among the Greeks*, translated by J. Fort, Zone Books, New York, 2006, p. 316.
13   Jose Ortega y Gasset, "Man the Technician", in Jose Ortega y Gasset, *History as a System and Other Essays Toward a Philosophy of History*, W. W. Norton & Company, New York and London, 1941, p. 147.

This being said, Plato acknowledges that there is some irrationality in any manual activity, even in those which belong to the true arts. "In the art of carpentering and all other handicrafts, the knowledge of the workman is merged in his work".[14] The intelligence of the workman is embodied, buried in the depths of his body. The technical operations constitute the unanalysable and irrational dimension of the manufacturing activity. They are accessible neither to knowledge, nor to interventions with the aim of controlling and eventually correcting the gesture of the workman.

In the Age of Enlightenment, the danger of alienation lies in the fragmentation of society into closed communities, exemplified by guilds.[15] The humanism promoted by the Encyclopaedists consists in bringing know-how out of the secrecy of the guilds (and out of the bodies of craftsmen) and in building a public space for technology. In a sense, it takes the opposite view of Platonic humanism. Attention is no longer focused on the conformity of the man-made thing to an immutable *eidos*, but rather on the technical operations themselves, i.e. on this irrational dimension of any manufacturing activity which must henceforth be brought to rationalisation, formalisation and public disclosure. A craftsman in one field must be able to adopt the ways of doing things and processes used in another field, in order to improve and progress – which supposes, explains Diderot, a standardisation of the nomenclature and the development of a grammar of the arts. This attempt at bringing technical activities to a new kind of rationality in fact had its origin two centuries earlier, when techniques began to be written (*redigere in artem*). However, in the eighteenth century, the capture of technical operations with a view to their formalisation goes hand in hand with disciplining the activities and the body of workmen. This intersects with economic issues: if the working body must be disciplined, it is because it is a productive body, a body from which maximum output must be obtained. In the ancient Greek world, the technique had been thought according to the coordinates of the *organon* (the extension of the living body) and of the manufactured object; it is now thought according to new coordinates: a disembodied form of intelligence on one side, an activity of pure execution on the other, reducing the executors to the rank of automaton. In this divide between intelligence and execution lies the origin of the alienation of man from technology, in the double sense pointed out by Simondon: from the top (the industrial boss, who holds the intelligence) and from the bottom (the simple worker, the productive automaton).

---

14   Plato, *Complete Works,* edited by J. M. Cooper, associate editor J. S. Hutchinson, Hackett Publishing Company, Indianapolis, 1997, 258d.
15   METO, p. 118/MEOT, p. 102.

Similarly, techniques, invoked as a liberation through progress during the Enlightenment, are today accused of oppressing man and of reducing him to slavery by denaturing him, of estranging him from himself through a specialisation that is a barrier and source of incomprehension.[16]

The danger of alienation that characterises industrial societies lies more precisely in the hyperspecialisation of productive tasks, which makes individuals nothing but mere cogs in a machinery that exceeds them.

The human world of technical action has once again become a stranger to the individual through its development and formalization, hardening itself into a form of machinism that has now become a new attachment of the individual to an industrial world that exceeds the dimension and possibility of thinking the individual.[17]

While the traditional craftsman is the true technical individual who, through his body, coordinates the manufacturing operations, workers in industries have lost this role, which is devoted to the machine. Through its operations, the latter coordinates the whole productive activity, the human being is relegated to subordinate functions (putting the machines into action, monitoring their proper functioning, etc.). The role of philosophy is to propose a new form of humanism capable of overcoming this situation of alienation in the industrial context. Therefore, according to Simondon, humanism in present times should include an understanding of technology.

2. Simondon beyond Marx, Heidegger and Bergson

Simondon's diagnosis therefore seems very classical and deprived of originality. It was posed in more or less similar terms by the three philosophers who respectively represent the three major orientations of contemporary philosophy of technology: Marx, Bergson and Heidegger.

Marx analyses the alienation of the industrial worker as a transformation in the relationship between life and technology, throughout the working process. While the craftsman alienated himself in the sense that through manufacturing, he produced his own objective reality outside himself (first meaning of alienation, *Entäusserung:* to objectify one's own reality in the outer world), he is now alienated in the sense that as soon as he is dispossessed of his productive activity and of the products of this activity, he is cut off from his own reality (second meaning of alienation, *Entfremdung*). By means of technology, the dead hold the living in their grasp – that is, the living labour of the worker is converted into fixed capital, into machines. As Marx says, the living labour is no longer realised

---

16 METO, p. 118/MEOT, p. 102.
17 METO, p. 119/MEOT, p. 102.

in the material work as in its objective organ; henceforth, machines absorb the living labour of the worker, so that the former becomes value creating value, capital in motion. It is thus within the framework of a philosophy of work that Marx analyses the danger of alienation characteristic of the capitalist industrial mode of production.

As for Heidegger, he analyses technology from the perspective of the history of Western metaphysics, more precisely as a history of "unveiling" or "revealing" – i.e. as a history of the way in which, at a given time, things are seen and thought of. Thus, in the age of modern technology, everything is understood according to its capacity to provide power. Everything is caught in the vice of the organisation, of the apparatus (*Ge-stell*) oriented to the extraction, transport, storage and supply of power.[18] In this respect, modern technology appears to be the cause of a form of decay of the world, whereas craftsman technology, on the contrary, participated in the structuring of the world.

Bergson considers technology as an activity of Man as a living being. Technology is part of the plan that nature had for humans. It is deeply grounded in life. However, as a vital phenomenon, technology should remain limited to the addition of artificial organs to our natural organs. Modern technology extends our power well beyond the modest extension of the possibilities of human action according to an organological perspective[19] – a situation that brings a contradiction into human life: between "being-in-life", that is to say being an organism that has imperative vital needs, and the life that each of us wants to live as a subject, and which blooms in an artificial world that grows indefinitely and is saturated with superfluous needs. Bergson then explains that this considerable extension of our power calls for a "supplement of soul" (*un supplément d'âme*), understood as a new perception: our perception is no longer proportionate to our action; we are not equipped to see what our technical action does to the natural world and to other living beings. This analysis is developed further by André Leroi-Gourhan.

Marx, Heidegger and Bergson/Leroi-Gourhan thus represent the three poles between which the various contemporary conceptualisations of technology have been distributed. Now, in this landscape, Simondon proposes an original approach.

From Marx, Simondon takes back the idea that the human is no longer the "bearer of tools" (*porteur d'outils*), and that from now on this role is devolved to the machine. However, this experience of alienation cannot, according to him, find both a satisfactory understanding and a solution within the framework of a

---

18   Martin Heidegger, *The Question Concerning Technology and Other Essays*, translated by W. Lovitt, Garland Publishing Inc., New York and London, 1977.
19   Henri Bergson, *The Two Sources of Morality and Religion*, translated by R. A. Audra and C. Brereton, University of Notre Dame Press, Notre Dame, Indiana, 2002.

philosophy of work. The Marxian analysis, like that of the *Aufklärung*, equates the emancipation of the human with the restitution to him, in the productive activity (of objects, institutions), of his full capacity to produce his own material and social reality. The liberated human is the human whose entire reality results from his own activity. Both the humanism of the *Aufklärung* and that of Marx refer to a doctrine of absolute artificialism. They do not acknowledge that the human being draws his reality, not only from his constructive activity, but also from his insertion within a natural order that he has not made. The constructivist humanisms of Marxism and *Aufklärung* respectively lack a philosophy of nature, which would refuse to limit human reality to what humans produce through their work.

From Heidegger, Simondon takes back the idea that technology, in its very essence, must be understood in metaphysical terms. Metaphysics (hylomorphism) prevents us from seizing the essence of technology. For Simondon, this recasting of metaphysics is phrased as a theory of individuation. However, contrary to Heidegger, Simondon refuses to seize modern technology by the prism of the *Ge-stell*, i.e. in terms of the capture and supply of power. A philosophy of technology, says Simondon, should not be confused with a "philosophy of human power through techniques".[20] Henceforth, Simondon refuses to blame the machine of modern technology for the decay of the world, as Heidegger does. For Simondon, machines organise the world and our relationship to it. A bridge (which is a passive machine), connecting a hill to another hill, makes each of them something more than a rock immovably placed in a given place; it actualises the potential that each one has to be a point of passage, an invitation to cross from one hill to the other. In this rock that dominates the valley, in this structure that seems full of its own reality, enclosed in its own limits, there is a call to movement. This call remains nevertheless a mere potentiality, deprived of effectiveness, as long as the human constructive gesture does not actualise it, by building a bridge.

From Bergson finally, Simondon takes back the idea that technology must be interpreted from the perspective of life, as a vital phenomenon. Simondon considers the human as a living being and that human behaviours must be described and understood according to the same categories as those which are used to interpret the behaviours of the non-human living. However, unlike Bergson, he refuses to oppose industrial machines and life. Machines are not univocally on the side of intelligence cut off from true duration (*la durée vraie*); they are part of the process by which the living human being continues his individuation at a non-vital level, giving birth to the "trans-individual".

Consequently, Simondon takes the opposite view of Marx, Heidegger and Bergson, on two essential points:

---

20 METO, p. 141/MEOT, p. 126.

Firstly, Marx as well as Heidegger and Bergson consider that technology is no longer comprehensible in the terms of the manufactured object. Technology is no longer indexed to the activity of the "Homo faber" (the expression is proposed by Bergson), i.e. the bearer of tools whose activity consists in making tangible and sustainable things intended to take their place within the world. All three interpret modern technology in terms of pure processuality – a process of capturing labour and accumulating capital in the form of machines for Marx; a process of exploiting everything as a "fund" (*Bestand*) of raw materials and energy, oriented towards the accumulation and supply of power for Heidegger; a process of turning life against itself for Bergson. This is also reflected in Arendt's analysis: technology consists less and less in making things (works) that ensure the sustainability of the world, and more and more in triggering new processes within nature.

Secondly, the three authors consider that modern technology escapes its traditional interpretation in terms of vital activity. In its industrial phase, technology no longer refers to the activity of humans as living beings.

3. The role of culture: linking humans to nature

At first glance, Simondon thus seems to return to the ancient Greeks' understanding of technology: on the one hand, he conceives the philosophy of technology as a philosophy of technical objects, whereas most of his contemporaries (and his successors) consider that the very essence of contemporary technology cannot be grasped philosophically from an analysis of technical objects; on the other hand, he conceives technology, including machines, as part of the vital individuation of human beings, which continues through psychosocial individuation. Technology contributes to creating collectives that are not completely organised by social norms. Simondon gives the example of the Greek engineer who introduces in the social order the relation to the non-social (i.e. to nature), and establishes a transindividual collective beyond the admitted social standards: the functioning of technology and its evolution are not subjected to social prejudices and established norms. They evidence a rationality of their own, irreducible to existing social norms, values and ways of thinking. However, technology also keeps a link to life; it is even that which, of all human achievements, keeps the greatest proximity to life. Technology makes the link between the vital and the transindividual. Simondon therefore reminds us of the two central themes of the ancient Greeks' conceptualisation of technology: the manufactured thing defined by its *eidos*, and the reference to life – except that the Simondonian technical object is no longer the object of use as with the Greeks, but the object as the seat of technological operations, mediation of the human and the natural world. Moreover, although he conceives technology as an activity of the living,

Simondon does not take back the idea that technological operations are unanalysable, sunk in the body and its obscure functionings. Simondon invents new coordinates for philosophically thinking technology, in the service of a new form of humanism – which means that, in his eyes, contemporary societies are confronted with an unprecedented danger of alienation, which is no longer that of a human being dominated by a world of machines that have become incomprehensible (which was the basic problem posed by Marx, Bergson and Heidegger).

This danger of alienation is exposed by Simondon in the first pages of *On the Mode of Existence of Technical Objects:* it lies in a "misoneism directed against machines",[21] consisting in excluding them from the culture. The main danger of alienation is not in the machines themselves, but in our attitude towards them. There is something Stoic in Simondon's thought: the evil is not in the beings and the events as such, but in the judgment that we carry on them. The culture is incomplete, truncated, because it excludes the technology. A true culture must include technology, including machines. Culture is not the set of beliefs shared by a social group forming a closed collective, and limited to a few accepted standards. This conception of culture is mystifying in the sense that it relies on oppositions: the opposition of the community to those who do not belong to it, the foreigners; the opposition of the human group which lives and thinks itself in opposition to nature, and which relates to it only through work. Here, culture is opposed to nature and this opposition reinforces the idea that humans are the only makers of their own reality. The human is the being cut off from nature, self-produced in an order of reality that is supposedly separated from nature. On the contrary, Simondon claims that a true and complete culture must include the relation to nature through technology. Technology must become an integral part of the culture insofar as it mediates the relationship between humans and nature. It establishes the relationship to nature by giving this relationship a consistency and objectivity superior to those produced by the collective work.

> The technical object, which is thought and constructed by man, is not limited to simply creating a mediation between man and nature; it is a stable mixture of the human and the natural, it contains human and natural aspects; it gives its human content a structure comparable to that of natural objects, and allows for the integration of this human reality into the world of natural causes and effects. The relation of man to nature, rather than being only lived and practiced obscurely, takes on a status of stability, of consistency, making it a reality that has laws and an ordered permanence. In edifying the world of technical objects and by generalizing the objective mediation between man and nature,

---

21   METO, p. 16/MEOT, p. 9.

technical activity re-attaches man to nature through a far richer and better defined link than that of the specific reaction of collective work.[22]

The machine brings into the human world a material consistency, giving it a certain stability and objective reality. Culture integrates the relation to nature and in doing so, it opens the society to the non-social, to what is not socialised – an opening that is necessary to every society, otherwise it dies. A completely closed society is not viable, it has no regenerative power; it cannot transform itself. To live, a society must be able to question itself, which implies that it can open up and integrate elements that are heterogeneous to its structures. This dimension of openness and heterogeneity is provided by technology. The technician has a social function, he is part of an established order which fixes the statuses and the places of everything and everybody, but he also imports into the society a non-social normativity – a normativity that does not depend on existing social norms, and which is heterogeneous to them. By integrating this heterogeneous normativity brought by technology, the society can be led to change its own normativity, to transform itself. Through technology, the penetration of a new normativity in a closed community is made possible. Any society that adopts a new technology accepts at the same time the values inherent to this technology, and by doing so it may be led to change its own values.

The technician is the true individual, i.e. the one who can enter into communication with other individuals without the mediation of social normativity. There are indeed two ways for society to organise the existence of individuals:

- either society is assertive and provides all that ensures their existence and the norms that structure it, in which case individuals communicate with each other only indirectly, through the social structures. The individual is defined by his integration into the group, he is the term of an asymmetrical relation whose other term is the society as a whole. The individual can relate to other individuals only through social structures and norms. Only inter-individual relations that are homogeneous to these structures are admitted. According to this perspective, the individual is entirely defined by his status and his social functions, he cannot bring any transforming dynamism into the society;
- or the society integrates individuals by providing them with the means to relate directly to one another – or rather, as Simondon insists, to individuate in a direct communication to each other, without the mediation of social normativity. The latter does not regulate the entirety of human existence and activity. Not everything is structured in society, nor in the individual. Not everything is socialised in the society, and not everything is individuated in the individual. The direct dialogue between one indi-

---

22 METO, p. 251/MEOT, p. 245.

vidual and another individual, communicating by that which is not socialised in them and is in the pre-individual state, makes the integration into the society of what is heterogeneous to the existing social structures and norms, and cannot be assimilated by them, possible. Technology introduces the direct dialogue with the natural world. As Simondon says, Greek engineers knew how to free themselves from the community and, in so doing, they gave it its first impulse to free individual thought and to stimulate disinterested reflection.

There is thus a close link between, on the one hand, the capacity of a society to integrate what is heterogeneous to its structures (this is the function of culture), and on the other hand, the capacity that an individual has to live and think according to norms that are not dictated by society, establishing a direct interindividual communication. The integration of the relationship to nature into the society (through culture) and the empowerment of individuals, making possible and even encouraging their emancipation from social structures and norms, are thus the two essential components of Simondonian humanism. This type of humanism is a technological humanism since this integration as well as this empowerment are based on technology, through which the non-social, i.e. normative features that are heterogeneous to current social structures and norms (nature), are introduced into the society.

4. Humanity in face of nature: from mastery to care

In others words (Simondon's words), the complete culture has a regulating function insofar as it renders compatible the "technical conditions" and the "organic conditions" of human existence. In a barely written and very allusive note, dating from 1952, i.e. long before the defence of the two theses (in 1958), Simondon provides a key to understanding this definition of culture as a compatibility of the organic and the technical:

> Techné, a great force conniving with the familiar world [...] [*Physis* is] full of potential and needs the organisers it has produced itself. We are natural beings who are indebted to the *physis* that is in us. *Techné* is our debt. The seed of *physis* which is in us must expand into *techné* around us. We [the human beings] cannot fulfil our very essence without radiating the organisers that we have in ourselves.[23] [author's translation]

We are natural beings and as such we are in debt to nature. We owe it our being, in the sense that it has put in us the seeds from which our being can blossom. This blossoming is achieved by means of *techné* and as Canguilhem said, in hu-

---

[23] SLT, p. 24.

man beings life blossoms in "technical plasticity".[24] Now, through technology, we do not only blossom according to the seeds of our being. We must also pay our debt to the *physis* by contributing to its development, to its fulfilment. Technology is not the expression of the power of humans and of their will to master a nature which is external to them. It is an operation accomplished on nature by a particular species of natural beings (humans) which belong to it; i.e. it is an operation accomplished on nature from within nature itself. More exactly, it is a concatenation of operations, a more or less extended operative chain, establishing a communication between two separate realities: nature within us, nature outside us. Far from distancing us from nature, technology makes the natural beings that we are, beings *for* this nature that made us (we are the organisers of nature). *Techné* does not mean a divorce of humans and nature, but on the contrary a close alliance between them, a relation of double actualisation, of double achievement: actualisation/achievement of both ourselves as natural beings, and of nature itself. The human/nature relationship is not a relationship between two constituted and completed realities, but between two unfinished realities, rich in potential and in continuous becoming. Simondon writes, about the Saint-Simonians: "for them, it is not about overcoming nature as a hostile force by attacking it, but rather about completing nature by adding communication routes"[25] [author's translation]. And also, as an exergue to the volume *Sur la technique (1953–1983)*, a citation from METO:

> In the absence of any end-point thought out and realized by living human beings on Earth, physical causality could not, in the majority of cases, have produced a positive and efficient concretization on its own.[26]

The human being is defined by his genesis more than by constituted structures. He can only be accomplished by actively organising his relation to nature, by actualising the potential it contains (what Simondon calls "radiating the organisers that we have in ourselves"). In a nutshell, *techné* is a constitutive dimension of human individuation.

As Emmanuel Mounier also said, the nature of man is artifice – a formula that may seem close to that of Simondon. But for Mounier, and for many of his contemporaries, technology is that by which human beings tear themselves away from nature to accomplish themselves. Nature is a set of positive mechanisms, it is deterministic. As we are living and natural beings, we are all that we can be. To be human is to overcome our natural being-in-life and to make ourselves something other than what nature has made of us. This is the definition of free-

---

24   Georges Canguilhem, *On the normal and the pathological*, translated by C. R. Fawcett, D. Reidel Publishing Company, Dordrecht, Holland, 1978, p. 118.
25   Gilbert Simondon, RP, p. 46.
26   METO, p. 51/MEOT, p. 49.

dom. As we can see, Simondon takes the opposite view of this conception. Nature, in us as well as outside us, is not what is given: it is what there is to accomplish. Simondon criticises the Cartesian dualism which reduces nature, including the human body, to a mere mechanism. By what makes him a human being, namely his soul, the human is outside of nature. For Simondon on the contrary, what characterises us as humans is not an extra- but an intra-natural process. *Techné* is not an emanation of human intelligence which is external to nature. It is an emanation of the *physis* within us. This analysis leads to an ethics of human action that could be formulated as follows, parodying Kant: act technically on nature in such a way that this action seems to emanate from nature itself. A consequence of this is that nature, within us as well as outside us, can always be improved by technical intervention. Any reality is full of potential and can be organised further, with the aim of optimising it. Simondon thus opposes the contemplative attitude, refusing to intervene on a reality because it is considered sacred, and the technical attitude:

> According to the perspective of sacredness, any being is judged entirely good or entirely bad [...] On the contrary, the technician carries the implicit assumption of a possible segmental, local intervention to repair, improve or optimize the being. An individual being that is seen technically is not entirely good or entirely bad: it is to be repaired in a local way; it is known as what calls for reparation, improvement and optimisation.[27] [author's translation]

This does not mean, however, that all is permitted – a conclusion that would be in total contradiction to the maxim of prudence, and let us say: of care, formulated above (to act technically as if nature were acting through us). A miscellaneous fact reported and commented by Simondon allows us to avoid this absurdity: a young farmer suffers from a serious hormonal imbalance which has made him obese. To heal and be able to continue to practise his profession, the young man must undergo expensive surgery. To finance it, he offers to sell one of his eyes. According to Simondon, the very fact of considering such a surgical act shows that a technical intervention may be void of any normativity adequate to the reality upon which it operates. It does not care for its intrinsic organisation and features. As such, it has no value. The problem raised here is that of the convergence between, on the one hand, the whole reality on which the technical action focuses, and on the other hand, the fragmented character of the technical intervention, which is always local. In others words, between an aspect of sacredness and an aspect of technicality. The surgical act enucleating the farmer is infra-technical because it makes these two aspects incompatible. On the contrary, an act of true technicality goes beyond its local performance and takes into con-

---

[27] *Sur la technique (1953–1983)*, p. 127.

sideration the organisation and/or the needs of the whole reality to which it is applied.

The same applies to the transforming action on outer nature. There are three modalities of this action:

- humans only intervene locally in nature, without trying to understand its underlying mechanisms in order to introduce some regularity in their action, making it more predictable and manageable. There is a natural law, humans cannot know it; they can only seize, locally, the right moment to act (*Kairos*). Nature itself has productive effectiveness, humans only intervene at certain points in the chain (or even at one single point). The aspect of totality dominates the local operation, there is no integration between them;
- the human being acts on a passive, homogeneous and constant matter; he imposes his law on things, he operates on nature without taking into account its organisation and its potential. He wants to master nature. Here, the aspect of totality is dominated by the technical operation, there is no integration either. Simondon calls this attitude technocratic, which consists in reconfiguring the world as a neutral field for the penetration of machines. As opposed to this attitude, Simondon conceives technology in terms of insertion, as an operation adequate to the geographical structures and the living possibilities of the Earth. In this last case, technology is not a rape of nature, a victory that humans would have over the natural elements; natural structures themselves serve as attachment points to the human technical operation;
- the relationship between humans and nature mixes humans' constructive efforts and a productivity that does not depend on this effort and is brought by nature itself. There is a conjunction of both the productivity of nature and human work; the productivity of nature is enveloped in human work. That's why Simondon defines the machine as a stable mix of nature and humanity. Human relationships to nature can be made more predictable and manageable.

Simondon thus considers the human being as a living being in constant becoming, who actualises his potential by means of technology. In doing so, humans do not substitute a second nature for their nature as living beings. Nature continues to impose its requirements. The surgical act is infra-technical as far as it is evaluated only with regard to the perfection of the act itself, cut off from any consideration for the general organisation of the reality to which it applies – here, the organism as a whole. The technical conditions of human existence can conflict with its organic conditions. We can forget that we remain living beings and think that we exist outside nature. Culture is a regulating force in that it reminds us that we are living beings, imbricated in nature. Technology is part of culture when it is a vector for the insertion of humans into nature (in us and out of us), and not a means to dominate nature and exploit it from an overhanging position.

Simondon opposes, to a definition of technology as a direct transformative intervention on nature, and treating it as a passive matter to be exploited, a definition of technology as the organisation of a stable relationship between humans and nature, i.e. as an objective mediation, coupling the human constructive activity and the "implicit forms" of nature. Conservation agriculture illustrates this. Instead of acting technically on soils with complete indifference to their complex and multi-scale organisation, these types of agriculture seek, on the contrary, to rely on it – microorganisms, fungi, earthworms, etc., perform very important functions such as providing oxygen or nitrogenous matter, from which farmers can benefit. Here, technology is not superimposed on nature as a set of operating schemes unrelated to natural operations, and incompatible with them; it fits smoothly into nature by integrating natural operations into its operating scheme. Technology relies on a science of operations in the Being.

Simondon discusses this point by distinguishing culture and breeding. In both cases, human activity is undoubtedly oriented toward a utilitarian appropriation of the living being, which goes hand in hand with a certain loss of coherence of the functions ensured by the latter (Simondon gives the example of a flower grown in a greenhouse:[28] it does not regulate the conditions of its conservation and its growth itself, this task is devolved to the gardener who regulates the hygrometry, the temperature). However, culture has another face; it can be an action on the vital milieu rather than on the living being itself. Simondon explains that culture, by developing the milieu, provides the opportunity for the birth of a second nature (i.e. an enrichment of nature), whereas breeding detaches itself from all nature, diverting nature into hypertelic paths with no exit for the species thus diverted.

There is thus no opposition between technology and culture, the latter also consists in technical interventions, but whereas certain technologies intervene directly on living beings, other technologies transform the living being by means of actions that transform the milieu, indirectly.

Breeding (be it applied to non-human living beings or to humans) relies on the will to intervene directly on the living being to tear it away from its nature and install it in a supernature, a closed group opposed to nature. The group is above individuals, it provides them with everything; human existence is entirely governed by the group. On the contrary, culture is indirect action. It does not consist in intervening on the human living being directly in order to transform it, but to make a detour and to intervene on the milieu, indirectly. The living human being is provided with an environment arranged for him but opened to

---

[28] METO, p. 49/MEOT, p. 47.

the exterior, inserted in a reality vaster than it, and populated by numerous other living beings. The group does not dominate the individuals, it does not seek to provide everything they need by supplying it to them. It aims rather to make them more capable, to help them develop their capabilities, by providing them with the appropriate environmental conditions.

For the technicised human, the milieu is virtually the whole world, which implies, Simondon says, an amplification of the human transforming action to the dimensions of the Earth. Technology can therefore no longer be evaluated according to intra-group norms, which are always local, limited and not universally participable. Technology can no longer be understood as a limited set of means, serving ends decided by groups; technology must be evaluated in the light of an ethic that goes beyond any constituted group – an ethic that is not based on particular cultural norms, but on the consideration of what technology does to the living beings on Earth.

The body schema of the human species is constantly undergoing change, it evolves by receiving new perceptive schemes and new schemes of intelligibility. Unfortunately, these schemes are not those that participate in the primary formation of humans as persons. In other words: we have not learned to see all that our technologies connect us with, establishing objective connections with all sorts of entities in the natural world. Aesthetics, i.e. the reflection on the structures of sensoriality and perception, is thus a very important aspect of Simondon's thought.

5. Conclusion: Simondon as a contributor to the philosophy of care

Simondon's philosophy of technology therefore points towards an ethics of care, according to three components:

- to shift from a technical act that relies on the will to master nature, to a technical act that inserts human operations into the system of natural operations;
- to give precedence to the individual and his empowerment over any constituted group;
- to reconfigure what Jacques Rancière calls the "distribution of the sensible",[29] that is to say the drawing of the border between what is admitted to visibility in the public space, and what is invisibilised. The consequences of our technology on the natural and living world are still largely

---

29   Jacques Rancière, *The Politics of Aesthetics. The Distribution of the Sensible,* translated by G. Rockhill, Continuum, London, 2004.

kept invisible by all sorts of economic and political forces. Making visible what is not visible is an essential component of care.

Insertion, empowerment, perception: these are the three coordinates according to which a version of humanism that is equal to contemporary challenges should be formulated. The coordinates of Greek humanism pointed to the political imperative of maintaining the stability of the human world, against the devastating power of *physis*; modern humanism was oriented towards the deployment of human power through technology; the coordinates of Simondon's humanism point towards care – care of living beings (human as well as non-human), care of nature. Now this type of humanism is necessarily technological as soon as:

> Humanity by itself creates much devastation. A highly technologised humanity, intelligently technologised through a network, which has a geographical sense, is much less dangerous for nature than humanity by itself.[30] [author's translation]

The main danger of alienation we face is no longer represented by the omnipotence of the industrial machine. It lies in the lack of care for nature and the living in general. Simondon's humanism can indeed be defined as a humanism of care, and technologies as an integral part of this humanism of care. As a consequence, care and its three essential components (insertion, empowerment, perception) must pervade the whole process of technological innovation and design. The humanism of care calls for humanistic engineers.

---

[30] SLT, p. 443.

Individuation and History

Transduction of Dialectics and Historical Epistemology

Taila Picchi

In this chapter, I question whether Simondon's theory of individuation allows for a philosophy of history or even individuation of history. History, as well as politics, is not a theoretical interest of Simondon's philosophical speculation. Nevertheless, individuation theory provides a fruitful toolbox to approach the historical becoming through a non-dialectical frame. Simondon's critique of dialectics reveals, on the one side, the influence of Hyppolite's reading of Hegel's phenomenology; on the other, a trans-dialectical *dispositif* introducing the notion of asymmetric synthesis. This translectical *dispositif* is based on the idea of a synthetic complementary relation exploiting the notions of metastability and disparation. The speculative proposal of a disparative dialectics or even translectics proceeds alongside Simondon's idea of human progress and represents a *transduction*[1] of dialectical thinking. The project of an axiomatisation of human sciences constitutes the theoretical frame for the historical issue and poses an epistemological problem concerning the conciliation between the temporality of ontogenesis and the temporality of human life. The necessity of a conciliation between genetic time and historical time represents the condition for an interrogation of history as historical epistemology. Such a reading will be based on the inner relation between a political reading of Simondon's theory and the irreducible discontinuous character of history, always implying possibility and invention of new solutions.

1. Hyppolite's debt between genetic time and historical time

Simondon stresses a critical approach to dialectics through the individuation process. As he argues in "Analyse des critères de l'individualité", the only postulate of individuation is that of realism of relation. This postulate has logical sense

---

1   Tra(ns)duction alludes to the proximity between Simondon's notion of *transduction* and the French word for translation that is "traduction". Thus, in French, it works as both transduction and translation of dialectical thinking. Moreover, Simondon's rectification of dialectics through translectics suggests the *transduction* (and thus a translation) of dialectics into a translectic situation.

and epistemological value and does not require a method or a doctrine based on "the identity of the rational and the real".[2] Through the realism of relation, Simondon presents a systematic theory that overcomes form-matter dualism and substantivism. Thus, dialectics would be a logical and ontological rethinking of the notion of substance, but it lacks the epistemological dimension. While Simondon's critique of dialectics could be read as a pioneer anti-dialectics or even an anti-Hegelianism such as Deleuze's,[3] it actually represents the answer to a methodological problem. According to Simondon, from an epistemological perspective ontology and history communicate, but dialectics does not provide a general and genetic method able to understand the process of becoming.

Simondon's search for a sort of universal structure of reality is based on the refusal of the notion of substance and his individuation theory outlines a common method for conceiving of ontological dynamism and historical progress. Thus, individuation theory represents the answer to the epistemological problem concerning the conciliation of ontology and history – or even process and progress. However, the epistemological problem at the basis of individuation theory is an extension of Hyppolite's reading of Hegel; more specifically, Simondon's thought is compatible with the peculiar reception of Hegel in France, along the lines established by Hyppolite's famous lectures.

Jean Hyppolite is the first French scholar who approaches Hegel's philosophy from a historical-philosophical perspective. Indeed, the French reading of the renowned German philosopher has been a very discontinuous phenomenon both on the chronological reception and on the theoretical one. According to Canguilhem, an unusual phenomenon occurs in France, i.e. the late discovery of Hegel. Before Hyppolite's studies in France there were two main trends: the ex-

---

2   ILNFI, p. 653/ILFI, p. 553.
3   Simondon's critique of dialectics interests one of his earliest readers, i.e. Gilles Deleuze, and contemporary interest in Simondon's anti-dialectics come from Deleuzian perspectives such as Toscano and Sauvagnargues's (Alberto Toscano, *The Theatre of Production. Philosophy and Individuation between Kant and Deleuze*, London, Palgrave Macmillan, 2006; Anne Sauvagnargues, *Deleuze. L'empirisme transcendental*, Paris, Presses universitaires de France, 2009). In *Difference and Repetition*, the Deleuzian notion of *asymmetric synthesis of the sensible* translates within the explicit frame of anti-dialectics – or even anti-Hegelianism – Simondon's notion of complementarity as synthetic relation. In Simondon's theory, a complementary relation implicates two terms not identical to each other nor even symmetric, like a positive or negative quality in relation to another with opposite sign. Complementarity means precisely another perspective for conceiving of the relation between the positive and the negative term: a kind of immanent relation which differs from identity criteria. Nevertheless, Simondon is not so anti-dialectical as Deleuze since he replaces the idea of the identity of structures with the identity of operations. Thus, being appears as plural and disparate and disparation is a recursive operation originating physical, biological, technical and psychosocial phenomena.

istentialist reading of Hegel and the Marxist one.[4] Thus, Canguilhem credits Hyppolite for having introduced French readers to Hegel.[5] Consequently, Simondon – and also Deleuze – is influenced by his reading.

Simondon's reading of Hegel – and also of Marx – is mediated by Hyppolite and the critique of dialectics should be understood against the background of Hyppolite's work.[6] Simondon's theory represents another way to answer the concluding question of *Logique et Existence*, i.e. how human time and logic time are related to each other. As we read in *Sur la philosophie*, Simondon argues that

> Hyppolite, giving up the research for a vertical transcendence that would refer human existence to another thing than itself, assigns philosophy the task of analysing the sense of historicity of this existence and of realizing the extension of historicity into history. The sense of historicity is given but it should be built as well. Hyppolite picks some features of Hegel and Marx's learning and the notion of project from Husserl. The main difficulty of Hegelianism is the relation between Phenomenology and Logics, between anthropology and ontology.[7]

First, exploring the existentialistic trend, Hyppolite replaces the idea of a vertical transcendence of history as dialectical movement with the contingence of history or even historicity. This interpretation of history, according to Canguilhem, is not ideological and not dogmatic but rather problematic.[8] In this sense, Hyppolite opens a third trend within French Hegelianism alongside the existentialistic and the Marxist ones. This fact makes individuation theory – which resonates with Hyppolite's questioning – a sort of translation of the rationality of being that dialectical thinking apparently accomplishes. Therefore, being should be conceived as a mediation between the time of logic and the time of life.[9] Sec-

---

[4] Canguilhem presents the two main trends of Hegel's reading in France split between the existentialist reading of Jean Wahl and the Marxist one of Alexandre Kojève.

[5] See Georges Canguilhem, "Hegel en France", in *Résistance, philosophie biologique et histoire des sciences 1940–1965. Œuvres complètes tome IV*, Paris, Vrin, 2015, pp. 321–341.

[6] Hyppolite replaces Merleau-Ponty as director of Simondon's dissertation on individuation [ILNFI]. Then, he takes interest in the concept of information and organises a conference with Simondon in 1962.

[7] "Les grands courants de la philosophie française contemporaine" (1962–1963), in SLΦ, p. 148.

[8] Canguilhem stresses the double trend of French Hegelianism: on the one hand, the religious reading in Fessard or Niel that restores Hegel as a thinker of the Christian faith as ultimate sense of human history; on the other hand, the instrumental reading of Hegel as political strategy and ideology of communism like in Kojève and then in Sartre. In this way, Kojève's work is overcome by Hyppolite. Indeed, Hyppolite's historical-philosophical approach takes account of the translation's issue of Hegel's thought in France, as Koyré before Hyppolite outlined. Canguilhem, "Hegel en France", *op. cit.*

[9] Both Hyppolite and Koyré have stressed the importance of the system of Jena for the later elaboration of Phenomenology that allows for an interpretation of dialectics far from dog-

ondly, according to Simondon, we can find in Hyppolite's work the idea of a constructive theory of progress and its crisis in opposition to the negative moment of dialectics. This would allow for the transition of historicity in history. Finally, Simondon's onto-epistemological problem translates Hyppolite's questioning concerning a possible conciliation between logical time and human time or even between ontology and anthropology.[10] Indeed, individuation theory proposes a possible conciliation through ontogenesis which defines a genetic time and a historical time in opposition to the existential one. The epistemological problem concerning a unified structure of human time (as anthropology and history) and logic time (as ontological dimension) is implicated in the proposal of the individuation theory as a proceeding and not as a principle.

What Simondon does not accept of dialectics is thus the symmetry between the logic of knowing and the physical genesis of being. For this reason, his search for a conciliation between genetic time and historical time does not postulate a philosophy of history such as Hegel's idealism or Marx's dialectical materialism. Rather, he distinguishes very clearly genesis and history since the question regarding the origin is ontological and must be replaced by the genesis; at the same time, history is a product or effect of ontogenetic dynamism: there is no history without a genetic process which is, at the same time, human progress.

2. The idea of progress in the light of technical evolution

A particular idea of progress can be detected in Simondon's thinking on technics and technology that can offer a pattern to conceive human progress in general. In Simondon, the question of progress is incidental with the project of a technological encyclopaedism which is at the same time a humanism. For this reason, he implies with the generic expression of human progress the historical process characterised by the self-consciousness of the transfer of cultural forms or the loss of some of them. Progress is linked with the humanistic project integrating technical knowledge within knowledge in general through reflexive thinking, i.e. philosophical thinking.

Progress is not simply a change; rather, it represents the cultural transfer of determinate modalities of relation between a human being and its *milieu*, its objects and its own society. The way Simondon conceives human progress suppresses the teleological element in relation to technical development, though "the evolution of technical objects can only become progress insofar as these technical objects are free in their evolution and not pushed by necessity in the

---

matic or ideological readings. Hegel's *Jenenser Logik*, according to Koyré and Hyppolite, focuses on the notion of relation and poses the condition of the later dialectical system.

10   This is properly the final question of *Logique et Existence*.

direction of a fatal hypertely".¹¹ Moreover, concerning the historical becoming, human progress is conceived as discontinuous. Indeed, "the idea of progress, or rather what is mythical about it, comes from this illusion of simultaneity, which presents as a fixed state what is merely a stage; [...] because this stage is still rich in virtuality; there is no determinism that presides over invention, and where progress is thought as being continuous, it masks the very reality of invention".¹² Not only invention actualises available potentials, but it also settles and builds a *milieu* where the evolution of technical objects is constructive. In other words, invention "calls forth the creation of this third techno-geographic milieu wherein each modification is self-conditioned".¹³

Even if technics presents a specific normativity concerning its autonomy in relation to biological and social regulation, Simondon's view is anti-technocratic and considers progress in the light of a humanistic demand.¹⁴ This fact is based on a peculiar relation between the idea of progress and universality which is not the historical becoming as the mere succession of inventions and their cultural impact. Consequently, the question of progress gathers not only the technical issue but also religious and linguistic issues as features of human progress in general.¹⁵ In METO, Simondon focuses on technical progress through the specific relation between progress and universality, which does not depend on technological development but rather on philosophical thinking caring about the humanistic demand. In this sense, the evolution of technical systems corresponds to technical progress since "each stage of development is the inheritor of previous ages, and its progress is all the more certain as each stage tends increasingly

---

11   METO, p. 58/MEOT, p. 56. Hypertely is a teleological excess and, according to Simondon, it is a negative effect produced within the evolution of technical objects. Instead of the adaptation with the *milieu* following material conditions of production or the purpose of their production, technical objects can specialise and then become unfit (*ibid.* p. 53/p. 50).
12   *Ibid.*, p. 122/106.
13   *Ibid.*, p. 58/56.
14   Simondon's humanistic demand is stressed since one of his first writings ("Humanisme culturel, humanisme négatif, humanisme nouveau" (1953), in SLΦ, pp. 71–75). Here, he questions the possibility of a new humanism extending the negative version presented by Sartre. In particular, Simondon revendicates the necessity of this new humanism in opposition to the three main trends of 20ᵗʰ century, i.e. German social democracy, Russian communism and American pragmatism. These three trends are based on specific representations of technology, as he writes: "three important recent social and political doctrines have thus incorporated, each in an original way, a representation and valorization of integrated technics" (METO, p. 231/ MEOT, p.223). According to Bardin, Simondon's new humanism is a hard humanism [*humanisme difficile*] against these three political reductions and the simple ontology [*ontologie facile*] of collective mythologies conceiving lightly human essence, Andrea Bardin, "De l'homme à la matière: pour une ontologie difficile. Marx avec Simondon", in *Cahiers Simondon* 5, 2013, p. 27.
15   See "Les limites du progrès humain" (1959), in SLT, pp. 269–278.

and more perfectly toward a state of sole beneficiary [*légataire universelle*]".[16] Again, the question of universality concerns the question of progress: universality manifests itself through the status of technics in which there are potentialities of societal transformations. Thus, technics is the universal legacy of every step of previous development.

The idea of progress taken between the continuity of technicity – as the genetic essence of technical evolution – and the discontinuity of the forms in which technicity manifests itself[17] leads to a necessary observation:

> The twentieth century seeks a humanism capable of compensating for the form of alienation that intervenes within the very development of technics, through a series of specializations that society demands and produces. There appears to be a *singular law of the transformation [devenir] of human thought*, according to which any ethical, technical, and scientific invention, which sets out as a means of liberation and rediscovery of man, becomes through its historical evolution an instrument that turns against its liberation and enslaves man by limiting him.[18]

The dark side of technological progress is not an intrinsic character of progress itself. It emerges as a moment where the technical development and the historical one are compared and overlapped following this *singular law of the transformation of human thought*. This is an immanent contradiction that notices the ambivalence of invention within human progress as a possibility of either liberation or domination. Consequently, the emancipatory potentials of technics must always be assessed in relation to their historical actualisation. In short, Simondon's humanistic project articulates technical progress as material and productive activity, self-consciousness and historical becoming in relation to the discontinuous idea of progress and the asymmetry between the introduction of innovation and historical evolution. Contemporary humanism, according to Simondon, retains something paradoxical i.e. the fact that the means of liberation from labour and the ideology of moral and scientific progress could become new chains for the human being. Consequently, alienation is implicit in technological development and has a historic determination but also an anthropological one that is inevitable and almost natural. There is an anthropological split of the idea of progress based on the different relation between activity and passivity in the conception of man in the 20th century.

---

16   METO, p. 76/MEOT, p. 76.
17   According to Simondon, "this transmission of technicity by its elements is what grounds the possibility of technical progress, above and beyond the apparent discontinuity of forms, domains, the types of deployed energy, and sometimes even beyond the schemas of functioning" (*ibid.*).
18   *Ibid.*, p. 118/pp. 101–102 (my emphasis).

The progress of the eighteenth century is a progress experienced by an individual through the force, speed, and precision of his gestures. The progress of the nineteenth century can no longer be experienced by the individual, because it is no longer centralised with the individual as the centre of command and perception in the adapted action. The individual becomes the mere spectator of the results of the functioning of the machines, or the one who is responsible for the organisation of technical ensembles putting the machines to work. This is why the notion of progress splits in two, becomes aggressive, ambivalent, and a source of anxiety; progress is at a remove from man and no longer makes sense for the individual, because the conditions of the individual's intuitive perception of progress no longer exist; this implicit judgment, which is very close to that of kinaesthetic impressions and to the facilitation of a corporeal dynamism which formed the basis of the notion of progress in the eighteenth century, disappear.[19]

Therefore, Simondon concludes that "an idea of progress that was conceived and desired substitutes itself for the impression of progress as something undergone [*éprouvé*]".[20]

> The technical object is not directly a historical object: it is subject to the course of time only as a vehicle of technicity, according to a transductive role that it plays with respect to a prior age.[21]

This transductive function allows Simondon to conceive the technical evolution endowed with a non-dialectical rhythm.

The different aspects of the technical being's individualisation constitute the centre of an evolution, which proceeds via successive stages, but which is not dialectical in the proper sense of the term, because, in regard to it, negativity does not play the role of an engine of progress. In the technical world negativity is a lack of individuation, an incomplete junction of the natural world and the technical world; this negativity is not the engine of progress; it is rather the engine of transformation, it incites man to seek new, more satisfactory solutions than those he possesses. This desire for change, however, does not happen directly within the technical being; it happens within man as inventor and user; this change moreover must not be confused with progress; a change that is too abrupt is contrary to technical progress, because it prevents the transmission, in the form of technical elements, of what an age has acquired to the one that follows.[22]

The refusal of a dialectical conception of progress represents a critique of the Hegelian logical perspective and also of the Marxist historical materialism.

---

19 *Ibid.*, pp. 131–132/p. 116.
20 *Ibid.*
21 *Ibid.*, p. 76/p. 76.
22 *Ibid.*, p. 71/p. 70.

Technics has potentialities and spontaneity like nature, while human being introduces the elements of historical transformation and thus determines the rhythm of progress as transmission of technicity. The incomplete connection between natural and technical world in terms of missing individuation revises the idea of negativity that is central in historical materialism.

3. The translectic situation and the tra(ns)duction of dialectics

Before approaching the topic of history in Simondon's thought we should introduce his conception of *translectics*. It is based on *transduction* as an operational synthesis between the terms of the relation and grounds a *translectic* situation in opposition to the dialectical one. Transduction "is called upon to play a role that dialectics could not play, for the study of the operation of individuation does not seem to correspond to the appearance of the negative as a second stage, but to an immanence of the negative within the initial condition through the ambivalent form of tension and incompatibility".[23] Dialectics in defining the negative as contradiction states a polarisation between positive and negative moment or even between subject and object. While, according to Simondon, there are not two moments or terms entirely in opposition to each other. This means that the negative is immanent in each term of the relation and their synthesis is based on the ambivalence of the two terms and not on their opposition.

For this reason, Simondon argues that "resolving transduction operates the inversion of the negative into the positive: that through which the terms are not identical to one another, that through which they are *disparate* (in the sense that this term assumes within the theory of three- dimensional vision) is integrated into the system of resolution and becomes a condition of signification".[24] Disparation is thus a correlative concept of transduction that Simondon introduces through the example of sight. Physiologically, when seeing, we compose two images caught by each eye into a unity. The homogeneous image of the observed object results from disparation.[25] Consequently, disparation is not properly a third moment of the seeing process, rather the unification of two separate and simultaneous moments. Therefore, through the notion of disparation Simondon underscores an original heterogeneity of being, manifesting itself in the coexistence of ambivalent elements. Disparation as asymmetric synthesis represents a kind of inchoative philosophy of difference without marking the ultimate break

---

23 ILNFI, pp. 14–15/ILFI, p. 34.
24 ILNFI, p. 15/ILFI, p. 34.
25 See also Sauvagnargues's comment on disparation as a third dimension, at the same time creative and problematic (Sauvagnargues, *op. cit.*, p. 254).

with dialectics. Instead of presenting a resolutive synthesis by which the contradiction is reconciled in a superior and homogeneous synthesis, Simondon does not solve the contradiction. Rather he conceives of a sort of ambivalent equivalence between conflict and solution: an asymmetric synthesis or even a *synthetic complementary relation*, in which the synthesis does not seem accomplished once and for all.

The logical proceeding of dialectics is thus criticised since "in dialectics with a ternary rhythm, the synthesis more or less *envelops* the thesis and antithesis by *overcoming* contradiction; the synthesis is therefore *hierarchically, logically*, and *ontologically* superior to the terms it joins together".[26] Moreover, the individuation process does not work according to a threefold rhythm as in the dialectics scheme; rather, it presents a constituent relation that keeps the symmetry – or even the asymmetry – of the terms it relates. In this sense, the identity between the real and the rational is replaced with the constituent reality of relation. Simondon's refusal of the dialectical rhythm depends on a specific idea of process and progress that makes these notions correlative: the individuation process requires the invention of a solution and in doing this represents a kind of progress; while progress means an open process where the invention of a new solution is not predictable. The negative moment of dialectical thinking is replaced by the immanence of the negative. The relation between thesis and antithesis is transferred to the transductive relation.

Simondon criticises dialectics for the logical inadequacy in understanding the ontogenesis since ontogenesis does not follow a ternary rhythm, but rather it is the perpetual emersion of individuated entities from the pre-individual being and does not properly have a rhythm. However, in "Pour une notion de situation dialectique", dialectics means firstly an epistemological subject, secondly an object and finally a situation where subject and object are reciprocally implicated. For this reason, Simondon prefers to employ the term situation. As he argues, "we can name true dialectical situation a translectical situation that implies an overcoming through a solution which continues crossing subsequent states of being".[27] This idea of subsequent states of being crossed by the translectic situation implies the postulate of the realism of relation which does not presuppose the identity between the rational and the real but rather the constitutive function of the relation itself as "a relation in being, a relation of being, a manner of being".[28] Simondon replaces dialectics with *translectics* or even with a *translectic situation*, where the term situation means precisely the relation between subject and object. Actually, Simondon does not refuse dialectics entirely, rather he wants to rectify this conception through the toolbox provided by individuation.

---

26   ILNFI, p. 111/ILFI, p. 111.
27   "Pour une notion de situation dialectique" (1960), in SLΦ, p. 103.
28   ILNFI, p. 12/ILFI, p. 32.

For this reason, he revises the dialectical situation – as an asymmetric relation of co-implication of subject and object that is not predictable in relation to the final result – considering the notions of negativity and crisis and translating them through the *dispositif* of metastable system.

In *Sur la philosophie* we find three writings which deal with the question of progress and dialectics.[29] What is significant in these writings is the refusal of negativity as motor of progress in opposition to dialectics which would identify becoming and logic time. In "Le progrès, rythmes et modalités", Simondon criticises Hegel and Marx's notion of negativity as motor of progress. According to him, in Marx "there is progress because there is the shift from an individual exploitation of nature to a collective exploitation of nature".[30] And this shift is due to the *jeu de la negativité*. In Hegel and Marx's conception, negativity determines the rhythm of progress but, according to Simondon, it does not allow for conceiving a "constructive theory of crisis".[31] The presence of crisis means a discontinuous idea of progress. In Hegel and Marx's theories, the notion of synthesis refers to "the triadic character of time, then progressive".[32] Nevertheless, the constitution of a finite synthesis as "the moment when there is a perfect state" represents "a kind of temporal egoism [*égoïsme temporel*]: history exists until us, but then time becomes a continuous time".[33] The idea of a non-negative motor of progress occurs again in "Négativité" and, especially, in "Pour une notion de situation dialectique" where Simondon opposes a constructive theory of crisis to the negative theory of historical materialism which presupposes a sort of inverted positivism under the sign of negation.

As Simondon argues,

> It is not exactly the contradiction or the negativity that represents the motor of progress; it is the ambivalence, the "yes-and-no", the uninvolved participation [*participation départicipée*] and *though* it strives for being: there is *more* a positive motivation rather than a negative motivation.[34]

Metastability is a key concept in individuation theory since it refers to a system only apparently stable but crossed through by potentials and information which lead it to individuate itself. Metastability means that an internal tension is occurring and this is a problematic state of the system or even a crisis. Thus, individuation represents the solution of the crisis through the stabilisation of tensions

---

29   "Le progrès, rythmes et modalités" (late 1950s), in SLΦ, pp. 83–100; "Négativité" (1955), in SLΦ, pp. 107–108; "Pour une notion de situation dialectique", in SLΦ, pp. 101–106.
30   "Le progrès, rythmes et modalités", in SLΦ, p. 95.
31   *Ibid.*, p. 96.
32   *Ibid.*, p. 97.
33   *Ibid.*
34   "Pour une notion de situation dialectique", in SLΦ, p. 102.

and potentials in an individuated entity. However, the individual occurring as solution of the internal tension through the individuation of the system is still metastable, because it can require a further individuation to solve a new internal tension. As Simondon writes, a dialectical situation implies "necessity of a tension. Metastability and tension. The dialectical situation is a metastable situation".[35] A metastable situation presupposes the presence of a crisis and its possible solution. For there to be a "situation", "there must be roots [*amorces*] of a relationship between the elements, and that these roots are strong enough to push to a resolutive action".[36] Moreover, "it is the ensemble constituted by fences and potentials that can produce a change. Thus, it is the antagonism or the sursaturation that makes the situation a constructive situation. It is *a situation*. Dialectics exists only in the form of a situation".[37] Therefore, Simondon argues that "optimizing dialectics is creating, with the potentials available, the more tense possible situation and though resolvable".[38]

Translectics indicates precisely a situation where a crisis arises and thus a solution is required. In relation to dialectics, translectics represents the implementation of the subject-objects relation through transduction. As Simondon argues, what is dialectical is the "discovery of a new dimension which integrates as new information what frames the two thesis – the framing itself is an integral part of the final discovery".[39] In the light of the short writing "Pour une notion de situation dialectique", it is clear that Simondon does not refuse dialectics but rather he considers it unsatisfactory. For this reason, he would improve the dialectical scheme through the relational onto-epistemology of individuation which is still compatible with dialectics.

4. History within the axiomatisation of human sciences

Though Simondon's theory is not concerned with history, it is possible to highlight that, in the light of his proposal for an axiomatisation of human sciences, history represents a part of this project. The inaugural lecture at the Société Française de Philosophie in 1960, "Forme, information, potentiels", presents the project of the axiomatisation of human sciences;[40] but here Simondon does not approach the topic of history. However, the publication of the volume *Sur la philosophie* shows a growing concern about history within this axiomatic project.

---

35 *Ibid.*, p. 104.
36 *Ibid.*, p. 103.
37 *Ibid.*
38 *Ibid.*
39 *Ibid.*, p. 102.
40 "Forme, information, potentiels" (1960), ILNFI, pp. 672–697/ILFI, pp. 531–552.

According to Simondon, the axiomatisation of human sciences through the analogic method necessarily follows the process of scientific axiomatisation that occurred between the 19th and 20th centuries. The issue is "Why are there multiple human sciences, when there is only one physics? [...] why are we obligated to distinguish different fields of study within psychology, sociology, and social psychology?".[41] The demand for axiomatising human sciences comes from a profound necessity for uniformity and universality of the individuation theory which strives for unifying the field of *individuated* knowledge and grounding an encyclopaedic systematicity. The complexity of this goal depends on the achieved degree of the scientific knowledge – or even the scientific formalisation – and mainly on the object and the application of human sciences, i.e. transindividual individuation that the conference "Forme, information, potentiels", unfortunately, does not approach. In brief, Simondon demands the unification of human sciences on the pattern of the sciences of nature.[42] As Toscano outlines, radicalising Simondon's thinking, "in his intervention [...] Simondon proposes, in a striking analogical short-circuit, and against the use of probabilistic theories in the social sciences, to 'transduce' the energetic theory of the metastability to the social domain and to think the pre-revolutionary situation as a privileged object (or medium) for the political application of a thinking of individuation".[43]

Within the axiomatic project of human sciences it is possible to understand the question of history and its eventual formalisation. As Worms points out, the historical issue appears in *Sur la philosophie* and it should be considered as an extension of the axiomatisation project.

"Human sciences should especially account for the changes of state, genesis and crisis processes that give rise to structures within the individual as well as the group; the genetic method would not only be a method, but the grasp of a dimension of the reality essential for the living being; human sciences and sci-

---

41 *Ibid.*, p. 674/p. 532.
42 As Simondon writes, "even concerning only one of these human sciences, the search for unity is quite problematic and that we must find an often reductive theory to arrive at the unity within each of these sciences. We observe a unity of tendencies rather than a unity of explanatory principles. If we compare the current situation of the human sciences to that of the natural sciences, such as this situation was in antiquity, in the sixteenth century, or at the beginning of the nineteenth century, we find that at the beginning of the nineteenth century there was a physics and a chemistry, perhaps even several physics and several chemistries. Conversely, little by little, at the beginning of the nineteenth century and at the beginning of the twentieth century, we have seen grand theories arise that have contributed various possibilities of axiomatization" (*ibid.*, pp. 674–675/p. 533).
43 Alberto Toscano, "The Disparate: Ontology and Politics in Simondon", paper delivered at the Society for European Philosophy/Forum for European Philosophy annual conference, University of Sussex (9 September 2007), p. 4. French edition: Alberto Toscano, "La disparation", in *Multitudes*, vol. 18, issue 4, 2004, pp. 73–82.

ences of nature would have a common field: that of processes of transition, of changes. In this way, history, which is the oldest but least formalized of the human sciences, could take the path of formalisation; unique among human sciences, history does not sacrifice transitory phenomena in favour of stable structures: the historical fact is essentially a notable transitory state, i.e. one that has a constitutive role and is as real as lasting states."[44]

In this propaedeutic class at the University of Poitiers between 1962 and 1963, history should take into account transitory phenomena which disappear in the stable and final form as "small deaths" which constitute the event fading away. Here, history is defined as the most ancient of human sciences. Temporality is defined as the dimension of being and historicity is presented both as a durable state and as a transitory state but significant in being a constitutive function of the event. History represents the common ground of the genetic method since it is an essential dimension of reality for the living being (*une dimension de réalité essentielle au vivant*). Thus, historicity corresponds to the emergence of this transitory dimension which constitutes stable structures and partially determinates their sense. In other terms, the ontogenetic negativity is immanent to the event. It is a dimension of reality that through disparation produces an asymmetric synthesis. Consequently, it neutralises the question of the determinate negation which in the Marxist tradition implies the question of the revolutionary action and the arising of the historical forces able to saturate the negation and then to begin a process of dereification. The historical fact as transitory phenomenon is based on the notion of metastable system and is linked with the social translation of metastability. The disparation of social metastability would solve conflictuality through an act of invention, as Toscano argues, radicalising Simondon's thinking.[45]

History as a dimension of being is a field where individuation occurs, thus it presents itself as continuity in being a specification of ontogenesis but also the discontinuity of the emergent individuation as the irruption of discontinuity in the background of a continuous genesis. This fact can be compared with Foucault's genealogical approach. Combes, for instance, argues that where Simondon works out an ontogenetic thinking as a new mode of knowing around ontology, Foucault builds a genealogical thinking around history.[46] This means that Simondon's onto-epistemology represents a germinal genealogical thinking and has a similar functioning to Foucault's historical genealogy. For this reason, Worms sees in Simondon's ontogenetic approach a plausible employment for the historical becoming and thus suggesting a possible philosophy of history.

---

44 "Sciences de la nature et sciences de l'homme" (1962–1963), in SLΦ, p. 234.
45 See Toscano, "The Disparate: Ontology and Politics in Simondon", *op. cit.*
46 Muriel Combes, *La vie inséparée. Vie et sujet au temps de la biopolitique*, Paris, Dittmar, 2011, p. 236.

More specifically, according to Worms, ontogenesis inevitably situates Simondon's conception on the ground of the ontological production and the coming of historicity that makes History an epistemological issue compatible with a constructivist perspective.

5. History and historicity in the economy of a disparative dialectics

In the light of the path presented within Simondon's thought, a question remains: is it possible to translate individuation into a philosophy of history? Simondon is not looking for a historical systematicity similar to Hegel's idealism or Marx's historical materialism; rather, his demand for an axiomatisation of human sciences shows a multidisciplinary view of knowledge and the complex and multilayered field of what is defined science as something not given once and for all. For this reason, history represents a partial and incomplete part of the knowledge concerning individuation and ontogenesis. In my opinion, individuation can be translated into a historical epistemology expanding Simondon's speculation from ontology to historical becoming. For understanding the significance of the individuation process I propose the speculative hypothesis of a disparative dialectics based on the critique of dialectics alongside the translation of individuation theory into a historical epistemology.[47]

Disparative dialectics is based on the definition of the translectic situation. In Simondon's critique of dialectics the concept of negativity seems to be inadequate for founding a constructive theory of progress and dialectics itself refers rather to a metastable situation characterised by the ambivalence of coexistent elements. Thus, the notions of metastability and disparation are key concepts in the rectification of dialectics as a synthetic complementary relation. Translectics is a polarised thinking of history or even the polarisation of history between historical time and genetic time. This fact allows for supposing the transition from the Hegelian notion of *Aufhebung* to Simondon's concept of transduction and translectic situation.

Simondon does not interact with Hegel but at the beginning of ILNFI his critique of the hylomorphic scheme puts a similar problem to that of Hegel's

---

47 The background of the idea of disparative dialectics comes from a comparison analysed in my PhD thesis with Marcuse's thought on technics and technology (T. Picchi, "*Tecnicità tra politiche della vita e politiche della memoria. Un percorso nella philosophie de la technique di Simondon e la teoria critica della tecnologia di Marcuse*"). In Marcuse, rather than in Simondon, the question of history is linked with the problem of determinate negation and represents the legacy of Hegel and Marx's thoughts. Thus, I found in Simondon's thought a dialectical or even translectical *dispositif* close to Deleuze's idea of the immanence of the negative without refusing totally the dialectical structure as in Deleuze.

Logic i.e. the relation between potentiality and actuality. He argues that "the logical force of this schema is so great that Aristotle was able to utilise it in order to sustain a universal system of classification that is applicable to the real both according to the logical path and according to the physical path, thereby guaranteeing the harmony of the logical order and the physical order and making inductive knowledge possible".[48] To the Aristotelian dualism Simondon opposes the technological paradigm of *informing (prise de forme)*, which "consists in *following the being in its genesis*, in accomplishing the genesis of thought at the same time as the genesis of the object is accomplished".[49] This means the refusal of the symmetry between the logic of knowing and the physical genesis and thus the adoption of a proceeding which catches reality during its happening. Consequently, Simondon prefers the epistemological perspective – or even onto-epistemological – and proposes a method able to account for the morphogenesis of being in every kind of its forms. The critique of dialectics and the proposal for the transductive method should be included in this picture. The individuation process is a logical operation that structures historical development as a proceeding and historical determination is a character of the contingency of reality. In other words, history rises up from the time flow in the background as historicity since "from this ontogenetic perspective, time itself is considered as an expression of the dimensionality of the being that is individuating".[50] Time is thus a dimension of a being individuating itself and historicity refers to individuals, i.e. the physical, biological, psychosocial or technical result of the individuation process. The notion of historicity occupies a peculiar role in Simondon's thinking since it refers to a historical discontinuity within the liquid substance of time that the individuation process crosses. As individuation concerns physical, biological, psychosocial and technical phenomena as well, historicity refers to every kind of individuated entity. In other words, historicity does not consist univocally in the human field, rather it considers every individuation level.

As Bardin explains, in ILNFI we find several meanings of historicity. As Bardin outlines, at the physical level Simondon defines *singularités historiques apportées par la matière*. In relation to the process of crystallisation he argues that there is a historical aspect to the coming of a structure within a substance: a structural germ must appear. Then, the individuation of an allotropic form starts from a historical singularity. Moreover, at the biological level he states that individualisation of the living is its real historicity. And at the psychical level, every thought is a relation, i.e. it entails a historical aspect of its own genesis. Consequently, Bardin concludes that historicity is linked to a mode of existence beyond the human one: it is linked to every kind of individuation from society to

---

[48] ILNFI, p. 21/ILFI, p. 39.
[49] *Ibid.*, p. 14/p. 34.
[50] *Ibid.*

matter through historical and local singularities.[51] Therefore, we have historicity of matter, historicity of life, historicity of society and also historicity of technical objects, because individuation realises the passage of the time flow in individuated and historicised entities. Historicity is not linked exclusively to human existence but it generalises and expands the historical dimension beyond the human field and thus suggesting also a historicity of the inorganic. In this perspective, a history purely human seems to collapse for a more complex totality in which mankind is included as a part of it. The notion of historicity requires an enlarged idea of history which also concerns inorganic phenomena and therefore is not exclusively a human science but rather it opens an ecological view of historical becoming.

Disparative dialectics and historicity as event-related phenomena are basic elements of a historical epistemology of individuation based on a discontinuous character of history. It is actually a sort of individuation of history through the toolbox provided by Simondon's individuation theory and represents a forerunner to philosophy of the event.

6. Towards a historical epistemology or even individuation of history

My reading of individuation as historical epistemology is based on the idea of history as polarised object and on the notion of historicity which articulates the correlative notions of metastability and disparation. Consequently, relying on Toscano's notion of politics of invention and Bardin's political epistemology, it will be possible to understand historical epistemology as individuation of history.

The idea of a plausible individuation of history comes from the speculative thesis of a disparative dialectics which would translate Simondon's critique of dialectics into a historical epistemology. In this sense, talking about individuation of history means to be placed within the framework of genetic epistemolo-

---

51 Bardin explains that in ILNFI the term historicity means a transductive chain beginning with a singularity introducing a discontinuity in the functioning of the system. From a physical perspective there are "historical singularities carried by the matter" (ILNFI, p. 43/ILFI, p. 57); in the crystallisation process "there is a historical aspect to the manifestation of a structure in a substance, insofar as the structural germ must appear" (*ibid.*, p. 70/p. 79). Then, "the individuation of an allotropic form begins with a historical type of singularity" (*ibid.*, p. 72/p. 80). From the biological perspective, "the individualization of the living being is its real historicity" (*ibid.*, p. 298/p. 268). From a psychological perspective, "every thought, precisely to the extent that it is real, is a *relation*, i.e. includes a historical aspect in its genesis" (*ibid.*, p. 77/p. 84). See Bardin, "De l'homme à la matière: pour une ontologie difficile. Marx avec Simondon", *op. cit.*, pp. 39–40.

gy. Simondon says in relation to the possibility of knowing ontogenesis that a science of the pre-individual being does not yet exist.[52] Consequently, in METO, he defines a *connaissance opératoire* that follows the genesis of being on the model of a handicraft activity as a kind of knowledge of operations – or even relations – and not of structures. Therefore, Simondon borrows from Piaget's study on the psychology of infancy the idea of a genetic epistemology applicable to ontogenetic processes of individuation following the operativity of being. Thus, we can recognise a genetic epistemology that allows for the knowing of temporality as genesis and a possible historical epistemology based on the conception of temporality as a peculiar phase of being, or even as a dimension of being springing from the individuation process.[53]

Simondon's idea of history implies the discontinuous aspect of reality that he compares to the cybernetic theory of information since information as well is a central notion for ontogenetic dynamism. As human progress is analysed through the technological evolution, the discontinuity of history is compared to the exchange of information. As Simondon argues

> the discontinuous aspect of the history of thinking may be considered through the cybernetic induction extended as a method for philosophical reflection: a temporal series such as that of history may be thought not only through its continuous and regular chains – in its permanence – as in the method of analytical determinism, but in its breaking-offs and revolutions, in these fundamental discontinuities.[54]

History is a field crossed by fundamental discontinuities and the notion of historicity corresponds to the informed information of individuated entities. The notion of historicity emerges at the intersection between genetic time and historical time. In other words, the ontogenetic perspective allows for a conception of time as a dimension of being and of history as a crisis that requires a solution. Historicity means properly the emergence of the solution of a critical situation

---

52 As Simondon writes, "an axiomatic of ontogenesis remains to be discovered, at least if this axiomatic is definable. It could be that ontogenesis is not able to be axiomatized, which would explain the existence of philosophical thought as perpetually marginal with respect to all other studies, since philosophical thought is what is driven by the implicit or explicit research of ontogenesis in all orders of reality" (ILFNI, p. 256/ILFI, p. 238).

53 This speculative approach in a philosophy of history would transfer Simondon's theory of ontogenetic becoming to a kind of historical epistemology. More specifically, it proposes to read history as a specific phase of ontogenesis and thus it would be plausible to understand historical phenomena as a product of the individuation process. In this sense, the postulate of individuation of *following the being in its genesis*, that founds Simondon's idea of onto-epistemology, can be applied to history. Consequently, more than a historical epistemology it is an individuation of history through the onto-epistemological postulate of following and thus knowing this specific phase of being that is history, characterised by the emersion of historicity.

54 "Cybernétique et philosophie" (1953), in SLΦ, p. 57.

and, consequently, genetic time and historical time are two perspectives that correspond respectively to the onto-epistemology of individuation and to the transindividual field where the event emerges within the inner relationality of being. Therefore, genetic time refers to a genetic epistemology that allows for knowing temporality as genesis, while historical time suggests a possible historical epistemology still to ground on the conception of temporality as a specific phase of being or even a dimension originating from the individuation process.

According to Worms, in the light of the volume *Sur la philosophie*, for the first time we discover Simondon as a thinker of history, even if it is not properly a history of philosophy: rather, a philosophy of history. In the introduction to the volume, Worms argues that we do not discover a dialectical thought but rather a polarised thought on history, as critical relation between man and its milieu. There is negativity as concrete resistance of milieu in relation to human action.[55] As mentioned before, dialectics is replaced by translectics that is a critical situation between subject and object requiring a solution. *Pensée polarisée* means not only the critical relation between the individual and the *milieu*, but also implicates the idea of history as polarised object. Whether history means polarisation of human practice between the subjective action and the objective dimension of the surrounding reality, the event is a transitory and not teleological phenomenon understandable through the notion of metastability.

Historicity corresponds to the emergence of a transitory dimension or even the event-related dimension of reality that through disparation produces an asymmetric synthesis. In Toscano's reading, metastability and disparation imply political consequence:

> the element of politics as analysis and intervention is not the genesis and the concretisation of social relations, but metastability (or disparation) "as such" and the event-invention which crystallizes it into a new configuration (carrying a further preindividual charge). Pre-revolutionary disparation is not held "in common". [...] Simondon displaces the false alternative between a causal density that would remove any singularity from revolution, on the one hand, and a mystifying decisionism, on the other, by seeking to think through the unforeseeable coupling between a pre-revolutionary disparation and political invention. The pre-revolutionary state is the "very type", according to Simondon, of the psychosocial state which a political science of metastability should concern itself with, "a state of supersaturation [...] where an event is very ready to occur, where a structure is very ready to emerge". What makes this state otherwise potential and accounts for its asymmetry vis-à-vis its resolution is the need for a structuring germ, a revolutionary crystal.[56]

According to Toscano, metastability authorises "a conception of politics as the invention of a communication between initially incompossible series; as inven-

---

[55] Worms, "Introduction", in SLΦ, pp. 11–12.
[56] Toscano, "The Disparate: Ontology and Politics in Simondon", *op. cit.*, p. 4.

tion of a common that is not given in advance and which emerges on an ontological background of inequality".⁵⁷ Although politics – no more than history – does not directly guide Simondon's theoretical endeavours, some critical readings, such as Toscano's or Bardin's, identify an implicit but still current political value in Simondon's thinking. Bardin's idea of a political epistemology based on individuation is also central for grounding a historical epistemology. The speculative idea of the individuation of history uses the same conceptual tools as a political reading of Simondon's thinking and thus presupposes a political view on human actions and relations. In other words, a historical epistemology of individuation is a politically situated perspective or even a politics of invention. And a politics of invention is "a coupling between the inventive and organizing capacities of several subjects [MEOT 253]".⁵⁸

Bardin implements the idea of a politics of invention through his political epistemology of individuation.⁵⁹ The proposal of a political epistemology allows for thinking social metastability and the possibility of a transformative action rising from potentials and tensions requiring a solution. The metastable nature of reality articulates the politics of invention alongside the production conditions of the event, the predictive limit of actualisation and the concrete possibilities of inventing new solutions and new forms of collective life. In my opinion, the perspective of historical epistemology translates individuation into a philosophy of history that would conciliate genetic time and historical time. Historical epistemology may ground the axiomatisation of human sciences on the historical character of transindividuality as a specification of Bardin's reading of Simondon's thinking, i. e. as political epistemology.

Simondon's thinking leads us to treat modern epistemology as a field of ideological struggle and therefore political. This epistemology would be able to deconstruct the imaginary conception of human nature that is essentially identical to itself and to suppress its ontological privilege without chaining man to any

---

57   Ibid., p. 3.
58   Ibid., p. 6.
59   As Bardin argues, "it is a question of building up a science of society that can be predictive with respect to homeostatic processes, but cannot be predictive with respect to the emergence and the outcomes of properly political interventions (thus the government is an 'invention' of compatibility rather than a regulation of the functioning of the existing) that are event-related and trigger processes of a discontinuous type. Such a science will be able to reconstruct the ontogenesis of the singularities that constitute the social system, and consequently to determine the ongoing tendencies and state conditions of the emergence of a synthesis operation that is not dialectically resolving, but 'metastabilizing'. The risk of such a properly political operation is constitutive and necessary to keep society open to the tension of the collective for which the political is not reduced to a defensive mythology of the established order" (Andrea Bardin, *Per una teoria delle società in Gilbert Simondon*, 2008, online, url: http://it.scribd.com/doc/29755776/Simondon-Per-unateoria-della-societa, pp. 5–6).

natural or historical determinism. Whether it is the "destiny" of metaphysics, technics, division of labour or market economy, Simondon's epistemology contributes to the elaboration of an alternative life in relation to the ontological opposition of the couples spirit-freedom/matter-necessity.[60]

In Simondon, human sciences and the sciences of nature are situated in an intermediary state between determinism and indeterminism. The idea of scientific truth as well as the notion of human essence is a metastable concept that authorises a conception of science as a system open to the future and able to receive new discoveries and progressive formalisations.[61] The conception of becoming is presupposed for a political epistemology oriented to continuous change and based on the inner metastability of the reality. In this perspective, political acting and historical analysis are caught between the genealogical tool of ontogenesis and the immanent possibilities within technical and scientific progress. History as well as political agency is a dynamic field requiring individuation: this means a non-predictable result arising from a critical situation, rich in potentials and tensions that keeps open the possibility of inventing new solutions and forms of life.

---

[60] Bardin, "De l'homme à la matière: pour une ontologie difficile. Marx avec Simondon", *op. cit.*, p. 42.
[61] Simondon's insistence on the fact that the sciences of nature are set between determination and indeterminacy is probably more provocative than the equivalent statement regarding history. If natural science as well as human history follow the same structure, it remains unclear what specific contribution Simondon makes to the specificity of historical development. Nevertheless, Simondon is not concerned with history and in the few passages he talks about it, it is for an exigence of completeness and systematicity of his idea of an axiomatisation of human science on the pattern of natural sciences.

Contributors

Jamil ALIOUI, who holds a Master of Arts in philosophy, computer science and mathematical methods, defended a doctoral thesis in philosophy entitled *Le "numérique" à la lumière de la philosophie de la culture de Gilbert Simondon* (University of Lausanne, 2023). In parallel to his teaching in high school, he is also involved in various cultural associations in French-speaking Switzerland, including the transdisciplinary journal *Arkhaï* and the Groupe vaudois de philosophie. He also holds a preparatory diploma for higher art and design schools (ECAL) and has followed, for several years, courses in musical composition which have led him to organise numerous concerts and to promote contemporary and experimental music.

Matthieu AMAT After a PhD in philosophy (University of Paris 1, 2016), and a postdoc at the University of Lausanne (2017–2022), Matthieu Amat is associate member of the research team "Pays Germaniques" (CNRS, France) and teaches philosophy in preparatory classes for entrance to the French "Grandes Écoles". His research focuses on philosophy of culture, especially in the German context: Neo-Kantianism, Lebensphilosophie, Simmelian studies. He published his dissertation in 2018 (*Le relationnisme philosophique de Georg Simmel. Une idée de la culture*, Paris, Honoré Champion) and, with Carole Maigné, *Philosophie de la culture. Formes de vie, valeurs, symboles* (Paris, Vrin, 2021) and co-edited *Simmel Educator* (special issue of *Simmel Studies. New Series*, 2019/1). He also works on relativism ("Relativism: A Practical and Theoretical Philosophical Program", in G. Fitzi (ed.), *International Routledge Handbook of Simmel Studies*, 2020) and on the place of analogy in philosophy.

Vincent BONTEMS, director of research at the Laboratoire de recherche sur les sciences de la matière (Larsim) of the CEA, co-director of the Master's degree in Management of Technology and Innovation (MTI) at the INSTN, and director of the collection "L'Âne d'or" at Les Belles Lettres. He is the author of *Bachelard* (Paris, Belles Lettres, 2010) and *Au Nom de l'innovation. Finalités et modalités de la recherche au XXIe siècle* (Paris, Belles Lettres, 2023). He is also co-author of *Les Idées noires de la physique* (Paris, Belles Lettres, 2016) and *Inventing a Space Mission: the Story of the Herschel Space Observatory* (Cham, Springer,

2017). He edited *Simondon ou l'Invention du futur* (Paris, Klincksieck, 2015) and *Bachelard et l'Avenir de la culture* (Paris, Presse des Mines, 2017).

Giovanni CARROZZINI holds a PhD in historical-philosophical disciplines from the Università del Salento (Lecce); he deals with French epistemology and history and philosophy of science and technology. He has translated Simondon into Italian and dedicated to him numerous scientific articles in several languages, four monographs (including *Gilbert Simondon, Filosofo della* mentalité technique, Milano, Mimesis, 2011 and *Variazioni su Simondon*, Roma, Castelvecchi, 2020) and two volumes of the Italian journal of contemporary history and philosophy *Il Protagora*.

Jean-Yves CHATEAU is Honorary General Inspector of Philosophy at the Ministry of National Education (France), specialist in ancient philosophy, Kant and Simondon. He has edited, presented and/or participated in the publication of numerous collections of Simondon's texts (*L'invention dans les techniques*, Paris, Seuil, 2005; *Imagination and Invention*, 2008, Paris, PUF, 2014; *Communication and Invention*, 2010, Paris, PUF, 2015 and *Sur la technique*, Paris, PUF, 2014). Chateau has also written, among other publications, *Le Vocabulaire de Simondon*, Paris, Ellipses, 2008 and *La technique de Platon à Simondon*, Grenoble, Millon, 2022.

Michaël CREVOISIER is associate professor in philosophy and member of the Logiques de l'agir laboratory at the University of Franche-Comté. His work focuses on contemporary French philosophy and in particular on the transformation of the concept of the transcendental in its relation to the evolution of technics ("La technique et le transcendental" in *Philosophique*, 2020) and aesthetic practices ("La nouveauté de l'image vidéoludique" in *Sciences du jeu*, 2019).

Ludovic DUHEM is a French artist and philosopher. He is currently Director of Research at the Ecole Supérieure d'Art et de Design of Valenciennes. He teaches philosophy of art and design in several higher education institutions (ESAD Valenciennes, ENSCI-Les ateliers in Paris and ENSAV-La Cambre in Brussels) and in universities (Lille and Valenciennes). His research focuses on the relationship between aesthetics, technology and politics within contemporary ecological issues. He is developing a critical exegesis of Simondon's work as well as a general theory entitled "techno-aesthetics". He is also developing an ecosocial thought of design based on mesology, bioregionalism and post-colonial thought. He has recently published *Crash metropolis. Design écosocial et critique de la métropolisation des territoires* (Monlet, T&P Workunit, 2022), *Écologie et technologie. Redéfinir le progrès après Simondon* (with Jean-Hugues Barthélémy,

Paris, Matériologiques, 2022), *Design des territoires. L'enseignement de la biorégion* (with Richard Pereira De Moura, Paris, Eterotopia, 2020).

Xavier GUCHET is professor of philosophy at the University of Technology of Compiègne (France), and head of the research lab Connaissance, Organisation et Systèmes Techniques (Costech). His research focuses on epistemological and ethical issues related to health and care technologies (personalised medicine, biobanking, engineering of organs and tissues, AI in oncology), but also on the philosophy of technology as such. He has written several books including one on the philosophy of Gilbert Simondon: *Pour un humanisme technologique. Culture technique et société dans la philosophie de Gilbert Simondon* (Paris, PUF, 2010).

Clémentine LESSARD is a PhD candidate at the École Normale Supérieure de Lyon, where she is completing a thesis on "Φύσις and Τέχνη in Simondon: Reception and Transduction of an Ancient Heritage". Besides the study of the contemporary reception of the pre-Socratics, Plato and Aristotle, her research focuses on the status of the philosophy of nature and the relationship to materialism in Simondon, as well as on the interactions between metaphysics and technology in the genesis of philosophical systems. She graduated from the ENS de Lyon and holds a master's degree in history of philosophy as well as an *agrégation* – highly selective certification for public education – in philosophy.

Sacha LOEVE is Associate Professor in philosophy of science and technology at the University of Lyon 3 – Jean Moulin, Faculty of Philosophy. Member of the Institut de Recherches Philosophiques de Lyon (IRPhiL). Co-editor of the books *Research Objects in their technological Setting* (Routledge, 2017), *French Philosophy of Technology*, Classical Readings and Contemporary Approaches (Springer, 2018), and co-author of *Carbone, ses vies ses œuvres* (with Bernadette Bensaude-Vincent, Paris, Seuil, 2018).

Carole MAIGNÉ is full professor of philosophy at Lausanne University. Her main research topics focus on aesthetics, philosophy of art and philosophy of culture. She edited recently: *Philosophie de la photographie* (special issue of *Archives de philosophie*, 2022, n° 85–1), *Austrian Herbartism*, (special issue of *Meinong Studien/Meinong Studies*, De Gruyter, 2021) and with Enno Rudolph and Magnus Schlette: *Logos* (special issue of *Zeitschrift für Kulturphilosophie*, 2020/2). She has also published lately: C. Maigné and M. Amat, *Philosophie de la culture. Formes de vies, valeurs, symboles*, Paris, Vrin, 2021.

Sarah MARGAIRAZ teaches philosophy in high school (France). She worked on the question of the pre-individual in Simondon and its metaphysical origins in authors such as the pre-Socratics, Nietzsche, Bergson and Merleau-Ponty.

Taila PICCHI devoted her PhD dissertation (University of Florence/University of Pisa) to a comparison between Simondon's philosophy of technique and Marcuse's critical theory of technology. Her research focuses on history of philosophy, epistemology, political thought and critical theory, and a particular feature of it is the renewal of marxistic issues through Simondon's work.

Julien RABACHOU holds a PhD in philosophy and is Program Director at the International College of Philosophy since 2022. He first worked on the metaphysical question of the individual and on that of the world, before becoming interested in political philosophy and social ontology. He encountered Simondon's work as he was writing his thesis (published under the title *L'Individu reconstitué*, Vrin, Paris, 2017) and has not ceased to return to this work since then and to be inspired by it for his own research.

Ashley WOODWARD is Senior Lecturer in philosophy at the University of Dundee. He is an editor of *Parrhesia: A Journal of Critical Philosophy*. Among other academic publications, he is co-editor of *Gilbert Simondon: Being and Information* (Edinburgh UP, 2013), the first collection of essays on Simondon to appear in English, and co-translator of Raymond Ruyer's *Cybernetics and the Origin of Information* (Lanham, Rowman & Littlefield, 2024).

References

Alioui, Jamil: "Interfaces and analogy", in: *Arkhaï 2021. Texte-Image-Interface*, Lausanne, 2021, pp. 167–193.
Amat, Matthieu and Maigné, Carole: *Philosophie de la culture. Formes de vie, valeurs, symboles*, Paris, Vrin, 2021.
Arendt, Hannah: *The Human Condition*, Chicago, The University of Chicago Press, 1958.
Aristotle, *Metaphysics*, trans. D. Ross, Oxford, Oxford University Press, 1924.
Aspe, Bernard: *Simondon, politique du transindividuel*, Paris, Dittmar, 2013.
Bachelard, Gaston: *Le Nouvel esprit scientifique*, Paris, Presses universitaires de France, 1934.
—: *La Philosophie du non*, Paris, Presses universitaires de France, 1962.
Bambrough, Renford: "Universals and Family Resemblances", in: *Proc. Arist. Soc.*, 1961, pp. 207–222.
Bardin, Andrea: *Epistemology and Political Philosophy in Gilbert Simondon. Individuation, Technics, Social Systems*, Dordrecht, Springer, 2015.
—: "De l'homme à la matière: pour une ontologie difficile. Marx avec Simondon" in: *Cahiers Simondon* 5, 2013, pp. 25–42.
—: Per una teoria delle società in Gilbert Simondon, 2008, http://it.scribd.com/doc/29755776/Simondon-Per-unateoria-della-societa.
—: "Simondon: transcendantal et individuation", in: Rametta Gaetano (ed.), *Les métamorphoses du transcendantal. Parcours multiples de Kant à Deleuze*, Hildesheim, Georg Olms Verlag, 2009, pp. 189–215.
Barthélémy, Jean-Hugues: *Ego Alter. Dialogues pour l'avenir de la Terre.* Matériologiques, Paris, 2021.
—: *La société de l'invention. Pour une architectonique philosophique de l'âge écologique*, Matériologiques, Paris, 2018.
—: *Penser l'individuation. Simondon et la philosophie de la nature*, Paris, L'Harmattan, 2005.
—: *Simondon ou l'encyclopédisme génétique*, Paris, Presses universitaires de France, 2008.
—: "Encyclopédisme et système de l'individuation du sens", in: *Klesis* vol. 42, 2018, pp. 148–181.
—: "Encyclopédisme et théorie de l'interdisciplinarité", in: *Hermès* vol. 67, 2013, pp. 165–170.
—: "Gilbert Simondon et le malentendu de l'encyclopédisme", in: iPhilo, 2020, https://iphilo.fr/2020/11/17/gilbert-simondon-et-le-malentendu-de-lencyclopedisme-jean-hugues-barthelemy/ [11.05.2023].
—: "Historique de la 'simondialisation'", online: https://sociologiassociativa.wordpress.com/projetos/simondon/historico-da-simondializacao/historique-de-la-simondialisation/ [11.05.2023].
—: "Quel mode d'unité pour l'œuvre de Simondon?", in: Barthélémy, Jean-Hugues (ed.), *Cahiers Simondon* 3, Paris, L'Harmattan, 2011, pp. 131–148.

—: "What new Humanism today?" transl. C. Turner, in: *Cultural Politics*, vol. 6, issue 2, 2010, pp. 237–252.
Barthes, Roland: *La Chambre claire*, Paris, Gallimard-Cahiers du cinéma, 1980.
Baudrillard, Jean: *Simulacres et simulation*, Paris, Galilée, 1981.
Beaubois, Vincent: "Un schématisme pratique de l'imagination", *Apparatus*, 16/2015, pp. 1–15 (http://journals.openedition.org/appareil/2247).
Bergson, Henri, *La pensée et le mouvant*, in: Bergson, Henri: *Œuvres. Édition du centenaire*, Paris, Presses universitaires de France, 1963, 1251–1492.
—: *L'évolution créatrice*, in: Bergson, Henri: *Œuvres. Édition du centenaire*, Paris, Presses universitaires de France, pp. 487–809.
—: "La philosophie de Claude Bernard", *La pensée et le mouvant*, in: *Œuvres*, Édition du Centenaire, Paris, Presses universitaires de France, 1963, pp. 1437–1489.
—: *The Creative Mind*, New York, Philosophical Library, Inc., 1946.
—: "The Philosophy of Claude Bernard", in: *The Creative Mind: An Introduction to Metaphysics*, translated by Mabelle L. Andison, Mineola, N.Y, Dover Publications, 2010, pp. 170–178.
—: *The Two Sources of Morality and Religion*, translated by R. A. Audra and C. Brereton, Notre Dame, IN., University of Notre Dame Press, 2002.
—: "Philosophical Intuition", in: *The Creative Mind: An Introduction to Metaphysics*, Mineola, N.Y, Dover Publications, 2010, pp. 87–107.
Bianco, Giuseppe: "Philosophie et histoire de la philosophie pendant les années 1950: Le cas du jeune Gilles Deleuze", in: Fruteau De Laclos, Frédéric and Bianco, Giuseppe (eds.), *L'angle mort des années 1950: Philosophie et sciences humaines en France*, Paris, Éditions de la Sorbonne, 2016, pp. 147–168.
Bontems, Vincent: "Quelques éléments pour une épistémologie des relations d'échelle chez Gilbert Simondon", in: *Appareil* [En ligne], vol. 2 | 2008, (accessed 30 October 2020). URL: http://journals.openedition.org/appareil/595.
Bouaniche, Arnaud: "Milieu et création dans la 'géophilosophie' de Deleuze et Guattari. Trois sources d'une théorie vitaliste de la création philosophique: Nietzsche, Canguilhem, Simondon", in: Carbone, Mauro, Broggi, Paride and Turarbek, Laura (eds.), *La géophilosophie de Gilles Deleuze: Entre esthétiques et politiques*, Paris, Éditions Mimésis, 2012, pp. 145–163.
Bradley, Marion Zimmer: "The Climbing Wave", *The Magazine of Fantasy and Science Fiction*, February 1955.
Politics, vol. 6, issue 2, 2010, pp. 237–252.
Bréhier, Émile: *Les thèmes actuels de la philosophie*, Paris, PUF, 1951.
—: *Transformation de la philosophie française*, Paris, Flammarion, 1950.
Canguilhem, Georges: *Essai sur quelques problèmes concernant le normal et le pathologique*, Clermont-Ferrand, La Montagne, 1943; trans. Fawcett, Carolyn R., *The Normal and the Pathological*, Zone Books, New York, 2007.
—: *La Connaissance de la vie*, Paris, Vrin, 1971.
—: "Dialectique et philosophie du non chez Gaston Bachelard", *Études d'histoire et de philosophie des sciences*, Paris, Vrin, 1970, pp. 196–207.
—: "Hegel en France", in: *Résistance, philosophie, biologique et histoire des sciences 1940–1965. Œuvres complètes tome IV*, Paris, Vrin, 2015, pp. 321–341.
—: *On the normal and the pathological*, translated by C. R. Fawcett. D. Dordrecht, NL, Reidel Publishing Company, 1978.

Carnap, Rudolf: *The Logical Structure of the World*, transl. Rolf A. George, Berkeley and Los Angeles, University of California Press, 1967.

Carrozzini, Giovanni: "Gilbert Simondon: brève histoire d'une réception difficile", in: Implications philosophiques, Feb. 2019, online: https://www.implications-philosophiques.org/gilbert-simondon-breve-histoire-dune-reception-difficile/ [11.05.2023].

Cassirer, Ernst: *Substance et fonction*, French translation by P. Caussat, Paris, Minuit, original ed. 1969, 1977.

Césari, Paul: *La valeur*, Paris, PUF, 1957.

Chabot, Pascal: *The Philosophy of Simondon*, translation by Graeme Kirkpatrick and Aliza Krefetz, London, Bloomsbury, 2013.

—: *Simondon*, Paris, Vrin, 2002, pp. 107–119.

Chateau, Jean-Yves: *Vocabulaire de Simondon*, Paris, Ellipses, 2008.

—: "Analogie, science et philosophie chez Simondon", in: Canal-U, 2019, https://www.canal-u.tv/82307 (22.01.2022).

—: "L'invention dans les techniques selon Gilbert Simondon" in: Simondon, Gilbert: *L'invention dans les techniques, Cours et conférences*, Paris, Seuil, 2005, pp. 11–72.

—: "Presentation: Communication et Information dans l'œuvre de Gilbert Simondon" in: Simondon, Gilbert: *Communication et information*, Paris, PUF, 2015.

—: "Technologie et ontologie dans la philosophie de Gilbert Simondon", in: Cahiers philosophiques, issue 43, 1990, pp. 97–138.

Châtelet, Gilles et Curien, Hubert (eds.), *Gilbert Simondon. Une pensée de l'individuation et de la technique*, Paris, Albin Michel, 1994, pp. 91–99.

Chevignard, Élie: *Qu'est-ce qu'un terroir?*, Beaune, Le souci de soi, 2019.

Combes, Muriel: *Gilbert Simondon and the Philosophy of the Transindividual*, translation by Thomas LaMarre, Cambridge, London, MIT Press, 2013 (first French edition 1999).

Crevoisier, Michael, *Être un sujet connaissant selon Simondon. Ontogenèse et transcendental*, Paris, Classiques Garnier, 2023.

Curien, Hubert (ed.): *Gilbert Simondon. Une pensée de l'individuation et de la technique*, Paris, Albin Michel, 1994, 91–99.

D'Alembert, Jean Le Rond: "Preliminary Discourse", translated by R. N. Schwab in: *The Encyclopedia of Diderot & d'Alembert*, Collaborative Translation Project, Chicago, University of Chicago Press, 1995, pp. 3–140.

Damisch, Hubert: *La Dénivelée. À l'épreuve de la photographie*, Paris, Seuil, 2001.

Debraine, Luc and Lugon, Olivier (ed.): *Photographie et horlogerie*, Gollion Infolio, 2022.

Deleuze, Gilles: *Negotiations*, translated by M. Joughin, New York Chichester, Columbia University Press, 1997.

—: *Pourparlers*, Paris, Éditions de Minuit, 1990, 2014.

—: and Guattari, Félix: *What Is Philosophy?*, translated by H. Tomlinson and G. Burchell, New York, Columbia University Press, 1994.

Déotte, Jean-Louis: "Simondon: les appareils esthétiques entre la technique et la religion", in: *Cosmétiques: Simondon, Panofsky, Lyotard*, La Plaine Saint Denis, Editions des maisons des sciences de l'homme associées, 2018 (https://books.openedition.org/emsha/222).

Didi-Huberman, Georges: *La Ressemblance par contact*, Paris, Minuit, 2008.

Dosse, François: *Gilles Deleuze & Félix Guattari: Intersecting Lives*, transl. by Deborah Glassman, New York, 2010, p. 162.

Duhem, Ludovic: "Apeiron et physis. Simondon transducteur des présocratiques", in: Barthélémy, Jean-Hugues (ed.), Cahier Simondon, n. 4, Paris, L'Harmattan, 2012, pp. 33–67.

—: "'Entrer dans le moule'. Poïétique et individuation chez Simondon", in: *La part de l'Œil*, issue 27–28, 2012–2013, pp. 227–257.

—: "La tache aveugle et le point neutre. Sur le double 'faux départ' de l'esthétique de Simondon", in: Barthélémy, Jean-Hugues (ed.), *Cahiers Simondon 1*, Paris, L'Harmattan, 2009, pp. 115–133.

—: "La théorie du cycle de l'image de Simondon", in: Wunenburger, Jean-Jacques (ed.), *L'histoire du concept d'imagination en France (de 1914 à nos jours)*, Paris, Classiques Garnier, pp. 233–246.

—: "L'idée d'"individu pur" dans la pensée de Simondon, *Appareil*, n. 2, 2008, online: https://journals.openedition.org/appareil/583.

Duhem, Pierre: *Sauver les apparences. SOZEIN TA PHAINOMENA. Essai sur la Notion de Théorie physique de Platon à Galilée*, Paris, Hermann, 1908.

Durand, Hermine and Anouch, Missirian: "L'usine marémotrice de la rance", Département Géographie et Territoire / ENS Paris [En ligne], 2009–2010, (accessed 19 October 2020). URL: http://www.geographie.ens.fr/Les-mecanismes-a-l-origine-d-une.html.

Dupréel, Eugène: *Esquisse d'une philosophie des valeurs*, Paris, Alcan, 1939.

Floridi, Luciano: *The Fourth Revolution*, Oxford, Oxford University Press, 2014.

—: *The Philosophy of Information*, Oxford: Oxford University Press, 2011.

Foucher, Kane X.: *Metastasis and Metastability: A Deleuzean Approach to Information*, Rotterdam, Sense, 2013.

François, Arnaud: "Pourquoi inverser les valeurs, ce n'est pas mettre de nouvelles valeurs à la place des anciennes", in: Yannick Souladié (ed.), *Nietzsche – L'inversion des valeurs*, OLMS, 2007, pp. 133–167.

Gagnon, Philippe, "Ruyer and Simondon on Technological Inventiveness and Form Outlasting Its Medium", in: *Deleuze Studies*, vol. 11, issue 4, 2017, pp. 538–554.

Garcia, Tristan: *Forme et objet. Un traité des choses*, Presses universitaires de France, Paris, 2011; transl. Ohm, Mark A. & Cogburn, John: *Form and Object. A Treatise on Things*, Edinburgh University Press, Edinburgh, 2014.

Gareli, Jacques: 'Transduction et information' in: Châtelet, Gilles (ed.), *Gilbert Simondon – Une Pensée de l'individuation et de la technique*, Paris, Albin Michel, 1994, p. 55–68.

Gayon, Jean: "Bergson entre science et métaphysique" in: *Annales bergsoniennes*, III, Bergson et la science, Paris, Presses universitaires de France, 2007, pp. 175–189.

Goldschmidt, Victor: *Le paradigme dans la dialectique platonicienne*, Paris, Vrin, 1947.

—: *Les dialogues de Platon. Structure et méthode dialectique*, Paris, PUF, 1947.

—: "Temps historique et temps logique dans l'interprétation des systèmes philosophiques", in: *Questions platoniciennes*, Paris, Vrin, 1970, first published in 1953, pp.13–20.

Gorz, André: *Capitalisme, Socialisme, Écologie*, Paris, Galilée, 1991.

—: *Écologica*, Paris, Galilée, 2008.

Granger, Gilles-Gaston: *Essai d'une philosophie du style*, Paris, Odile Jacob, 1988.

Grenet, Paul, *Les Origines de l'analogie philosophique dans la dialogues de Platon*, Paris, Boivin, 1948.

Guchet, Xavier: *Pour un humanisme technologique. Culture, technique et société dans la philosophie de Gilbert Simondon*, Paris, Presses universitaires de France, 2010.

—: "Évolution technique et objectivité technique chez Leroi-Gourhan et Simondon", in: *Appareil* [En ligne], vol. 2 | 2008, (accessed 19 October 2020). URL: https://journals.openedition.org/appareil/58.

—: "Merleau-Ponty, Simondon et le problème d'une "axiomatique des sciences humaines". L'exemple de l'histoire et de la sociologie", in: *Chiasmi International*, vol. 3, 2001, pp. 103–127.

Gueroult, Martial: *Descartes selon l'ordre des raisons*, Paris, Aubier, 1953.

—: "La voie de l'objectivité esthétique", in: *Mélanges d'esthétique et de science de l'art offerts à Etienne Souriau*, Paris, Nizet, 1952, 95–124.

—: "Logique, architectonique et structures constitutives des systèmes philosophiques", in: *Encyclopédie française*, volume XIX, 1ᵉ partie, sect. C, 1957, 24.15–16.

—: *Philosophie de l'histoire de la philosophie*, Paris, Aubier-Montaigne, 1979.

Halloy, José; Nicolas, Nova and Alexandre, Monnin: "Au-delà du low-tech: technologies zombies, soutenabilité et inventions. Interview croisée de José Halloy et Nicolas Nova par Alexandre Monnin", in: Attard, Isabelle et al. (eds.), *Low Tech: face au tout numérique, se réapproprier les technologies*, Paris, Passerelle, 2020, pp. 120–128. [En ligne] (accessed 14 January 2021): https://www.ritimo.org/Au-dela-du-low-tech-technologies-zombies-soutenabilite-et-inventions.

Haumont, Alice: "L'individuation est-elle une instauration? Autour des pensées de Simondon et de Souriau", in: Chabot, Pascal (ed.), *Simondon*, Paris, Vrin, 2002, 69–88.

Hegel, Georg Wilhelm Friedrich: *Encyclopedia of the Philosophical Sciences in Basic Outline*, K. Brinkmann and D. O. Dahlstrom (eds.), translated by Dahlstrom and Brinkmann, Cambridge University Press, 2010.

Heidegger, Martin: *The Question Concerning Technology and Other Essays*, translated by W. Lovitt. New York and London, Garland Publishing Inc., 1977.

Heredia, Juan Manuel: "Simondon y el problema de la analogía" in: *Ideas y Valores*, vol. 68, issue 171, 2019, pp. 209–230.

Hottois, Gilbert, *Simondon et la philosophie de la culture technique*, Bruxelles, De Boeck, 1993.

Hui, Yuk: *Recursivity and Contingency*, London, Rowman & Littlefield, 2019.

—: "Simondon et la question de l'information", in: Jean-Hugues Barthélémy (ed.), *Cahiers Simondon 6*, 2015, pp. 29–47.

Iliadis, Andrew J.: "Informational Ontology: The Meaning of Gilbert Simondon's Concept of Individuation", in: *Communication+1*, vol. 2, issue 1, 2013, Article 5.

Jankélévitch, Vladimir: *La mort*, Paris, Flammarion, 2017.

Joly, Bernard: "Prolonger la vie: les attrayantes promesses des alchimistes", in: *Astérion. Philosophie, histoire des idées, pensée politique*, vol. 8, 2011, https://doi.org/10.4000/asterion.1993.

Juffé, Michel: "Gilbert Simondon: una testimonianza", in: *Il Protagora* vol. 42, issue 23/24, 2015, pp. 219–224.

Kant, Immanuel: *Critique de la raison pure*, translated by A. Tremesaygues and B. Pacaud, Paris, Presses universitaires de France, 2012.

—: *Critique of Pure Reason*, translated by P. Guyer and A. W. Wood, Cambridge University Press, 1998

Lafitte, Jacques: *Réflexions sur la science des machines*, Paris, Vrin, 1972.

Lanouzière, Jacqueline: "Gilbert Simondon", in: *Il Protagora* vol. 42, issue 23/24, 2015, pp. 205–208.

Lavelle, Louis: *Traité des valeurs*, 2 vol., Paris, Presses universitaires de France, 1951, 1955.

Lecourt, Dominique: *Georges Canguilhem*, Paris, Presses universitaires de France, 2008.

—: *La philosophie des sciences*, Paris, Presses universitaires de France, 2018.

Le Senne, R.: *Obstacle et valeur*, Paris, Aubier, 1934.

Loeve, Sacha: "Du récit au design, et retour: des modes de résolution du problème de l'unité de la technologie chez Simondon", in: Bontems, Vincent (ed.), *Gilbert Simondon ou l'invention du futur*. Colloque de Cerisy, Klincksieck, Langres, 2016, pp. 113–124.

Lotze, Rudolf Hermann: "Le monde des Idées", in: *Philosophie*, vol. 91, 4/2006, Minuit, pp. 9–23.

Maigné, Carole: "Sauver les phénomènes: la beauté vitale en photographie. À partir de Simondon et de Marker", in: Zernik, Clélia and Worms, Anne-Lise (eds.), *Actes du colloque de Cerisy. Beauté vitale* (forthcoming).

Marquet, Jean-François: *Le Vitrail et l'énigme: Dialogue avec Pierre Soual*, Paris, Les Petits Platons, 2013.

Marx, Karl: *Capital*. eds. Ernest Mandel and New Left Review, transl. Ben Fowles. London, Penguin Classics, 1990

Mills, Simon: *Gilbert Simondon: Information, Technology and Media*, London and New York, Rowman & Littlefield International, 2016.

Marcuse, Herbert: "Über den affirmativen Charakter der Kultur", in: *Zeitschrift für Sozialforschung*, vol. 6, 1/1937, pp. 54–94.

Merleau-Ponty, Maurice: *La structure du comportement*, Paris, PUF, 2013.

—: *L'institution – La passivité – Notes de cours au Collège de France (1954–1955)*, Paris, Belin, 2003.

—: *Le Visible et l'invisible. Suivi de notes de travail*, Claude Lefort (ed.), Paris, Gallimard, 1964.

—: *Phénoménologie de la perception*, Paris, Gallimard, 1945, 1976.

—: "Le doute de Cézanne" in: *Sens et Non-sens*, Paris, Nagel, 1948, pp. 15–50.

—: *Phenomenology of Perception*, English translation by Colin Smith, London and New York, Routledge Classic, 1958.

—: *In Praise of Philosophy and Other Essays*, transl. by John O'Neill, Evanston, Northwestern University Press, 1970.

Micoud, André: "Gilbert Simondon et la posture herméneutique: quelques notations", in: Chabot, Pascal (ed.), Simondon, Paris, Vrin, 2002, pp. 107–119.

Morizot, Baptiste: *Pour une théorie de la rencontre. Hasard et individuation chez Gilbert Simondon*, Paris, Vrin, 2016.

Moutaux, Jacques: "Sur la philosophie de la nature et la philosophie de la technique de Gilbert Simondon", in: Bloch, Olivier (ed.), Philosophies de la nature, Paris, Éditions de la Sorbonne, 2000, our translation, pp. 489–499.

Mol, Annemarie et al. (eds.): *Care in Practice. On Tinkering in Clinics, Homes and Farms*, Bielefeld, transcript Verlag, 2010.

Mouillaud, Maurice: "Frammenti per Gilbert Simondon", in: Il Protagora vol. 36, issue 12, 2008, pp. 401–404.

Naegel, Paul: "Une première mondiale énergétique française: l'usine marémotrice de la Rance", HAL [En ligne], 2012, (accessed 19 October 2020). URL: https://halshs.archives-ouvertes.fr/halshs-00746910/document.

Nancy, Jean-Luc: "Le système, hier et aujourd'hui", in: *Les Temps Modernes* vol. 682, 2015, pp. 180–197.

Ortega y Gasset, Jose: "Man the Technician", in: Ortega y Gasset, Jose (ed.), *History as a System and Other Essays Toward a Philosophy of History*, W. W. Norton & Company, New York and London, 1941, pp. 87–161.

Petit, Victor: *Histoire et philosophie du concept de "Milieu": individuation et médiation*. PhD dissertation, University of Paris 7 Denis Diderot, 2009.

—: and Deldicque, Timothée: "La recherche en design avant la 'recherche en design'", in: *Cahiers COSTECH*, vol. 1, 2017, https://www.costech.utc.fr/CahiersCOSTECH/spip.php?article16.

Pieuchard, Marion: *La photographie et l'automatisme: histoire d'une utopie du Photomaton au procédé Polaroïd*, PhD thesis, Université Paris 1 Panthéon Sorbonne, 2013, https://tel.archives-ouvertes.fr/tel-03007927.

Plato: *Complete Works*, edited by Cooper, J. M., associate editor Hutchinson, J. S., Indianapolis, Hackett Publishing Company, 1997.

Polin, Raymond: *La création des valeurs: Recherches sur le fondement de l'objectivité axiologique*, Paris, Presses universitaires de France, 1944.

Pols, Jeannette: *Care at a Distance. On the Closeness of Technology*, Amsterdam, Amsterdam University Press, 2012.

Quine, Willard v. Orman: "Two Dogmas of Empiricism" in: *The Philosophical Review*, Vol. 60, No. 1 (1951), pp. 20–43.

Rancière, Jacques: *The Politics of Aesthetics. The Distribution of the Sensible*, translated by G. Rockhill, London, Continuum, 2004.

Rabaud, Étienne: "L'interdépendance générale des organisms", in: *Revue philosophique de la France et de l'Étranger*, vol. 118, 1934, pp. 171–209.

Rantala, Juho: "The Notion of Information in Early Cybernetics and in Gilbert Simondon's Philosophy", Paper presented at Doctoral Congress in Philosophy 22, University of Tampere, Finland, 2018. (Available online: https://www.researchgate.net/publication/337670231_The_Notion_of_information_in_early_cybernetics_and_in_Gilbert_Simondon%27s_philosophy)

Robin, Léon: *Platon*, Paris, PUF, 1935.

Rosa, Hartmut: *Aliénation et Accélération. Vers une critique de la modernité tardive*, Paris, La Découverte, 2014.

Ruyer, Raymond: *La Cybernétique et l'origine de l'information*, Paris, Flammarion, 1954.

—: *La Genèse des formes vivantes*, Paris, Flammarion, 1958.

—: *Le monde des valeurs*, Paris, Aubier, 1948.

—: *Paradoxes de la conscience et limites de l'automatisme*, Paris, Albin Michel, 1966.

—: *Philosophie de la valeur*, Paris, Armand Colin, 1952.

—: "Les Limites du progrès humain", in: *Revue de métaphysique et de morale* vol. 63, issue 4, October–December 1958, pp. 412–427.

Sauvagnargues, Anne: *Deleuze. L'empirisme transcendantal*, Paris, Presses universitaires de France, 2010.

Scheler, Max: *Der Formalismus in der Ethik und die materiale Wertethik*. Bern and München, Francke, 1966.

—: *Le formalisme en éthique et l'éthique matériale des valeurs*, transl. M. de Gandillac, Paris, Gallimard 1955.

Schnädelbach, Herbert: *Philosophie in Deutschland. 1831–1933*, Frankfurt a.M., Suhrkamp, 1983.

Sebbah, François-David: "The Philosopher and (his) Techniques: From the Work of Pierre Ducassé, in: *Diacritics*, vol. 42, issue 1, 2014, pp. 6–21.

Sennett, Richard: *The Craftsman*, New Haven and London, Yale University Press, 2008.

Simmel, Georg: *La tragédie de la culture*, French translation by S. Cornille and P. Ivernel, Paris, Payot-Rivages, 1988.

Simondon, Gilbert: *Communication et information*, Paris, Presses universitaires de France, 2010, 2015.
—: *Cours sur la perception. 1964–1965*, Paris, Presses universitaires de France, 2013.
—: *Deux Leçons sur l'animal et l'homme*, Paris, Ellipses, 2004.
—: *Du mode d'existence des objets techniques*, Paris, Aubier, 1958, 1969, 1989, 2001, 2012.
—: *Imagination et invention. 1965–1966*, Paris, Presses universitaires de France, 2014.
—: *L'individuation à la lumière des notions de forme et d'information*, Grenoble, Millon, 2005, 2013, 2017.
—: *Sur la philosophie. 1950–1980*, Paris, Presses universitaires de France, 2016.
—: *Sur la psychologie. 1956–1967*, Paris, Presses universitaires de France, 2015
—: *Sur la technique, 1953–1983*, Paris, Presses universitaires de France, 2014.
—: *La Résolution des problèmes*, Presses universitaires de France, Paris 2018.
—: "Culture et technique", article published in 1965 in the *Bulletin de l'Institut de philosophie* of the Université libre de Bruxelles, in: *Sur la technique. 1953–1983*, Paris, Presses universitaires de France, 2014.
—: "Cybernétique et philosophie", text from 1953 in: *Sur la Philosophie. 1950–1980*, Presses universitaires de France, 2016.
—: "De l'implication technologique dans les fondements d'une culture", in *Sur la Philosophie. 1950–1980*, Presses universitaires de France, 2016.
—: "Epistémologie de la cybernétique" (1953), in: *Sur la philosophie. 1950–1980*, Paris, Presses universitaires de France, 2016, pp. 175–199.
—: "Fondements de la psychologie contemporaine", in: *Sur la psychologie. 1956–1967*, Paris, Presses universitaires de France, 2015
—: "Humanisme culturel, humanisme négatif, humanisme nouveau" (1953), in: Gilbert Simondon, *Sur la philosophie. 1950–1980*, Paris, Presses universitaires de France, 2016, pp. 69–75.
—: "Imagination et invention", in Simondon, Gilbert: *L'invention dans les techniques. Cours et conférences*, Paris, Seuil, 2005, pp. 273–304.
—: "Impression de la réalité souveraine", in: *Sur la technique. 1953–1983*, Paris, Presses universitaires de France, 2014.
—: "Introduction. (Note sur l'attitude réflexive, autour de 1955)", in: *Sur la philosophie. 1950–1980*, Paris, Presses universitaires de France, 2016, pp. 17–25.
—: "Invention et créativité", course from 1976, in: *La résolution des problèmes*, Paris, Presses universitaires de France, 2018.
—: "Le progrès, rythmes et modalités", in: *Critique*, no. 816, May 2015, pp. 384–400.
—: "Les encyclopédies et l'esprit encyclopédique", text from ca. 1950, in: *Sur la Philosophie. 1950–1980*, Presses universitaires de France, 2016.
—: "Les grands courants de la philosophie française contemporaine", in: *Sur la Philosophie. 1950–1980*, Presses universitaires de France, 2016.
—: "Lettre de Gilbert Simondon à Jean Le Moyne, datée du 29 mars 1970", in: *Revue de Synthèse* vol. 130, issue 1, 2009, p. 130.
—: "Les encyclopédies et l'esprit encyclopédique", text from ca. 1950, in: *Sur la Philosophie. 1950–1980*, Presses universitaires de France, 2016.
—: "Les Limites du progrès humain", in: *Revue de métaphysique et de morale* vol. 64, issue 3, July–Sept 1959, pp. 370–376.
—: "L'invention et le développement des techniques" in: Simondon, Gilbert: *L'invention dans les techniques. Cours et conférences*, Paris, Seuil, 2005, 227–272.

—: "L'objet technique comme paradigme d'intelligibilité universelle" in: *Sur la technique. 1953-1983*, Paris, Presses universitaires de France, 2014.
—: "Note sur l'attitude réflexive", preparatory document, ca. 1955, in: *Sur la philosophie. 1950-1980*, Paris, Presses universitaires de France, 2016.
—: "Objet technique et conscience moderne", text from 1961, in: *Sur la technique. 1953-1983*, Paris, Presses universitaires de France, 2014.
—: "Optimisme et pessimisme", in: Gilbert Simondon, *Sur la philosophie. 1950-1980*, Paris, Presses universitaires de France, 2016, pp. 109-115.
—: "Place d'une initiation aux techniques dans une formation humaine complète", in: *Cahiers pédagogiques*, vol. 9/2, 15 November 1953, p. 115
—: "Psychosociologie de la technicité", text from 1960-1961, in: *Sur la technique. 1953-1983*, Paris, Presses universitaires de France, 2014.
—: "Prolégomènes à une refonte de l'enseignement", text from 1954, in: *Sur la technique. 1953-1983*, Paris, Presses universitaires de France, 2014.
—: "Psychosociologie du cinéma", text from ca. 1960, in: *Sur la technique. 1953-1983*, Paris, Presses universitaires de France, 2014.
—: "Quelques éléments d'histoire de la pensée philosophique dans le monde occidental", course of 1971-1972, unpublished.
—: "Recherche sur la philosophie de la nature", in: Simondon, Gilbert: *Sur la philosophie. 1950-1980*, Paris, Presses universitaires de France, 2016, pp. 29-34.
—: "Réponse aux objections", text from 1954, in: *Sur la technique. 1953-1983*, Paris, Presses universitaires de France, 2014.
—: "Sciences de la nature et sciences de l'homme", in: *Sur la philosophie. 1950-1980*, Paris, Presses universitaires de France, 2016.
—: "Technique et eschatologie", text from 1972, in: *Sur la technique. 1953-1983*, Paris, Presses universitaires de France, 2014.
—: "Voyage aux États-Unis (Extraits sur le Pragmatisme, 1952)", in: Gilbert Simondon, *Sur la philosophie. 1950-1980*, Paris, Presses universitaires de France, 2016, pp. 77-81.
—: *Imagination and Invention*, translated by Joe Hughes and Christophe Wall-Romana, Minneapolis, University of Minnesota Press, 2022.
—: *Individuation in Light of Notions of Form and Information*, translated by Taylor Adkins, Minneapolis, University of Minnesota Press, 2020.
—: *On the Mode of Existence of Technical Objects*, translation by Cécile Malaspina and John Rogove, Minneapolis, Univocal Publishing, 2017.
—: *Two Lessons on Animal and Man*, translated by Drew S. Burk's, Minneapolis, Univocal Publishing, 2011.
—: "Allagmatics", in: *Individuation in Light of Notions of Form and Information*, translated by Taylor Adkins, Minneapolis, University of Minnesota Press, 2020.
—: "Analysis of the Criteria of Individuality", in: *Individuation in Light of Notions of Form and Information*, translated by Taylor Adkins, Minneapolis, University of Minnesota Press, 2020.
—: "Complementary Note on the Consequences of the Notion of Individuation", in: *Individuation in Light of Notions of Form and Information*, translated by Taylor Adkins, Minneapolis, University of Minnesota Press, 2020.
—: "Form, Information, Potentials", translated by Andrew Iliadis, in: Bardin, Andrea, Carrozzini, Giovanni and Rodríguez, Pablo (eds.), *Philosophy Today*, vol. 63, issue 3, Summer 2019, pp. 571-583.

—: "History of the Notion of the Individual", preparatory work written between 1952 and 1958, in: *Individuation in Light of Notions of Form and Information*, translated by Taylor Adkins, Minneapolis, University of Minnesota Press, 2020.

—: "Invention and Creativity", 1976 lecture, in: *La résolution des problèmes*, Paris, Presses universitaires de France, 2018.

—: "Technical Mentality", trans. Arne de Boever in: Arne de Boever, Alex Murray, Jon Roffe, and Ashley Woodward (eds.), *Gilbert Simondon: Being and Technology*, Edinburgh, Edinburgh University Press, 2012, pp. 1–15.

—: "The Limits of Human Progress: A Critical Study", trans. S. Cubitt, in: *Cultural Politics*, vol. 6, issue 2, 2010, pp. 229–36.

Simondon, Nathalie: "Biography", transl. by Joe Hughes and Drew Burk, http://gilbert.simondon.fr/content/biography [10.04.2022]

—: "Biographie de Gilbert Simondon", sur *Gilbert Simondon. Site d'information sur l'œuvre et les publications*, http://gilbert.simondon.fr/content/biographie [11.05.2023].

Soulez, Antonia: *Comment écrivent les philosophes?*, Paris, Kimé, 2003.

Souriau, Étienne: *L'Instauration Philosophique*, Paris, Alcan, 1939.

—: *Les différents modes d'existence*, Paris, Presses universitaires de France, first ed. 1943, 2009.

—: "Du mode d'existence de l'œuvre à faire", in: *Les différents modes d'existence*, Paris, Presses universitaires de France, first ed. 1943, 2009.

—: "On the mode of existence of the work to-be-made", in: *The Different Modes of Existence*, translated by E. Beranek and T. Howles, Minneapolis, Univocal Publishing, 2015, pp. 219–240.

Stengers, Isabelle: "Pour une mise à l'aventure de la transduction", in: Chabot, Pascal (ed.), *Simondon*, Paris, Vrin, 2002, pp. 137–159.

—: "Résister à Simondon?" in: *Multitudes* 18, 2004, pp. 55–62.

Stern, A.: *La Philosophie des valeurs. Regard sur ses tendances en Allemagne*, 2 vol., Paris, Hermann, 1936.

Stiegler, Bernard: *La technique et le temps. 1. La faute d'Épiméthée*, Paris, Galilée, 1998.

—: *Qu'appelle-t-on panser? Tome 2: La leçon de Greta Thunberg*, Paris, Les liens qui libèrent, 2020.

—: "Chute et élévation. L'apolitique de Simondon", in: *Revue philosophique de la France et de l'Étranger*, volume 131, issue 3, July 2006, 325–341.

Toscano, Alberto: *The Theatre of Production. Philosophy and Individuation between Kant and Deleuze*, London, Palgrave Macmillan, 2006.

—: "La disparation", in: *Multitudes*, 18, 2004, pp. 73–82.

—: "The Disparate: Ontology and Politics in Simondon", paper delivered at the Society for European Philosophy/Forum for European Philosophy annual conference, University of Sussex (9 September 2007).

Trenti, Gregorio: *Estetica e morfologia in Gilbert Simondon*, Sesto San Giovanni, Mimesis, 2020.

Tronto, Joan: *Moral Boundaries. A Political Argument for an Ethic of Care*, New York and London, Routledge, 1993.

Turquety, Benoît: *Politiques de la technicité. Corps, mondes et médias avec Gilbert Simondon*, Mimesis, 2022.

—: "Charles Cros et le problème "cinéma": écrire l'histoire avec Bachelard et Simondon", in: *1895. One Thousand Eight Hundred and Ninety-Five*, 72/2014, 11–35 URL: http://journals.openedition.org/1895/4801.

Uexküll v., Jakob: *A Foray into the Worlds of Animals and Humans, with a Theory of Meaning*, transl. by Joseph D. O'Neil, Minneapolis, London, 2010.
Veblen, Thorstein: *Théorie de la classe de loisir*, Paris, Gallimard, 1970.
Vernant, Jean-Pierre: *Myth and Thought among the Greeks*, translated by J. Fort, Zone Books, New York, 2006.
Vieillard-Baron, Jean-Louis: "Lettres inédites de Bergson", in: Worms, Frédéric (ed.), *Annales bergsoniennes II*, Paris, Presses Universitaires de France, 2004, pp. 473–474.
Vuillemin, Jules: *Nécessité ou contingence: l'aporie de Diodore et les systèmes philosophiques*, Minuit, Paris, 1997; partially transl. in Vuillemin, Jules: *Necessity or Contingency: The Master Argument*, CSLI Publications, Stanford 1996.
Weber Max: "Science as Vocation", in: H. H. Gerth and C. Wright Mills (Translated and edited), *From Max Weber: Essays in Sociology*, New York, Oxford University Press, 1946, pp. 129–156.
Windelband, Willhelm: *Einleitung in die Philosophie*, Tübingen, Mohr, 1914.
Wittgenstein, Ludwig: *Philosophical Investigations*, transl., G. E. M. Anscombe, New York, Macmillan, 1959.
Worms, Frédéric: "Présentation", in: Gilbert Simondon, *Sur la philosophie. 1950–1980*, Paris, Presses universitaires de France, 2016, pp. 5–14.

Schwabe Verlag's signet was Johannes Petri's printer's mark. His printing workshop was established in Basel in 1488 and was the origin of today's Schwabe Verlag. The signet refers back to the beginnings of the printing press, and originated in the entourage of Hans Holbein. It illustrates a verse of Jeremiah 23:29: 'Is not my word like fire, says the Lord, and like a hammer that breaks a rock in pieces?'